Our Own Snug Fireside

Our Own Snug Fireside

Images of the New England Home
1760–1860

Jane C. Nylander

Alfred A. Knopf
New York
1993

THIS IS A BORZOI BOOK
PUBLISHED BY ALFRED A. KNOPF, INC.

Library of Congress Cataloging-in-Publication Data
Nylander, Jane C.
Our own snug fireside : images of the New England home, 1760–1860
Jane C. Nylander. —1st ed.
p. cm.
Includes bibliographical references and index.
ISBN 0-394-54984-8
1. New England—Social life and customs. 2. Home—New England—History. I. Title.
F8.N95 1993
974'.03—dc20 92-17148 CIP

Manufactured in the United States of America
First Edition

For Richard

Contents

PREFACE *Great Neatness and Convenience* ix

CHAPTER I *Introduction: Glimpses of the New England Home* 3

CHAPTER II *Our Great Family* 20

CHAPTER III *Going to Housekeeping* 54

CHAPTER IV *Frosty Mornings and Stinging Fingers: The Effects of Winter* 74

CHAPTER V *Clean, Bright, and Comfortable: Dimensions of Housework* 103

CHAPTER VI *Clean and Decent: A Family's Clothing* 143

CHAPTER VII *Toward Our Mutual Support* 163

CHAPTER VIII *A Comfortable Sufficiency: Food and the New England Kitchen* 183

CHAPTER IX *The Pleasure of Our Friends and Neighbors* 221

CHAPTER X *The One Day Above All Others: New England Thanksgiving* 261

ACKNOWLEDGMENTS 283

NOTES 287

BIBLIOGRAPHY 301

INDEX 311

Preface

Great Neatness and Convenience

THIS BOOK EXPLORES THE INTERSECTION BETWEEN REALITY AND REMINISCENCE in the broad scope and minute details of everyday life in New England during the years 1760–1860. Its goal is to define the appearance and confirm the daily activity within the early New England home, which was to become enshrined as a result of nineteenth-century literary, historical, antiquarian, and artistic movements. By using sources ranging back to the middle of the eighteenth century, it includes the experience of the parents and grandparents of the nineteenth-century antiquarians—those who knew the olden times firsthand and were able to enrich the story as it was told and retold in later generations.

The years 1760–1860 encompassed the transformation of New England households from a time of mutual production to an idealized domesticity and were characterized by increasing gentility, materialism, and personal privacy. The high point of this change coincided with the childhood of those who wrote the books, staged the photographs, established the museums, wrote the pageants, gave the Lady Washington tea parties, labeled their grandmothers' tea cups, and suffered through the disruptions of the Civil War—an experience that undoubtedly stimulated their activities as well as shaped their understanding. Because they viewed the preindustrial New England society as a unit, they disregarded the political consequences of the events of 1776 and the reality of mill towns and burgeoning cities, often referring to the entire period as "colonial" and regarding the region as "rural."

Although this book presents the material aspects of New England's domestic life, it is neither a decorating guide nor a history of the decorative arts, household furnishings, or changing domestic technology. There are many excellent books and articles that explain the appearance and placement of objects within the home.[1] This volume explores the idea that the domestic objects of an earlier time were selected for their utility as well as for ornament. It therefore considers objects and their arrangement from the point of view of function and makes understanding the routines of everyday life itself the basis for understanding the New England home.

This book characterizes the personal experience of selected individuals as it is revealed in their own writings: their diaries, letters, travel accounts, and reminiscences. It is amplified by carefully chosen illustrations, all of which are of American scenes and most of which are of New England origin. The result is admittedly selective and subjective, focusing on households in the middle and upper end of the economic spectrum—those prosperous families who shared mutually acceptable attitudes and values, as well as a comfortable standard of living. Their New England was centered in Boston, and they lived mostly in small villages or on settled farms in Massachusetts, the Connecticut Valley, Rhode Island, southern New Hampshire, and southern Maine.

The ideal New England home was perceived in the late nineteenth century as warm, welcoming, comfortable, and unchanging—a stable center—which formed a counterpoint to the surging forces of change in contemporary society. This book explores the evidence of those qualities. Traditional patterns of everyday life and household furnishing are compared to the changes in domestic spaces that occurred in response to factors as diverse as prosperity and poverty, summertime and wintertime, advancing age, or a houseful of children. The sense of internal order that characterized everyday life in early New England encompassed many kinds of change. When Sarah Orne Jewett wrote about the ideal home with its "chairs all in their places," she knew that those chairs were frequently moved and used by diverse people for diverse tasks; yet the proper places were as important in the overall scheme of things as the person who used them and put them back.

The ideal New England home was also characterized by hard work, frugality, and a degree of self-sufficiency. The thump of the churn and the whir of the spinning wheel were seen by the antiquarians as the dominant rhythm of daily life. Recent historical studies have rightly challenged these concepts of self-sufficiency,[2] defined the barter economy,[3] and recognized the spinning wheel as the ultimate icon of the New England homestead.[4] Yet there was once a solid basis for these assumptions, and perhaps we can place them in context: identify the degree to which they are justified, acknowledge gender roles, define the complex nature of household and neighborhood economy, and preserve the essence of the image through definition.

The sources are selective, chosen from wills and inventories, early newspapers, published and manuscript diaries, letters and account books, the published accounts of European travelers, and the beginnings of New England's prescriptive literature in the advice books of Robert Roberts, William A. Alcott, Lydia Maria Child, and Catharine Beecher. These are amplified by the superb descriptive writing in the homesick letters of the first New England missionary women in Honolulu, the richly detailed reminiscences of Sarah Anna Emery and Caroline King, the semiautobiographical novels of Harriet Beecher Stowe, and the vivid description in the short stories of Sarah Orne Jewett and Alice Brown, as well as by paintings, engravings, and pictures of all kinds, documented cups and saucers, chairs and tables, bedsheets, and baby clothes.

Because this book is centered in the home and its primary characters are women, the earliest sources are the most limited. The writings of eighteenth-century New England women are scarce indeed, reflecting a time of limited female literacy, demanding schedules of daily work in a highly productive household economy, and the stress of supervising and caring for large and complex extended families. Eighteenth-century diaries that describe daily routine throughout a lifetime are even more rare; many of the journals of that period were kept by unmarried girls who abandoned them under the pressures of housekeeping; others focus almost exclusively on spiritual concerns. For these reasons, Sarah Snell Bryant, Elizabeth Porter Phelps, and Ruth Henshaw Bascom are important characters in this book, and its rhythms reflect their lives. As diarists, they have become historical heroines, sharing with us the intimate details of their household work and management, their contributions to the household economy, and their care and concern for their families and for the common community.

Almost every day from 1794 until her family departed for Illinois in 1835, Sarah Snell Bryant (1768–1847) picked up her pen and made an entry in her diary.[5] After noting the state of the weather, she wrote brief comments about her daily work, the health and activities of other members of the household, the names of those who came to call or to whom she paid visits, and other details of her life in Cummington, Massachusetts. Because the diary was kept for so long a time, it reveals the influence of changing circumstance—the arrival of children, the supervision of restless adolescents, the pain and diminished circumstances of widowhood, and the temptation to seek a new life in the West. Above all, it defines the never-ending nature of daily work and permits a kind of analysis that is revealing. Not at all introspective, Sarah Bryant's diary is most useful for the picture it provides of the patterns of everyday life, with its complex and changing cast of characters and the daily round of housework, food preparation, dairying, textile making, sewing, and laundry.

At Forty Acres, the "convenient mansion" built by her father, Moses Porter, in Hadley, Massachusetts, in 1752, Elizabeth Porter Phelps (1747–1817) kept a similar diary, from the time she was a young girl. While the early and later entries of the fifty-four years of this diary are primarily spiritual in nature, the entries made during the middle years of Elizabeth Phelps's life are expanded with rich detail about the management of the family's large farm and the complexities of providing for a household that eventually included her son Charles, daughter Betsy, and adopted daughter Thankful; her widowed mother; a highly mobile husband; two slaves, Caesar and Phyllis; a shifting number of farmhands, hired girls, orphan children, cousins, in-laws, and travelers; impoverished, injured, or insane neighbors; hired dressmakers, weavers, tailors, and milliners; and almost daily visitors. In the diary, Elizabeth Phelps made notations about births, sicknesses, and deaths among her neighbors and recorded her own participation in these events as assistant, watcher, or mourner. The brief diary entries offer an outline of domestic activity and community interaction that are greatly amplified by the regular correspondence that Elizabeth exchanged with her husband and children whenever they were separated. Perhaps the most revealing of these letters are those of domestic advice sent to her daughters and daughter-in-law when they were newly married, and those to her husband when she was away from home for weeks at a time waiting to assist at the births of her grandchildren.[6]

In central Massachusetts and southern New Hampshire, Ruth Henshaw Bascom (1772–1847) also kept a daily journal throughout most of her life, beginning in 1789 at the age of seventeen and continuing for fifty-seven years. During the years when she was responsible for management of a parsonage for her second husband, the Reverend Ezekiel Lysander Bascom, she also recorded household expenditures and kept careful records of the letters she sent and received. Some of her diaries include charts noting the size of the family and counting the numbers of people present for each meal, callers, and overnight visitors.[7] Ruth Bascom's descriptions of everyday household routine began at an earlier age than those of Sarah Snell Bryant, and she was more concerned with concrete details than the young Elizabeth Porter. Through her eyes, we see the

1. SARAH SNELL BRYANT (1768–1847), OIL ON CANVAS, BY "MR. CLARK," 1829. COURTESY OF THE TRUSTEES OF RESERVATIONS, BRYANT HOMESTEAD, CUMMINGTON, MASSACHUSETTS.

On October 29, 1829, Mrs. Bryant's diary records: "Mr. Clark came from New York to take my portrait." William Cullen Bryant may have been thinking of his own mother when he wrote to his brother John on November 21, 1831: "Marry a person who has a good mother, who is of a good family that does not meddle with the concerns of their neighbors, and who, along with a proper degree of industry and economy, possesses a love of reading and a desire of knowledge. A mere pot-wrestler will not do for you." (William Cullen Bryant II and Thomas G. Voss, The Letters of William Cullen Bryant, *vol. 1, 1809–1836 [New York: Fordham University Press, 1975], p. 308.)*

degree of textile production expected of the teenaged daughter of a prosperous Leicester, Massachusetts, family; her problems as a young schoolteacher; the joys of marriage and establishing an independent household turn to the ashes of widowhood, the breakup of a home, a second marriage with stepchildren and parishioners to care for, an unstable husband, and the satisfaction of a financially rewarding and independent career as a profile artist. Through it all there were beds to make, floors to wash, laundry to hang out, and sick neighbors to care for. To obtain cash income, Ruth turned first to her needle, making

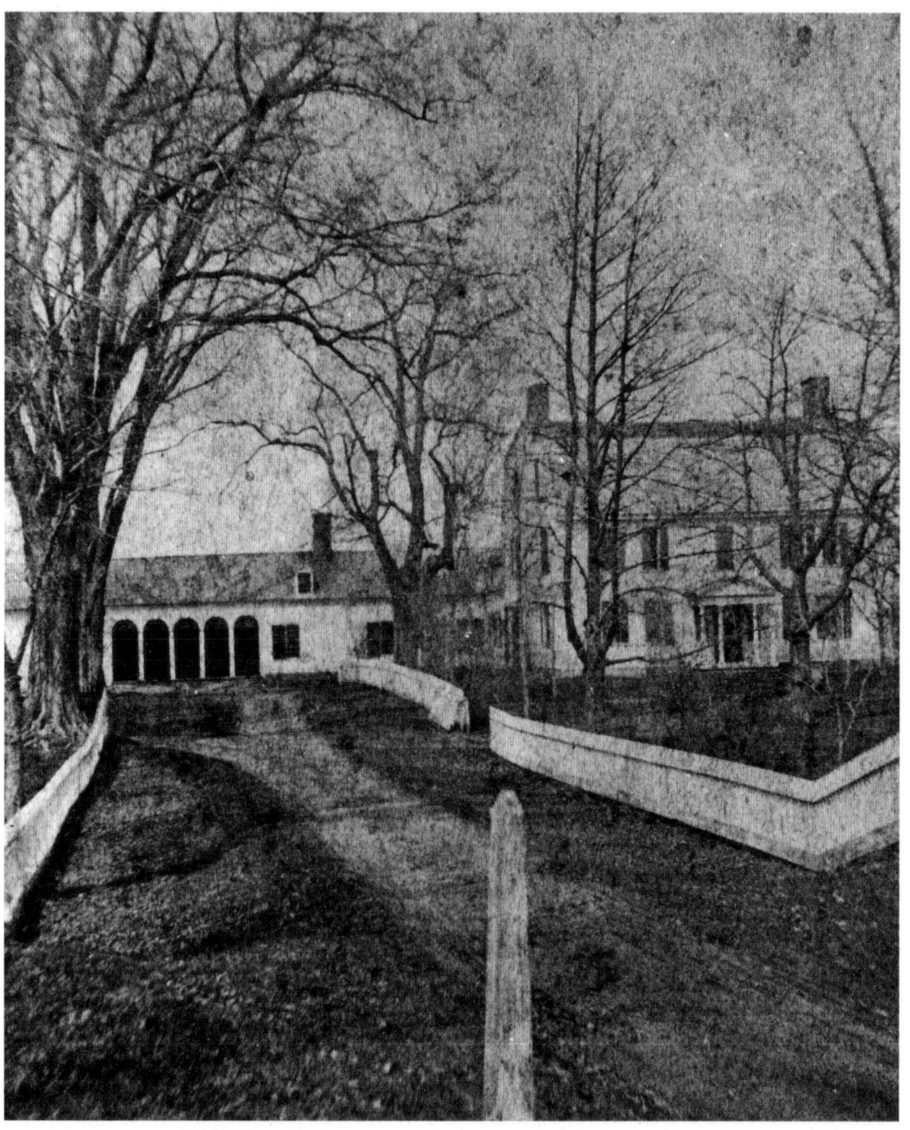

2. FORTY ACRES, HADLEY, MASSACHUSETTS, ONE-HALF OF A STEREOGRAPH, C. 1865. PORTER-PHELPS-HUNTINGTON FOUNDATION, AMHERST COLLEGE LIBRARY.

Elizabeth Porter Phelps was born at Forty Acres and lived there until her death in 1817. The house was enlarged and extensively remodeled at the time of her marriage to Charles Phelps in 1770 and again in 1799, when they hoped that their son, Charles, and his bride, Sally Parsons, might live with them in the old homestead. Timothy Dwight described the property in 1801: "This estate lies on the eastern bank of the Connecticut River, and contains about six hundred acres . . . , on one border are excellent mills; on another a river furnishing cheap transportation to market. It is intersected by two great roads leading to Boston and to Hartford . . . and within very convenient distance all the pleasures of refined and intelligent society may be easily enjoyed." (Travels, *I*, *259–60.)*

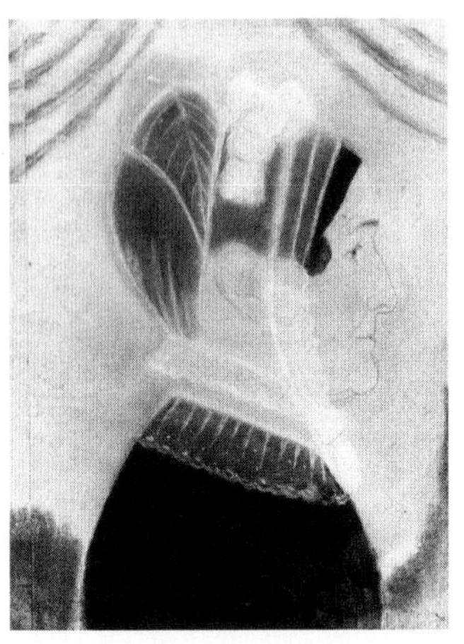

3. RUTH HENSHAW BASCOM (1772–1848), SELF-PORTRAIT, PASTEL, C. 1835–40. HISTORIC DEERFIELD, INC., DEERFIELD, MASSACHUSETTS.

gowns and bonnets for her neighbors, sometimes interpreting a new fashion in a rural community, and often being called to the home of a recently deceased person to spend all night sewing mourning garments and bonnets in order to have them ready in time for a funeral or for the bereaved family to wear to meeting on the following Sabbath. Beginning in 1819, she made fewer mourning bonnets and began instead to make the profile portraits for which she is now well known, completing thirty in that year alone. Though childless, her role as a minister's wife required her to care for hundreds in her time, and the life revealed in Ruth Bascom's journal defines yet another kind of New England home.[8] Despite life's many uncertainties, it was home that formed the stable center of this woman's life. On New Year's Day 1825, Ruth Bascom described its importance in her diary: "This year opens upon us, surrounded by every external necessity and convenience. a warm and convenient House and outhouse. food, fuel, & fire & ten thousand blessings more than we deserve bestowed by a kind Providence."

While traveling through northern Massachusetts in 1793, that practiced observer the Reverend William Bentley noted, "There are a number of fine houses in the great road which have a fine effect upon the Traveller, astonish him noticeably with the idea of ease by affluence. The Farms have great neatness, & convenience."[9] Sarah Snell Bryant, Elizabeth Porter Phelps, Ruth Henshaw Bascom, and Sarah Anna Emery lived in such places. They, and many others, can open the doors of those fine houses and share the complex reality that was everyday life in old New England.

Our Own Snug Fireside

I

Introduction: Glimpses of the New England Home

AMERICAN LITERATURE IS RICH IN IMAGES OF THE NEW ENGLAND HOME and of women's central role within it. From Longfellow's depiction of Priscilla Mullins at her spinning wheel in "The Courtship of Miles Standish" to the vivid word-pictures of Harriet Beecher Stowe in *Oldtown Folks,* or those of Francis Underwood in *Quabbin,* we are given glimpses of another world that seems somehow to have been frugal, hardworking, and guided by stern moral principles yet at the same time warm, satisfying, and firmly centered on the home and family. Such an ideal home was located in the rural countryside or a small village, and it was envisioned as a haven from the impact of modern technology and the rapid pace of change. In these writings, the old-fashioned country ways were idealized and seen as a reflection of an earlier, more desirable time.

The domestic images that have enchanted New England writers and artists since at least the mid-nineteenth century offer a window to a complex reality. Both the romantic visions of regional poets such as Longfellow and Whittier and the more careful descriptions of the local colorists bring life and greater understanding of the furnishing and functioning of New England homes as they are described today by academic historians and re-created in the period rooms of museums. Although Sarah Orne Jewett sought to convey only "the tone of things" in her fiction, and her observations are sometimes castigated as the romanticism of a summer visitor, her descriptions of rural homes are vivid with myriad concrete details that she had observed while making visits to old people when accompanying her father on his rounds as a physician. A different point of view was offered by authors of family reminiscences and town histories, yet their descriptions of households and domestic events were rooted in an effort to portray a complex everyday reality. Selected images from these homes provide the background for the narrative illustrations in nineteenth-century juvenile fiction and temperance literature. They became fully developed in the paintings of Frank Shapleigh and the lithographs of Currier and Ives, and the carefully staged photographs of Emma Coleman, Frances and Mary Allen, Chansonetta Stanley Emmons, and Wallace Nutting

Almost all of these people—authors, artists, and antiquarians—were New England natives who were born in the late eighteenth or early nineteenth century to people who had been born in the eighteenth century. Many of them knew the rhythms of rural life from personal experience. The rigid moral canon and patterns of work and activity they had learned as children and the stories they had heard by firelight informed their understanding and gave structure to their daily lives. They had heard firsthand the stories of hard work and hard decisions, Indian attack and revolution. To them there was an immediacy about the past, as well as an awareness that the way of life they cherished was gravely threatened by factors beyond their control. Their work was

4. EAST CHAMBER IN THE PETER CUSHING HOUSE, HINGHAM, MASSACHUSETTS, WATERCOLOR, BY ELLA EMORY, 1878. PRIVATE COLLECTION.

A room furnished in the late eighteenth century, and still in use nearly one hundred years later, reflects the unchanging qualities of the domestic environment known by many nineteenth-century New England antiquarians.

devoted to documenting and memorializing a past that they felt was rapidly disappearing in the face of immigration, urbanization, and industrialization. These authors and historians also feared that as the oldest people in each town lost control of their faculties and died, there would be no reliable evidence of the earlier times. Hence, the labors of the antiquarians were at once inspired and shaped by the experience of their elders. They began to write down the stories, to describe the settings, and to draw the scene as it then appeared or as it was described to them by someone who had seen it a generation or two before. Their motivation was well expressed by J. H. Temple in his 1872 history of Whately, Massachusetts: "Part of the design of this book is to preserve a record of the manners and customs of our fathers; and as the generation that saw these early homes is now so nearly gone—with whom will perish the *first-hand* knowledge—it will not be out of place here to draw a rough sketch of one of those houses, and the family life within. Perhaps our grand-children may be interested in looking at it."[1]

It should not surprise us that these writings often centered upon the home or that some of the best of them were created by women. Their vivid literary and artistic images arose from actual daily experience in household management, and they were certainly influenced by the point of view encouraged by the authors of nineteenth-century domestic advice literature. They were also victims of the Civil War, which had left a large number of unmarried women in modest circumstances in village homes or on family farms throughout New England—a world of widows and spinsters at once unwilling and unable to reap the benefits of the industrial age.

These authors are now often criticized for their subjective and romantic points of view, yet their work should be considered in light of their own goals and circumstances. They understood that the details of everyday life might be considered trivial, yet they also understood that the intimate world of the home is at the core of human experience. By preserving the details of New England life as they had known it, these authors hoped to strengthen the foundation of a society confronted by dramatic social and economic change. Caroline King of Salem warned us that her writing of reminiscences did "not pretend to any historical or statistical accuracy" and acknowledged that she was "not sure" of her dates. Her impulse for writing *When I Lived in Salem* came from a mind "full of detached pictures" of the Salem of her childhood, and the work was undertaken in the hope of giving "the young people of the present day some details of the lives of their grand-mothers and great-grandmothers."[2] In the same vein, Eliza Orne Sturgis, also of Salem, penned her wonderful "Recollec-

5. *The Old Arm Chair,* SHEET-MUSIC COVER, THAYER & COMPANY, LITHOGRAPH, BOSTON, 1840. PRIVATE COLLECTION.

In this sentimental ballad, a piece of furniture is honored for its associations with a beloved family member who was central to an idealized home.

tions of the 'Old Tucker House,' " which, "without pretending to be accurate in detail, gives a faithful picture of life in the home of those who are now all departed."[3]

The home the New England authors described and many people yearned for was envisioned as large, commodious, welcoming, and sheltering—a place where the fire never went out. It was a center of personal and community values: a physical reflection of strength, frugality, hard work, rugged individualism, neighborly trust, and community concern. It should not be surprising that these authors also imagined such a home as always warm and clean, self-sufficient and unchanging, immune to the influences of the outside world and the pressures of the marketplace. The well-thumbed Bible and worn threshold, the carefully stitched sampler and the chest of snowy linen redolent with the scent of crumbling lavender were important in the definition of place; the vacant chair personified an influential patriarch or nurturing mother. Most important, the spinning wheel, the kitchen fireplace, the tall case clock, the cradle, and the butter churn became domestic icons, celebrated in poetry and paint for generations yet unborn. A home that contained such objects provided identity, for it had been lived in by one's ancestors and contained relics of their daily life: locks of their hair, trunks of their clothing, and bundles of their letters. Such a home also provided a sense of continuity—a firm ground from which one could set forth to face whatever life had to offer in the city, the Far West, or abroad.[4] With home as an anchor, one could be secure in the knowledge that there was a firm, unchanging center to which one could return in prosperity or adversity, whenever one was in need of moral replenishing or a fresh start.

Such a home was usually envisioned as a commodious farmhouse or a comfortable village dwelling, with overarching trees, a tidy dooryard, bountiful fields, and a large barn that was somehow both mysterious and productive. The house itself was described as either a two-story mansion or a quaint saltbox; both had multiple rooms clustered around a central chimney. In reality, the majority of eighteenth- or early-nineteenth-century New England houses was much smaller, especially in rural areas. The most common house type was what

6. JONATHAN SAYWARD HOUSE, YORK, MAINE, PHOTOGRAPH, C. 1890. COURTESY OF THE SOCIETY FOR THE PRESERVATION OF NEW ENGLAND ANTIQUITIES.

This venerable pile was the home of two sisters, Mary and Eliza-beth Barrell, who lived their entire lives in their great-grand-parents' house, making very few changes. As early as 1868, the sisters welcomed summer visitors to their home, where they delighted in showing the ancient furnishings and historical relics in the parlor.

is today known as a "cape"—a one- or one-and-a-half-story house with three or four rooms around a central chimney, the upper floor containing either unfinished space or a few plastered chambers. These houses ranged in size from 10 by 14 feet to up to 15 or 16 feet square.[5] A much smaller number of houses were a full two stories in height and measured as much as 25 by 45 feet square; a few were even larger. Many of these early buildings were so unsubstantial that they have not survived; others have been added on to and remodeled into the larger houses that later served as the ideal.[6]

As early as 1826, circumstances combined to help make one tiny rural house a symbol of the hardworking New Englander's confrontation with an unsympathetic environment. Deep in New Hampshire's Crawford Notch, where the sun sets in the early afternoon in wintertime, the home of the ill-fated Willey family stood unscathed while the family and their hired man were killed outdoors seeking safety from an avalanche in 1826. The house remained standing until 1890, with many of the family furnishings left in place—a monument to hard work, determination, and bad luck that was frequented by travelers, celebrated in fiction, and whose image spread round the world on stereographic cards. Usually the ideal home was set in a more sympathetic place and circumstance, yet its concrete details seem to float through both. A country village, an upland farm, or even a quiet city street could serve as a setting for the ideal. The authors agreed that New England was a special place where life was indeed different—a factor that was recognized and cherished by New Englanders, who have always had a strong sense of place. The residents of early New England

7. THE WILLEY HOUSE, PENCIL AND WATERCOLOR, BY JAMES ELLIOTT CABOT, 1845. NEW HAMPSHIRE HISTORICAL SOCIETY.

were strongly influenced by the traditions of Calvinism and the routine of the established Congregational church, honoring a certain stoicism, hard work, and stern independence, which were interpreted as self-sufficiency. They were proud of observing Thanksgiving as the most important day of the year and self-righteous in refusing to observe Christmas day, which they considered an emblem of popery. Respect for the established social order characterized their relationships and were symbolized in the use of the honorifics "sir," "ma'm," "grandsir," and "grandma'm." Most women referred to their husbands as "Mister" or "Doctor," even within the privacy of their own diaries.

As early as the 1850s, Samuel Goodrich defined the particular New England point of view as a "moral sense, in every man's bosom, impelling him to seek improvement in all things, cooperating with this liberty, giving him the right and the ability to seek happiness in his own way—which forms this univer-

8. FURNITURE BELONGING TO THE WILLEY FAMILY, STEREOGRAPH BY CLOUGH & KIMBALL, C. 1870. NEW HAMPSHIRE HISTORICAL SOCIETY.

A summer traveler who visited the White Mountains in 1831 recalled in 1880: "Our next stop was at the Willey House in the Notch, which had remained closed, just as it was left by the frightened inhabitants, when the awful avalanche occurred—where, amid the war of the elements, and the descending rocks and trees, the whole household perished—No one had then been found willing to occupy the house—we could see through the windows, the table with the crockery left as by an unfinished meal, a tea kettle, an iron pot, and some other cooking utensils on the hearth and the brands that had fallen apart and died out—It still stands there I believe or as much of it as relic hunters, with yankee blades have allowed." ("Reminiscences of the White Mountains by Mary Jane Thomas," Historical New Hampshire *28 [Spring 1973]:1, 48.)*

sal spirit of improvement—the distinguishing feature of the New England people."[7]

New Englanders perceived themselves as deeply religious people, and they observed the hand of God in everyday occurrences. The minister was both an honored member of the community and a role model, the head of both his own household and his congregation. Although he was supported by taxes, he often managed a farm as well as his clerical duties. Early in his ministerial career the Reverend William Bentley affirmed that "New England has been remarkable in my day for the most careful observance of Sunday,"[8] although fewer than half of the total population were actually church members, and many women's diaries testify to the ease with which they stayed at home on Sundays when the weather was poor or they felt ill. An English visitor in 1827 observed that "at sunset the Sabbath began, finishing at the same hour upon Sunday evening.

This is very common in many parts of New England. After sunset on Saturday no one walks or drives out, and they would not even drink tea in a quiet way with a neighbor."[9] For those who did attend the day-long weekly meetings, with their sociable nooning, church-going served as both an affirmation of community and a tangible expression of rank and privilege. Seats were assigned or purchased according to social and economic standing, and the clothing of the congregation underscored the differences. As a young bride, Eliza Susan Morton Quincy attended the Brattle Street Church in Boston and observed "many peculiarities in dress, character and manners, differing from those of New York and Philadelphia," which the New York native found "very Striking."[10] As urban American society became less homogeneous, these New England differences were even more marked in country villages.

Both literate and literary, New England townspeople placed great value on education and early on supported common school education. A certain intellectual rigor characterized the thinking of both men and women, many of whom prided themselves on their high-mindedness and regarded *Pilgrim's Progress* as a road map for life.

Because Colonial New Englanders had their roots in England and were confined to trade with the mother country through the restrictions of British mercantile law, their tastes were profoundly influenced by London fashion and the products of British manufacturers. By placing standing orders for fashionable goods with London agents, wealthy New Englanders could be assured of delivery in just a few weeks. A restrictive and unfashionable country taste was defined by British exporters who chose to send outdated merchandise or items of inferior quality to be sold by storekeepers in rural areas, where consumers had little choice. Still, even in New England's cultural center and largest city, Boston, there seems to have been a kind of conservative norm that expressed itself in disdain for those who were overly concerned with conspicuous consumption and a simmering envy of those who were.

New England singularity went far beyond hard work, high-mindedness, and a peculiar or conservative style in dress or furnishings, however. Most highly valued was a strong sense of family and community, which expressed itself in frequent visiting, sociable exchanges of work, and tangible evidence of neighborly concern. People expected to assist each other on occasions of birth, illness, serious accident, fire, or death. They took over farm chores, provided meals, gave medical advice, brought remedies, coached laboring mothers, watched through the night, cared for each other's children and livestock, laid out the dead, sewed mourning garments, attended funerals, and prayed for each other. Small acts of personal charity were expanded and institutionalized in the early nineteenth century in maternal associations, social libraries, charitable organizations, and a variety of movements advocating temperance, prison reform, vegetarianism, and abolition. Seeking to define the special quality of New Englanders within the brotherhood of mankind, Mrs. Susanna Rowson, the proprietress of a young ladies' academy in Boston, summed up the chief characteristic of New Englanders as "that humanity and spirit of brotherly love, which cannot behold a fellow creature in distress, without extending the hand of comfort and assistance. They are friendly, hospitable, and well inclined toward strangers; so much so, that few who have resided in New England any considerable time, but quit it with regret, and remember its inhabitants with sentiments of respect and esteem."[11]

The period of intense interest to the nineteenth-century New England antiquarians was usually referred to as the "olden time." An imprecise term, it seems to have encompassed two or three full generations—the time within the actual memory of the oldest people. Anything beyond living memory was considered "ancient." For someone like Sarah Anna Smith Emery, born in 1787 in West Newbury, Massachusetts, this time ranged back to the girlhood of her grandmother in the early eighteenth century. Sarah Emery's *Reminiscences of a Nonagenarian* contains descriptions of many aspects of life in the family homestead, built in 1707. She acknowledged that the book was "chiefly derived from the recollections of my mother; but recitals by my father, grandparents and other deceased relatives and friends have aided the work," and she added that she had obtained "many anecdotes and facts from several aged persons still living."[12] Her book includes physical descriptions of the homes of friends and relatives on nearby farms as well as in Newburyport and Boston. Within its pages the author has wrought a rich web of detailed description of everyday experience and social interaction that recognizes the impact of the changing seasons, the demands of daily work, the expectations of gender roles, and a changing cast of characters as family members moved in and out of the house, married and gave birth, prospered and grew old, sickened and died. Sarah Emery knew from firsthand account that her mother had been in the garret "giving it a spring cleaning" and that "candles were lighted for the dinner table" on the memorable "dark day" of May 19, 1780.[13] Even though Sarah herself was not born until seven years later, there is no reason to doubt the veracity of this or many of her other accounts, even though few of them are as precisely dated. In the same way that modern Americans remember where they were and what they were doing on the day Neil Armstrong first set foot on the moon or John

9. THE SMITH PLACE, CRANE HILL, WEST NEWBURY, MASSACHUSETTS, ANONYMOUS LITHOGRAPH, IN SARAH ANNA EMERY, *Reminiscences of a Nonagenarian* (NEWBURYPORT, 1879), FRONTISPIECE.

This was the childhood home of Sarah Anna (Smith) Emery and is the setting of many of the scenes and activities described in her Reminiscences of a Nonagenarian. *The original part of the house (shown here as a rear lean-to) was built in 1707, and additional rooms were soon built; the whole was remodeled by Sarah Smith's grandfather at the time of his marriage in 1748. Successive generations of the family set up housekeeping here, adding their own new furnishings to the accumulations of their forebears.*

F. Kennedy was assassinated, remarkable public occurrences, such as the "dark day" or receipt of the news of the battle of April 19, 1775, or of George Washington's death in December 1799, and particular personal events, such as births, marriages, and deaths, are the milestones that have always defined historical time. Although the selection of the topics covered by Sarah Emery's reminiscences was undoubtedly influenced by her own later experience and focused by the times in which she was writing, her book contains a great deal of information that can be confirmed by research in more traditional academic sources. For this very reason, *Reminiscences of a Nonagenarian,* and many other books like it, should be valued for the rich detail with which they illustrate everyday life in a specific place and time. Although not quite primary sources, they are certainly not fiction. Like any fine work of art, they add depth to the record and help to fill in the outlines of a picture with a wealth of vivid, carefully selected details that richly illustrate the subject at hand.

During the last half of the nineteenth century, a number of talented artists and photographers also turned their attention to documenting the pastoral New England scene and the idealized activities of the home. Ignoring the hubbub of the city marketplace and the noisy confusion of the factory, these artists sifted through the complex visual stimuli of the modern world around them and produced tranquil images that personified the unchanging ideals they admired. The dutiful spinster was idealized by Thomas Eakins in a work like *The Courtship,* while Frank Shapleigh and E. L. Henry depicted domestic interiors in which modern technology was unknown and everyday life was governed by the weather and the rhythms of agriculture and ancient processes, their occupants apparently unaware of any alternative. In Deerfield, Massachusetts, and York, Maine, Frances and Mary Allen and Emma Coleman set up their heavy and bulky photographic equipment, unpacked their trunks of old-fashioned clothing, and made narrative photographs that documented household processes, such as flax processing and candle dipping, that seemed somehow endangered, or re-enacted social occasions, such as quilting parties and preparing Thanksgiving dinner, that seemed central to the New England domestic experience. Neither the painters nor the photographers seemed to notice that they created visual anachronisms by juxtaposing in their "old-fashioned" costumes the bonnets of 1830 with the gowns of 1860 and by ignoring the influence of the late-nineteenth-century aesthetic in their own work or their neighbors' interiors. For these artists, capturing a mood of old-fashioned simplicity was the goal, and there was satisfaction in knowing that each completed picture helped to preserve an image of a precious part of New England life.

A more detailed antiquarian sensibility arose early within some nineteenth-

10. OLD KITCHEN, BARTLETT, NEW HAMPSHIRE, 1883, OIL ON CANVAS, BY FRANK H. SHAPLEIGH. COLLECTION OF GERTRUDE AND DAVID TUCKER. PHOTOGRAPH COURTESY OF THE NEW HAMPSHIRE HISTORICAL SOCIETY.

Shapleigh's popular interior views focused on a capacious hearth and recognizable antique furnishings.

11. GARRET OF THE STEPHEN ROBBINS HOMESTEAD, EAST LEXINGTON, MASSACHUSETTS, PHOTOGRAPH, C. 1900–10. COURTESY OF THE SOCIETY FOR THE PRESERVATION OF NEW ENGLAND ANTIQUITIES.

"What a museum of curiosities is the garret of a well-regulated New England house. Here meet together, as if by some preconcerted arrangement, all the broken down chairs of the household, all the spavined tables, all the seedy hats, all the intoxicated-looking books, all the split walking sticks that have retired from business (weary with the march of life). The pots, the pans, the trunks, the bottles—who may hope to make inventory of the numberless odds and ends collected in this bewildering lumber-room? But what a place it is to sit of an afternoon with the rain pattering on the roof! What a place in which to read Gulliver's Travels!*" (Thomas Bailey Aldrich,* The Story of a Bad Boy *[Boston, 1870].) The antiquarian treasures that survived here were carefully labeled by Miss Ellen Stone, the last occupant of the family homestead.*

century New England households, where family relics were identified, labeled, and set aside, either as curiosities or as icons. For some, it was enough to save a few things that were associated with the most revered ancestors: the signers of the Declaration of Independence, the royal governor, the honored pastor, the Pilgrim father, or the Indian captive. Coats of arms, painted or embroidered family records, and portraits were honored and carefully preserved by those interested in genealogy. For others, there was interest in objects associated with family rituals, and they saved the wedding gowns, the samplers, and the infant garments.

In some unusual households the antiquarian interest extended to almost every little thing. In such places, labels naming former owners and identifying specific functions or singular circumstances were placed on each object, box, or trunk as it was carefully packed away in the attic or in a bureau drawer. As much as it was hoped that these objects would find future usefulness within the family, it was recognized that they could evoke an image of an earlier time through association with an individual personality or by documenting information that might otherwise be lost. This kind of informative labeling was done by people with a particular historical awareness who were often members of the generation that had actually used the items themselves or had grown up with those who had. In East Lexington, Massachusetts, Ellen Stone labeled her family's possessions in this way, using information given to her by her aunt,

Caira Robbins, who was born in 1796. Ellen labeled samples of bed ticking as well as homespun sheets, tablecloths, and bed coverings; she saved examples of simple window curtains and highly fashionable bed valances; and she did not overlook the towels, toothbrushes, bars of soap, and papers of pins at the same time that she saved and labeled the tea cups, looking glasses, and trunks of clothing that caught the interest of many of her contemporaries. From this rich contextual hoard have come some of the best documented artifacts of the New England home—another dimension added by someone who preserved information as well as objects, which is the best kind of antiquarian activity.[14]

12. "WHY DON'T YOU SPEAK FOR YOURSELF, JOHN?," CAST PLASTER SCULPTURE, BY JOHN ROGERS, C. 1860. COURTESY OF THE SOCIETY FOR THE PRESERVATION OF NEW ENGLAND ANTIQUITIES. PHOTOGRAPH BY J. DAVID BOHL.

Rogers's popular sculpture brought the figure of Priscilla Mullins at her spinning wheel into many American parlors, where Longfellow's 1858 poem "The Courtship of Miles Standish" was already well known.

Even without antiquarian labels, the practical tools of daily life—especially the brass kettle, the warming pan, and the spinning wheel—were elevated to special status as they became the quintessential symbols of the New England home. These things were highly sought after by early antique collectors and found a new usefulness when they were enshrined as relics in the parlor. Indeed, as old houses were remodeled and expanded, the old kitchen itself was sometimes used as a parlor or sitting room, and the broad hearth became an important symbol of family unity, even as iron stoves or central heating greatly improved upon its original function.

A formal memorializing movement established itself in New England as early as the first centennial anniversaries of settlement, battle victory, or Indian massacre. Usually these occasions were observed by religious ceremonies, and those sermons that were published are important records of both historical fact and later interpretation and commemoration. By the end of the eighteenth century, a minister in Deerfield, Massachusetts, called for the preservation of historical relics associated with earlier times. By the first round of bicentennial observances in the 1820s, some of these objects began to be presented to the public in formal exhibitions, the first permanent repository being at Plymouth, Massachusetts, where Pilgrim Hall opened on Forefathers' Day, December 22, 1824, and exhibited furniture and a spinning wheel that were thought to have come over on the *Mayflower.*

Sometimes household relics were gathered together and exhibited in settings

13. "THINGS OLD AND NEW," ILLUSTRATION IN CLARENCE COOK, *The House Beautiful* (NEW YORK, 1877), P. 190.

"A 'restoration' effected in an old house at Newport, by Mr. McKim, one of the foremost of our young architects," in which the large old kitchen fireplace has been made the center of a modern living room and given "a new lease on life, and whatever new was added kept true to the spirit of the old time, without any antiquarian slavishness."

14. "OAKEN CHAIR BROUGHT OVER BY GOV^R CARVER IN THE MAYFLOWER IN 1620, & NOW IN PILGRIM HALL, PLYMOUTH," LITHOGRAPH, BY WILLIAM S. PENDLETON, BOSTON, 1826–34. PRIVATE COLLECTION.

An important relic of the first settlement at Plymouth, the Carver chair had already entered a New England museum collection by the time this print was published. Although modern wood analysis now disproves the idea that this chair was brought over on the Mayflower, this may be the earliest published image of a piece of American furniture.

that suggested domestic interiors—tangible visions of the ideal. One of the earliest historical re-creations of a New England home was the "scenic representation of the old Franklin House in Milk street, Boston," with two rooms arranged as they were thought to have looked on that momentous occasion on "which the illustrious Philosopher was born January 17, 1706." This "novel exhibition" was set up from December 21 to 30, 1858, in the new Boston Music Hall as part of a benefit fair to raise money for the building fund of the Boston Young Men's Christian Association.

The re-creation of the Benjamin Franklin birthplace was constructed from plans and drawings furnished by D. W. N. B. Shurtleff[15]; and the rooms were "furnished, as nearly as can be, in the Manner of the olden time, many persons having kindly lent articles of furniture for the purpose." Not only did the fair committee attempt to re-create the furnishings of the chamber in which Franklin was born, but they set up the parlor as well. At regular intervals throughout the fair, costumed volunteers performed tableaux and led visitors in Psalm singing, "after the manner of our forefathers."[16] In this exhibition, the cradle, tall case clock, blazing hearth, and spinning wheels were firmly established as essential components of New England period rooms, and living history may have been born.

Interest in the domestic settings of earlier times spread rapidly in the next quarter century, and generic exhibitions were arranged at the Brooklyn Sanitary Fair in 1859, at the Essex Institute in 1875, in the New England Kitchen at the Philadelphia Centennial Exhibition in 1876, and at countless church fairs

15. "BIRTH PLACE OF [BENJAMIN] FRANKLIN, IN MILK ST. JAN. 6, 1705–6 O.S. AS REPRODUCED AT THE FAIR OF THE BOSTON YOUNG MEN'S CHRISTIAN ASSOCIATION, DEC[R] 25, 1858," LITHOGRAPH, BY J. H. BUFFORD. COURTESY OF THE SOCIETY FOR THE PRESERVATION OF NEW ENGLAND ANTIQUITIES.

16. INTERIOR OF THE FRANKLIN BIRTHPLACE, AS REVEALED IN A PEN AND INK SKETCH, MOUNTED BELOW THE HINGED LEAF OF BUFFORD'S LITHOGRAPH.

In this print, the front wall of the house is a hinged sheet of paper that may be lifted up to reveal the interior of the Franklin house. At the YMCA fair, people dressed in period costume re-enacted everyday life at the family fireside, and the spinning wheel, roaring fire, and tall case clock were displayed as established icons of the past.

and historical commemorations at the local level. Usually these featured military relics, household objects, or clothing associated with prominent citizens; lavish displays of flags and bunting; and an assortment of household goods featuring at least one large spinning wheel. There were seldom attempts to recreate room settings, but these events were important in developing a regional historical awareness and in identifying particular objects.

Although the local-history movement became widespread throughout New England, several centers were extremely influential, especially Plymouth, Salem, and Deerfield, Massachusetts; Hopkinton and Warner, New Hampshire; York, Maine; Lexington and Concord, Massachusetts; and Hartford and Litchfield, Connecticut. Some of the earliest historical museums were established in these towns, and there literary and artistic impulses often converged with the antiquarian interest.

At Deerfield, George Sheldon, the president of the Pocumtuck Valley Memorial Association, wrote throughout the 1870s of the organization's desire to have a permanent home in which to preserve and display its collections of domestic artifacts: "We have the spinning wheel, the household utensils, and the door once hung and attacked by assaulting foes, and we need with these to set up housekeeping again."[17] When the PVMA opened Memorial Hall in 1880, its members had arranged a Colonial parlor, bedroom, and kitchen—the first New England displays of household objects in period settings shown to the public on a basis that was intended to be permanent.

17. A WOMAN, PROBABLY THE ANTIQUARIAN C. ALICE BAKER, ARRANGING PEWTER IN MEMORIAL HALL, DEERFIELD, MASSACHUSETTS, SHORTLY AFTER THE BUILDING WAS COMPLETED AND OPENED TO THE PUBLIC IN 1880. COURTESY OF THE SOCIETY FOR THE PRESERVATION OF NEW ENGLAND ANTIQUITIES. PHOTOGRAPH BY EMMA COLEMAN.

Today the people who established these collections, conducted the first local research, set up the first exhibitions, and wrote town histories, historical novels, and personal reminiscences are often castigated as "antiquarians." Although it may be easy, and even politically correct, to dismiss their work as romanticized and inaccurate, it is important to recognize that these nineteenth-century historians knew what they were doing. Most of them had talked with many people who were born before the American Revolution. Their work was informed by experience and etched in memory. Statistical models did not interest them.

The authors of local history and personal reminiscence were content to draw upon the evidence of the past as they found it in trunks of letters, public archives,

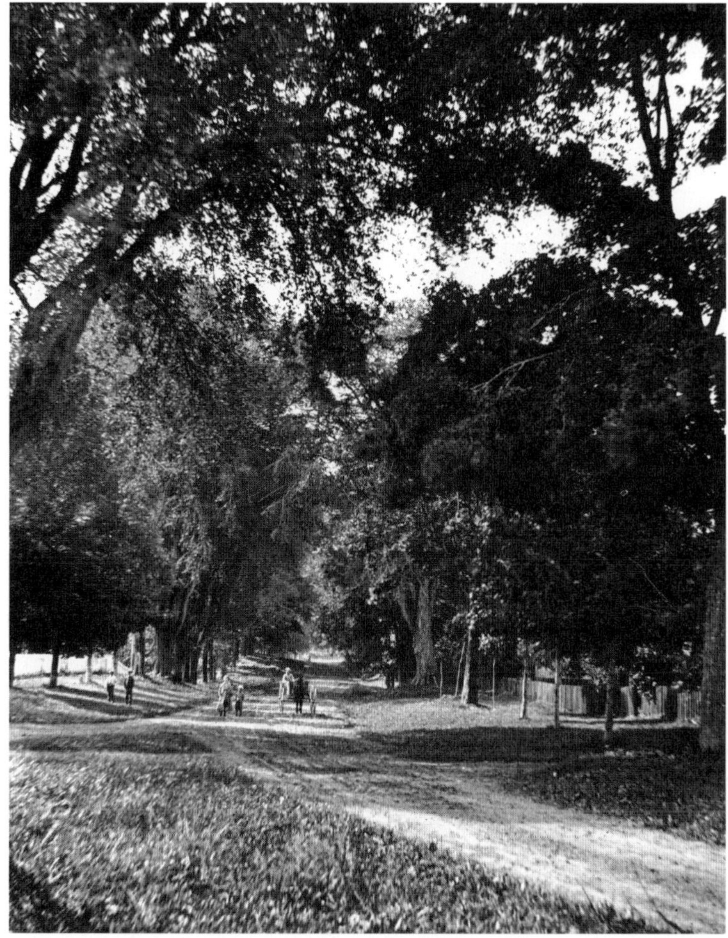

18. "THE STREET," DEERFIELD, MASSACHUSETTS, STEREOGRAPH, BY P. BRADFORD, GREENFIELD, MASSACHUSETTS, C. 1868. POCUMTUCK VALLEY MEMORIAL ASSOCIATION, DEERFIELD, MASSACHUSETTS.

The quintessential village scene.

historical libraries, or desk drawers. They used the resources of their own lives, writing of life as they lived it within the well-ordered and traditional ways of specific homes and communities. Their writings were intended to preserve the evidence of everyday life and to memorialize those who had gone before. In Deerfield, Massachusetts, "the eighteenth century was still alive" when local historian George Sheldon "was a boy—and the seventeenth century a close memory."[18] Sheldon learned not only from those who could tell him of the past but from the evidence they had left behind in private manuscripts and public records. For him and for others like him, the objects of the past told stories as vivid as the written or spoken word.

II

Our Great Family

WHEN DAVID EMERY CAME TO TELL TWENTY-FIVE-YEAR-OLD SARAH Smith that he had rented the old Pillsbury place and they could soon be married, her "preparations for marriage were nearly complete, but nothing definite had been decided upon." On hearing what David had to say, Sarah "was completely dumbfounded. The Pillsbury domain consisted of a farm of sixty acres, on which was a large, old-fashioned house, which for many years had been a noted tavern for drovers and country traders. With the most perfect *sang froid* Mr. Emery stated his intention of immediately putting up a large slaughtering house, and that he had already hired Mr. James Carey to assist in the butchering business. Mr. Carey, his wife and two children were to occupy a part of the house." Sarah soon recovered her composure. She inspected the premises; made plans for alterations, fresh paint, wallpaper, and whitewashing; and began to assemble her furnishings. When Sarah and David were married, only six weeks later, on April 22, 1812, Mr. and Mrs. Carey "with their two oldest children were already settled in rooms at the upper end of the house." Upon arrival at her new home, Sarah found herself "not only the landlady of a public house, but the mistress of a family numbering seven persons, besides Betsy Downing, the maid servant, there were three hired men, Daniel Smith, Aaron Palmer, John Webster and a boy of fourteen named Guy Carlton Mackie."[1]

Sarah Emery's responsibility for "a family numbering seven persons" and the psychological pressures of sharing even a large house and dooryard with another family of four people may seem like a lot for a new bride, but her expe-

19. THE PILLSBURY PLACE, ANONYMOUS LITHOGRAPH, IN SARAH ANNA EMERY, *Reminiscences of a Nonagenarian* (NEWBURYPORT, 1879), FACING PAGE 270.

The home in which David and Sarah Anna Emery first set up housekeeping after their marriage in 1812.

rience was not unusual. Sarah had grown up in a house shared by two families, and she clearly understood her obligation to care for hired men and girls as well as her new husband. Many early New England families extended far beyond the nuclear family that is the late-twentieth-century norm. Indeed, the very concept of family differed widely from that held today, embracing everyone who lived within the same household. People were expected to live in functioning families, and few people of any age lived alone. Those who did were apt to be regarded as strange or even dangerous, and "old maids" were often the targets of cruel jokes. People who were unmarried usually lived with their aging parents or with unmarried relatives.

Sarah Emery described a family of four old maids and their two brothers, "pleasant, estimable men" and "precise genteel bodies" who were noted for the "harmless idiosyncrasies" of their housekeeping: "Though the food was bought in common, each brother and sister provided their own tea and coffee, and each had a separate pot. Uncle Joe drank chocolate, Uncle Josh, coffee, Miss Nabby, strong old hyson, Miss Lizzie liked hers weaker, Miss Nannie preferred young hyson, while Miss Hannah never drank anything but Souchong. It was exceedingly diverting to see the six small pots . . . sizzling on six little mounds of embers before the capacious fire."[2] Such idiosyncrasy was acceptable within the family structure that these siblings had developed. Had these people chosen to live separately, they would have been considered queer.

This was clearly an unusual situation. More commonly, for a variety of reasons, old or young widows; children and step-children; elderly grandma'ms and grandsirs; maiden aunts and uncles; nieces and nephews; young men preparing for college; unsettled single people in their twenties; students of law, medicine, or divinity; hired men and hired girls; apprentices, servants, and slaves; orphans; and cousins of all ages might be grafted onto the basic family structure. Those with fragile health, chronic or terminal illness, or physical handicaps, the mentally retarded, the senile, and the insane, were not excluded. Young widows and widowers with children often remarried, introducing the complications of step-parent relationships at the same time that they enriched their personal lives and found help with the routine of household management and child care.[3] Whether they were related to each other or not, by living, working, sleeping, and eating together in a single household, people were considered to be members of that family. When census takers visited New England's houses at the end of the eighteenth century, they usually found eight or ten people in each family. Because of the impermanency of relationships with household help, this number was subject to change at any moment, but the concept of family remained stable. Those who lived together, for however long or short a time, were bound together in their dependence on one another for the necessities and comforts of everyday life, by the structures of work, and by the bonds of caring.

20. GOOD COMPANIONS, OIL ON CANVAS, BY J. WELLS CHAMPNEY. COLLECTION OF EDITH N. MILBURY. PHOTO COURTESY OF VOSE GALLERIES, BOSTON.

21. THE SARGENT FAMILY, OIL ON CANVAS, ARTIST UNKNOWN, CHARLESTOWN, MASSACHUSETTS, C. 1800. NATIONAL GALLERY OF ART, GIFT OF EDGAR WILLIAM AND BERNICE CHRYSLER GARBISCH.

The earliest New England genre scenes are family portraits that tend to illustrate the nuclear family, which was the innermost circle of a complex domestic unit.

Sarah Emery grew up in a house (figure 9) in West Newbury, Massachusetts, in which her parents occupied one side and her widowed grandmother, an aunt, and a married uncle and his family lived on the other. Sarah's mother and grandmother each had her own "front" room and chambers furnished from her bridal portion, but all of these people ate together and shared the kitchen, garret, barns, and "back chamber—the large one under the long, sloping back roof—[which] was set apart for household manufacture."[4] When her uncle and his family were able to purchase an adjacent farm and moved out of the old homestead, Sarah noted that "though we were glad of the additional room, the house seemed strangely still and lonely, with only grandm'am and Aunt Sarah."[5]

Similarly, Stephen and Olive Walkley occupied a newly built one-and-a-half-story house in Southington, Connecticut, after their marriage in 1811, sharing living space with his father, Jonathan, and his two unmarried sisters from the beginning. One nephew lived with them until 1822, and the young Walkleys themselves had nine children between 1812 and 1832. Once the first three children were born, the family never seems to have included fewer than nine people.

22. COFFIN HOUSE, NEWBURY, MASSACHUSETTS, C. 1870, ONE-HALF OF A STEREOGRAPH. COURTESY OF THE SOCIETY FOR THE PRESERVATION OF NEW ENGLAND ANTIQUITIES.

*This house grew through time to accommodate expanding and changing families. The earliest portion, about 1654, has a single room with a fireplace on each of the two stories; this became the ell when the larger portions of the house were added in the eighteenth century. According to Peter Benes, the house was in the late eighteenth century "lived in simultaneously by as many as four related families and an estimated eighty occupants," an estimate based on inheritance patterns and demographic studies. (*Old Town and the Waterside *[Newburyport, 1986].)*

Complex living situations did not always result in domestic harmony. Sarah Emery described what happened when Daniel Colman married Nancy Pike, and "the young couple commenced housekeeping in half of Col. Jeremiah Colman's house. . . . A large L was soon added to the house, giving accommodation to the two families; but for some months the sisters-in-law shared the kitchen, one having a fire in one corner of the capacious fireplace and the other in the opposite, the brick oven being used alternately."[6] Flexibility and a spirit of compromise were necessary in order to achieve any level of domestic order within shared living spaces.

During the early years of their marriage, Sarah and Peter Bryant moved frequently, sharing space with other families, living in rented rooms or small houses in both Cummington and nearby Plainfield, Massachusetts. In 1801 they settled in Cummington, building a four-room addition to the Snell farmhouse, which provided an office for the doctor and some privacy for their growing family.

When Ruth Bascom married Dr. Asa Miles on St. Valentine's Day in 1804, she and her husband did not leave at once to set up housekeeping, nor did they move eventually into a cottage for two. At first the couple stayed with her parents in Leicester, Massachusetts; after a few weeks, Dr. Miles departed alone for Westminster, and Ruth remained behind, purchasing furniture and housekeeping equipment in Worcester and organizing her "things." On May 16, a messenger came to tell Ruth that her husband was unwell, and she departed at once for their new home.[7]

Although childless herself, Ruth cared for one child or another throughout most of the first twenty years of her married life. Dr. Miles had been married before and had a son, Clough Rice Miles, who stayed with Ruth for a short while after Dr. Miles's untimely death in the spring of 1805. Later, Clough went to live with one of his father's brothers, but he kept in touch with Ruth and she continued to express concern for him and saw him occasionally. Widowed less than a year, Ruth was married to the Reverend Ezekiel Lysander Bascom, on February 26, 1806. The following year, on March 10, she brought home four-year-old Priscilla Elvira Estabrook to care for; within a week, the child's mother had died, and Ruth referred to the child in her diary as "now our own."[8] Before New Year's Day 1812, her husband's motherless nephew, Lysander, was also

23. DR. BRYANT'S OFFICE, PHOTOGRAPH, C. 1888. COURTESY OF THE SOCIETY FOR THE PRESERVATION OF NEW ENGLAND ANTIQUITIES.

This is the "new house" described in Sarah Snell Bryant's 1801 diary. It was actually an addition to her father's house that Dr. Peter Bryant built to accommodate their growing family and provide himself with a medical office. The new construction effectively doubled the amount of living space that was shared by the Snell and Bryant families until Sarah's parents died in 1813. In his will, Ebenezer Snell left almost all of his household furnishings and half of the buildings on the farm to Sarah herself and the other half of the farm to her son Austin. Austin Bryant sold the family farm in 1835; in 1842, this part, Peter Bryant's 1801 addition, was moved to a new location and used thereafter as an independent house. After William Cullen Bryant bought back the homestead as a summer retreat in 1865, he remodeled it drastically and reconstructed a slightly smaller version of this section as an office for himself.

living with them at the parsonage in Gerry (now Phillipston), Massachusetts, in northern Worcester County near the New Hampshire border.[9] Ruth and her husband began to take in young people as boarding students; on March 12, 1813, nine were in residence. These boys and girls attended school in the afternoons and evenings and were considered members of the family, with responsibility for performing certain chores, observing house rules, and attending meeting on Sundays. Even while she was taking in young students as members of her own family, Ruth Bascom sent Elvira to her close friend, Miss Catherine Fiske, who had opened a new boarding school in Keene, first leaving her there on June 6, 1813.[10] Never having had the pleasure of caring for an infant of her own, Ruth brought dozens of young people through the trials of adolescence. Throughout her long diary, the entries reveal the complexity of running a large household and the anxiety of having a large family.

Elizabeth Phelps's adopted daughter, Thankful, lived with her husband, Mr. Hitchcock, in Northampton after their marriage in 1796, but she returned to Forty Acres in 1798 in time to be attended by her mother and her sister Betsy during a "severe travel." Betsy wrote to their brother Charles, telling of the new baby's impact on the household: "Our sister Hitchcock has given us a nephew . . . what with sickness and this little urchin to engage my attention, I have found no time to scribble—Mary is cleverly—has left her room—her infant has the appearance of being perfectly healthy—it is three weeks since she became a mother." Elizabeth then added a postscript to her letter that must have been of great interest to Charles: "Mr. Hitchcock talks of calling his boy Charles—have you any objection? not Charles Phelps."[11] Charles must not have raised any serious objection, for his mother noted in her diary on a Sunday in April that "Mr. Hitchcock's son this day [was] christened by the name of Charles Phelps—Lord he is thine & I rejoice in it. Dearly do I love him—but Monday morning early he and his mother & father left us to go to live at Brimfield. . . . Betsy went with 'em. The last waggon of goods went this day."[12] Mr. and Mrs. Hitchcock finally set up housekeeping in Brimfield a year and a half after their marriage; their family already included this infant son.

Two years later, Charles's wife, Sally, wrote to her mother-in-law, saying, "Betsy no doubt informed you, that a time was coming when I should greatly want a Mother's company, that time if nothing particular happens will be about the last of August." After some negotiation, Elizabeth Phelps agreed to leave her "great family" in Hadley and went up to Boston to encourage and assist her daughter-in-law, who was expecting the birth of her first child. Sally's own mother had died, and although she had engaged a good nurse, it would have been unthinkable for her to have experienced her first delivery without a close female relative at hand. The baby was not born as soon as expected, and Elizabeth's long absence complicated the family situation in Hadley. Her husband wrote to her plaintively on September 10, "We shall get along—whether the Cheese will be as good as yours, I will not take upon me to say, but be assured we will do as well as we can," and again on the twenty-second, "I was [in] hopes you would have been home before the Peaches were gone, but that cannot be, they will not last more than a day or two more. . . . I cannot say I am free of anxiety for Sally, I hope she will do well, although the Time is long—am very glad you are with her, for I am sure it would be distressing to her to be alone." Less guardedly, he wrote to their daughter Betsy after Sally's son was born, "Your mother has been gone from home five weeks this morning. . . . [I] am almost worn out, I have had more than is common for me to do, since your mother left us, although Polly is as good a Girl as I ever saw of her age." Although he recognized the importance of his wife's mission, Charles Phelps sorely missed Elizabeth's superb management skills and significant personal contribution to the work of their large farm and family.[13]

Like many women of her time, Sarah Bryant had seven children: five boys and two girls, who were born at roughly two-year intervals between 1793 and 1807.[14] Sarah Bryant nursed each of her children for a year or more. Like many of her contemporaries, she was either pregnant or nursing almost continuously for fourteen years. When we think of the women of those days as skilled managers who made important personal contributions to the household economy, it should be remembered that they were usually pregnant or nursing an infant; sometimes they were both.

Throughout Sarah Bryant's diary, there is very little direct reference to either the discomforts or the concerns of pregnancy. Mrs. Bryant maintained a regular schedule of work right up until the very last days before each child was born, sometimes cutting down on strenuous physical labor like weaving and increasing the amount of time spent cutting out clothing or working on other projects that were less taxing.

Usually, Sarah Bryant's diary entries were suspended for a few days when a child was born, but the record was soon filled in. "Unwell. Seven at night a son born. Mamma and Mrs. Shaw were here" indicated William Cullen's birth on November 3, 1794; the following July, "unwell at night . . . a son born a little before sunset" [the next day] announced the arrival of Cyrus. Two women came to assist during Cyrus Bryant's birth, but his mother did not linger long in bed. Two days after delivering she "got up," and she soon resumed care of her family. When her first daughter, Sarah, was born, on July 24, 1802, the new mother "sat up" the next day, "walked in the kitchen" on the twenty-sixth, "went outdoors" on the twenty-seventh, and soon resumed her sewing.

Most young mothers delivered their babies at home, with their own mothers, sisters, some neighbor women, and usually a midwife in attendance. Although not a midwife, Elizabeth Phelps was frequently called to her neighbors in times of travail, and she had assisted at dozens of births before her own grandchildren were born. Having observed many different situations, she was well qualified to coach her daughters and daughter-in-law when their time came. The gathering of women for the rituals of "social childbirth"[15] provided support and encouragement for new mothers, as well as extra hands and long experience should an emergency develop.

Although women spoke of one's being "brought to bed" to describe delivery, laboring women delivered not in a bed but supported on a chair, on someone's lap, or on a specialized birthing stool. As soon as the afterbirth was delivered, they sought the comfort of a fresh bed.

New mothers were encouraged to rest after delivery, but the amount of time actually spent in bed and the social rituals associated with "lying-in" varied widely, the result of standards set by community or social class, the amount of help available, and personal inclination. In eighteenth-century Salem, Mary Vial Holyoke paid a "setting up visit" to Mrs. C. G. Pickman after a child was born. On September 9, 1771, Mrs. Holyoke herself felt "very poorly" and took necessary action: "Put up bed." The next day she still felt "very ill," and although she knew why, her labor must have progressed very rapidly, for no one else was present when she was "brought to Bed quite alone 11 A.M. of a Daughter. Child very well." Four women were present in the house the next day, and the same four came to call four weeks later, when Mrs. Holyoke observed the formal ritual of "sitting up week. Mrs. Epes, 2 Pickman's, Mrs. Rowth & Miss Dowse here. Club here."[16] It seems unlikely that she had stayed in bed the entire time, but this was not her first child and she may have welcomed an opportunity to rest peacefully in her chamber. Being ready to receive formal callers and display the new baby took some time.

In Portsmouth, New Hampshire, in the 1820s and 30s, Sarah Goodwin employed a doctor instead of a midwife to attend her deliveries, but she still expected to have to entertain friends and neighbors after her deliveries, and she prepared herself during the last few weeks of her pregnancies by arranging for a "monthly nurse" who would take care of her and the baby as well as pass cake and wine "to all who called on the fourth and fifth weeks." Sarah Goodwin's later reminiscences include detailed descriptions of these occasions and the nurse's work during her seven confinements. The nurse slept with the baby, did laundry, and "also kept the baby and myself in elegant toilets and waited on all the company upstairs and to the street door. . . . I had white flannel wraps trimmed down the front and all round with satin ribbon. For one occasion my wrap was trimmed with broad blue satin ribbon and tall blue bows on my cap. I used to receive in dear Aunt Dennett's great easy chair and I hope she knew how much I enjoyed it. Before every confinement a great batch of plum cake was baked in the great brick oven. After being put to bed the Doctor and such friends as were being useful had a great feast of good things downstairs." Mrs. Goodwin also tells us that by the time her last child, Susan, was born in 1844, the attending doctor put an end to the custom of serving cake and wine in the mother's room, calling it "unsanitary."[17]

Sarah Bryant's diary shows clearly that customs in a rural community were far less formal, and the requirements of her family did not permit the luxury of a month of pampered privacy or the formality of a "sitting up week." In Leicester, Massachusetts, Ruth Bascom's sister had a little more time: "Mrs. Denny in chamber, her son a fortnight old."[18]

In a Northampton household with live-in help, Anne Jean Lyman was usually "able the very next day to sit up in her large easy-chair, with her mending basket and book beside her, making first one and then the other her pastime for

24. SEWING IN A CHAMBER, WOODCUT, ALBERT ALDEN PROOF BOOK, C. 1840. COURTESY AMERICAN ANTIQUARIAN SOCIETY.

Although icy cold in wintertime, chambers were often used by women as summer sitting rooms. Miss Beecher recommended straw matting for permanent carpets in chambers, since they "are used most in summer." (Catherine Beecher, A Treatise on Domestic Economy, *[Boston, 1841], p. 359.)*

some hours of each day . . . [and by the second week] she had resumed all the duties of the house and was driving all over the country with my father."[19] Regardless of her social obligations, the goal for each woman was to be restored to "strength and usefulness" as soon as possible.[20]

In preparation for a woman's confinement, many families set up special beds. In wealthy households, these were fashionably curtained high-post beds, which would provide both warmth and privacy for the new mother as well as make a strong social statement to those who came to call on her. When Sally Foster Otis was preparing to give birth to her seventh child in Boston in the winter of 1798, her husband, Harrison Gray Otis, wrote anxiously from Philadelphia, where he was serving in Congress. He urged his wife to keep warm and, if necessary, to have her bed set up in the drawing room, where it would be easier to maintain a good fire. He also cautioned her to see only her mother and sister in the first days after giving birth, no matter how well she found herself feeling. Having her bed set up in the most fashionable room in the house would have her well placed to receive callers once she had recovered her strength.[21]

In less formal households, where women expected to resume their duties soon after delivery, the ideal was to make use of a comfortably warm first-floor bedroom. If the room was centrally located, a woman could conveniently supervise the kitchen and family activity, receive visitors, and comfortably nurse the baby or take a quick nap whenever the baby was asleep. Such a chamber would also be convenient for nursing a sick person or supervising children's naps. Although there seems to be no formal documentation of a room actually called a "borning room" in New England historical sources, the need for such a place certainly existed. In many households there were already beds in almost every room except the kitchen. The regular use of one of them by a new mother may well have given rise to the informal designation of such a space as a "borning room." For a new mother who wanted or needed to remain in charge of her household, probably nothing could have been more welcome.

When a new baby was expected, it was important to be prepared with more than a warm and conveniently located bed. The dangers of infection were not yet known, so large quantities of boiling water were not part of the picture, but baby linen needed to include nightgowns, caps, and quantities of absorbent napkins for both mother and baby. Bands for wrapping the infant's umbilicus and a pair of strong scissors were also useful. Midwives and others who were frequently called to attend at childbirth may well have kept such equipment in a special basket, such as that listed in the estate inventory of Daniel Fowle, Esq., a Portsmouth, New Hampshire, printer, as "a Basket with a Christning Blanket & sundry matters in the Women's Way."[22]

Caring for a newborn child is never easy, and the extended family structure provided important support to tired parents in the early weeks. When Elizabeth Phelps checked on Sally one morning after the baby was born, she found "another pair of eyes which she says have been open considerable part of the night—for you must know he has found out that it is much better lying with a mother than a dry nurse."[23]

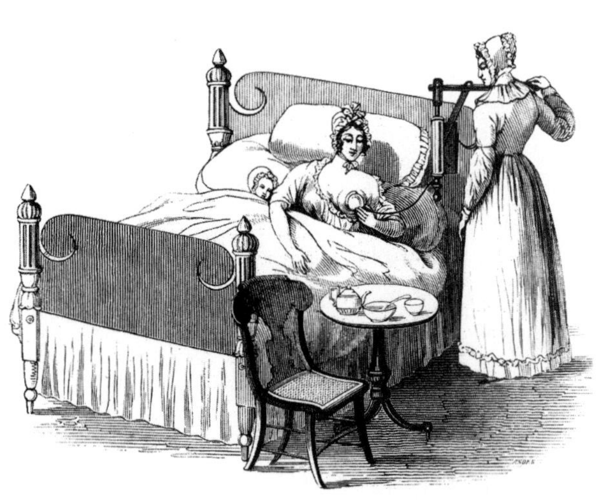

25. Woodcut, Alexander Anderson Scrapbooks, Vol. V. Print Collection, Miriam & Ira D. Wallach Division of Art, Prints and Photographs, The New York Public Library, Astor, Lenox and Tilden Foundations.

Within the privacy of a lying-in chamber, a breast pump could be used to relieve pressure in cases of infection or when an infant had died.

Most mothers nursed their babies for more than a year, but sometimes they ran into difficulties with breast infections. Mary Holyoke was seized with a "violent pain" in her breast on November 15, 1771, ten weeks after giving birth to her daughter Elizabeth. Her breast was lanced the next day and treated with both a "poultice" and a "frog plaster."[24] Without antibiotics, she was lucky to recover.

Sarah Bryant made frequent references to her newborn children in her diary in the months after they were born, but she never referred to them by name until four to six months after the birth. Instead, the entries refer to the "babe," a term that may have been a reflection of their mother's hesitancy to become too closely attached to them for fear they might die, as so many of their young cousins and neighbors did. Earlier, in Salem, Mary Holyoke had the same hesitation, referring to three-month-old Edward as "The Child" when he died in November 1766.[25]

Perhaps for the same reason, Sarah Bryant never seems to have made infant clothing until after she was safely delivered. Her first task after childbirth was usually sewing infant's "clouts," or diapers. The overriding concern in making infants' shirts, caps, and gowns was that they be sewn neatly, with smooth seams that would not chafe. Infant clothing was often made of used linen, which was soft and absorbent. Most of these garments were made without fastenings. Until the invention of the safety pin in the middle of the nineteenth century, baby clothes were secured by weaving long straight pins through them.

At night, very young children slept with their mothers; like "little Master Royall" Tyler, they sometimes slept with their fathers as well. However, in some families it was the nurse rather than the father who joined the mother and the demanding newborn in bed. By the 1830s, authors of maternal advice books were recommending "the infant should sleep near its mother though not in the same bed." In order to prevent children from becoming too warm, being crushed to death by an adult, or falling out of bed, as well as to provide free circulation of fresh air, these authors advised the use of a crib the same height as an adult bed, with one side that could easily be let down so the infant could be taken into the mother's bed for nursing.[26] Despite a plethora of such advice, many people continued to sleep with their babies and to put toddlers into a trundle bed placed at the foot of their own beds. Probate inventories document the furnishings of such bedchambers, such as the "South Chamber" on the second floor of the Boston home of Ebenezer Rockwood, which contained a cradle, a trundle bed, and a crib, in addition to a mahogany bed with gilt cornices and dimity curtains, when it was listed in 1815.[27] One author recalled that "Grandmother, when her first baby came, took it into her own bed. When another baby came to crowd it out, there was the trundle-bed that stood under the big bed all day, and rolled out at night with a sleepy rumble. And when more babies still came to crowd the trundle-bed, the first baby, a big boy, six years old now, had a bed made for him at the head of the back stairs or up garret, under the sloping eaves. The rain lulled him to sleep, and the snow drifted in sometimes. In the spare chamber, a big bed loomed untouched. It hovered in his dreams, a presence not to be put by."[28]

In the daytime, infants were placed in cradles in sitting rooms, kitchens, dooryards, or wherever it would be quiet enough to promote the child's sleep and still be easy to monitor the occupant. Young Sally Phelps found that she was

26. "On Guard," oil on canvas, by Thomas Waterman Wood, 1874. St. Johnsbury Athenaeum, St. Johnsbury, Vt. Photograph by Jenks Studio.

During the daytime, an infant's cradle might be placed in a comfortably warm spot where the baby's cries could be heard easily yet it would not be disturbed by household activity.

"so foolish I cant yet sit patiently and hear my little darling cry, and though he is a charming good Boy yet he will be in my arms the greatest part of the time."[29] As they began to move about, most young children found themselves handed from one caretaker to another within the complex family structure. The concept of a formal and separate nursery was unknown except in houses with a large retinue of servants. Probably no early–New England child grew up thinking of one particular room as his or hers alone. It was customary to separate boys and girls from a fairly early age, and boys often had their beds in unfinished loft or attic spaces, like those described in *Oldtown Folks.*

In all of these households, children made a tremendous impact. They were a drain on the emotions as well as the economic resources of a family. Concern for their education, safety, and spiritual well-being was paramount. Their incessant activity and noise and their unpredictable natures added to the complexities of shared and multigenerational households. Elderly grandparents, aunts, and uncles were convenient caregivers and good storytellers, but they were also apt to be infirm and easily irritated. The mothers of large families were usually in their forties by the time their last child was born, and parents were over sixty when their youngest children established their own households.

Those who lived in what today would be called an extended family—the blessed patriarch, the fragile grandma'm, the maiden aunts and clever uncles, the boarders, and the faithful lifelong servants—all developed emotional ties to the members of the household in which they lived.

The diarists William Bentley and Thomas Robbins were both unmarried Congregational ministers who rented rooms and lived with families. Bentley lived with Widow Crowninshield in her Salem, Massachusetts, household, which varied in size as children, help, and other boarders came and went throughout his long pastorate. Robbins lived first with the Wolcott family in East Windsor, Connecticut; later he lived in Bridgewater and Mattapoisett, Massachusetts. When one of the Wolcott daughters was married, in November 1826, Robbins "assisted . . . in getting Eveline's furniture" and noted in his diary: "Have a good deal to do in connection with the wedding. . . . At evening married Edgar Bissell to Eveline Wolcott. I came to this family when she was four years old, and have had considerable care of her education. She seems to me like a daughter. We had a very pleasant wedding—above forty guests." On

November 30, the day after her wedding, Robbins noted: "Eveline went away. She has very good furniture." The next day, Robbins couldn't stay away; he "rode to the Hill and dined at Mr. Bissell's. Assisted in putting up some of their furniture."[30] Because they had lived in the same household for many years, the ties of family were well established between Thomas Robbins and Eveline Wolcott, even though they were not blood relations.

Despite the complicated relationships and interrelationships of people who shared dwelling spaces, the central focus, authority, and responsibility seems always to have been in the head of household and his wife. After Dr. Peter Bryant died, authority shifted to his son Austin, while the doctor's widow continued to live and work in the same house where she had been both daughter and mistress. Sarah Bryant lived with at least some of her children for twenty-nine years after the doctor died. Elizabeth Phelps's widowed mother lived with her for twenty-eight years after her marriage. Inevitably, conflict would develop as a recently widowed woman was asked to yield her authority at what had been her own fireside and table to her son and his wife while she continued to be active in the work of the family.

Within families, daily interaction with the elderly resulted in the informal transmission of cultural values between generations. Some old people clung to the elaborate fashions of their youth even in the face of infirmity, reluctant to give up these status symbols. Sarah Emery paints an unforgettable picture of calling on Madam Eben Parsons, who was "habited in a white dimity wrapper, her head adorned by a crape turban, surmounting a frisette of light curls; her gouty feet encased in velvet slippers . . . still further assisted by a gold-headed cane."[31]

27. SALLIE, RICHARD, AND CAROLINE GARDNER CARY, BOSTON, 1842, SILHOUETTE BY AUGUSTE EDOUART. BOSTON ATHENAEUM.

Even active games like "ring pin" and "graces" were sometimes played indoors.

28. MRS. RUSSELL STURGIS (1756–1843) AND MRS. ROBERT BENNETT FORBES (1773–1856), BOSTON, SILHOUETTE, BY AUGUSTE EDOUART, 1842. BOSTON ATHENAEUM.

Women of two generations enjoying reading and conversation in a Boston parlor.

29. MRS. NICHOLAS SALISBURY (MARTHA SAUNDERS) (1704–92), OIL ON CANVAS, BY CHRISTIAN GULLAGER, 1789. WORCESTER ART MUSEUM, WORCESTER, MASSACHUSETTS.

Mrs. Salisbury was usually referred to in family correspondence as "Honored Mother." She lived with her bachelor son Stephen in a commodious house in Worcester, Massachusetts, which served as both their home and an active commercial store. Five years after she died, the fifty-one-year-old Stephen married twenty-nine-year-old Elizabeth Tuckerman of Boston. The couple made major changes in the house, moved the store to another building, and brought handsome new furnishings from Boston, both at the time of their marriage and again twenty years later.

The rooms that were set aside for widows under the provisions of dower must have been crowded with the personal accumulations of a lifetime. These wonderful "old-fashioned" possessions also bore a special role in the transmission of a sense of family and place. One great-grandmother, Deborah Lewis, "had a room with a corner fireplace, over which was two cupboards, a low bedstead, two chairs, a low round table, a tall chest of drawers and a covered chest. This dear room was where the whole household often gathered to talk over and decide many family matters, for she was amiable and wise."[32] Another favored grandmother "valued the old and took kindly to the new."[33]

Nelson Walkley of Southington, Connecticut (1812–78), recalled a special relationship with his grandfather in letters written in 1877. "When I was a boy my grandfather was a paralytic & sat in the corner east of the fire place in the south room under the book cupboard & I had to wait on him. . . . In those days his bed was in the S. W. corner of the kitchen. . . . He had an arm chair on rollers . . . [and] he was lifted out onto that & sat on the east side of the fireplace directly under the book cupboard. . . . He sat there all day except he was rolled up to the table to eat. . . . I had to sit by & wait on Granpa to light his pipe & get him drink & to while away the time he would tell me tales of the deep and teach me navigation. This may seem strange to you but it is nevertheless true he taught me Geometry & Mathematics before I knew how to read."[34] Grandfather must have been a real challenge to those who had to empty his chamber pot and lift, bathe, shave, and dress him in the corner of the kitchen, but he was still honored as the patriarch and useful as a teacher.

Younger widows who were able to live alone might take advantage of their inheritance of real property and take in boarders. "Found mother quite comfortable. In her circumstances she is well accommodated. She keeps boarders, who are a great comfort to her."[35] By taking in boarders, this woman created a new family, as well as providing herself with a source of income.

The practice of renting a portion of one's house to another family was not restricted to widows. Until he was married, Abner Sanger lived with his sister Rhoda and their mother, but they never seem actually to have occupied a separate dwelling. In the fall of 1780, he went "up to Ezra Metcalf's and agree[d] with him about hiring part of his house." After the men drew up a formal indenture and signed it, Abner constructed "a hovel by Ezra Metcalf's barn door" to shelter his animals and built a trundle bed in anticipation of the three adults living in one room. On January 1, 1781, they finally moved.[36] In the spring Abner bought the farm, and the Metcalf family moved out; but almost immediately Sanger rented their part of the house to another family. Sharing such a small household must have become intolerable, even for people who were used to it. On October 15, 1782, anticipating new tenants, Sanger wrote, "I think I collect old boards and make a partition between Lawyer Stiles's part of our kitchen and the part that I improve."

30. MOSES BROWN (1738–1836), OIL ON CANVAS, BY MARTIN JOHNSON HEADE, C. 1858, BASED ON AN EARLIER DRAWING BY WILLIAM HARRIS. RHODE ISLAND HISTORICAL SOCIETY.

The hard contours of a Windsor chair were sometimes softened by padding and cushions for an elderly person. Moses Brown was more than ninety years old when the original image was made.

Even where family relationships were well defined and the definition of responsibilities clear, the coming and going of friends, family, help, travelers, young people, daytime workers, and some seasonal laborers made change a household constant. Complex personalities and people with diverse political and religious opinions gathered around the family table, bringing news and sparking the conversation. Excessive use of alcohol sometimes resulted in violent or unpredictable behavior. Members of the nuclear family came and went to watch over the sick and the dead, to assist births, to help out with seasonal work, to visit relatives, to embark on business ventures, or to seek information and advice. In 1807, while her husband was away from home for nearly six weeks, Sarah Bryant had a trying experience. On February 18 an "old sow got into the kitchen at night & tore the children's clothes to pieces." By the nineteenth, she had accepted the reality of the experience and moved forward. Since there was no one else to do it, she "mended the children's clothes."[37]

In the homes of professional men, especially doctors, ministers, and lawyers, students might board with the family while undertaking a period of instruction in preparation for college admission or as professional training. Dr. Peter Bryant gave medical instruction to as many as ten young men at once, many of them boarding in his own household. Dr. Bryant's second son, William Cullen, spent the winter of 1809 in North Brookfield, Massachusetts, with his uncle, the Reverend Thomas Snell, studying Latin; the following winter he was closer to home, studying Greek with another minister, the Reverend Moses Hallock, in Plainfield.[38]

Cullen studied at Williams College in 1810 and 1811 and practiced law for a while, but after the publication of "Thanatopsis" in 1817, he was launched on what was to become a celebrated journalistic and literary career. Austin Bryant, the eldest son, settled down to farming when he reached maturity, but his brothers, who did not inherit land from their father, were much more unsettled in their career choices. Cyrus, Rush, and John tried college, taught school, and studied medicine and law; Rush was even admitted to West Point and remained there briefly. After several trips exploring lands in Michigan and Illinois, both Rush and Cyrus married and settled permanently in Illinois. They were joined by their mother, their sister Louisa, and Austin and his entire family in 1835.

Family relations were complicated not only by intergenerational conflict and stepparents, but by the informal adoption of orphaned children or the children of people who were unable to support them, and by the presence of mentally retarded, physically handicapped, chronically ill, senile, intemperate, or insane persons.

In October 1782, the Phelps family had a serious and potentially dangerous problem to deal with. Elizabeth described it in her diary: "This Eve. my husband had a most dreadful Fray at the Widow Warners with Brother Solomon he very crazy." The following Sunday, "Sol got loose (he was chained in the Barn)" and "our folks went got him home." On Wednesday, "Sol [was] put into the shop chained there. Satterday my Husband gone. Sol got Loose—son come home, Sol hurt none of us—praised be God."[39] After this, there is no mention of what happened to poor Sol.

Caring for someone who was mentally or emotionally unstable was a taxing burden. In 1809, the sixty-two-year-old Elizabeth Phelps took pity on Mary Andries, an elderly woman whose husband had just died. "I went over and told her she must come and live with me, but that she must have all her dirt and rags there. . . . After the corpse was taken away, . . . she was put into the waggon and brought here and set directly before our kitchen fire—having been previously washed, and cleansed, and dressed in decent clean clothes. . . . We have got that old great chest which Phyllis died in, and put against the outward east door in the kitchen, put straw in the bottom, then a bed—that is her night accommodation. . . . As to her health it is as well as could be expected, but she is assisted, in dressing,

31. "Evils of Drink," woodcut, Alexander Anderson Scrapbooks, Vol. X, Print Collection, Miriam & Ira D. Wallach Division of Art, Prints and Photographs, The New York Public Library, Astor, Lenox and Tilden Foundations.

The disruptive behavior of intemperate people was often vividly described and illustrated in publications that advocated the cause of temperance in the 1830s.

and undressing, like a child—I was in hopes we should learn her to walk, but pretty much despair now."[40] Although the old woman spent much of her time in prayer, she was certainly a worry to Elizabeth and a care to the household.

32. SARAH (SALLY) CUTTS, DRAWING, C. 1830. PHOTOGRAPH BY J. DAVID BOHL. COURTESY OF JOSEPH W. P. FROST.

An unfortunate woman, said to have been "demented, but not dangerous," in contrast to the behavior of her insane brother, Charles, who was kept chained in the attic for many years.

For those faced with the prospect of months or even years of care for a senile or deranged person, more than a "great chest" was needed. Some invalids preferred the comfort of a large upholstered easy chair. When Jabez Puffer died in Keene in 1794, Abner Sanger noted that it had been "years since he has been capable of sleeping in a bed by reason of his decrepit condition, by the rheumatism, he has always slept in his great chair."[41] Adult-sized cradles were useful for their soothing motion as well as for the protection they offered to a person who might be injured by spastic movement or rolling out of bed. Such cradles could also provide short-term comfort to people in pain. In Leicester, Massachusetts, in the late winter of 1802, Sally Scott developed a bad scrofulous sore on her ankle. Mr. Scott built her a cradle on December 29 and 30, and on New Year's Day Ruth Bascom noted, "Sister Scott took possession of her new cradle & knit on Andrew's mittens."[42] When a person was "not so feeble in her animal as her rational faculties, which had sunk into a second childhood,"[43] careful watching was necessary in order to avoid accidents. When "Uncle Diman," the "oldest man" of Dr. Bentley's church, died in Salem in 1795, the minister explained what had happened to the poor man: "In the close of life, he became intemperate, not having the best care taken of him. By falling into the fire he hastened that death which was fast approaching."[44]

It was customary for someone to stay up all night and watch over people who were seriously ill. This task often fell to young women, who were called to the homes of neighbors or nearby relatives to observe the sick person for signs of sudden change and to fulfill whatever needs might develop. Sarah Emery described a long night in which she stayed up with an aunt who was "a confirmed invalid." After the family's regular Bible readings and prayers, Sarah was left alone with the sick woman, who asked that herb tea be kept hot for her and then soon fell asleep. Sarah added wood to the fire and "placed a pewter

33. LADY PEPPERRELL HOUSE, KITTERY POINT, MAINE, DRAWING, C. 1820–30. PHOTOGRAPH BY J. DAVID BOHL. COURTESY OF JOSEPH W. P. FROST.

The kind of "comfortable house of the last century . . . from which life and vigor had long been ebbing, until all instincts of self-preservation seem to have departed," described by Sarah Orne Jewett in her story, "The Landscape Chamber." This was the home of the Cutts family in the nineteenth century. The owner, Lieutenant Cutts, had committed suicide after suffering severe financial losses resulting from Jefferson's embargo of 1807; his unfortunate children Sally and Charles lived on in the decaying house for many years.

34. "AUNT PATTY'S CRADLE," GENERAL ARTEMAS WARD MEMORIAL FUND MUSEUM, SHREWSBURY, MASSACHUSETTS, OWNED AND MAINTAINED BY HARVARD UNIVERSITY. PHOTOGRAPH BY RON WHITE.

An adult-sized cradle used by a family member for more than a decade. "Aunt Patty" is said to have been "not right, you know, simple." A special low table with a revolving top was made so she could reach it from her cradle.

porringer of balm tea on the embers." Trying to stay awake and to maintain both boiling tea and a comfortable temperature in the room, Sarah read newspapers for several hours and then snoozed in an easy chair. Suddenly waking, she "sprang for a candle, but . . . it was difficult to find the table; at length the candle, a small dip with a tow wick, was lightened, the fire replenished, and . . . the herb tea boiling when aunt Susy awoke." Sarah was relieved by another aunt at dawn, in time to walk home and begin her own morning chores.[45]

35. VISITING THE SICK, WOODCUT PUBLISHED IN BOTH *Eliza Van Wyck* AND *Tommy Wellwood* (BOTH NEW YORK, N.D.). PRIVATE COLLECTION.

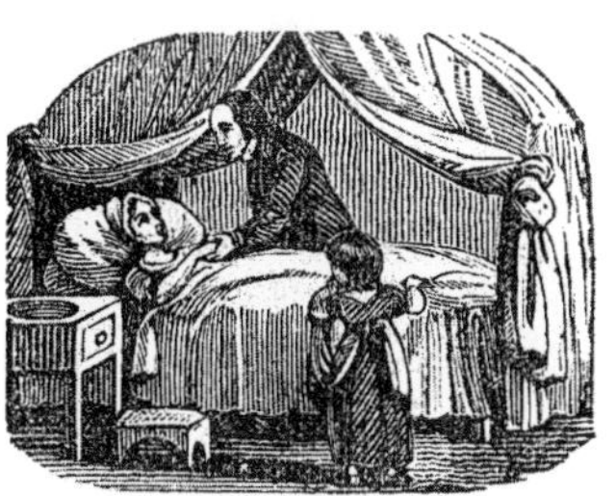

Sometimes young women were called to watch in houses that they did not know well. Susan Dickinson in Amherst, Massachusetts, described listening one night to "the steady talk of the clock of time and eternity, the wild scramble of the rats in the wall, the cracking and snapping of the old house itself, the soft scurry in the grass outside the open window of things I could not name but worse did imagine." Another time she "ventured down to the kitchen for broth," passing through a darkened hallway with only a faint oil lamp in her hand, past "stairs painted in wild grey scrawls and the walls papered in landscape designs with strange animals," which terrified her as she passed by.[46]

These families were fortunate to be able to call on young neighbors to watch; twenty-four-hour care of a demanding patient could wear down family resources very quickly. In those days it was customary for sick people to be confined to bed for long periods of time—months, or even years. Those who found that an upright position facilitated breathing were cared for in easy chairs. Keeping the patient warm, providing hot broth and tea, and offering comfort and prayer were the primary duties of watchers.

36. VIEWING THE DECEASED, WOODCUT PUBLISHED IN *The Narrative of Catherine Helfenstein* (D. C. 1830), (NEW YORK, N.D.).

The shaped coffin typical of the early nineteenth century is here laid on a bed. The corpse within it is dressed in grave clothes consisting of a shroud and a special cap.

When a person died, it was customary for someone to stay with him and "watch" until he was buried. The corpse was usually laid out and dressed in a shroud or other "grave clothes" soon after death. As soon as the coffin was ready, the body was placed inside and the coffin usually remained open until the funeral began. Because bodies were not embalmed, funerals were not delayed, especially in summertime.

Most coffins were displayed on tables or sawhorses in parlors, where the mourners assembled to hear words of comfort and sympathy. When a distinguished person died, it was customary in the countryside to display the open coffin on a bier in front of the house so that people might pay their respects without having to intrude on the bereaved family. When Peter Bryant died, his open coffin stood in the snow in front of the house for two days while people came from miles around to pay their respects to the honored doctor.

Before the funeral ceremony, the principal mourners put on black garments, veils, ribbons, and other tokens of their grief. The minister arrived. When it was time for the funeral service, people were called together by the ringing of a church bell. With the house surrounded by horses and vehicles, friends and family bade their last farewells before the coffin lid was closed and fastened tight. Prayer was offered at the home of the deceased before the procession made its way to the grave. The coffin was carried by strong young bearers, and the pall, a black cloth, was supported over it by pallbearers, who were usually the most socially important people in attendance. On June 14, 1814, Mr. and Mrs. Bascom walked out "to see the funeral procession [of Captain Smith], in which were the disconsolate widow & 5 children, their aged parents, bowed down with grief—and many brothers and sisters to mourn the loss of their beloved friend and brother."[47] Having a number of carriages in a funeral procession was considered a mark of gentility, but many people simply walked as they followed the coffin to the graveyard. After the burial, the mourners usually returned to the home of the deceased, and refreshments were offered. At other times the bearers were entertained elsewhere.

Sarah Goodwin remembered impressive quantities of food at country funerals at the time of her grandfather's death in 1815. "Extra help was brought in and the bushels of doughnuts that were fried, the ovensfull of pies that were

37. THE FIRST, SECOND, AND LAST SCENE OF MORTALITY, EMBROIDERED PICTURE. PRUDENCE PUNDERSON, PRESTON, CONNECTICUT, 1780. CONNECTICUT HISTORICAL SOCIETY, HARTFORD.

This allegorical embroidery depicts three stages of a genteel woman's life. At the left, a closed coffin lid is embellished with a border of brass nails and the initials "P.P." To emphasize the somber scene, the looking glass has been covered with a cloth, because vanity was considered unseemly in the presence of death. In the earlier segments of this vignette, in the center, Prudence Punderson is shown as an adult tracing an embroidery design and, at the right, as an infant being rocked in a cradle by a young black servant. Surviving tables, chairs, embroidered pictures, and a looking glass from the Punderson family now at the Connecticut Historical Society closely resemble those depicted in this scene, heightening one's belief in the truthfulness of the narrative.

baked, the geese, turkeys, chickens and beef that were roasted, amazed me. Piles of cooked food stood round the great kitchen and on the day of the funeral a long table was set in the largest front parlor and liquors of all sorts abounded. People came from Barrington, Madbury, Nottingham, Durham, and Dover [New Hampshire] (for my Grandfather was well known and much beloved) and everybody ate and drank." Mrs. Goodwin also remembered that "on the return of the procession the mourners went upstairs and seated themselves in a front chamber. Presently a solemn-looking man with a cue appeared, bearing a great waiter full of wine glasses, containing each Madeira wine, a lump of sugar and a teaspoon."[48]

38. THE SORROWING FAMILY, WOODCUT, C. 1825. ALEXANDER ANDERSON SCRAPBOOKS, VOL. X, PRINT COLLECTION, MIRIAM & IRA D. WALLACH DIVISION OF ART, PRINTS AND PHOTOGRAPHS, THE NEW YORK PUBLIC LIBRARY, ASTOR, LENOX AND TILDEN FOUNDATIONS.

A widow weeps after her husband's death. Although the body has not yet been placed in a coffin, the artist has shown the looking glass covered with a cloth in order to convey the idea that the man has died.

In *Oldtown Folks,* Mrs. Stowe tells us that "it was a doctrine of those good old times . . . that a house invaded by death should be made as forlorn as hands could make it. It should be rendered as cold and still, as unnatural, as dead and corpse-like as possible, by closing shutters, looking glasses pinned up in white sheets, and the locking up and hiding out of sight of any pleasant little familiar object which would have been thought out of place in a sepulchre."[49] A house invaded by death was transformed in appearance as well as in emotion. Still, the family within it was left to carry on. Time had stopped for only one of them.

Help

Because the concept of family included help as well as relatives, households not only were large and diverse but changed in size frequently. Hired girls and agricultural laborers came and went, depending upon the work requirements of the season, the management skills of their employers, the stability of their temperament, and the demands of their own families.

In some households, day laborers joined the family at dinnertime. Elizabeth Phelps often wrote about the rigors of harvest time; on July 17, 1773, she served meals to "twenty five Reapers" at Forty Acres.[50] Susan Lesley later recalled that in the Lyman family in Northampton in the early nineteenth century, "all were provided for in the house. It was not unusual for us to have eight or ten men in the summer, which complicated the housekeeping very much."[51] Although the number of day laborers fluctuated with the seasonal demands of farm work, those hired men who were retained on a long-term basis were usually considered part of the family. This was the case at the Phelps farm in Hadley, although there was considerable mobility among the workmen. Not everyone employed at Forty Acres was an ideal employee. Some were lazy; others were intemperate. On December 20, 1802, Mrs. Phelps wrote to Betsy that she was alone at Hadley, and she complained, "This is the second night, two drunken men have been all the dependence we have had to take care of the barn & house—I did fasten my doors last night & intend to tonight. They have been both drunk eno' three days past." She wrote again of hired men in December 1809, telling Betsy of the arrival of new men, who made some welcome changes in everyday life: "Our workmen are all changed except John [Morison, the Scotch gardener], Nair has got his 9 pence as John says, your father has hired Bill Till . . . and his brother, and your father likes 'em well, it seems clever [agreeable] not to have the kitchen full of talk and brawl, as it used to be with Nair and Ralf."[52] Such men were part of the family circle of care and concern, but they were certainly not considered equals.

Including short-term help in the arms of family reflects not only paternalism but also mutual responsibility. If hired men and girls entered a family to provide services, they expected care if they fell sick, laundry service, mending, and some new clothing in addition to their room, board, and wages. Immoral behavior and bad habits caused problems and reflected badly on the family. The

39. VIEW OF THE SEAT OF MOSES GILL, ESQ. OF PRINCETON, ENGRAVING, *Massachusetts Magazine*, 1792. BOSTON ATHENAEUM. COURTESY OF THE SOCIETY FOR THE PRESERVATION OF NEW ENGLAND ANTIQUITIES.

Gill's country seat included a house 50 feet square, with an adjacent "farm house" of 40 by 36 feet, together with a large barn, coach and chaise house, sheds, and other agricultural outbuildings. In contrast to the direct involvement of Charles and Elizabeth Phelps in managing the agricultural economy of Forty Acres, the Gills used their seat as a fashionable summer residence, with distinctly separate accommodations for their workers.

burdens of care and governance fell on both husband and wife. During the years 1744 and 1745, Samuel Lane of Stratham, New Hampshire, deliberately limited the number of apprentices he took on, instead hiring journeymen when he needed help in his tanning business, in order to save his "weakly Wife the trouble of a great family."[53]

The hiring of household help has always been based on a balance of need and the ability to pay. Among most prosperous families in early–New England towns and cities, there was a general expectation that both household and farm work required some outside help, especially when there were no strong young people in the family. Among the wealthy, there were always fairly formal servant relationships and, in the eighteenth century, some household slaves.

In city and country alike, there were informal arrangements for help within neighborhoods or within the extended family structure. Young girls went for long visits with their married siblings or cousins to perform a wide range of unpaid services; and, as historian Laurel Ulrich has pointed out, "Women exchanged daughters as they exchanged kettles."[54] These visits and exchanges helped young women hone their skills at a wide variety of useful tasks, absorb a knowledge of traditional housekeeping methods, and mature outside the structure of their immediate families. When country girls visited their city relatives, they were exposed to urban manners, fashions, and shopping opportu-

40. RALPH WHEELOCK'S FARM, OIL ON CANVAS, .641 × 1.22, BY FRANCIS ALEXANDER, C. 1822. NATIONAL GALLERY OF ART, WASHINGTON, D.C., GIFT OF EDGAR WILLIAM AND BERNICE CHRYSLER GARBISCH.

Many seasonal laborers were employed at harvest time on this large and productive farm on Denison Hill in Southbridge, Massachusetts.

nities, but many were also expected to help with household chores, cooking, family sewing, and entertaining.

In the eighteenth century, formal indentures, apprenticeship agreements, and chattel slavery ordered some of the relationships between masters and servants and defined the educational responsibilities of employers, as well as their obligation to provide adequate food and clothing. However, since there was no requirement that documentation of these agreements be filed in court records, it is difficult to know how these contracts governed general household help. Colonial newspapers carried many advertisements for runaway slaves, apprentices, and indentured servants, but they tell us more about the clothing of the runaways than about the agreements that governed their work. Although Sarah Emery tells us that in late-eighteenth-century Newbury, "in most families there was a boy or girl bound to service until the age of eighteen,"[55] formal apprenticeship was not the norm for household help, and few young girls were actually bound until they were eighteen.

41. JERSEY NANNY, MEZZOTINT, JOHN GREENWOOD, BOSTON, 1748. GIFT OF HENRY LEE SHATTUCK. COURTESY, MUSEUM OF FINE ARTS, BOSTON.

This rare print illustrates the everyday work dress of a black woman named Ann Arnold who lived in Colonial Boston.

Among more prosperous families in rural towns,[56] girls from less fortunate families were hired to assist with certain aspects of the household work. They came with the expectation that in addition to their room and board they would receive modest cash wages or store credits, as well as thorough instruction in reading and housekeeping; that they would be provided with clothing; that they would be cared for and their services replaced whenever they were sick; and that they would have opportunities to return home to visit their families and could respond to family emergencies when needed. They participated in church and community activities, such as singing schools, quilting parties, husking bees, and the observation of holidays, often in conjunction with daughters in the family. In return, they knew that they might be called upon to fulfill an expanded range of responsibilities at harvest time and Thanksgiving, whenever the family entertained, or if the mistress of the household gave birth, fell ill, or died.

Ideally, these relationships extended over a long period of time. Nancy Wood lived at service with the family of Jonathan Sayward for ten years before going to Boston to live with another family.[57] Elizabeth Sturgis of Salem tells us: "It was the custom in those days for young

American girls to enter families to be initiated into the work of a house and it was not uncommon for them to remain for years or until they were married; and sometimes for their whole lives, identifying themselves with the family and sharing all their joys and sorrows. They were taught all kinds of housework, together with sewing, reading, etc."[58] Such a settled, long-term relationship was ideal from an employer's point of view.

42. PHYLLIS, A PAINTED DUMMYBOARD, NEW ENGLAND, PRE–1753. COURTESY OF THE SOCIETY FOR THE PRESERVATION OF NEW ENGLAND ANTIQUITIES. PHOTOGRAPH BY J. DAVID BOHL.

This life-sized painting on wood is believed to depict a mulatto servant of Elizabeth Hunt Wendell (c. 1716–99). After the death of her husband, Jacob Wendell, in 1753, Mrs. Wendell married the Reverend Thomas Smith and moved to his home in Falmouth, Maine, taking both Phyllis and the dummyboard with her.

"Neat handed Phillis" was a table maid in Milton's 1632 poem "L'Allegro," and thereafter the name was commonly used in pastoral poetry for an attractive rustic maiden or rural sweetheart. In the eighteenth century, "Phyllis" became a common name for female servants in literature, and in New England it was widely used for female slaves, who had no choice of English name. In Hadley, Massachusetts, Elizabeth Porter Phelps's female slave was also named Phyllis.

When hired girls were from the lower classes or less fortunate families, the relationship between mistress and maid was ideally one of mutual respect and affection, the young person being considered a member of the family. Ruth Bascom made repeated reference in her diary to "our girl," reflecting at once a definition of role and a sense that the girl was indeed a member of the Bascom family. Older women who worked as servants did not always enjoy or expect a settled relationship, although that was the ideal for both mistress and maid. In the spring of 1815, Elizabeth Phelps bewailed the speedy departure of a hardworking servant: "Our Indian woman left us in one week & one day, her husband came and took her with him. thus are our pleasing prospects often cut off—& well so, teaches patience, & a proper submission to all allotments, it was clever to have her so long, she did a deal of dirty hard work, & it indeed very well,—we anticipated a great benefit from her strength & good management, where we can find [another] one we know not."[59]

A newly married woman who was on a tight budget and lacked confidence in her new role might have difficulty in establishing her authority and keeping help. This was the situation in which Betsy Huntington Phelps found herself soon after her arrival in Litchfield in 1801. At first she was confident that she could manage, then she wrote to her mother: "My girl . . . intends leaving us a week from today—what I shall do then is uncertain. . . . This I am sure—if nothing happens I am able to do my own work—it may come hard, as you say, but perhaps it will be good for me." Still, she was hopeful: "If you hear of a good girl that we could take, it would be a fine thing for us." Gradually things became even more complicated, and Betsy wrote again, explaining her predicament: "Chloe has been with me almost a fortnight—she has a pretty little girl, not troublesome, but with her she talks of having five shillings a week, we cannot give it—and if she will not stay for three shillings and the board of her child we must part." Finding herself with "no company and no cleaning house to do" in early September, Betsy tried to economize by sending Chloe out to earn day wages working for other families. Although she felt sure that she could get along "cleverly," it didn't work; Chloe left, and Betsy tried to get along with even more inexperienced help. Trying to save money, she was soon exhausted, writing to her mother: "I am in great haste for a fortnight's ironing, baking and churning to do, and . . . only a little girl of 13 years to assist me. . . . I thank you for your wishes that I had good help—and that Sally's girl had offered to get one for me—but our income will not allow us to hire good help, because they ask so great a price—I have been counting the number of girls I have had since I came to Litchfield and find the number to be ten, the one I have now will leave me tonight or tomorrow night—and then I am destitute." Then good fortune fell in her lap. A week later, she wrote again to Hadley: "And now I must call upon you to help me praise the Lord—you know the difficulty we have had about help—Monday . . . I was almost worn out with work, and did not wash me up until almost sunset—but while I was doing it, a black girl came and offered her services, how providential!—it had such an effect on me that the tears gushed into my eyes and my heart returned its grateful tribute. . . . Mrs. Deming, one of our most respectable women has had this girl all summer, but their family being larger, she was not able to do all the washing, being only fifteen—she now has one that can do all her work and will stay with her till spring—she therefore sent this one to me, that if I had no one engaged I might have her thro' the winter—how kind, and how much I am favored—she is large of her age, and quite handy—and was desirous of coming—I shall treat her well."[60] Hopefully, Betsy had learned a good deal about how to manage servants in the first year of her marriage; she certainly had a variety of young women from whom to learn.

Some hired girls received weekly or monthly cash wages. Others were paid with store credits and settled with their employers once a year. Consider Dickinson of Deerfield kept an account book from 1806 until 1823 in which he recorded a wide variety of family expenditures, including store credits and wages for a succession of hired girls. Each girl earned room and board plus four shillings a week, with pay deducted for days on which she might be absent to visit her family or to "work for herself." Some of the girls worked almost exclusively for cash, but others used credits for ribbons, pins, gloves, shawls, bonnets, shoes, combs, dressmaking services, shoe repair, and yards of calico, gingham, or sheeting. On March 24, 1824, Dickinson gave Betsey Guellow four dollars "to keep election," and on June 18 she received twenty cents "to see the Elefant." Of the $21.67 which Betsy earned that year, she spent $19.53, leaving only $2.14 in cash to show for her year's work.[61]

43. THE HAPPY FAMILY, WOODCUT IN MRS. SHERWOOD, *Home* (NEW HAVEN, 1833). PRIVATE COLLECTION.

Although serving girls were considered part of the family structure and economy, they knew their place and were not depicted as equals in contemporary artwork.

In some families unmarried daughters in their teens and twenties were permitted to record the cash value of their work within the family and were also responsible for their personal expenditures. One of Sarah Bryant's neighbors, Ruby Packard, kept an account book in which she recorded her "work for mother" and the store credits she was able to earn thereby. In York, Maine, Jonathan Sayward's great-granddaughter Mary Barrell kept careful records of money earned by spinning and knitting, as well as her expenditures for clothing, textiles, household furnishings, and a few charitable contributions.[62] In Plymouth, Vermont, Sally Brown noted in her diary that she "sold Mary my Navarino bonnet for a weeks work in spinning for Mother."[63]

Hired girls usually shared beds with each other or with daughters of the family. Since they were accustomed to sharing beds with siblings and visiting female cousins, many of them would have been uncomfortable sleeping alone.

It was customary for the clothing of hired girls to be provided by the families with which they lived and for them to assist in the family sewing. As part of her instruction, Sarah Bryant cut out gloves and gowns for her hired girls, which she expected them to sew for themselves,[64] but Sarah also sewed for her help, making shirts, frocks, gowns, caps, pelisses, tuckers, and bonnets for the girls, and leather mittens, waistcoats, vests, spencers, coats, pantaloons, and trousers for the hired men.[65]

Hired girls usually dressed in simple, practical work clothes during the day. "The dress of these girls . . . consisted of a gown of stuff or calico, with a high-necked and long sleeved tire which completed the costume. Their hair was cut short or parted neatly and out behind their ears. Bangs and fringes were unknown in those days and would not have been tolerated for a minute."[66] However, not all families provided for their young female helpers as they did for their own children. Outraged by the treatment of some "little bound girls in families," Sarah Anna Emery recalled their inadequate clothing and sloppy appearance: "I have often seen such children going to the pump in mid-winter, clad only in a homespun short gown and petticoat, with slipshod shoes, disclosing huge holes in the heels of their stockings, and an old hood tied over their tangled hair."[67] Such conditions suggest that girls sometimes worked in families who either did not bother or could not afford to keep them nicely, and who were not offended by their ragamuffin appearance.

Frequently, help was recruited from within one's own circle of acquaintances, or a suitable candidate might be recommended by a distant friend or relative. Some people, however, resorted to newspapers, and their published advertisements define the work and remuneration expected.

> A Place in the Country Wanted
>
> For a smart active girl, 11 years of age, in a Small family where her services would be useful, All her clothing would be furnished.[68]

Eleven or twelve was considered a normal age for girls to begin to live outside their own families and provide services for others. When Francis Robbins was newly married in 1818, he and his brother rode together to the nearby town of Enfield, Connecticut, "and got a girl of twelve years old, to be kept if she suits."[69] Although the Reverend Thomas Robbins never married or established his own household, he often made ventures seeking girls to assist in household chores in the families with which he lived. His detailed diary reveals that in some cases the hired girls were recruited from black families in nearby cities.

Because hired girls were considered members of the family and were counted upon to perform basic services, a settled relationship was the goal. It was always jarring when a change occurred. In March 1825, Robbins noted: "Our black girl, Harriet, that I procured at Norfolk, went away. Her mother took her away, as I think, unjustifiably." Harriet had been living and working in East Windsor since July 17, 1822.[70]

Many newly hired girls had never slept away from home before and were miserably homesick even when they were only a few miles from home. Some hired girls were clearly immature, cantankerous, dishonest, or unreliable; some were all of these and more. When Sarah Bartlett was "discovered to make false ties" in some yarn she had been spinning, she was so angry at being found out deceiving her employer about the amount of work she had done that she set his house on fire and it burned to the ground.[71]

Kindhearted young Elizabeth Phelps found herself in a pickle in the fall of 1768 when she took in a young woman who wanted work. Her diary entry describes what happened: "Monday about 9 o'clock at night came here Sarah Goodrich with her sister. . . . Betty being with child had no setled place of abode therefore my mother was a going to set her spinning for her for a week or two she not expecting to lie in the three months—soon after they got in they with the rest of us that was up went to bed. . . . But we had not been a bed long before Sarah was obliged to get up Betsy was so poorly. She grew ill. Worthington went into town after Aunt Porter then turned straight around after Mrs. Dickingson a midwife tho the child was born a half hour before she came. Thomas Smith his wife got here a little after the child was born—it lived not an hour." Sarah Goodrich left her hapless sister alone in the care of the Phelps family for nearly a month.[72]

Adding an attractive young woman to the family circle sometimes caused almost unimaginable trouble. In Landaff, New Hampshire, Abigail Bailey had problems with both her husband and her help: "In September 1770, we hired a young woman to live with us. She had been a stranger to me, I found her rude and full of vanity. Her ways were to me disagreeable. But to my grief I saw that they were pleasing to Mr. B. Their whole attention seemed to be toward each other; and their impertinent conduct very aggravating to me, and (I was sensible) provoking to God. I learned to my full satisfaction, that there was improper conduct between them."[73] This must not have been an unusual situation, at least in the city, for William Bentley noted in 1797 that "remarks have been made that of all the girls sent into families to provide their own maintenance those who have gone to Boston have been the most unhappy. Almost all of thm have returned heavy laden to their friends in Town. The difference of morals is great, but the force of parental presence and advice is greater."[74]

Diarists like Sarah Bryant expressed considerable satisfaction when a difficult girl left of her own accord, yet the tremendous amount of work that needed to be done made help a necessity, and personal circumstances, especially childbirth, sometimes put the mistress in the position of having to retain a lazy or unreliable servant. The winter of 1806–07 was a particularly bad time for Sarah Bryant. Nancy Thayer had lived with the family only since July 17 and had gone home for six weeks between August 1 and September 17, when suddenly, on the twenty-fourth, she "went home bag and baggage." Left with her six young children to care for in addition to her husband, her parents, and a number of boarding students, Sarah was without settled help throughout the difficult harvest season, cold winter, and busy spring, employing five different women, including the temperamental Nancy Thayer, on a sporadic basis for weaving, candle dipping, spinning, and general housework until Nancy's sister

Sukey came to stay for six weeks beginning May 29, 1807. Sukey's employment may well have been related to Sarah Bryant's impending maternity, for John Bryant was born on July 22. Sukey Thayer went home on August 3, and thereafter Temperance Barber came weekly to do the washing until Polly Hamilton came to live in on September 7. Although Polly remained with the Bryant family for a year, it was not until 1814, when John, the youngest child, was seven years old, that a hired girl named Martha arrived and the situation was stabilized. Martha remained in the Bryant household for nearly five years. Perhaps her situation was made more interesting by the companionship of the Bryants' daughter Sally, who was twelve years old when Martha arrived. Sally and Martha often did chores together, visited mutual friends, and attended apple-paring bees and other work parties during the time Martha was part of the household.

Routine chores assigned to hired girls included most of the heavy indoor work. Sarah Bryant's girls worked at washing; ironing; dishwashing; cleaning; scouring pots, kettles, floors, and pewter; spinning wicking and making candles; picking geese; making starch; and hatcheling, spinning, and bleaching linen. Apparently, Sarah Bryant—and her mother, while she was alive—did much of the cooking, leaving the task of food preparation to the hired girls. After butchering was done on December 6, 1800, for example, Chloe "cleaned the creature's feet."[75]

Hired girls were often trusted with errands to neighbors and the store, and these ventures may have been treated as rewards for work well done or perceived as an escape from more onerous tasks.

In some households, additional help was employed for particularly burdensome tasks, especially laundry, nursing, and seasonal housecleaning. Within a community there were often single women, or desperately poor people, who supported themselves with short-term work, but some young women from fairly prosperous families worked by the day as spinsters or assisting with sewing until they were married.

Everywhere, hired girls carried much of the responsibility for spinning. Sarah Emery's "Aunt kept a hired girl through the year. In the summer she helped in the dairy and housework, but her chief employment was spinning."[76] In February 1780, Mrs. Ebenezer Parkman hired two women for one week to spin. One of them, Lucy Maynard, must have continued her employment for a longer period because Ebenezer Parkman's diary noted on March 22 that he "Gave Mrs. P.—33 Dollars to pay Miss Lucy Maynard."[77] In the Bryant household, Sarah herself usually warped and set the looms, but the hired girls did all of the spinning and much of the routine weaving while the Bryant children were small.

When children grew up and left home, family size decreased and the remaining children were of an age to do more work themselves, so the urgency of finding help decreased, and fewer outsiders were hired. Sarah Bryant employed less help when her own daughters were teenagers and later, when she shared her home with her son and daughter-in-law.

Within the daily work routine, the housewife assumed certain responsibilities herself, and others were reserved for the daughters of the family. In Northampton, Judge Lyman's wife "always superintended the kitchen department herself, including the dairy; but all the daily care of the house, the sweeping and dusting, and arrangement of the table, with a small girl or boy to wait, came to the young ladies of the house, with only occasional help from the second woman."[78] Elizabeth Phelps herself often did the cooking and cheesemaking on a very large farm. In the spring of 1813, she wrote to her daughter Betsy that "Martha & your old mother, are all the females that at present cook, & take care of 7 men." Still, she felt certain that her daughter-in-law Sally could not get along in Boston without four house servants: "The Cook certainly must be had—the chamber maid cannot be wanting—a man or boy to do errands & split wood &c—& little Sally is daughter's right hand almost."[79]

44. HARDWARE FOR BELLPULLS, ENGRAVING, CATALOGUE OF YATES & HAMPER, BIRMINGHAM BRASS FOUNDERS, C. 1821. COURTESY WINTERTHUR LIBRARY, PRINTED BOOK AND PERIODICAL COLLECTION.

Intricate systems of wires and bells facilitated formal relationships between masters and servants in some prosperous households.

By the mid-nineteenth century, Sarah Goodwin decried the lack of specialized skills among many native-born help, who could not be relied upon in the kitchen and which made it necessary for ladies "to be in their kitchens all the morning hours. They had to make all the deserts, jellies, preserves, pickles, cake, and iron all the ruffled shirts and other starched things."[80] Mrs. Goodwin preferred the more formal kind of servant relationship which was characteristic of many prosperous urban households of the Victorian era.

As sensibilities changed among the rising middle class, a preference began to develop for deferential behavior among servants, and the rituals of everyday life became more formal. In some cases, problems arose in enforcing new standards of morality, cleanliness, and dress. As expectations changed, the sense of help being truly part of the family declined. In her 1839 book *The Good Housekeeper,* Mrs. Hale felt a need to include a list of "Rules for Domestics." One of these expressed the author's wish for an identifiable servant role: "It would look neater and keep your hair much smoother; if you would wear a cap or handkerchief while at work, as English servants do."[81]

Shying away from the formalization of domestic service, Lydia Maria Child in her 1832 book *The American Frugal Housewife* still preferred that young girls spend "two or three years with a mother, assisting her in her duties, instructing brothers and sisters, and taking care of their own clothes," insisting that "this is the way to make them happy, as well as good wives, for, being early accustomed to the duties of life, they will sit lightly as well as gracefully upon them."[82]

In her 1841 *Treatise on Domestic Economy,* Catharine Beecher offered a whole chapter titled "On the Care of Domestics." Recognizing the advantages of more formal relationships with servants, Miss Beecher stressed the educational and quasi-parental role of employers, yet she advised "that domestics use a different entrance to the house, and sit at a distinct table, not because they are inferior beings, but because this is the best method of securing neatness and order and convenience."[83] Patient instruction, consideration, and consistency were advised to bind domestics to their employers and to inspire satisfactory work.

In no matter was the increasing formality of relationships between mistresses and servants more clearly defined than that of where the servants should eat. When she moved to Concord, Massachusetts, shortly after her marriage to Ralph Waldo Emerson in 1835, Lidian Emerson consented to "adopt the country practice of having but one table in the house." When she explained this new practice in the kitchen to the two servants she had brought with her from Plymouth, Louisa, the housemaid, agreed to eat with the family, but Lydia, the cook, objected. The next morning, she flatly refused to leave what she regarded as her place in the kitchen, and Louisa chose to stay with her."[84]

In many rural homes, the help continued to be treated as part of the family. Informality in these relations was so characteristic of country families until nearly the end of the nineteenth century that it became a literary convention. Harriet Beecher Stowe's "Dolly" in *Oldtown Folks* and the outspoken "helps" in some of the stories of Sarah Orne Jewett exemplify widespread social practice.

The families in which these people lived considered them as full participants in the patterns and rituals of everyday life and work. The family structure was diverse, and governance was unquestionably paternalistic. Although the composition of the family changed in response to circumstance, the stability of the family was the central focus of human concern. People were aware that it could be broken by death at any moment, yet family solidarity was celebrated at weddings, important anniversaries, and Thanksgiving Day. On June 11, 1752, Samuel Lane enjoyed another kind of family gathering: "I raised an Addition to my House and had my Father and Mother and all their 14 Children together at my Table." Unfortunately, the family circle was soon broken: "That Day [a] week after we were all together at Br. Jabez James Funeral who Dined with us at Raising."[85] Even in the face of death, the unity of the New England family was of paramount importance to its members.

III

Going to Housekeeping

When newly married couples went to housekeeping in early New England, their situations varied widely. Many parents were able to provide their daughters with the basic essentials for housekeeping, and this was a widely shared goal. For some fortunate brides there might be a brand-new house, already filled with expensive furnishings in the latest Boston or London fashion. For others, home would be no more than a single room in a crowded household of strangers or a flimsy house no larger than a room. For them there was little more than a bed and bedding, a chest, a cooking pot, and a spoon. Some were already widows and mothers themselves. Others faced widowed or domineering mothers-in-law who required their sons to stay in the family homestead and were reluctant to yield their traditional authority and management role. Some, like Elizabeth Phelps, an only child whose father had died when she was eight years old, never left their childhood homes. Many, like Sarah Bryant, waited until their own parents died before becoming truly independent, moving from place to place with an increasing number of young children while their husbands came and went, attempting to earn an adequate living, serving in the legislature, or seeking improved health. For others, like Ruth Henshaw Miles, the dream of wedded bliss turned to ashes far too soon, when their young husbands died. Less than a year after their wedding and just a month after Asa Miles's death, Ruth witnessed the appraisal of his real estate and furniture; on May 27 her things were packed up and returned to her father's house. The next day, about six in the evening, she left their "once pleasant, but now gloomy house."[1] Clearly, newly married people wanted to establish independent households, but their success depended on wealth and circumstance.

In the fall of 1759, nearly a year after her marriage, Mary Fish Noyes began unpacking some long-awaited boxes in New Haven. She had been living as a guest in the home of her husband's parents since the beginning of the year. Despite the fact that the wealthy Noyes family could provide every comfort for the young couple, custom dictated otherwise, and Mary's parents were gratified that they were able to provide for their daughter. Mary and her husband, John, were eager to set up housekeeping in rooms designated for their specific use, and it must have been with considerable satisfaction that Mary received in a coasting vessel a hair trunk, a chestnut box, a hogshead, and some furniture shipped to her by her parents. The containers were accompanied by a letter from Mary's father, a minister of modest means in Southington, Connecticut, who reminded the couple that the objects being sent were, in fact, the property of God and assured them that he and his wife considered themselves "Pleased and Rewarded, if we may be used as [God's] Instruments of Contributing anything to your Conveniency of Living."

The "Few Articles for Housekeeping" that were sent to Mary must have been very welcome indeed, for they included enough furniture and furnishings to ensure a modest level of hospitality and domestic comfort and to make it possible at last for her to move from the status of guest to housewife with some degree of independence. Polished iron "Hand Irons" and a shovel and tongs were provided for one fireplace. There were also two bedsteads, "one with a Sacking Bottom; The other Common, bound up with a Bed Cord," as well as a tea table, a dressing table, and a "mahogany leaf" (table), but there were no chests or chests of drawers, no desk or bookcase, and, most surprisingly, no chairs. It may be that Mr. and Mrs. Fish were confident that chairs and perhaps some additional furniture were being provided by the Noyes family, or it may be that chairs were shipped separately from Southington along with a china table that was late in coming from William Welden's shop.

Mr. Fish assured Mary that although the large looking glass with a shell on it had been "Somewhat hurt, in coming from Boston" it was not seriously damaged, and Mary was advised that "The Pieces, that broke off are in your Trunk, wrap'd in a paper & writ upon. Any ingenious hand may easily Glue them on again." Her father expressed his concern that her "common Bedstead" might be too long; they had "intended to have it altered; But failed of it." It would not be difficult to have it "Cut Shorter" if she thought it would be best. Mr. Fish was also worried about the bed cord, writing: "Tis to mean, I intended you a *New Hemp Cord,* but Could not get one in Town, so was obliged to Send Such a one as we had at Hand"; he hoped the cord would last a while. Mr. Fish also expressed his apologies that he had no news about additional goods that had been ordered in Boston. He did not mention chairs, but he was most concerned about his failure to get any yardage of Persian silk for a quilt, assuring her that if she could find any in New Haven, she should get it if possible and count on having her parents reimburse her when they next visited.

Mary's father cautioned her that after her things were delivered and she obtained the key to her trunk from the master of the coasting vessel, she should be careful in unpacking. His letter contained very specific instructions: "In Opening the Chestnut Box, where the Glass & Brittle ware are Stow'd, Observe the following Directions—viz. The First you may cut the Walnut Band of each Side of the Lid. Then prie up on each end of the Lid, which is nail'd, & the Nail, that goes thro the Back Lid into the Lid, will I suppose give way. Then be careful in Taking out the wool, lest the Small Vessels, wh[ich] are Dispersed through ye Whole, should hang to it, & Receive Damage." Such attention would be rewarded, for her mother had packed the box with great care, "Beginning at [the] Bottom [with] 1 Pr. Dutch Blankets, Next a large Looking Glass, with Back down the Face covered, first with Paper, then with a thin Board. Next are Stowd away amongst ye Wool . . . 2 Stone Platters. 1 Doz. Stone Plates, ½ Doz. China Tea Dishes & Saucers. ½ Doz. Custard Dishes 1 Sugar Dish & 1 Slop Bowl. Besides, your China Punch Bowl, Stone Tea Pot & Water Pot, China or Glass mug, 2 Green Jugs, &c: On ye Top of all, is 1 pr Homemade white woosted Blankets." Once the box was unpacked, Mary was supplied with basic articles for serving food and tea, the expected role of any wife.

Among the other things brought up from the wharves for John and Mary Noyes were a new feather bed made of homemade ticking and sewn up in a blanket; a hogshead containing another feather bed, this one made of "bought Tickin"; and the other necessary bedding for both beds: four pillows, two bolsters, and an Ozenbrig underbed of sacking, which was folded and stitched to make a protective covering around the piece of lining fabric and the dyed wool batting that Mary was to use in making up her Persian bed quilt.

There was also a hair trunk in which, her father wrote, "We have put up and hope you'll find" a worsted gown, a quilted petticoat, and a pair of stays, and additional bedding, table linens, and towels. These included eight pairs of sheets, eight pillow cases, twelve towels, three tablecloths, two smaller tablecloths with six homemade napkins, a damask tablecloth with six napkins that still needed to be hemmed, a calico bed quilt, a silk damask blanket, a worsted blanket, a worsted coverlet, flannel for a blanket, and "some small articles not mentioned." Although many of these items were made of imported textiles such as worsted and damask, and only a few of them were identified as being homemade or homespun, it is clear that Mary's mother had been busy making pillowcases and hemming sheets, towels, and tablecloths right up until the trunk was taken to the wharf, for Mr. Fish had been obliged to open it after it had been packed and inventoried in order to add more things.[2]

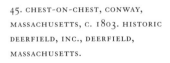

45. CHEST-ON-CHEST, CONWAY, MASSACHUSETTS, C. 1803. HISTORIC DEERFIELD, INC., DEERFIELD, MASSACHUSETTS.

This impressive and expensive piece of furniture was made to order by Jonathan Smith of Conway, Massachusetts, as part of the wedding furniture of Lydia Batchelder, who married Simon De Wolf in December 1803.

Mary Fish had not been weaving, sewing, and quilting for years in order to assemble a "hope chest" full of bedding and table linens in anticipation of a marriage that was yet to be negotiated. Indeed, her parents did not even place the orders or begin to assemble the things until after Mary and her husband had departed for New Haven. Her mother was busy hemming napkins a year after Mary's marriage, and the last things were being packed in her trunk even as the coasting vessel approached the wharf in Southington.

The provision of large quantities of bed and table linen was central to the idea of provision for housekeeping, but in eighteenth-century New England very few of these goods were set aside for years before a marriage. Daughters participated in the textile production of a family throughout their teenage years by spinning, weaving, sewing, knitting, and quilting, but it was not until a wedding was agreed on that the focus of this work shifted to the preparation of things for their own homes. Once the effort began in earnest, many family members turned their attention to producing or assembling the necessary items. In some cases, the work continued after the wedding itself, and the newly married couple did not actually go to housekeeping for several months, or even years.

Even though many of the newly completed articles of bedding and table linen were eventually stored in wooden chests, there is no documentation of a "hope chest" in early–New England family records or diaries, nor is there evidence of the tradition that a girl must make thirteen quilts before she could make her best, or "bride's," quilt. Like so many other romantic ideas about life in the preindustrial era, the "hope chest" seems to be late-nineteenth-century in origin.[3]

There is, however, considerable truth to the popular image of the period of betrothal being characterized by anxious consultation between the engaged couple, bulk purchasing of household goods, large-scale commissions to cabinetmakers, parental anxiety, unusual amounts of dressmaking, vivacious quilting parties, and extensive shopping expeditions. But this is certainly overstated in many fictional accounts.

Among settled New England families, it was normal practice for daughters to be outfitted with a basic stock of goods for housekeeping, known as a "marriage portion." This was part of a long-established custom in England and was common throughout Europe and America. Sons were usually given land upon which to establish their own families and, if it could be afforded, a house. Since there was no legal obligation for these transfers, detailed records of them are scattered among family papers rather than documented in the public record.

Twelve days after twenty-four-year-old Samuel Lane married Mary James of Hampton, New Hampshire, on Christmas eve in 1741, the couple went to housekeeping in his unfinished house in nearby Stratham. Mary's parents had supplied a basic inventory of household furnishings and implements, and Lane noted in his diary with some satisfaction: "I Mov'd my Wife and her goods to my own House."[4] From this time forward, Mary's goods became Samuel's. Under the common law, men controlled the goods women brought to marriage unless there was a written agreement between them stating otherwise. These were unusual for first marriages except in the most prosperous families; such agreements were much more common when the bride was a wealthy widow.

Mary's goods had been given to her by her own parents as part of the expected provisioning of daughters. Evidence of these gifts is abundant in the legal record, although the details are often hinted at rather than spelled out in detail. The dates on deeds of land and buildings being transferred from father to son can sometimes be coordinated with that of the young man's marriage. Paternal wills often specified that when bequests were made, consideration had been given to goods and land that had already been transferred from parent to child. Because of the considerable value involved and the importance of good records in avoiding legal squabbles in the future, fathers made detailed lists of the goods that were given to daughters as well as of the lands that were given to sons. Samuel Lane's son Jabez took care to record his daughter Martha's marriage portion in 1808 in a document titled: "The within is the Account of the Things I give my Daughter Martha Mathes Towards her Portion out of my Estate which is to be considered as part payment of the Legacy I have given her in my will as it now stands."[5] Similarly, in Shrewsbury, Massachusetts, in 1827, Nathan Howe recorded the value of the furniture and furnishings of his daughter's portion in his account book under the heading: "Harriet Howe, Dater for the following account to be accounted for hereafter as part of her portion of her Father's estate."[6] In making formal bequests to daughters, fathers often mentioned that these were in addition to what had been previously given. As much as twenty years after his first daughter's wedding, Samuel Lane added to his account of her marriage portion the value of his gifts of some ceramics, clothing, and a clock. Ebenezer Snells's bequests to both his son Thomas and his daughter Abigail were clearly given "in addition to what I have heretofore given." Thus, the transfers of household goods and land that were made when a young couple set up housekeeping were actually the first transfer of property from one generation to another, and along with later gifts were carefully accounted as a kind of advance on an inheritance.

The Marriage Portion

In eighteenth- and early-nineteenth-century New England, the term "portion," or "marriage portion," was used to describe the goods given when a daughter was married. The term "dowry" was not used to describe such goods until at least the middle of the nineteenth century, when it appears in some short stories in *Peterson's Magazine* and *Godey's Lady's Book*. The custom and traditions associated with the marriage portion are well defined in a series of essays published in 1890 titled "Shall Our Daughters Have Dowries?"[7]

It must have been considered very important for a young man to select a bride whose parents could provide generously for her. Soon after Royall Tyler had convinced Mary Palmer that she should marry him, he brought her "a large trunk tightly packed with everything a parent could wish for an outfit for a daughter,"[8] and she was grateful to him for allowing her impoverished family to keep up appearances. While Tyler was establishing a law practice and building a new home for Mary in Vermont, she continued to live with her parents in Watertown, Massachusetts, even after they were married and a son was born.

During these years, Tyler supplied his wife with household furnishings for their future home as well as with food and clothing for her current use. He came to visit in February 1796, bringing more household goods, including a dozen teaspoons and three large spoons marked with her own initials, "M.P.," rather than the initials "M.P.T." or "R.M.T.," which would have indicated for their whole lives that the spoons were acquired after the couple was married. Mary felt that "this was delicate and kind in him, for he knew I could not purchase them, and he wished to make it appear that my parents did so. In this was he was doing everything in his power to make me forget everything that was unpleasant in my situation."[9]

During the winter of 1796, Mary and her sisters were busy sewing bedding and table linen from textiles that Tyler provided. By the time she left for Vermont in March, her trunks were packed with "linen, sheets, tablecloths and towels, and the bed curtains, which were dark purple and white chintz, trimmed with white knotted fringe," which she had made herself according to a style Tyler had drawn for her and to fit a bed that had been "made half a foot wider than usual for the accommodation of little Master Royall."[10]

Although Mary Palmer Tyler's long wait to marry and then to join her husband in Vermont was unusual, it was not at all uncommon for a young couple not to leave immediately after their wedding, travel alone for a period of time, and then return to their new and independent household. Indeed, many couples waited weeks or even months before leaving the parental home and going to housekeeping. Anticipating her son Charles's marriage to Sarah Parsons of Newburyport, Elizabeth Phelps wrote to her future daughter-in-law on September 18, 1799: "We are . . . in such confusion, you would not know this solitary antique habitation; the house is undergoing a complete repair—and may I not hope you will soon make it your dwelling?"[11] Sarah's parents had died, and Elizabeth hoped the young couple would move permanently to Hadley; but she was disappointed in the long run. Sarah and Charles were married in Newburyport on New Year's Day in 1800, and Sarah remained with her uncle Theophilus Parsons for three months while Charles came alone to stay in Hadley until the spring. On April first, the young couple went to Boston together and stayed with two different cousins of hers until the beginning of June, when he took her to Hadley to spend the summer with his parents at Forty Acres. Charles stayed with her two weeks before returning to Boston. During the summer, Sarah visited friends in Greenfield, Brimfield, Hadley, Hatfield, and other nearby towns, spending her time "more pleasantly, than profitably." Charles returned to spend most of August with his wife and parents in Hadley before the young couple returned to Boston on the twenty-fifth, when they finally took rooms and "went to housekeeping the first day of September," fully nine months after their wedding.[12]

In New Hampshire, Samuel and Mary Lane lived out their lives in Stratham, completing the house Samuel had begun in 1741 and eventually having three sons and five daughters. When each girl was married, she received a generous supply of household goods and furnishings, which were either purchased especially for her or chosen from the general family supply. Samuel Lane kept detailed lists of the household furnishings that were supplied to each one. The value of every item was carefully noted on a document titled: "An Account of things I give my Daughter . . . toward her Portion." Lane tried hard to divide his property fairly among his children, and these lists were useful to him in determining the value of each girl's share.

Lane's eldest daughter, Mary, married John Crocket on October 26, 1762. Her father's account book indicates that her household goods were being gathered up during more than ten months prior to the wedding and that he paid for most of the things with shoes he made himself. On March 10, Lane bought nine yards of bed ticking for one of the new beds he had ordered for Mary from Charles Tredwell, a merchant in Portsmouth, and soon after he set aside another "homespun ticking," which had been woven by a neighbor, for another of Mary's beds. Lane then began to gather up the forty-two pounds of "choice feathers" and the thirty-eight more pounds, "Some of them mixed," that would be used to fill the two beds. The feathers were acquired from neighboring farmers; from Portsmouth merchants, including Tredwell; and from poultry on Lane's own farm; the purchased feathers came in quantities ranging from two to twenty-two pounds, and it took nearly a year to obtain the desired amount.

Lane also bought pewter plates and platters for Mary from merchants in both Newbury and Portsmouth. His debit account at Tredwell's during this period included buckles, a frying pan, a kettle, a tea pot, tea cups, curtain rings, shalloon for a bed quilt, and a dozen plates, as well as sewing supplies and fabric for clothing for other family members, indigo, nutmeg, tea, molasses, and rum. Local people were paid to help prepare Mary's household goods, including Samuel Allen for weaving "coverlids," Daniel Allen's wife for weaving blanketing, Lydia Nokes for weaving 13½ yards of ticking, and Mary Haley for "Quilting a Bed Quilt." The last debt was for fourteen pounds, the amount charged in Lane's account of Mary's portion for "Quilting" her shalloon bed quilt—a remarkable bit of proof that one young woman's best, and only, marriage quilt was made neither at a quilting party nor by her own hand.

Like Mary, each of her sisters was outfitted in her turn with two beds, one set of bed curtains, numerous sheets and pillowcases, a brass warming pan, blankets, coverlids, and just one quilt. In the way of furniture, there were two pieces of case furniture with locks, three tables, and an assortment of chairs for each girl. Two candlesticks were the only portable sources of light for any of the new households. For food preparation and service, the daughters were given fine tea cups and punch bowls, common earthenwares, a few pieces of glass, iron pots and kettles, pewter plates and dishes, ironware, tin, and woodenware, and spoons and knives. (Only Sarah, who was married in 1783, received forks.) Trivets and toasters, trammels and hooks were provided for hearth cooking, but none of the daughters was given a spit or a roasting jack. Each must have set up housekeeping in a kitchen equipped with a bake oven, for every list includes a "peal" and bread pans. To establish a dairy, each girl was given a cow, wooden milk pails, and a churn. Her other domestic implements included both a great wheel and a foot wheel, a washtub, cards, and a pair of "sizzers." Although none of the daughters was given a horse, each received a pillion, which would enable her to ride behind her husband or a friend, and was her father's way of ensuring her an opportunity to travel long distances within her new community, or even to return home for a visit. Lastly, more as an expression of parental wealth than for its utility, each girl received one silver teaspoon.

46. CAST-IRON KETTLE, BERKSHIRE COUNTY, MASSACHUSETTS, 1801. OLD STURBRIDGE VILLAGE. NEGATIVE NUMBER B14070.

This kettle was cast with the inscription: "This I give to my daughter Lydia J. Clap 1801, R. Cady." It measures 20¼ inches in diameter and is 13½ inches high; it weighs about sixty-five pounds. Samuel Lane's daughter Susanna received a "larg Iron Pott" that weighed sixty pounds as part of her basic housekeeping equipment; her sister Bathsheba's largest kettle weighed fifty-five pounds.

Dower Right

Samuel Lane's provision of basic household necessities for his daughters was not at all unusual in eighteenth-century New England. However, the survival of all five lists within one family makes it possible to understand the methodical way in which these goods were selected and the careful balance made by a father determined to treat his children equally. Even in the face of changing taste and fashion, economic and political upheaval, wartime inflation and postwar depression, Samuel Lane provided each of his daughters with the same basic inventory of household goods—objects that were expected to serve them a lifetime. Throughout the remainder of his life, all he saw fit to add to each of their households was a clock, some pewter, and a set of black-and-yellow cups and saucers.[13]

It is important not to confuse the informal provision of a marriage portion, later known as a dowry, with a widow's right of dower. The latter is a legal provision that was adapted from the English common law and was adhered to in all of the American colonies. Dower was a form of legal protection intended to provide support for a widow and her minor children. Under the right of dower, a widow had an uncontested right to one-third of the real property owned by her husband at any time during their marriage. Her right to this property held true even in cases of insolvency, and a widow's third was paid before obligations to any creditors. In some states the provision of one-third was increased to one-half of the husband's estate if the couple was childless.

By will, a husband could leave his entire estate or any portion of it to his wife, but if a man died without a will, or intestate, the right of dower was applied in the settlement of his estate. In cases of intestacy, executors were required to set aside one-third of a man's estate for the support of his widow and any minor children. A widow's actual ownership of personal property did not extend beyond her own clothing, jewelry, and miscellaneous very personal property. The goods set aside as her dower were a life right only, intended to provide for the sustenance of a widow during her lifetime. After her death, this property reverted to her husband's children.[14]

Whether established by a husband's will or by the decision of executors appointed by the probate court, the provision made for a widow usually resembled that made for a new bride. Few widows inherited large quantities of land and permanent title to a house; these usually were passed along to sons or grandsons, while the widow received life tenancy in at least a portion of a house, household goods, access to a hearth and well, specified quantities of foodstuffs, and firewood. In order to prevent quarrels with those with whom they were required to share living space, the division of property was usually very specific, and male heirs were instructed to provide wood, water, and certain services. Some widows received a cow, but other animals and agricultural tools were usually passed along to male heirs.[15]

Before he died in 1797, Jonathan Sayward prepared a will in which he made a typical provision for his widow, Elizabeth, whom he had married as his second wife in 1779. Although he bequeathed his "homestead, with the buildings of every kind thereon, and appurtenance there unto belonging" to his grandson Jonathan Sayward Barrell and instructed that his "clock, a large Map of North America, the Family and other Pictures are to be taken and considered as appurtenant to my Mansion House," Sayward specified that Elizabeth should receive during her widowhood the northwest end of the "dwelling house from the Garrett to the Cellar, inclusively and authority to open a passageway from

47. PARLOR IN THE SAYWARD HOUSE, PHOTOGRAPH, C. 1890, YORK, MAINE. COURTESY OF THE SOCIETY FOR THE PRESERVATION OF NEW ENGLAND ANTIQUITIES.

This is one of the rooms at the northwest end of the dwelling house, which Jonathan Sayward specified in his will would be used by his widow, Elizabeth. Despite the fact that the room contains a portrait of Sayward's first wife, as well as one of himself and one of his daughter Sally, apparently Elizabeth Sayward made few changes in the furnishings, for this is the room that her step-great-granddaughters, Mary and Elizabeth Barrell, showed to visitors as a relic room in the middle of the nineteenth century. By the time this photograph was taken, around 1885, the room had new wallpaper, carpeting, and a hearth rug, but Jonathan Sayward's chairs retained their original upholstery, and the relics of his adventure to Louisburg were still displayed with pride by his descendants.

the West Room thro' the bed room to the Kitchen, if she pleases." For her sustenance, Elizabeth Sayward was to have one-third of the currently owned liquors and provisions, as well as a quarter of a specific garden, "the keeping of a Cow Summer and Winter" at the homestead, and "five cords of hard Wood and five cords of hemlock or Pine, to be delivered Anually at the House." In order to maintain her station within the community, Elizabeth was permitted to retain the seat in the meeting house "Pew where she usually sits on the Sabbath" and, in common with her husband's grandson, "the use and improvement" of his horse and chaise. Elizabeth also received specific bequests of household furniture "in addition to the agreement made with her before marriage . . . all the household goods she brot me at marriage to dispose of as she pleases [and] one third part of the bedding, sheeting and Table Linen, which she has or shall make while she is my wife" [and] "the use and improvement" of her husband's "Easy chair, two leather chairs, and one Cane Chair" during her widowhood.[16] The provisions of the will were intended to define limits for both the elderly Elizabeth and her fortunate step-grandson, but each of them also inherited a responsibility to share the family kitchen, garden, pew, vehicle, and some of the chairs. If repairs or reupholstery was needed, she had the right to make the necessary "improvements."

Understanding that shared living quarters might be awkward, Jonathan

Sayward offered his widow Elizabeth the right to make a separate entrance from the kitchen into the portion of the house in which she would dwell after his death, and she did so. She did not, however, break through a doorway between her first-floor chamber and the front parlor (fig. 47). Although that room had also been set aside for her use, she could enter it only by passing through the sitting room of her step-grandson and his family; by going out the kitchen door, around the house, and entering the front door; or by going up the back stairs and down the front.

Some men made even more specific provision for sectioning off the widow's new living quarters. Legal language described the woman's right to pass and repass over one-third of the staircase; to obtain regular access to the well, the cellar, and the oven; and to be supplied with specific quantities of food and fuel. These provisions were intended as protection for widowed women. In practice, multigenerational households were seldom this rigid in their functioning, but all parties agreed that it was wise to back up potentially difficult situations with the force of law.

No matter how harmonious the relations between generations in a household, the dynamics of the family shifted when the seat of authority passed from one person to another or infirmity set in. It helped everyone if a first-floor chamber could be set aside for an elderly widow; if a private entrance door could be cut to the outside, so much the better.

Jonathan Sayward's will is not unusual in providing that certain kinds of property be passed along to male heirs and other to female heirs. It was normal for sons and grandsons to inherit land and buildings, and for the eldest or most favored son to receive title to the family homestead and serve as executor of his father's will. Usually daughters inherited personal property, ranging downward in value from silver and fully curtained beds to clothing, furniture, cows, and kettles. Although Ebenezer Snell made a specific bequest of his clock to his daughter Sarah Bryant and left her to divide "all" of his household furniture with her sister Abigail, specific exception was made for his "Desk and Book case" and a "Great Bible," which were left to his son and namesake, Ebenezer Snell, Jr.[17] Having already established Eben on a nearby farm, the father left the family homestead and most of his land in equal shares to his daughter Sarah Snell Bryant and her son Austin. Since Sarah was already living there and had cared for her parents through their last illnesses, it must have been difficult for her to part with furnishings that she was accustomed to using every day. Her only comment in her diary was: "Ebenezer moved away Sir's desk"; she made no mention of Abigail's claims.[18]

Taste and Fashion

In trying to understand the factors that influenced choice and the impact of taste and fashion over circumstance, correspondence can be more revealing than legal and financial accounts. In 1785, twenty-year-old David Spear was working as a clerk for his father in an elegant new store on Foster's Wharf in Boston. Nineteen-year-old Marcy Higgins of Eastham, on Cape Cod, was spending the winter with relatives in the city when she met David and their courtship began. When Marcy returned to her parents' home, she and David began an exchange of letters that reveal a great deal about the contrasts of urban and rural upbringing and taste, as well as the expectations of an engaged couple at the end of the eighteenth century.

When the date for their marriage was finally set, in the spring of 1787, the subjects of the letters changed from taste and manners to the details of housekeeping and plans for furnishing their future home—those items that David described as "matters more immediately important to our Future Manner of Living." Apparently, David's father planned to set aside and remodel two rooms in an existing house as a parlor and chamber for the young couple and to provide most of their furniture. It is unclear from the correspondence or from subsequent probate records whether David and Marcy were to share the house with David's parents or were permitted to live in an entire house, of which only two rooms were remodeled at the time of their marriage. The latter appears most likely, for they remained in this house throughout their married life, making a home for their own twelve children before Marcy died in 1803.

In 1787, David looked forward to setting up a fashionable household with some satisfaction, writing to Marcy: "Now, my Dear for the Furniture. My Father told me in plain words that he means to make me a present of all we shall want, I mean the most Bulky part. This is very clever my Dear. He tells me that he does not wish me to lay out my Money in this way. But means to have me keep it for a help to me in getting into Business for myself." This is directly opposed to the normal New England tradition of household furnishings being provided by the bride's father and considered as part of her "portion" of his estate, but the correspondence between David Spear and Marcy Higgins does not explain why his father rather than hers provided for them.

For the young Spears' best furniture, consideration was given to quality of materials and workmanship as well as to style. To ensure the very best, Mr. Spear engaged George Bright, who was "esteemed the neatest workman in town." David wrote to Marcy: "Mr. Bright, who is an old Friend and Acquaintance of my Father's is to make all the Mehogany Furniture—and he tells me that he has the best of Wood, and will as he comes across good pieces, lay them by a seasoning for this purpose, that we may have the very best he has. He professes a great deal of Friendship for my Father—and this, added to his being reckoned a very honest Man, and an extraordinary good Workman, is much in our favor, and I doubt not but that we shall have very good Furniture from him. . . . He tells me he can finish the whole in about 3 weeks after he begins."

Although he had confidence in Bright's workmanship, reliability, and the quality of his materials, David Spear was not certain that his fiancée would be pleased with the design of some of the pieces. He cautioned her that "the Chairs are different from any you ever saw, of the newest Taste." David's vocabulary and sensibility apparently did not offer further words to describe these chairs, and we are left to wonder whether they were square-back or shield-back, carved or inlaid, Hepplewhite or Sheraton. When David Spear's parlor was inventoried in 1806, it contained "10 mahogany hair bottom chairs" valued at fifty dollars, in addition to a pair of mahogany lolling chairs with covers, valued at twenty dollars. Presumably, these are the very pieces that were made by George Bright in 1787. Still in use after nearly twenty years, they had indeed proved to be of good quality.

David also wrote to Marcy describing the plans for the remodeling, which had been drawn "in the most Genteel manner and at the same time to be as convenient as possible." The more elaborate "Front Room is to be done in a more elegant Manner, according to the newest Taste. It is to have no Closets, but instead thereof to have Arches, excepting a small Closet at one side of the Chimney, which will be convenient, but will not be perceived unless when the door is opened. In these Arches there will be two of those Lolling Chairs you wished to have—one of them to stand in each Arch instead of Tables—these Chairs being more Fashionable." In addition to the concealed chimney closet, David proposed to have the window seats made with either drawers or "Lids to lift up at the Top for the Convenience of containing Bottles." Marcy had wanted a pair of silver candlesticks, and these may have been more than David could afford. Hoping to mollify her, he wrote: "I have not got real ones. But I have got a pair that are much more durable and full as handsome, so much so that they have been taken to be Solid Silver. I have two other pair that are Brass and a pair of Steel Snuffers. This is something towards Housekeeping." The couple agreed on a design for a "painted Carpet," or floorcloth, but when it came to the matter of selecting wallpaper, David was not so confident. He had seen several styles and wrote to Marcy: "There are a great variety of Fashions; I am totally at a loss what Kind to get. As this principally depends upon Fancy, I wish to have your opinion."[19]

For someone so concerned with current fashion, establishing a household was an exciting opportunity. Little has yet been discovered about David and Marcy's life together, but, sadly, only a few months after Marcy's death, in 1803, David was declared *non compis mentis* [*sic*] and he was sent to Dr. Willard's in Uxbridge for specialized care. At that time, a guardianship inventory was taken of his property. The appraisers found that there had been little change; the lolling chairs were still in place in the arches in the parlor, and the best bed was still hung with copperplate curtains, nearly twenty years after they had first been placed there for an excited bride and groom. Taste and fashion had changed in the city around them, but the statement of convenience and style that had been made at the time of the establishment of their household was fundamental.

A World of Difference

From 1819 to 1821, Elizabeth Margaret Carter of Newburyport kept a small account book detailing the preparations for her marriage to William Reynolds and the establishment of their new home in Boston. Although Elizabeth's father spent the extraordinary sum of over three thousand dollars in anticipation of his daughter's wedding, her house was outfitted with the same basic range of things the Lane daughters had received two generations before in rural New Hampshire: beds and bedding; chairs and tables; articles for food preparation, storage, and service; lighting devices; and fireplace and laundry equipment. There were significant differences in the quantity and quality of the individual pieces, of course, but there were also additions to the list that reflect important changes in attitude about comfort and convenience, or different expectations about important functions within the home, new standards of cleanliness, privacy, and housekeeping practice.

Elizabeth's furniture was much more highly differentiated in terms of its intended use than that of Samuel Lane's daughters. Their furniture was serviceable, but it was intended to serve many different kinds of functions; only their breakfast and kitchen tables and kitchen chairs had names that defined the intended use. Much more of Elizabeth Carter's furniture was designed to serve a specific purpose. This reflects new standards of comfort and luxury,

48. FAMILY OF THE REVEREND JEDEDIAH MORSE, WATERCOLOR, BY SAMUEL F. B. MORSE, C. 1809–10. NATIONAL MUSEUM OF AMERICAN HISTORY, SMITHSONIAN INSTITUTION.

Jedediah Morse married Elizabeth Breese on May 14, 1789. If this is actually a picture of the interior of the Morse family home on Main Street in Charlestown, Massachusetts, it depicts a common situation: furniture that appears to have been acquired in 1789, when the couple was married, was still in use along with a thoroughly modern carpet purchased twenty years later.

as well as decreasing flexibility in the use of space within the New England home. Elizabeth's furnishings included card tables, dining tables, chamber tables, a Pembroke table (a type usually used as a breakfast table), a kitchen table, and parlor and chamber chairs. None of the Lane girls owned more than one looking glass or one piece of upholstered furniture; Elizabeth Carter owned lolling chairs and a sofa, a rocking chair, and several looking glasses.

By the time Elizabeth Carter was married in the early 1820s, industrialization had both reduced the price and transformed the appearance and availability of cotton cloth and other textiles. Although cotton sheeting was both easy to care for and comparatively inexpensive, linen seems to have remained the standard for quality bedding and tablecloths. Elizabeth purchased more than 81 yards of linen sheeting, 11½ yards of linen damask, and only 22¼ yards of cotton sheeting to be cut and hemmed as sheets, pillowcases, bolster covers, tablecloths, and napkins. She also purchased 6 yards of dimity, 12½ yards of "patch,"[20] and 20 yards of blue-and-white copperplate, apparently intending to have dimity and patch window curtains in two rooms. There was enough of the copperplate to make a full set of bed hangings for either the high-post bed or the field bed.

49. WILLIAM HANCOCK'S FURNITURE WARE ROOMS, LITHOGRAPH, BY WILLIAM PENDLETON, BOSTON, 1829–30. BOSTON ATHENAEUM.

The extensive furniture warerooms of William Hancock in Boston offered consumers a wide range of ready-made goods from which to choose.

50. "WAREHOUSE OF J[OSIAH] BUMSTEAD & SON, NO. 145 WASHINGTON STREET, BOSTON," LITHOGRAPH, BY WILLIAM PENDLETON, C. 1826–34. COURTESY, AMERICAN ANTIQUARIAN SOCIETY.

In this handsome store with abundant natural light streaming down from skylights above, shoppers could make selections from a large stock of imported and domestic wallpapers, including those manufactured by Bumstead himself.

Elizabeth Carter's choices for floor coverings reflect the recent availability of factory-made carpeting, as well as the expansion of international trade. Shortly before her marriage she purchased green-and-white Kidderminster carpet for one of the chambers and Venetian carpets for the parlors and the staircase. Fifty yards of straw carpeting from India or China were laid on the floors of two other chambers.

The detailed accounts of Elizabeth Carter's household expenditures also illustrate new standards of personal and domestic cleanliness in the early nineteenth century. Two of the chambers were furnished with wash stands, ewers and basins, and chamber pots. There were more chamber pots available, a good supply of clean sheets and table linens, brooms, brushes, and a dust pan, as well as a washing machine and plenty of other specialized laundry equipment: wash tubs

51. EDWARD CHAMBERLIN'S "WHOLESALE CHINA AND GLASS WAREHOUSE" AND RETAIL SALESROOMS, CORNER OF HANOVER AND BLACKSTONE STREETS, BOSTON, LITHOGRAPH, BY WILLIAM PENDLETON, C. 1835–36. BOSTON ATHENAEUM.

Ornamental and useful wares are displayed in the windows on three floors.

52. MITCHELL AND FREEMAN'S CROCKERY, GLASS & CHINA WAREHOUSE, CHATHAM STREET, BOSTON, LITHOGRAPH, C. 1825–35. PRIVATE COLLECTION. COURTESY OF THE BOSTONIAN SOCIETY.

The hogsheads and the rectangular crates on the curb in both figure 51 and figure 52 are typical of the containers in which British goods were shipped to New England. When designs and forms were selected and packed in England "for the country trade," taste and fashion were dictated by exporters and the pressures of the marketplace rather than by individual choice. Seconds and wares that were out of fashion in Europe may well have been exported wholesale to rural America, where storekeepers could count on a balanced selection of cups and saucers, plates, bowls, and mugs at modest prices. For more elaborate forms and a greater selection of more fashionable designs, storekeepers or individual customers had to make their own selections at places like Chamberlin's or Mitchell & Freeman's in Boston or in other urban centers.

53. DRESSING TABLE, BY GROVER SPOONER, BARRE, MASSACHUSETTS, C. 1835. OLD STURBRIDGE VILLAGE, PHOTOGRAPH BY HENRY E. PEACH. NEGATIVE NUMBER B20065.

This piece of chamber furniture was purchased for three dollars by thirty-two-year-old Miss Martha P. Robinson of Barre shortly before her marriage to Ephraim L. Marsh in 1835. Marsh's first wife was Martha's sister Alice, who had died in 1822, leaving two small children and an established household. Having no need to purchase basic housekeeping supplies, Martha apparently felt free to buy a piece of furniture for her own personal pleasure.

and a wash bench, a clothes horse, sad irons and a folding board, special baskets, a clothes line, and pins.

Elizabeth's purchases reflect the transformation and dominance of the British ceramic industry, with full sets of dinnerware and a dessert set, as well as several tea sets and other dishes with specialized functions, such as pudding dishes, a soup tureen, covered sauce tureens, salad dishes, covered custard cups, and fish dishes. Her table would be set in a way that reflected new standards of individual food and beverage service, including not one but several sets of forks and knives, tumblers, and wineglasses by the dozen. It could be lighted by lamps as well as by candles, and there was the expectation that household help would be employed to carry things about on waiters or trays, and that dishes of food needed to be covered in order to be kept warm while they were brought from the kitchen to be served in the dining room.

The careful selection of these objects ensured that Elizabeth would have the necessary equipment to fulfill her anticipated role as wife, hostess, and household manager, but very few of the words she used to describe her purchases of household furnishings or her wedding gifts indicate that she was aware of contemporary trends in architectural or interior design. Although she identified one bed as a "field" bed and described her card tables and a Pembroke table as "Grecian" and a dozen of her chairs as "fancy," she described the rest of her things in terms of their function (dining table, parlor chair, book shelf, bread trough, oil pot, tea tray, carving knife, cake pan, ginger bread pan, hearth brush, warming pan, candlestick, candle box, chamber pot, dressing glass, looking glass, knife tray, fish dish, and coffee, tea, or cream pot), size (large, small, one-pound, one-quart), color (white, yellow, blue, blue-and-white), ornament (blue-printed), appearance (high post bed, armchair, covered dish, flat-back, odd chair), quantity (a pair, a piece, a set, yards, a dozen, or other specific number), material (tin, ivory, straw, birdseye, glass, china, Britannia, linen, wool, cotton), or means of decoration (japan, cut, planished, copperplate). Apparently she was more concerned about being well supplied with things she regarded as necessary, durable, and suitable than with the details of fashion and the abstract concept of style.

Although the early nineteenth century saw a tremendous increase in the ready availability and lowered cost of household furnishings, as well as a general increase in wealth, New England as a whole was experiencing profound economic stress and change. Despite the improving economic conditions and rising expectations of the middle class at the time, most people lived modestly. Rural families throughout the region considered their chances and weighed new opportunities. Some people succumbed to the promise of cash wages and left their farms to enter factories; others, like the Bryants, tried to improve their farms but eventually decided to move west to New York State, Ohio, Illinois, or Michigan.

Authors of prescriptive literature like Mrs. Child cautioned newlyweds to be conservative in their expenditures for household furnishings and ornaments. "The prevailing evil of the present day is extravagance. I know very well that the old are prone to preach about modern degeneracy . . . but, laugh as we may at the sage advice of our fathers, it is too plain that our present expensive habits are productive of much domestic unhappiness. . . . Do not spend all your money, be it much or little. Do not let the beauty of this thing, and the cheapness of that, tempt you to buy unnecessary articles. Doctor Franklin's maxim was a wise one, 'Nothing is cheap that we do not want.' Buy merely enough to get along with at first. It is only by experience that you can tell what will be the wants of your family. . . . Begin humbly. As riches increase, it is easy and pleasant to increase in hospitality and splendour; but it is always painful and inconvenient to decrease."[21]

54. JOHN ROBBINS AND HIS PEDDLER'S CART, WALTHAM, MASSACHUSETTS, DAGUERREOTYPE, C. 1843. COURTESY OF THE SOCIETY FOR THE PRESERVATION OF NEW ENGLAND ANTIQUITIES.

Peddlers brought a variety of manufactured goods to rural doorsteps. Sarah Bryant purchased useful kitchen equipment from peddlers over the years: a teapot in 1820, earthen milk pans in 1822, and two coffeepots in 1830. Ruth Bascom relied on peddlers for sewing supplies as well as for incidental kitchenwares. Both women occasionally permitted peddlers to spend the night in their houses.

IV

Frosty Mornings and Stinging Fingers: The Effects of Winter

New England winters are always measured by comparative extremes of cold weather and depth of snow. Nineteenth-century writers of local-color fiction and nostalgic reminiscences sketched dramatic word-pictures of these conditions, epitomized by Harriet Beecher Stowe's description in *Oldtown Folks:*

> One of my most vivid childish remembrances is the length of our winters, the depth of our snows, the raging fury of the storms that used to rage over the old farmhouse, shrieking and piping and screaming round each angle and corner, and thundering down the chimney in a way that used to threaten to topple all down before it. Those were cold days, par excellence, when everybody talked of the weather as something exciting and tremendous,—when the cider would freeze in the cellar, and the bread in the milk-room would be like blocks of ice,—when not a drop of water could be got out of the sealed well, and the very chimney-back over the raked-up fire would be seen in the morning sparkling with a rime of frost crystals.[1]

New Englanders have always countered these images of winter cold with those of the coziness and warmth associated in many minds with home. At the very least, it could be agreed that "the comforts and delight of winter depends on adequate shelter, plenty of fuel and warm garments,"[2] and the blazing hearth was the center of it all. People treasured the thought of friends or relatives enjoying a comfortably warm home. "I know of no place in the wide world so cozy as the occupancy and free range of your parlour in a cold winter,"

55. NEW ENGLAND WINTER SCENE. LITHOGRAPH, CURRIER AND IVES, 1861. COURTESY OF THE SOCIETY FOR THE PRESERVATION OF NEW ENGLAND ANTIQUITIES. PHOTOGRAPH BY J. DAVID BOHL.

The hand-colored lithographs of Currier and Ives brought images of the picturesque rural New England scene into American parlors all across the country. Although this early winter view seems benign, the amount of snow on the roof of the house shows that the temperature in the attic was well below freezing.

wrote George Tuckerman to his sister Elizabeth Salisbury in 1818.[3] Added to these ideas of warmth and coziness were images of sociability and hospitality, for the cold days of winter gave a degree of respite from field chores, and with good sleighing, transportation between homes and towns was easier than when the roads were muddy. In those days, "Bright eyes, and kind hearts, and cheerful fires within, deprived the country of its solitude, and winter of every thing disagreeable."[4] By 1840, a Portsmouth merchant could see the beauty in "a real old fashioned Snow Storm . . . very large flakes lodging on the trees, & adhering thereto make a most singular & beautiful appearance—about 12 inches of Snow fell."[5]

Contemporary sources indicate that normal indoor temperatures were often less than what would be considered comfortable today. On December 21, 1797, John Innes Clark of Providence wrote to a friend: "This month has been more pleasant. It is however, exceeding cold, the thermometer in our dining room with a good fire being about 48°."[6] Sarah Emery recalled that "the winter of 1820 and 1821 was remarkably cold. . . . China cups cracked on the tea table from the frost, before a rousing fire, the instant the hot tea touched them; and plates set to drain in the process of dishwashing froze together in front of the huge logs, ablaze in the wide kitchen fireplace."[7]

Even in the homes of prosperous New Englanders, provision of unusual warmth, like bright light, was considered a sign of hospitality. On cool days in spring and fall, many people lighted fires in parlors and sitting rooms only when company was expected. Describing preparations for a tea party in Salem about 1835, Eliza Sturgis recalled that when "the eventful day had arrived, the parlor and guest chamber were opened and a fire lighted in the former, so it would be warm before the arrival of the ladies."[8] William Bentley's diary entry for November 1, 1819, underscores the idea of fire as a symbol of welcome: "We have as yet had not serious occasion for fire tho hospitality has kindled it."[9]

Those who wrote reminiscences in the last half of the nineteenth century felt strongly that times had changed with the advent of iron stoves and furnaces, although New England winter weather was still severe. "Truly," wrote Mrs. Royall Tyler, "the people of this age know little of the horrors of winter."[10]

In contrast to the vivid descriptions of winter in reminiscences and fiction, contemporary diarists and letter writers usually commented on the cold only when it was extreme. On January 4, 1835, Thomas Robbins described "an extreme cold day" when the thermometer in the back chamber registered four degrees in the early morning and did not rise above fourteen indoors all day long. On December 17 of that year he noted: "thermometer this morning about 3 [degrees]. My ink and other things were frozen hard in my chamber."[11] William Pyncheon noted that on December 12, 1786, in Salem, the night was so

56. "There is no school like the family school," *The Mother's Assistant and Young Lady's Friend* (Boston, 1842), engraving, by O. Felton, based on *The Wife*, a painting by Samuel F. B. Morse, engraved by A. B. Durand and published in *The Lady's Book*, December 1831. Private collection.

Prescriptive literature of the 1830s and 40s idealized this kind of image of an idle woman with just one child, seated near a parlor fireplace while her husband reads aloud. This is in direct contrast to the nostalgic view seen in figure 67, only a decade or two later, where the ideal family was seen gathered about the kitchen fireplace and engaged in productive work during the reading.

cold that "few could sleep."[12] Sarah Bryant's diary also includes regular comments about the annual deepening of the cold. Her entry for December 5, 1830, is typical: "colder than it has been this season, froze in the house last night."

But New England weather can be chilly even in the summertime, and unseasonable weather was also a subject for comment. The elderly Jonathan Sayward confessed to his diary that on July 16, 1787, he had "built a fire in my sitting room to make me comfortable for it was cold."[13] Pyncheon tells us that on August 30, 1787, the weather was "cooler than often in February; at night people are uncomfortable abed without warming."[14]

The unsettled weather patterns of spring and fall stimulated diarists' comments, such as the pleased "I have but little occasion for fire"[15] and Thomas Robbins's rather disgusted notation on September 5: "Rainy all day. Cold; had a fire in my chamber."[16] Indeed, cold, raw spring weather could provoke almost anyone. Sarah Connell Ayer described such a day on May 29, 1809, when it "rain'd all day, and was so cold in the forenoon we all hovered round the kitchen fire." Twenty years later, Christopher Columbus Baldwin noted on May 26 that it was "so cold that every morning my water in my wash *bole* [*sic*] *freezes* quite hard."[17]

Sarah Bryant frequently recorded her concern for the loss of new lambs in April, the safety of newly planted crops and blooming fruit trees in May, and the freezing of food supplies. On the Bryants' Massachusetts hill farm, cold spring weather was a disaster that could strike at any time. Snow fell in Cummington on May 27, 1817, while the apple trees were in bloom, and it would be many weeks before the safety of the crop was assured that year. In the fall of 1833, people were "late about their fall work on account of the weather—many potatoes frozen and spoiled in the ground . . . cyder apples frozen in the Orchard—some have their winter apples frozen not picked."[18]

Many diarists described exceptional cold in March and April, when hopes of spring must have been rising. Robbins noted on March 6, 1833, that it was still cold enough that wine stored in a room without a fire was frozen solid.[19] Far more satisfying must have been the occasions in early spring when a diarist could record, "Sat in my chamber without any fire, went to meeting without a great coat," or "took off my Waistcoat and shifted to finer stockings," or "took off my flannel."[20] Sarah Bryant's diary is rich in its mentions of the delights of spring: maple sugaring in the woods soon followed by the ice breaking up in the river; the first sound of frogs peeping; the greening of grass in the dooryard and the blooming of peach, plum, and apple trees; the first blush of green on the lilac bushes followed by the intense fragrance of their blooming; the hiving and swarming of bees; going to pick cowslips in the lower meadow; taking off her winter gown and replacing it with a "linen loose gown"; going to lecture without a shawl; watching the men plant barley, corn, and wheat; "sewing" the garden in a "fine growing time"; and turning the sheep and cows to pasture in the tall new grass. The softness of the spring air tempted the hardworking Sarah on March 30, 1799, when she "lay abed after [the] sun rose." On May 6, 1819, she had to cope with an unseasonably warm day ("very warm—so warm as to melt tallow in the house"), whereas the year before, spring had been slow. In 1818 the weather was not settled until May 23, "the first clear warm morning we have had since March." As often happens in New England, it seemed as if the long-awaited spring were over in a few days; by the twenty-eighth, Sarah could note "vegetation comes on rapidly—but 3 or 4 days since the trees began to show their leaves & now they are almost at their bigness."[21]

Fires were kept going all day long in most New England kitchens, and for many this comfortably warm room was the place where daily living was centered for a large part of the year. In more formal, upper-class households, additional daytime fires were regularly kept going in some other rooms during cold weather, but many rooms were closed off in wintertime, halls and passageways were dark and frigid, and few chambers saw a warm fire on a daily basis. Susan Lesley described the parlor of her family home in Northampton, "where we lived 8 mos of year,"[22] and later assured her son in a letter, "Our home is warm enough, that part of it which we use."[23]

Fire insurance records for prosperous households document the small proportion of rooms that were heated on a regular basis. In 1807, for example, "two sometimes three or four fires" were all that were reported kept at Moses Brown's large "Dwelling House in Providence Neck."[24]

In some of these households, servants mitigated the worst impact of cold winter mornings by rising early and establishing a fire in the room where the family would take their breakfast, as well as in the kitchen. Even in wealthy households it was unusual for a servant to enter a bedchamber and light a fire in order to warm the room somewhat before the sleepers arose. Mrs. Packard described her experience on such a cold morning, when she "arose at eight and found snow patches in every crevice of my windows, a tracery of frost work on the panes of glass, and the water in the ewer a mass of ice. With chattering teeth and purple fingers I descended to the parlour. It was in perfect order, a cheerful fire blazed on the hearth, and Edward's boots, polished to the highest, were warming by the fender."[25]

Brick chimney stacks retained some heat throughout the night, keeping at least a portion of the rooms through which they passed somewhat warmer than the outside walls. If such heat could keep the temperature above freezing, indoor plants and flower bulbs could be forced into bloom. There is little evidence of this in eighteenth-century households, but after about 1820, many people developed an interest in indoor gardening. In late February 1828, Julia Smith reported that her sister Abby had daffodils growing in the house and that she sent blossoms to four friends.[26] Thomas Robbins, a minister boarding with a family in East Windsor, Connecticut, often confided to his diary that he was worried about his indoor trees. Sometimes these concerns were justified: on January 14, 1820, his best orange tree was injured by cold during the night.[27] Flowers grown indoors included gillyflowers, cactus, heaths, and sweetly scented roses, geraniums, mignonette, and stock.[28]

Even with a fire going all day long, on extremely cold days a kitchen might not be warm all the way to the outside walls. A daughter of the Knight family of Hancock, New Hampshire, recalled her mother hanging blankets from hooks in the ceiling to make a sort of tent near the fireplace inside which the children huddled for warmth.[29] Harriet Beecher Stowe described it best: "There was always something exhilarating about those extremely cold days, when a very forest of logs, heaped up and burning in the great chimney, could not warm the other side of the kitchen; and when Aunt Lois, standing with her back so near the blaze as to be uncomfortably warm, yet found her dishtowel freezing in her hand, while she wiped the teacup drawn from the almost boiling water."[30]

The cold made dishwashing not only uncomfortable but sometimes impossible. The Bryants had a piped water system that conveyed water from a spring to the house and barn, but it sometimes froze solid. In the coldest weather it was difficult to keep even deep wells free of ice. In the winter of 1780, it was so cold in Westborough, Massachusetts, that the family of Ebenezer Parkman was without water for weeks: "Our lowest and best well has been ever since ye great Storm [in January], froze up and filled with Snow that we have not been able to use it, till today, when we got it open."[31]

Samuel Lane described an even more difficult situation in 1786, when after "a remarkable Dry fall . . . Difficult getting Water for Household Use: Wells being generally Dry; people are obliged to hall their Water from Brooks; an after the weather grew Cold in Winter; to put it in Cellers, to keep it from freezing for Daily Use."[32]

Severe winter weather also made food preparation difficult. Since both food and water were apt to be frozen hard, careful planning and ample time were required to put a meal on the table. Unexpected company could present a real problem if their arrival did not coincide with normal mealtime. For Mary Tyler on such an occasion in 1794, "it was very inconvenient, the fire in the kitchen had been out for hours and everything was frozen. We concluded that a cup of tea, some toast and cheese would do"; but water, bread, and cheese all had to be thawed before hospitality could be offered.[33] Ruth Bascom complained of such a day, even in April, in 1826: "snow flying, winter-like indeed—liquids freezing hard *in* doors."[34]

At such a time, people recognized the danger of touching a freezing latch or spoon with wet hands. "The axe, the saw, the hatchet, all the iron tools, in short, were possessed of a cold devil ready to snap out at any incautious hand that meddled with him."[35] Setting the handle of the pump high and covering it with a blanket before going to bed were recommended to keep it from freezing. Mrs. Child warned of the necessity, for "a frozen pump is a comfortless preparation for a winter's breakfast."[36] Ebenezer Parkman had just such a problem in the winter of 1737. On February 19, he "cast a handful or two of Salt" into the pump and two days later was pleased to record "the small matter of Salt which I cast into my pump on the 19th wonderfully loosened the Spire though it had been frozen for a long time."[37]

Anne Jean Lyman recalled that during her girlhood at Brush Hill in Milton, Massachusetts, "The winters were long and cold; the appliances for heat not what they are now, the large open chimneys and wood fires being cheerful to the eye, but with their ample draughts not warming to the body. 'We wore our great coats in the house half the time, Sally and I,' she said 'and even then could not have been warm without the active employments that kept us constantly busy.' "[38]

Unfortunately, active employment for women could not always be conducted near a comfortable fire, for spinning and weaving required bulky equipment, flammable raw materials, and a large amount of floor space. Yet both also required nimble fingers, and there are many diary references to the relocation of spinning wheels and even to days so cold that the work was interrupted or made impossible. Faced with a quantity of wool to spin on a cold winter morning in 1828, Julia Evelina Smith of Glastonbury, Connecticut, made a fire in a little room and asked someone to move her great wheel in there so that she could spin.[39]

Men's winter work usually involved considerable physical activity, even in winter. Caring for animals; cutting, moving, and splitting firewood; sharpening tools and repairing buildings; butchering; and threshing grains required the space that was found only in unheated barns and sheds and outdoors itself. On November 27, 1794, Abner Sanger of Keene, New Hampshire, described a cold day's work: "I do no great more than get wood and take back wood, tend cattle and keep fires, mend my house floor under the outer door."[40] Although almost all men, especially in the country, worked at these sorts of tasks, some men's professional occupations were more sedentary. Lawyers and ministers, especially, spent a good deal of time indoors, and the contemplative nature of their work required a comfortable and quiet study.

Even a minister in rented quarters was responsible for splitting firewood and maintaining his own fire. On December 21, 1844, Thomas Robbins noted that the early-morning temperature reading was five degrees and complained, "It requires much heat to warm my great room."[41] On the following February 7, he was still struggling with the cold and noted, "The cold abates a little. Difficult to warm my room sufficiently."[42]

Weather Records

Considering the impact of the cold on daily activity and the work required to maintain a modicum of comfort, it is no wonder that weather records are included in all kinds of diaries. Indeed, a typical diary entry, whether for men or women, begins with a brief description of the weather. Not everyone owned a thermometer—a good thing, according to Samuel Goodrich in his 1856 *Recollections of a Lifetime,* for without one people would not be frightened "with the revelation that it was 25° below zero."[43] Still, many diarists seem to have had access to these instruments and recorded the temperature on rising in the morning.

Some farmers owned thermometers, as did educated men interested in scientific observations, who often owned other kinds of scientific instruments as well.[44] Charles Peirce of Portsmouth, New Hampshire, advertised thermometers for sale in 1805, saying "shew me an affluent gentleman of taste and observation without a thermometer in his house, and you shew me a miser."[45]

Yale president Timothy Dwight recognized that temperature readings were influenced by circulation of air as well as direct sunlight. Seeking accurate and consistent readings, he placed his thermometer "on a wall with paper on the north side of the house, and in a room admitting the freest passage of the external air, which, however, does not blow directly on the instrument."[46] Thermometers were seldom recorded in probate inventories, so it is as difficult to know how many people were capable of taking accurate temperature readings as it is to know where thermometers were usually hung. Barring such evidence, it is often unclear whether thermometers were hung indoors or out. Apparently, not everyone who owned a thermometer hung it in a permanent spot. A farmer, Horace Clark of East Granby, Connecticut, implied this when he commented in his diary entry for February 19, 1836, that "those that hung their thermometers early in the morning found it 15^{d} below."[47]

Thomas Robbins seems to have had bad luck with thermometers or was careless in their use. More than once, he recorded in his diary that he had broken his thermometer and "felt it to be quite a misfortune."[48] In both 1843 and 1844, he recorded two reasons for broken thermometers—once a result of "hanging out in my absence" and once being "broken by the wind in my absence."[49] Robbins also noted more than once that his thermometer appeared to have been stolen, which suggests that the instrument was left hanging outdoors all the time.[50] In the middle of the winter of 1817, Robbins broke his thermometer, and he expressed his frustration in his diary: "I feel very much the want of a thermometer."[51] Finally, after a year of complaining to himself, on January 29, 1818, he rode to Hartford with a friend and "Paid for a handsome thermometer with a mahogany case, $8.00."[52]

Firewood

Most New Englanders relied on wood for heat, although as the amount of forested land near cities was cleared and prices rose, some coal was imported to Boston and other coastal towns. At the beginning of the seventeenth century, New England had been fully forested, and this abundance gave rise to habits of building large fires, which used huge quantities of wood. This was in contrast to contemporary practice in England, where smaller wood supplies promoted both frugality and the use of coal and peat for fuel. New England Tories who took up residence in London during the American Revolution commented on the resultant difference: "The fires here not to be compared to our large American ones of oak and walnut, nor near so comfortable."[53]

Many agreed that clear-cutting of woodlots was the most efficient way to produce new supplies of firewood.[54] "When a field of wood is, in the language of our farmers, cut clean, i.e. when every tree is cut down, so far as any progress is made, vigorous shoots sprout from every stump; and, having their nourishment supplied by the roots of the former tree, grow with a thrift and rapidity never seen in stems derived from the seed. Good grounds will thus yield a growth amply sufficient for fuel once in fourteen years. A multitude of farmers therefore, cut their wood in this manner, although, it must be confessed, there are different opinions and practices concerning the subject."[55]

Firewood was usually cut in December, January, or February, when snow in the woods made it relatively easy to move heavy loads by sled. The *New England Farmer* cautioned families to obtain their entire season's supply of wood early in the winter, before the snow became so deep as to make it difficult to enter the woods with a team and a sled.[56] This is exactly what happened in the Berkshire County town of Cummington in late January 1827. Sarah Bryant described the problem in her diary: "Snow very deep. Difficult getting wood. Snow dry like sand which does not tread." The previous year, the Bryant family had the opposite problem. Even though Austin and a hired man had been busy chopping in the woods, they had difficulty bringing their firewood into the yard. This was a problem throughout the town, and on March 4 Sarah Bryant expressed her concern: "Sloppy going snow wastes fast—almost everyone cutting wood but few have got their wood. There has been little snow."[57]

Cutting and splitting wood in wintertime meant that it could dry and season before it would be needed. "Finished my large pile of wood to lie over the winter,"[58] wrote Thomas Robbins in 1840, after he had learned the hard way the importance of allowing sufficient time for wood to dry. Five years earlier, in early January 1835, Robbins had complained of frost in his chamber when he was forced to burn green wood, having no other on hand.[59]

Snow made it easier to transport wood supplies to urban areas as well.[60] If it was a dry winter, with no snow cover so that sleds could be used to move wood, shortages might develop. On January 25, 1760, badly needed "wood was among the 1001 loads of provisions brought into the city of Portsmouth during the day."[61] In January 1776, William Pyncheon noted in his diary that an ample snowfall had made sledding easier and that the price of wood in Salem fell significantly as a result. In late February 1789, Pyncheon noted that despite some moderation in the weather and occasional thawing, the sledding remained "good, and

57. BRINGING IN WOOD, *Peter Parley's Method of Teaching Arithmetic.* OLD STURBRIDGE VILLAGE, STURBRIDGE, MASSACHUSETTS. NEGATIVE NUMBER B17915.

Splitting and carrying in more than twenty cords of firewood in the course of one winter was a laborious task for men and boys.

wood is brought in plenty; many loads remain [unsold] in the street from a.m. to 2 and 3 o'clock."[62] The coming of snow brought the prospect of physical comfort to city dwellers who lacked fuel. One observed "With great satisfaction we at length behold the ground covered with snow, for we are almost freezing here; it has been impossible almost to obtain wood to keep us warm."

The Reverend Timothy Dwight noted in his 1801 *Travels in New England and New York* that wood was the only fuel used in New Haven, but it was very expensive, "hickory being from seven to eight dollars the cord of 128 feet; oak, five; and pine, three."[63] In 1807, Bentley reported that Eastern wood was selling for eight dollars a cord, with loads that contained from sixty to ninety-one cords arriving by sea.[64] In inland towns, even in what Dwight called "old and thrifty settlements," where there was still some forest remaining, the price was much lower—usually not more than one-third as much as in the coastal communities.[65]

Careful management of fires and a knowledge of the properties of different species of wood enabled a family to get the most heat for their labor or investment. Hickory, birch, and good cuts of white oak and ash provided a good steady fire for baking, while lesser kinds of oak, chestnut, or hemlock could be used for a more moderate fire. If no dry wood was available, ash and hickory would be the best to use. Green or rotten wood was regarded as useless, although either one was sometimes found buried in the center of purchased cords.[66]

During woodcutting time, men and boys spent long, hard days in the woods. Many households, like the Bryants', hired additional help for this arduous task. Abner Sanger of Keene, New Hampshire, was frequently employed as a day laborer in cutting and hauling wood for others, exchanging his services for a wide variety of household necessities. Although he cut a lot of wood, there is no indication that he cut a winter's supply at a time for any one person, especially for himself. On January 31, 1778, he noted in his diary, "I chop me a load of wood on Lieutenant Benjamin Hall's land. I have Jeremiah Stiles's oxen to sled it home."[67] Sanger cut up wood and split it throughout the year, usually working logs that had been cut the previous winter. He described preparing specific kinds of firewood, such as backlogs, foresticks, and oven wood, or cutting wood for specific needs, such as heating water for laundry and heating the oven for baking. Apparently, Sanger tried to avoid cutting wood on Sundays, for he often cut an extra supply "for Sunday" and left it near the door.[68]

It is difficult to know how much wood was actually needed to maintain a

58. FARMHOUSE WITH A DISORDERLY WOODPILE, CHARLTON, MASSACHUSETTS, OIL ON CANVAS, C. 1820–40. COLLECTION OF DR. AND MRS. BARNES RIZNIK.

Abner Sanger's experience shows that firewood drawn to the dooryard in wintertime might not ever be completely cut, split, and neatly stacked. Management of the woodpile reflected the amount of available labor, circumstance, and individual work habits.

kitchen fire for a full winter, much less what incremental amount was needed to heat each additional room. We are right to doubt the need for that "very forest of logs" described by Harriet Beecher Stowe, but there are few documented sources on which to rely. Some say that a fair estimate is an amount equal in volume to the volume of the space to be heated, but this is very hard to judge.

Family account books sometimes contain detailed information about the total quantities of wood used in a single season for heating, cooking, and baking and for heating water for dishwashing, laundry, and bathing. Although these records are usually for fairly wealthy families, the data are still useful. Jonathan Sayward burned forty-four cords of wood during the twelve-month period beginning July 1, 1789, in a house with seven fireplaces, a bake oven, and two chimneys. Sullivan Dorr of Providence recorded in his family expense book that he had burned twenty-seven cords, two feet of wood between May 3, 1826 and May 4, 1827.[69] This smaller amount of wood fueled a kitchen fireplace with Rumford roaster and range, heated water for dishwashing, laundry, and bathing, and heated a sixteen-room house with fourteen fireplaces and three chimneys that was occupied by at least seven people. Unfortunately, we do not know how many fireplaces either family used on a regular basis.

The Minister's Wood Supply

Most congregations made a contractual arrangement to supply a quantity of firewood to their minister as part of his annual compensation, but they were not always prompt in delivery. In January 1753, Ebenezer Parkman nearly ran out of wood. On the twenty-seventh, there was "but a Stick or two left at the Door, and yet a Stormy, raw Cold Day—P.M. Snowy. Lieutenant Tainter came to See how 'twas with us as to wood . . . but there came none. But I was oblig'd to make what we had in the House and the few Sticks at the Door, do over the Sabbath." Fortunately, three of his parishioners each brought a load of wood on Tuesday.[70] In contrast to Parkman's scanty situation, some towns provided a minister with more wood than would actually be needed for heating and cooking in the parsonage, and he was expected to trade the surplus for other useful articles. Until 1770, the town of Hadley, Massachusetts, regularly voted to provide its settled minister with one hundred cords of wood each year. On November 30, 1779, the town of Westborough, Massachusetts, voted to supply just forty cords for Ebenezer Parkman.[71] Sometimes the wood was delivered in an almost ceremonial fashion, as on New Year's Day in 1824, when forty cords of wood, along with "other valuable presents," were presented to the Reverend Ezekiel Lysander Bascom by his Ashby, Massachusetts, congregation. One of the loads was described as being 8½ feet wide, 14½ feet long, and 12 feet high, containing almost twelve cords of birch and maple. So large was the load that thirty-seven pairs of oxen were used to pull it![72] For several days the load remained on four sleds that were chained together, and many people came to view it as a curiosity. Some stopped to visit with Mrs. Bascom, but many others came "to view the great load of wood without calling." More than fifty men appeared at the parsonage on January 7 and "unloaded the Great Load by piecemeals as they cut away & finally before sunset all this twelve cord [was] unloaded and . . . more was all cut & by dark all piled & the chips carried under cover or got in a winnow."[73] Not all ministers received such a generous supply, and many had to cut it up themselves.

Wood was sometimes used as a reward or extra benefit for ministers in good standing. In March 1833, Thomas Robbins was pleased to report that the annual meeting of his society was "very harmonious," with the result that "they voted me a kind donation of three cords of wood." Three days later, just as the frost was "getting out of the ground," and the going must have been very muddy, Robbins was happy to receive "a large load of seasoned maple wood . . . at the rate of $6 per cord."[74] At other times, the amount supplied by the congregation was insufficient for a cold season or was delivered at an inconvenient time of year. Robbins was happiest when his wood was delivered in the spring, so that it could season before the next heating season; but in 1838 he was obliged to purchase firewood in November and paid $6.43 for two cords of pine; in November 1849 he bought part of a cord of seasoned walnut, valued at $9.21 a cord.[75]

Maintaining Fires

In most households, maintaining a supply of appropriately cut, split, dry wood seems to have been the responsibility of men and boys, but it is much less clear who carried the responsibility of building and maintaining a good fire. These are tasks so central to daily life that they are almost never mentioned in diaries. In the parsonage at Blue Hill, Maine, the Reverend Jonathan Fisher built a fire in the kitchen fireplace and another in his study each morning before beginning an hour's reading in Hebrew.[76] In many households, banking the fire at night, carefully raking up the coals, and covering them with ashes in order to preserve a few pieces with which the morning fire might be lighted appears to have been the responsibility of men; but laying a fire and kindling a flame in the morning was a task that usually was done by women. Many references suggest that the management of fires was women's work—a job that was intimately related to successful cooking and baking, in addition to allowing some degree of control over the temperature of indoor workspaces.

It was a serious matter if the coals on the hearth went out during the night, for then it would be necessary to strike a spark from a flint and steel or to send to a neighbor's house for some hot coals. Mary Tyler recalled a terrible accident that happened one day when "mother rose pretty early to prepare breakfast and found all the fire gone out; our custom then was to rake up the fire carefully at night under the ashes so as to preserve it in case of sickness in the night or convenience for kindling the fire in the morning. Lucifer matches were not yet invented, and, to save herself the trouble of striking fire in a tinderbox, she awoke little George, gave him a pair of small light tongs and bid him run to the next neighbor's house in sight, and get a coal of fire." Unfortunately, "when he came out of the house where he had been, and got a fine lively coal in his little tongs, the sun, as usual, made it appear to the child as if it was gone out, and he lifted up the tongs to blow it and keep it alive as he thought; the action broke the coal and half of it fell into his bosom and lodged near his hip." His clothing caught fire, and the child was terribly burned; fortunately, after many weeks of agony, he recovered.[77]

In addition to banking the fire and finding a light, women also had to cope with the related tasks of sweeping up wood chips, bits of bark, pine needles, insects, and other dirt that fell from the incoming wood, and cleaning up ashes that blew from the fireplace or were scattered when the hearth was cleaned.[78] Some people kept their firewood and kindling in a wood box to contain the mess, and in Concord, Massachusetts, Ellen Emerson kept stove wood in her parlor closet.[79] Sometimes a day's supply of wood was stacked in the corner of the kitchen or in an adjacent shed. In some old New England houses, the walls of the corner nearest the kitchen fireplace were badly dented and had their moldings entirely worn away by the stacks of wood that had been piled there.[80]

Thomas Robbins, who rented second-floor rooms, kept his wood stacked conveniently in the garret of the house in which he lived.[81] Some farmhouses had separate woodhouses or conveniently attached woodsheds,[82] but both travelers' accounts and contemporary landscape pictures make it clear that some people stored a large portion of their wood outdoors in untidy piles.

By the early nineteenth century, much of southern New England was deforested, and the price of firewood increased dramatically. Some wood was brought by sea from northern Maine and the Maritime Provinces of Canada to coastal towns, but it was still expensive. After 1833, Pennsylvania coal was commonly available for fuel in cities, and it provided an economical alternative. The use of coal required grates and pokers and a different fire management style. For many, the difficult transition was a necessity. Later one remembered "the first anthracite coal fire I ever saw was in an open grate in my brother's house in Boston, about 1830. It was regarded with curiosity; and the idea of using such material for fuel elicited considerable discussion in the community. Now a wood fire is the curiosity."[83]

Danger from Fires

The continuous burning of open fires has its own dangers, and inevitably many house fires were started by careless disposal of hot ashes, sparks that clung to a hearth broom, or stray coals or sparks that escaped from open fireplaces at night, through faulty chimneys, or in untended rooms. Many escaping sparks resulted only in holes burned in bed coverings, hearth rugs, or table linen, but housewives complained of the mending that was required as a result. The potential for much more serious damage was always recognized, however. William Pyncheon of Salem was cognizant of his good fortune when he awoke on the morning of April 21, 1783, to find the "chambers full of smoke [and] the office floor burnt through into the cellar, a hole 4 inches in diameter."[84] Mrs. Royall Tyler recalled an evening in which she had intended to stay awake to watch a sick son but fell asleep while nursing her infant and awoke to find that the fire she had left burning on the andirons had thrown a spark that had ignited the woodwork and burned a place as large as her hand. Fortunately, the fire had gone out by the time she awoke, and many years later she could speculate upon the hand of Providence in her affairs.[85] To prevent such a happening, Ebenezer Parkman put five sheets of tin over the floorboards next to the hearth in the chamber of the new house he was building in 1755.[86] Not everyone was so careful, however, and New England newspapers and town histories contain many stories of houses that burned to the ground as a result of fires that were started in just this way. Such a tragedy befell the family of John Wendell in Portsmouth, New Hampshire, in April 1763, when "Fire happened by a Defect in the Hearth of the Kitchen thro' which it was communicated to the Pannell Breast-Work of the next Room, and raged with such Violence that in a few Minutes it got through the Roof." This "distressing Instance of Fire . . . intirely consumed the Dwelling House," but fortunately, "he with his Family escaped the Jaws of the devouring Element, yet in a naked, melancholly Condition. . . . The Town being soon alarmed, such uncommon Assistance was afforded, as that he saved most of the Furniture in the lower Part of the House,

59. HEARTH RUG WITH PUPPIES, EMBROIDERED WOOLEN YARN ON A LINEN BACKING, MADE BY ELIZA WILLIAMS, DEERFIELD, MASSACHUSETTS, C. 1825. HISTORIC DEERFIELD, INC., DEERFIELD, MASSACHUSETTS.

In 1825, at the Brighton Cattle Show (the annual fair of the Massachusetts Society for Promoting Agriculture), Eliza Williams of Deerfield received a gratuity of one dollar for a hearth rug—perhaps this very one. Mrs. Williams was the second wife of Dr. William Stoddard Williams, having married him in November 1822. This hearth rug with its charming image of curled-up puppies would have been placed directly in front of a fireplace to protect a carpet from flying sparks and from the wear and tear caused by people pacing back and forth in front of the fire. Some imported British hearth rugs of the 1820s show cats and dogs curled up in front of the fire; one of them may have served as the design source for Eliza Williams's rug.

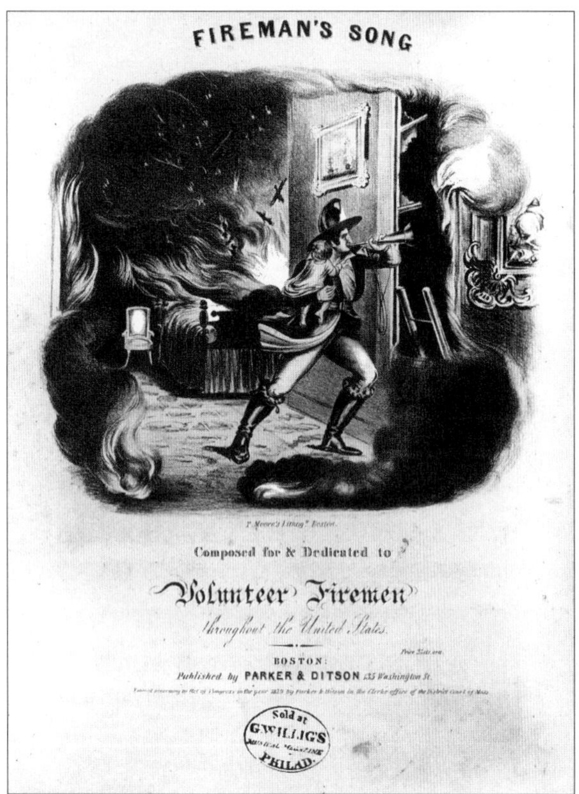

60. *Fireman's Song,* SHEET-MUSIC COVER, LITHOGRAPH BY T. MOORE, BOSTON, 1839. COURTESY AMERICAN ANTIQUARIAN SOCIETY.

with near all his Books and Papers; but all in the Chambers, where was Trunks of many valuable Things, chief of his own and Family's Cloathing, with all the Furniture, was consumed." Fortunately, Portsmouth's three fire engines were able to prevent the fire from spreading to two neighboring houses less than ten feet away.[87]

Some fires were started when coals ignited flammable materials, particularly flax, which was often brought in to dry near the fire before being broken. In January 1780, the Reverend Ebenezer Parkman of Westborough, Massachusetts, noted in his diary that he was worried about some flax that had been dressed by Ephraim Parker and brought into the house on a pole on which it was hung before the fire to dry. Parkman wrote, "I had a good deal of Reluctance at it, remembering that Capt. Gouge's House at Hopkinton was, some years ago, burn't down by Flax taking Fire." Parkman was right to be worried. The next day, "As ye Flax aforesaid hung before ye Fire; notwithstanding ye distance it was placed at, a Coal was snapped out from the Fire & began immediately to burn in it, which had it occurred last night, while we Slept, what would have been ye Event!"[88]

Flax was not the only combustible material stored indoors that could accelerate a house fire. The New Hampshire *Gazette* carried an account of a child who was trapped on the second floor of a burning house and died in flames that had been "instantly communicated to a large quantity of dried herbs which were hanging in the chamber." Such events were apparently not infrequent, and newspaper editors often concluded their accounts of the resultant fires with a caution "against the too frequent practice of drying flax and other combustible material near a fire."[89]

Open fires and large containers of boiling liquids presented even more direct dangers to children. In Henniker, New Hampshire, alone, seven children were scalded to death in the forty years between 1790 and 1830, and two more died by falling into the fireplace.[90] On March 28, 1826, two children, ages 2 and 3½, neighbors of Ruth Bascom, were "sadly scalded . . . by the falling of a kettle of boiling soap from the crane!" Both died the next day and on the thirty-first they were buried in the same coffin.[91]

61. THE GREAT FIRE IN SCHOOL STREET, WORCESTER, MASSACHUSETTS, 1838, DRAWN BY GEORGE L. BROWN, LITHOGRAPHED ILLUSTRATION ON AN INSURANCE COMPANY BROADSIDE. WORCESTER HISTORICAL MUSEUM.

Efforts to save household furnishings during a major fire often created congested and chaotic conditions in the nearby streets.

Fires also presented dangers for adults. In 1816, the Connecticut *Courant* reported the death of seventy-two-year-old Miss Elizabeth Knight of Worcester, Massachusetts, who was discovered to have "fallen into the fire, and was almost entirely consumed. Shocking to relate, her whole body was destroyed, her head, which was in one corner of the fire-place, so far disfigured by being burnt, that her face could not be identified; and her legs below her knees, were in the other corner, with her stockings remaining on them."[92]

Another danger of fire arose from dirty chimneys. William Pyncheon had such a problem in January 1777: on the twenty-third, a fire in the chimney "nearly burnt the keeping room"; a week later, the same chimney was on fire again.[93] Even a small spark could ignite a chimney fire, as it seems to have done at the Bascom parsonage in 1826. Mrs. Bascom described it in her diary: "This day we were quite alarmed by the smoke issuing from the study chimney at every cranny and at the top large columns of smoke occasioned by the chimney's being much on fire though there has been no fire in the study and but little in the stove. . . . All in suspense and anxiety for an hour about noon—O may we feel truly grateful, that it was but an *alarm,* that our house and property was not consumed as we had reason to fear it would be."[94] Fires could also be ignited when sparks fell down an unused flue and landed in a pile of soot, bird's nests,

62. standing stool, woodcut, alexander anderson scrapbooks, vol. ii, print collection, miriam & ira d. wallach division of art, prints and photographs, the new york public library, astor, lenox and tilden foundations.

A standing stool, or baby tender, offered some protection from falling into the fire or into a large tub of boiling liquid. Some were made without wheels, offering the additional advantage of keeping the baby in one place. (See EWPH to EPP, January 18, 1803. PFP, box 13, folder 1.)

63. child with clothes on fire, woodcut, alexander anderson scrapbooks, new york public library.

or spider webs, or against a wooden fireboard in an unused fireplace.[95] Thomas Robbins described his reaction to such a situation succinctly: "Got a fright in burning my chimney."[96]

Chimney fires were a community concern, especially in towns and cities where houses were close together and fire could easily spread from one building to another. Regulations governing the employment and pay of chimney sweepers were enacted in large towns, and laws were passed to require that people keep their chimneys clean and notify official firewardens of any defects they observed.[97] When an alarm occurred, people assembled to assist in putting out the fire, removing valuables, offering advice, and providing empathetic support for those directly affected. Thomas Robbins was on hand for such an event in 1839, noting in his diary: "In the evening we had in the village an alarm of fire from a burning chimney. Was out late."[98]

A Warm Bed in a Cold Room

As long as the chimney was functioning and wood was available, people maintained at least a kitchen fire in all seasons. In cold weather, many indoor spaces were unheated, even when they were occupied for sleeping. William Davis recalled that "fires in chambers were in my day far from being universal," and he asserted that he "never slept in a heated chamber, except when sick, until . . . sixteen years of age."[99] In *Oldtown Folks,* Harriet Beecher Stowe describes a house heated only by the great kitchen fireplace and where "duly at nine o'clock every night *that* was raked up, and the family took their way to bed-chambers that never knew a fire, where the very sheets and blankets seemed so full of stinging cold air that they made one's fingers tingle; and where, after getting into bed, there was a prolonged shiver, until one's own internal heat-giving economy had warmed through the whole icy mass. Delicate people had these horrors ameliorated by the application of a brass warming-pan—an article of high respect and repute in those days."[100]

Mrs. Stowe went on to describe the experience of a boy who slept in an attic even during the winter, when "the thermometer must have stood below zero, and where the snow, drifting in through the loosely framed window, often lay in long wreaths on the floor" and when, on awakening, "Aunt Lois . . . opened the door and set in a lighted candle, one of my sinful amusements consisted in lying and admiring the forest of glittering frost-work which had been made by our breath freezing upon the threads of the blanket."[101]

It was not only in attic chambers that one's breath froze in the sheets and blankets and snow drifted across the floor. Abner Sanger reported that December 19, 1793, "was spent to clear out chambers of snow"[102]; other diarists had similar experiences.

During the coldest months, it was not uncommon for people to constrict or otherwise rearrange their living space. On December 6, 1742, Samuel Lane "moved into my New Shop, where I and my Wife lived Chiefly this Winter, to Save Wood."[103] Throughout the 1770s, Jonathan Sayward of York, Maine, moved his bed seasonally from one room to another.[104] While her husband was away in the winter of 1810, Mrs. Royall Tyler made the north parlor of her Vermont home into a bedroom for the winter, using a trundle bed under her for her two young sons and taking the two youngest children into her own bed.[105] In December 1816, Isaiah Thomas of Worcester moved from the back chamber to the south front chamber for the winter, in order to take advantage of the additional warmth provided by the sun.[106] In late January 1806, seventy-year-old Martha Ballard of Augusta, Maine, took what seemed even to her to be extreme measures to deal with the cold: "I have put my bed into the bedroom; corkt the cracks and hung up sheets to make the rooms more comfortable."[107]

In households where beds were spread on the floor without a bedstead, there was a real danger in being too close to the fireplace. In 1802, the Greenfield *Gazette* published a report of a house that had burned to the ground when four small children "spread a bed before the fire and laid down to sleep." Fortunately, the children, as well as "two very aged people . . . who lived in one part of the house by themselves, and had gone to bed," all escaped."[108] Despite the danger, beds on the floor near the fire were not at all uncommon in those very

64. DR. WILLIAM GLYSON, OIL ON CANVAS, BY WINTHROP CHANDLER, C. 1795. OHIO HISTORICAL SOCIETY.

Fully enclosing bed hangings provided some privacy as well as warmth.

crowded households where every inch of space was at a premium, or in certain unusual situations. Even Ruth Bascom found herself resting on a straw "bed on the floor by the west room fire" for several nights in November 1809 while she watched over her husband and another sick person.[109]

For those who could afford them, bed curtains offered some protection from arctic blasts of air in unheated bedchambers. A full set of bed curtains included a tester cloth, or fabric roof, for a bedstead; a headcloth permanently fixed behind the headboard; and four movable curtains, two at the head and two at the foot of the bed. These curtains could be pulled up by cords or drawn horizontally on a series of brass rings or tape loops that passed over curtain rods mounted below the tester cloth at the sides and foot of the bed frame. Usually the top of the bedstead and the curtain mechanisms were concealed by ornamental valances. Because bed curtains required large quantities of fabric, they were expensive. Statistical studies of New England probate inventories show that by the 1770s, in some towns at least half the households had curtained beds in one room, and many had them in more than one room.[110] This is not surprising, for although bed hangings were expensive, they served an important purpose. Within tightly closed bed curtains, body heat would moderate the temperature inside the bed frame, and people in bed would not have to breathe frigid air.

Unfortunately, bed curtains were also flammable. This was underscored by Dr. Bentley in his description of a "melancholy event" that took place in Salem in 1816, when "the maid servant, in the absence of the parents, put a child to bed & by the candle carelessly put fire to the bed curtains. The fire was not discovered till the fate of the child was decided. It was terribly burnt & expired in the night & the bed & its fine vallance destroyed." Bentley lamented the loss of both the child and the valuable bed hangings.[111]

Bed hangings might also be ignited by the flame of a candle held by a person checking on the health of an invalid or a child during the night, by a night light with an open flame left too close to a curtain, or by the "absurd and reprehensible practice of reading in bed."[112] The danger of such fires increased as more people began to use cotton for bed hangings in place of the fire-retardant wool that had been more popular in the mid-eighteenth century.

Sleeping with another person also generates warmth, and New Englanders were used to sharing beds. From earliest childhood, they had slept together—as infants in their parents' bed, then with their youngest siblings in a nearby trundle bed, and later with siblings, cousins, and perhaps friends, apprentices, or domestic help of the same sex. When visitors decided to tarry, or stay overnight, they expected to be put up in beds with the family. So unused were many people to sleeping alone that they often sought out sleeping partners.

65. BED HANGINGS ON FIRE, WOODCUT, ALEXANDER ANDERSON SCRAPBOOKS, VOL. X, PRINT COLLECTION, MIRIAM & IRA D. WALLACH DIVISION OF ART, PRINTS AND PHOTOGRAPHS, THE NEW YORK PUBLIC LIBRARY, ASTOR, LENOX AND TILDEN FOUNDATIONS.

Edward Jenner Carpenter, an apprentice cabinetmaker in Greenfield, Massachusetts, described in his diary his feelings about sleeping alone. On July 9, 1844, he wrote, "I got Jo. Moore to sleep with me last night"; and the next day, "I got Albert Field to sleep with me last night, & I must go and get somebody to sleep with me tonight for it is rather lonesome to lie alone." The quest continued, and on the sixteenth, Carpenter wrote, "I got John Smith to sleep with me last night, but I have got to sleep alone tonight." On the twentieth, "I slept alone last night & have got to tonight. Dexter sleeps down to the house with his brother till Lyons gets back."[113]

Of course, sleeping with a marriage partner was more desirable. When Esther Edwards Burr wrote to her friend Sarah Prince in January 1775, she declared herself to be in a silly mood, and she could not refrain from sharing an entertaining idea: "Pray what do you think everybody marrys in, or about Winter for? Tis quite merry, isn't it? I really believe tis for fear of laying cold, and for the want of a bedfellow. Well, my advice to such is the same with the Apostles, LET THEM MARRY—and you know the reason given by him, as well as I do—TIS BETTER TO MARRY THAN TO ______."[114]

Some New Englanders also practiced bundling, especially during the last half of the eighteenth century. An unmarried man and woman, usually young people who had begun courting, were permitted to spend the night in bed together, keeping at least some of their clothes on.[115] The earliest published study of the practice, by Henry Stiles in 1871, suggests that the custom of bundling was practiced by those whose limited means compelled them to economize strictly in their expenditure of firewood and candlelight."[116] The same reason is given in "A New Song in Favour of Courting," also published by Stiles:

Since in a bed a man and maid,
May bundle and be chaste,
It does no good to burn out wood,
It is a needless waste.[117]

Before climbing into their bed at night, some people took time to warm it. Stones or bricks that had been heated by the fire and were wrapped in pieces of old blankets could serve this purpose, or one could use a special warming pan. Long-handled brass warming pans were kept in kitchens or in the cellarway,[118] where they could be filled with coals from the dying fire at the end of the day and carried quickly to the cold bedchamber. Such a pan was placed between the sheets and rubbed briskly to warm the bed and eliminate any lingering dampness. The effect upon the sheets was very much that of ironing, but a more lasting warmth was absorbed by blankets and by the feathers or straw that filled the bed itself. Rubbing a long-handled metal pan full of hot coals demands a steady hand, strength, and speed if one were not to scorch the sheets or spill the coals. Once used, a warming pan could be laid upon the hearth until the next morning or returned to the kitchen. In either case, it was essential for the person who was to occupy the bed to climb in quickly in order to enjoy the transitory effect of the warming.

Although warming pans seem to have been fairly common,[119] it is difficult to know with what frequency they were actually used. The task is easily performed, but some people felt that having one's bed warmed was a sign of weakness. Having contracted a cold, Isaiah Thomas of Worcester had his bed warmed on December 30, 1826, and later noted in his diary that he felt that such an indulgence was "a very unusual thing for me."[120]

Taking Advantage of Severe Cold

Not all bedchambers were used exclusively for sleeping. Their space might also be used for spinning, weaving, or food storage. Harriet Beecher Stowe described "a great cold northern chamber, where the sun never shone, and where in winter the snow sifted in at the window-cracks, and ice and frost reigned with undisputed sway, [which] was fitted up to be the storehouse of . . . surplus treasures. There, frozen solid, and thus well preserved in their icy fetters, they formed a great repository for all the winter months; and the pies baked at Thanksgiving often came out fresh and good with the violets of April."[121]

Unoccupied chambers, unfinished lean-to spaces, and shed chambers were ideal storage places for foodstuffs that would be best preserved by freezing. Although most fruits and vegetables had to be protected from freezing, one cookbook author suggested that "cranberries keep well in a firkin of water. If they freeze, so much the better."[122] The only concern was unseasonably warm weather. When Sarah Bryant experienced a day "warm enough to keep the door open" on December 30, 1829, she was seriously concerned about her supply of frozen meats and pies.

Because of the radiant heat of an active central chimney, the temperature in many attic spaces remained above freezing. Meal, flour, and dried foodstuffs such as corn, apples, pumpkins, and herbs could be safely stored in attics regardless of how cold it became. Whole apples, squashes, and onions stored well in the dry heat of an attic during the fall, but they would be damaged if it got too cold. Potatoes, carrots, beets, and cabbages would be damaged by either extreme heat or cold. William Pyncheon of Salem noted on October 30, 1788, that when the weather was "excessively cold, people's roots were frozen in the garret."[123]

Cellars were more reliable for storing root vegetables, apples, and cider, which needed to be protected from freezing. After spending the summer of 1791 at home in Braintree, Abigail Adams wrote from Philadelphia on October 30 to her sister Mary Cranch that she had forgotten to make arrangements for "cider and potatoes to be put into the cellar." Abigail was anxious about the temperature in the cellar, for although she had given directions to have the cellar banked up, she was not confident that it had been done. She asked Mary to make sure that it was "secured before the Frost."[124]

Banking of the cellar served to reduce draughts of cold air at the sill level, thereby helping to warm the first floor as well as protecting the contents of the cellar itself from freezing. In banking, piles of "forest leaves, sawdust or tanbark"[125] were stacked against the lower part of the house as insulation. The practice was known at least as early as the mid-eighteenth century, for Ebenezer Parkman had his sons bank the foundation of their house in early November 1750.[126] Noah Blake of Deerfield, Massachusetts, noted in his diary on December 2, 1805, that he had "Banked the house with cornstalks and pompion vines,"[127] and Ruth Bascom noted similar activity on November 1, 1810, when two men and a team worked together banking her house.[128] Abner Sanger often was employed to bank up people's houses; he used "chip dung" or sand.[129]

Many New England farmhouses were sited so that they faced south, in order to take advantage of the warmth of the sun. Some houses were constructed with unfired brick or seaweed used as nogging, or filling, inside the walls. Either served well as a form of insulation, helping to keep the house warm in winter and cool in summer. Low ceilings helped to conserve heat, and massive central chimneys radiated some warmth to all rooms. In many houses, interior window shutters were kept closed in winter in order to reduce the infiltration of cold, but this was inconvenient in rooms that were in constant use, for closing the shutters also darkened the room.

In *The House Book,* Eliza Leslie suggested that preparations for winter should include the stopping up of cracks and the prevention of drafts around doors and windows. She recommended stuffing wadding, or cotton batting, around window sashes and over obvious cracks, as well as the use of pieces of wood wrapped in green baize and nailed to the bottom of doors through the baize only, or the preparation of long, narrow bags of carpet or some other thick cloth, which could be filled with sand and laid across thresholds. Her most obvious advice was to "keep the key always in the lock."[130] Miss Leslie also asserted that in the north, "most of the windows are made with double sashes, as preventives to draughts of cold air,"[131] but there is little documentation of this practice in New England before 1850.

Many country people sealed up their front doors for the winter and hung blankets over them to reduce drafts. Ralph Waldo Emerson found this an analogy to human personality, recording in his journal in 1836 that every man has both a sunny and a pompous side, which can be compared to "the two entrances of all our Concord houses. The front door is very fair to see, painted green, without a knocker, but it is always bolted, and you might as well beat on the wall as tap there; but the farmer slides around to the house to the quiet back door that admits him at once to his warm fireside and loaded table."

No matter how much money they spent or how hard they tried, even people who were well off could not always be warm in winter. The broad hearths and huge chimneys that characterized eighteenth-century New England architecture and were romanticized by late-nineteenth-century antiquarians pulled vast drafts of air through the house, while only a little heat radiated from them directly into the room. In other words, most of the heat of those great fires went straight up the chimney.

Technological Improvements in Heating

During the late eighteenth century, cast-iron stoves were imported to New England from Pennsylvania, and some were made at foundries in Salisbury and Stafford, Connecticut, and at the Revere foundry and others in Massachusetts. "Rittenhouse Fire places, 10 plate and 6 plate Stoves; Cast Iron Backs and Jambs for chimnies," probably all imported from Pennsylvania, were advertised by John Goddard of Portsmouth in the New Hampshire *Gazette* on May 21, 1793. All of these stoves were thought to increase the amount of heat from a fire by increasing the area of radiating surfaces or moving the fire farther into the room.

As nearby woodlots were emptied and wood became more expensive in cities, some men began to turn their attention to the problem of improving the efficiency of heating systems. These studies went hand in hand with late-eighteenth-century scientific inquiry into the nature of heat and combustion. Benjamin Thompson, Count Rumford, published an influential series of essays in 1796 in which he explained basic scientific principles and proposed solutions that would be far-reaching in their effect on New England households. Most significant was his suggestion that scientifically designed fireplaces with smaller fireboxes and a smoke shelf in the chimney opening would emit less smoke, be more effective in controlling drafts, and radiate more heat. Many builders incorporated these ideas into new houses, and soon many of the large old fireplaces were reconstructed according to Rumford's principles and smaller hearths built inside the yawning fireplaces of old. The backs and sides of these new fireplaces were plastered to reflect heat, and the throat of the chimney contained a smoke shelf to prevent downdrafts. The romantic picture of the hearth so broad that people could actually sit inside it came abruptly to an end, and it was finally possible to describe a winter room as cozy.

Simple cast-iron fireplaces (popularly known as "Franklin" stoves) and six-plate box stoves were the basic types of stoves used in early-nineteenth-century New England parlors, sitting rooms, and chambers. Beginning in 1816, stove manufacturers patented a variety of innovations, such as smoke domes, which increased the radiating surface of a stove or improved combustion efficiency;

but it was not until the 1830s that these were produced in very large numbers. Once these technologically improved stoves were readily available, "Franklin Stoves, of old patterns" were advertised for sale at "reduced prices."[132]

The installation of cast-iron stoves in parlors, sitting rooms, and even some bedchambers in the years after 1820 resulted in a more efficient and reliable source of evenly distributed heat than had been possible with open fireplaces. People were also relieved from at least some of the dangers of fire and from the necessity of being on guard for flying sparks and the expense of replacing hearth rugs. The stoves themselves were ornamental, being both sculptural in form and embellished with cast designs of all sorts.

66. Wilson's patent stove, 1829, installed in the General Artemas Ward Memorial Fund Museum, Shrewsbury, Massachusetts, owned and maintained by Harvard University. Photograph by Ron White.

By moving the fire out onto the hearth and adding a cone-shaped device to capture smoke and radiate heat, Wilson's design increased the amount of heat radiated from a small fire, thus saving fuel.

However, stoves also created a drier indoor atmosphere, which some felt resulted in an increase in respiratory infections. Houseplants were suggested as a means of ameliorating the dry air in rooms heated by stoves, for it was recognized that the plants provided both oxygen and humidity.

Stoves also had other disadvantages. In order to burn evenly, stove wood needed to be cut into small pieces of consistent size and thoroughly dried. Stovepipes became clogged with creosote, which sometimes dripped from the joints onto scrubbed floors or expensive carpets. Overheating was common, and scorched woodwork or even fires resulted. Often stoves were installed without insulation under them and too close to flammable walls and woodwork, without any recognition of the potential dangers they posed.

Uninsulated stovepipes were commonly passed through wooden overmantel panels, fireboards, or lath-and-plaster walls with only a thin pottery sleeve or no protection at all. In some houses, stores, and public buildings, stovepipes were carried through several rooms in order to obtain the maximum amount of radiant heat before the smoke entered the chimney; placing several bends or turns in the course of these elongated pipes was thought to increase the amount of heat from a single fire, although it actually increased the dangers of dripping creosote and fire in the pipes themselves.

Hot stoves projecting into active living spaces presented their own dangers, especially to children, who could be seriously burned by falling against a stove. On January 21, 1844, two-and-a-half-year-old Elizabeth

Babcock Leonard "fell against the hot stove, while walking with the little lamb in her arms, burning her face slightly and both hands badly leaving the skin on the stove."[133] Almost every New England town history or reminiscence contains a description of a similar experience.

Cleaning stoves was a messy chore. Wood ashes were easy to spill while being removed through narrow stove doors, and hot coals hidden among the ashes could easily start a fire. Rust often developed on the iron exterior, especially during periods of infrequent use. Black lead was advertised for restoring stove surfaces,[134] but it was difficult to use. In the early years, it was common practice for stoves to be removed for the summer, and this procedure could easily result in blinding airborne soot and cascades of crunchy creosote.

Still, stove heat was more efficient and easier to manage than large open fireplaces. Zilpah Longfellow of Portland, Maine, wrote enviously to her husband Stephen in 1822 describing a neighbor's new heating system: "I think we *must* have ours warmed in the same manner. . . . It would be so delightful to have every part of the house comfortably warmed in winter." Mrs. Longfellow was convinced that having a "furnace" would not only be delightful but also contribute to an improvement in her health, "as Mrs. Gardiner's is."[135] Mary Palmer Tyler was also hearty in her praise of improvements in heating devices: "When I think of our sufferings from cold . . . during my early married life, I

67. "A NEW ENGLAND FIRESIDE," IN *Ballou's Pictorial*, BOSTON, MARCH 10, 1855. COURTESY OF THE SOCIETY FOR THE PRESERVATION OF NEW ENGLAND ANTIQUITIES.

In direct contrast to the image presented in figure 56, here are three generations of a family, welcoming their neighbors in "a very felicitous presentation of the interior of a good old-fashioned New England homestead, many of which yet exist, remote from cities and towns, in all their primitive purity and attractiveness. The picture abounds with character and truth of detail. That wide yawning fireplace, with its blazing pile of walnut and oak, resting on the andirons, the merry children nestling in the chimney corner . . . the row of flat-irons and candle-sticks upon the mantle-piece, the strings of dried apples so airily festooning the ceiling, the cat by the fireside, and the gun upon the rack. . . . It is pleasant to dwell upon a scene like this. . . . From such firesides great and noble men and women have gone forth into the world."

feel disposed to vote for a monument to the memory of the first inventor of family stoves."[136]

However efficient stoves may have been, and no matter how welcome the warmth they provided, in retrospect, New Englanders missed the roaring fire that had served as a focal point for family gatherings. Stoves and central heating, which made possible the enjoyment of a free range of evenly heated space, had a negative effect on interpersonal relationships, destroying the physical force that had brought people together and threatening the centrality of home: "We children missed the bright fire light in the evenings. With the big back log and fore stick and pine knots between, it made our great kitchen look very bright and cheerful in the evenings. . . . And we used to love to sit around on the hearth and tell stories or listening to some older person telling a story. And when company would come in, they would all take turns in singing a song or telling a story."[137]

People quickly forgot the frozen bread and water in the pantry, the frost upon the windowpanes, the icy hallways and the damp, cold beds, and the family fireside became an overpowering image of home.

V

Clean, Bright, and Comfortable: Dimensions of Housework

AFTER THE RIGORS OF WINTER, IT WAS A DELIGHT TO FLING OPEN THE doors and windows and savor the soft spring air. On March 22, 1825, Sarah Bryant took time to walk to the store. On Saturday, April 16, it was "clear very pleasant and warm" in Cummington, and an invigorated Sarah accomplished a lot: "opened the doors and windows—and cleaned out the west chamber—baked bread and pies—the buds of Lilacs opened—Ironing done," while "Austin sewed his wheat." Three days later, she "scoured the pewter."[1]

For New England women, the pleasure in the first spring days was tempered by an awareness that there was hard work to be done. By spring the house was really dirty. Winter's crackling fires and long hours of candlelight had deposited smoke and soot on almost every surface. Bits of bark, pine needles, and wood chips had fallen from stacks of firewood, and the hearths were packed with ashes. The kitchen and sitting room had been the centers of intense family activity, and there was all sorts of detritus from whittling, knitting, sewing, spinning, and other work to be cleared away. Paint was chipped and woodwork dented in corners behind the woodbox, on the fireplace surrounds, and on the doorjambs. Since people had tracked in plenty of dirt along with snow and ice, and now their feet were often covered with mud, the floors were badly stained, and whatever carpets there were needed to be taken up and cleaned. The banking around the foundation had begun to decay and now harbored mice and other vermin amid partially frozen vegetable matter. Some of the winter vegetables had begun to rot, and the apples were getting soft. Mushy potatoes needed to be made into starch, and the winter's accumulation of fat needed to be made into soap before it turned rancid. The difficulties of procuring large quantities of water and of drying things thoroughly in freezing weather had resulted in badly yellowed sheets, shifts, shirts, and baby clothes. Linens that had been hung to dry before the fire had holes from flying sparks and needed to be mended. Woolen clothing worn for weeks on unwashed bodies really smelled. Flannel undergarments began to itch instead of providing comfort. Moths were waiting to attack. Soon the calves would be born and there would be butter to make; the sheep would be washed and there would be wool to break. No one disagreed with the author of one of the new advice books when she stated firmly: "Spring is particularly the time for house cleaning and bleaching linen."[2]

Spring was the time for a ritual turning out and thorough cleaning of the entire house, from cellar to attic. Each room in turn was emptied and scrubbed and freshened with new whitewash, the furniture rubbed and polished, the windows washed, the ashes removed from the fireplace, and the hearth swept and scoured. Order was restored. The work involved in all of this was, of course, tremendous; but it had to be done. Anne Kane described the debilitating effect of spring cleaning in a letter to her mother in 1812: "I hardly know when I wrote to you dearest mother we have been so engaged in white washing and cleaning house and such a large smoky house as ours with so much woodwork that I have been fatigued to death both in mind and body."[3] She was not alone.

After touring New England in 1800, the Reverend Timothy Dwight reported that the households were noted for their order and neatness, even "among those who are in humble circumstances."[4] This may well have been the ideal, but as Dr. William Bentley traveled about eastern New England between 1789 and 1819, he found that order and neatness were not necessarily the same as cleanliness, and standards varied. Returning from a journey through southern New Hampshire and Vermont in 1793, Dr. Bentley was forced to spend the night in Bernardston, Massachusetts, "without clean linen. . . . I lodged upon the bed, & in no sense in it."[5]

It is difficult to know what was considered a minimal standard of cleanliness in these crowded houses that were active centers of productivity. Any space that was thoroughly cleaned was quickly dirty again, for the daily activity of a large number of adults and children created dust and brought in dirt. Cooking, ironing, spinning, sewing, and other work generated more dust, distinctive trash, and the appearance of clutter. Steel knife blades, brass candlesticks, copper tea kettles, and pewter plates all corroded easily and needed to be polished. Only a few people had continuously running water piped in from a spring. Strong odors were generated by the fires and cooking at the fireplace, processing milk and making cheese in the buttery, burning tallow candles, using chamber pots, piling dirty laundry in baskets, and warm wet wool; some people hung infants' diapers to dry on kitchen clotheslines without washing them; and no one used deodorant.

There is no question that most people aspired to a clean house in perfect order. As was true in England, people in New England associated cleanliness with moral purity, and women measured themselves, and were measured by others, by their success in achieving this ideal.[6] The special desire to have a clean and orderly house on Sunday propelled women to a flurry of activity on Saturday, when many also did additional cooking in order to avoid excessive work on the Sabbath. The day of rest was well deserved, but it could not be conscientiously enjoyed until community expectations and one's own personal standards had been met.

As the nineteenth century progressed, there was a definite increase in the general standards of cleanliness—which, of course, resulted in more work. New domestic rituals and increasing demands for privacy resulted in the intensive use of more rooms and much more specialized equipment. This is particularly true in the matter of food service and dining, but it is true in other areas as well. The increase in housework resulted in a change in the way both housewives and household help structured their time, with much more being given over to the repetitive tasks of housekeeping and less to the productive activities that were an important part of the household economy. In middle-class homes, and especially in rural areas, where the processing of agricultural products continued within the home, this resulted in considerable economic and psychological stress among those who were responsible for compliance with the new ideals.

In both the eighteenth and the early nineteenth centuries, the idea of regularity in household arrangements applied to the hours of eating, sleeping, and rising as well as to tidiness. Catharine Beecher, the author of *A Treatise on Domestic Economy,* believed in systems, and she recommended that "night hours . . . be regarded as the ordinary period required for sleep, by an industrious people, like the Americans. According to this, the practice of rising between four and five, and retiring between nine and ten, in Summer, would secure most of the sunlight and least of the noxious period of the atmosphere." Because she believed that night air was less dangerous in winter and people were more tired during the colder months, she felt that then "the proper rule would be, to rise as soon as we can see to dress, and retire so as to allow eight hours of sleep."[7]

Some people followed her advice, and some didn't. Susan Lesley recalled that her mother rose at dawn, threw open the windows, and began housecleaning. "The two parlors, dining-room, entry and stair case are all carefully and thoroughly swept before six o'clock. She then calls up her domestics, if they are not already up."[8] On a cold January morning in 1828, Julia Evelina Smith "had breakfast this morning by candlelight at 6:30. It was cloudy, and a bit rainy"; a week later, she noted that they had had breakfast before sunrise every morning for seven days.[9] Anticipating a busy day on January 20, 1812, Ruth Bascom lit a fire and "began to wash at half past 4 this morning."[10]

Not everyone went to bed with the chickens, either. Few families retired before eight or nine in the evening, although in some areas of New England the winter sun sets as early as three o'clock in the afternoon. Sometimes the press of necessary work kept farmers, housewives, mechanics, or professional people up very late. On October 24, 1776, Abner Sanger husked "for Henry Ellis's wife until one or two o'clock at night."[11] In 1813, Thomas Robbins had a long day: "Worked late on sermons—began 1st 9 AM, 2d 8:15 PM, finished 2nd at 3:15 AM. I believe I never wrote so much in one day. About midnight drank a cup of tea."[12] When Robbins's uncle died in 1836, he found himself again working unusually late and noted: "Wrote laboriously and seven hours by candle-light, and finished my sermon a little before one o'clock.[13]

The Luxury of Light

Although Dr. Bentley tells us that on the unusually dark day of May 19, 1780, Captain John White of Salem was "obliged to have a Candle to do the ordinary business of the house & for dinner, for the space of three hours or more,"[14] candles were not usually lighted in daytime. People were used to working by available light, and it was customary to move one's work into the sunshine, wherever that might be.

Candles were used sparingly even at night. It was not unusual for people to sit without a candle and "keep blind man's holiday" during the early evening or when there was bright moonshine reflected through the windows. In a room with a brightly burning fire, people could see to eat, wash dishes, spin, iron clothes, knit, set candlewicks, peel apples, whittle clothespins or candle rods, or accomplish any of a hundred other simple tasks. On a "bright moonshine evening," especially when the ground was covered with snow, it might be light enough to read inside the house. Usually no more than a single candle was used for those who needed additional light. One woman recalled that "when evening came we used to set a candle on the candle stand and pull the stand to the centre of the room so that four people could sit around it and see to work."[15] During the long evening, one person might tell stories to entertain the children and the other adults while they worked. A person near a candle or the fire could read aloud, if imagination and conversation failed.

68. READING BY A WINDOW TO UTILIZE NATURAL LIGHT, WOODCUT IN *Anecdotes for Children* (NEW YORK, N.D.). PRIVATE COLLECTION.

Among poor families, knots of pitch pine, called "candlewood," were saved and burned at the side of the hearth for additional light. Sylvester Judd's *History of Hadley* tells us that "candlewood was used also for kindling fires, when few people had wood-houses and dry wood. . . . It appears from the account books of Deac. Ebenezer Hunt of Northampton, that he brought a cart-load of candlewood every year from 1739 to 1776. Many others on both sides of the river had a load yearly. Some men belonging to Northampton, Hadley and Granby, born between 1780 and 1790, affirm that when they were young many farmers got a quantity of candlewood from the pine plains every year, both knots and pieces of fat wood, for lights and kindlers. The knots were burnt in the fire-places; some splinters were used for candles, to go to the cellar for cider, apples, etc."[16] Judd's description is confirmed by Abner Sanger's diary, which contains many references to searching for, digging out, carting, and splitting "candlewood." On one occasion he brought in two loads.[17]

In most households there was no artificial light at all except in the room where the family sat in the evening. Many people recalled that "candles were a great luxury and little children were obliged to find their way to bed in the dark."[18] On evenings when there was a full moon shining outside, it was not hard to find one's way upstairs. Usually, however, it was very dark indeed, and it could be dangerous to grope about, especially in an unfamiliar place. An unfortunate man staying at a tavern in New Haven in June 1796 "was going to bed without a light . . . [and] opened a cellar instead of a chamber door, and falling down the cellar steps fractured his Scull, of which he expired the next morning."[19]

Tiny wax tapers floating on a thin layer of oil in a glass of water were used as night-lights in some families. These were commercially available at least as early as 1812,[20] but they could easily be made at home by cutting out small circles of cork and inserting a short, thin, tightly twisted wick through them. The amount of light provided was minuscule, but it was enough to see one's way across a room to care for a crying baby, use a chamber pot, or find a larger light source. In any case, these lights were much safer than leaving a candle burning all night, especially near a fully curtained bed.

In order to get about safely in the dark, many people carried a light with them, but there was still a serious danger of setting something on fire while looking for a lost article at night, or of bumping into something while carrying a candle. Chambersticks were specially designed to make it safer to carry candles from room to room, having broad drip pans to catch running wax or tallow and offset handles to prevent burning one's hands if the candle dripped badly. There were also lanterns, which protected candle flames from the wind and helped to prevent the spread of sparks. Carrying some kind of light was absolutely necessary on moonless nights in order to move about the dooryard; to reach and enter the cellar, barn, privy, or woodshed; and to obtain water from the well.

Even in stationary candlesticks, lighted candles were a fire hazard. Many newspaper accounts document tragic house fires, in which people were killed and much property lost, that were accidentally started by candles, especially when carried by children or used for reading in bed.

69. "Going to Bed," woodcut in *The Rose Bush; or Stories in Verse* (New York, n.d.). Private collection.

When one moved through dark hallways on moonless nights, it was necessary to carry some kind of light. When lighted candles were carried from room to room, it was important to hold them steady and upright in order to prevent burning the hand and spilling wax or tallow on the floor or carpet.

Despite the dangers associated with their use and the availability of whale oil and lamps, candles remained the standard source of light, especially in rural areas. They were made of animal fat, usually the hard tallow from beef and sheep. Some people spun their own candlewicks of cotton or tow, which had to be thoroughly dry before they were used. On March 3, 1801, Elizabeth Phelps wrote to her daughter Betsy: "Tomorrow I propose to make candles the wicks are made and in the warm Oven."[21] Country stores usually stocked candle wicking, but it is impossible to tell if it was plainly spun or braided. A special kind of braided candlewicking was developed in France in the late 1820s. It was made with one thread pulled tighter than the others in order to keep the end of the wick in the outside of the candle

70. SILVER OR PLATED CHAMBER CHAMBERSTICKS, OR HAND CANDLESTICKS, ENGRAVING IN TRADE CATALOGUE, GREAVES & HOYLAND, SHEFFIELD, ENGLAND, C. 1780, PLATE 36. COURTESY OF WINTERTHUR LIBRARY, PRINTED BOOK AND PERIODICAL COLLECTION.

Chambersticks, or hand candlesticks, were made with broad pans, to prevent dripping wax or tallow from staining the carpet, and offset handles, to protect the bearer from being burned by hot wax. The conical device is an extinguisher; the slot under the candle socket is intended to secure a scissorlike candle snuffer used for trimming candlewicks. Number 51 is described as "double beaded," while number 52 is "a single beaded vase hand candlestick"; each style was available in small, medium, and large sizes.

flame, where it would be consumed by the flame. Wicks that consist simply of twisted fibers burn rapidly and turn into a long strand of glowing snuff that must be regularly trimmed from the candle and extinguished.

Studies of nineteenth-century country store inventories show that storekeepers usually stocked far more candlewicking than they did whale oil, indicating that candles made of locally grown tallow were the most common source of artificial light in those rural areas.[22]

Candle Making

Dipping was the usual procedure for making candles in families, for then a large quantity could be made at one time, and the bulk of a year's supply prepared. Candle-making day involved a prodigious amount of concentrated work, "sevenfold worse in its way even than the washing day," according to Harriet Beecher Stowe in *Poganuc People*.[23] As early as 1807, an advice book suggested what many women already knew: "Candles made in cool weather are best . . . they are better for keeping for eight or ten months, and will not injure in two years, if properly placed in the cool."[24]

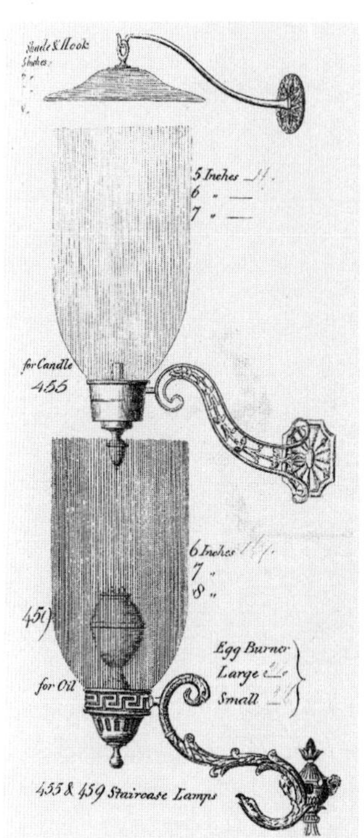

71. STAIRCASE LAMPS FITTED WITH A CANDLE SOCKET OR AN EGG-SHAPED WHALE-OIL BURNER, ENGRAVING IN *Birmingham Trade Catalogue: A Book of Lamps*, BIRMINGHAM, 1812. COURTESY OF WINTERTHUR LIBRARY, PRINTED BOOK AND PERIODICAL COLLECTION.

In a wealthy household, hallways and staircases might be lighted continuously with this kind of device, which had a large glass shade to protect the open flame from drafts and a separate glass cover, or smoke dome, to deflect smoke and prevent unsightly stains on the ceiling.

Susan Blunt described the process in her reminiscences: "Mother used to dip candles in the fall, enough to last all winter. When a beef was killed in the fall, she would use all the tallow for candles. On the evening before we would help her prepare the wicks. The Boys would cut a lot of Rods and she would cut the wicks the length of a candle and then string them on the rods. In the morning she would commence her day's work. She had an old fashioned chair, with a very long back, which she would turn down so the back would be right side up to hold the rods and put the big kettle of tallow at one end. And then seat her self so she could reach the rods easily and then dip each one in the hot tallow and straighten out the wicks so the candles would be straight when they were finished. When she had gone over them once, she would commence again at the other end and so keep on until the candles were large enough. She kept the kittle full by turning in hot water."[25] By raising the candles at just the right speed and working on a day with a moderate temperature, the fine quality of the candles would be assured. The candles would be cooled overnight and the bottom ends cut off neatly. The finished candles were packed away in a mouse-proof container for safe storage.

Some people also had tin or pewter candle molds in which six, eight, or as many as twelve candles could be made at once. When one had run out of candles or had a small amount of tallow that might be wasted unless it was made into candles, using candle molds was an efficient procedure. Susan Blunt recalled that her mother used candle molds only when her supply of dipped candles was gone.[26] Margaret Baker tied the wicks tightly, "stuck the small end into a potato" so the tallow would not run out at the bottom, filled the molds with melted tallow, and then hung them up to harden.[27]

A variety of techniques was used to improve the quality of homemade candles, such as dipping the wicks in limewater with saltpeter to purify rancid tallow and to prevent dripping or running,[28] or adding beeswax, bayberry wax, or camphor to the tallow to give a very clear light and also to prevent running.[29] In 1825, the *New England Farmer* suggested placing finely powdered salt at the top of a burning candle, deep enough to reach the bottom of the black part of the wick. A candle treated in this way was said to "burn very slowly, yielding a sufficient light for a bed chamber."[30] Candles could also be made whiter by bleaching in the sun; hanging them in a cool attic near the window was a good way to accomplish this.[31]

Since tallow has a low melting point and is an edible fat that is very attractive to rodents, it was important to store candles in a cool place and to secure them from rats and mice. A small quantity could be kept handy in the kitchen or pantry in a tin candle box, but the bulk of a year's supply required careful storage. While visiting in Boston in June 1818, Elizabeth Salisbury sent directions concerning this to her son Stephen in Worcester: "You will have the candles put down cellar—on the Cider Horses I should think the best place, not on the floor. Charge Melinda to keep them covered on account of the Rats."[32]

Even some of those who did not make their own candles preferred candles to oil lamps. Thomas Robbins noted that he had paid $2.25 for seventeen pounds of candles on December 14, 1841. The following October, he did much better when he "paid for twenty-three pounds of candles and a box, $3.65"; and in the spring of 1846, he noted in his diary: "I get good mould candles for eleven cents a pound."[33] Twenty-three pounds of candles may well have been nearly a year's supply for an unmarried minister who often read or wrote sermons in the evening. Sarah Bryant dipped candles once a year, making between twenty-two and thirty pounds at a time, depending on the available supply of tallow. In Princeton, Massachusetts, Elizabeth Fuller made sixteen dozen candles in December 1790 and another eighteen dozen the following March.[34] On George Washington's birthday in 1812, Ruth Bascom "made twenty four dozen candles, baked, &c." Fortunately, "Olive assisted."[35]

Both dipped and molded candles were commercially available in cities, where individual households did not have large supplies of tallow. Ashbel Wells, Jr., advertised both dipped and molded candles in Hartford in 1790, as did Stephen Frothingham in Portsmouth, New Hampshire, in 1791, offering to pay cash for tallow or to trade it directly for candles.[36] Candle dipping continued at home in rural areas at least until the advent of kerosene in about 1869, and throughout the nineteenth century in some very frugal households.

Using candles was a messy process, for they dripped and they guttered and they smoked. After gathering up the used candlesticks from the mantels or tables where they had been left the night before, one needed to clean off unburned tallow and bits of charred wicks before setting the sticks in a convenient place. Each morning the cleaned candlesticks were fitted with candles long enough to last an evening and then stored in the kitchen, where they would be easy to find and to light when darkness fell. This task usually fell to children or hired girls, although in houses where there were more formal servants their task was the same. In 1827, Robert Roberts advised young servants: "You should always make it a regular rule to set up your candles in the morning."[37]

Lamplight

Roberts's book of advice also reflects changes in the sources of light in urban households by suggesting to servants that "lamps are now so much in use for drawing rooms, dining rooms, and entries, that it is a very important part of a servant's work to keep them in order, so as to show good light."[38] This may have been true in city mansions, but for country people candles remained an important source of light until the widespread use of kerosene in the post–Civil War period.

72. PARLOR SCENE, ADVERTISEMENT FOR *The Boston Weekly Magazine*, IN *Boston Directory*, 1839. COURTESY OF SOCIETY FOR THE PRESERVATION OF NEW ENGLAND ANTIQUITIES.

"Nothing looks more cheerful than a parlor with a bright fire in the grate, a brilliant argand lamp on the table, and this table, which had better be a round one, covered with books and work." (The Book of the Seasons *[Boston: B. B. Mussey, 1842].)*

THE BOSTON WEEKLY MAGAZINE,
A QUARTO JOURNAL OF EIGHT PAGES,
Published every Saturday.....Devoted to
Moral and Entertaining Literature, Science, and the Arts,

Thomas Robbins did not give up candlelight until 1848, despite his need for light to write and read by. Apparently, even then it took some convincing. He noted on December 28, while boarding with Mr. and Mrs. Gleason, that "my host and hostess have persuaded me to use at their house a lamp. They take the labor of procuring the requisite articles and keeping them in operation."[39] Perhaps the Gleasons thought it would be safer for the old man to use a lamp than candles and were glad to take care of it for him. These new lamps burned whale oil and required even more daily care than candles. Each morning the lamps were carried to the kitchen or the scullery to be cleaned, refilled with oil, and have their wicks trimmed, chimneys and shades washed, and bodies polished. They were easy to light but difficult to regulate, producing as much smoke and glowing snuff as candles if they were not managed carefully.

Elizabeth Sturgis of Salem recalled that the early lamps were not reliable, either. Her description of a tea party given by Mrs. Tucker about 1835 tells of a hostess who used borrowed candlesticks in order to ensure adequate light for an evening party, even though the family owned lamps by this time, for "Mrs. Tucker had learned by former experience not to trust to oil lamps when she had company. They would burn perfectly for weeks when the family were alone, but with the natural depravity of inanimate things, so sure as they were required for a special occasion, it seemed as if evil spirits posessed them. They went out, they smoked, the oil ran over and there was no conceivable wickedness that oil lamps could not indulge in when it was important they should be on their best behaviour."[40]

Despite their unreliability and expense, ornamental table lamps seem to have been a standard feature on center tables in parlors of middle-class households by 1835 or 1840. Small mats, called lamp rugs, were placed under them to protect tabletops and tablecloths from spots and stains caused by dripping lamp oil. Directions for lamp rugs were published in Miss Leslie's *The American Girl's Book* in Boston in 1831 and republished in Louis Godey's *Lady's Book* in the spring of 1835. These rugs were squares made of carpet scraps and trimmed all around with ravelings of green and brown carpet, which were thought to look like a bed of moss in which the lamp would stand. In an 1843 edition of *The House Book,* Miss Leslie suggested that cheaper versions could be made of oilcloth, but she preferred those that were handsomely worked in crewel or other embroidery and bound with upstanding fringe.

73. "THE HOBBY HORSE," OIL ON CANVAS, AMERICAN, C. 1835–40. NATIONAL GALLERY OF ART, WASHINGTON, D.C., GIFT OF EDGAR WILLIAM AND BERNICE CHRYSLER GARBISCH.

The puffy woolen object at the base of the lamp stem is a lamp rug, intended to protect the table and tablecloth from seeping lamp oil.

Fire and Water

In the coldest weather and on the shortest days, it was usually the responsibility of a hired girl or other servant to light fires, heat water, and begin the chores long before it was light. In houses where there was no servant, these jobs fell to the most active and responsible adults. Occasionally a sense of charity or helpfulness broke through rigid custom and the gender barrier. On a cold morning in February 1778, William Pyncheon "rose at 5 . . . and made the fires for the servant, who has often made them for me; I felt gratitude, and she showed it."[41]

In the best-regulated households there was an informal indoor schedule of sweeping floors, making beds, emptying chamber pots, cleaning and fixing candlesticks, tending fires, cooking, serving meals, carrying water, and washing dishes. Most water was carried in buckets from wells in the dooryard, but shallow dug wells were not always dependable. In late November 1829, Ruth Bascom must have been delighted to be able to record in her journal: "Last

74. THE OLD OAKEN BUCKET, IN *The Mother's Assistant and Young Lady's Friend* (BOSTON, 1842). PRIVATE COLLECTION.

This illustration was published with a letter in which the associative values of home and the objects of everyday life were valued for the "permanent moral and religious impression" they cast upon young people. The "old oaken bucket" was chosen in order to underscore the importance of "pure cold water" and total abstinence. Although romanticized in poetry and song long before the Civil War, the wooden water buckets were breeding grounds for bacteria.

Wednesday we had our well cleared for the first time since we came here nearly 9 yrs., and Saturday began to have *some* water from it, the first for some seven or eight weeks on account of the loweness of the water, lower than ever known, so the chain would not reach it."[42]

Piped water systems were set up in cities at the end of the eighteenth century, and some prosperous farmers constructed private water systems as well. By 1793, Richardson's Tavern in Keene, New Hampshire, had a "spring which runs under the Street & a for a small expense is led to the respective houses & furnishes already water for his troughs & is intended for every domestic use. The convenience is hardly imagined until it is seen."[43] In 1796, plans were first put forward for an "aqueduct from Spring pond" to Salem, and the Portsmouth aqueduct was begun the following year. When these systems were completed, water flowed by gravity from a spring or reservoir through log water pipes to a tap in the cellar, the kitchen, the scullery, or the woodshed of individual houses.[44] Sometimes there was enough pressure to raise the water to the first floor.

Traditionally, privies were independent buildings located in a far corner of the kitchen garden or dooryard; archaeologists have found that urban privies were often located on the lot line at the rear of the yard, sometimes back-to-back with that of a neighbor. They were undoubtedly aromatic, and Dr. Bentley mentioned the "extreme heat of our necessary houses, shut up in hot days, easily rendered almost suffocating."[45] As early as the 1780s, when prosperous families enlarged their houses with ells designed to accommodate specific workspaces and defined storage areas, some privies were relocated indoors, to a distant corner of such an ell. Miss Beecher felt that the traditional outdoor location of wells and privies was dangerous to the health—not because of their proximity to each other, but because "persons in the perspiration of labor, or in the debility of ill health, are obliged to go out of doors in all weathers."[46] She preferred that the privy be located in an attached shed and recommended that "the privy should have two apartments, as indispensable to the healthful habits of the family."[47]

Neither the diarists nor Miss Beecher mentions the care of chamber pots as

75. "COLONIAL WASH KITCHEN" (OLD ELIOT HOUSE, HYDE PARK, MASSACHUSETTS), OIL ON CANVAS, BY JOHN ENNEKING, 1883. NEW BRITAIN MUSEUM OF AMERICAN ART, HARRIET RUSSELL STANLEY FUND. PHOTOGRAPH BY E. IRVING BLOMSTRANN.

In a house without piped water or drains, scrubbing and laundry often took place in a "sink room," or scullery, separated from the main kitchen. This 1883 painting shows that the process and the equipment had changed little in one hundred years, and the artist was attempting to convey a scene that was fast disappearing in urban areas.

76. SINK IN A CELLAR IN SALEM, DRAWING MADE TO INSTRUCTIONS GIVEN BY JOHN ROBINSON TO ILLUSTRATE THE APPEARANCE OF THE "OLD WOODEN AQUEDUCT ARRANGEMENT" AS IT WAS IN HIS BOYHOOD HOME, NO. 2 CHESTNUT STREET, IN SALEM, MASSACHUSETTS. COURTESY OF THE SOCIETY FOR THE PRESERVATION OF NEW ENGLAND ANTIQUITIES.

The standing pipe with its wooden faucet was a terminus of a piped city water system first constructed in 1796. Gravity forced the water up to the level of the faucet in the cellar; later, a pump was used to raise the water to the first floor. Robinson remembered that the wooden faucet often popped out of the pipe and had to be hammered back in place; while it was out, water flowed freely from the standpipe.

77. PRIVY AT JUDGE SAMUEL HOLTON HOUSE, DANVERS, MASSACHUSETTS. PHOTOGRAPH COURTESY OF THE SOCIETY FOR THE PRESERVATION OF NEW ENGLAND ANTIQUITIES. PHOTO BY THE HISTORIC AMERICAN BUILDINGS SURVEY, C. 1936.

This late-eighteenth-century form of privy is seen in landscape paintings and documented by archaeologists but rarely survives. It has two chambers, each with two or more seats. The interior was plastered above a plain wooden dado. Small windows provided necessary light and ventilation.

part of daily housework or of the weekly task of cleaning bedchambers. Chamber pots are listed in a few inventories, but they are conspicuously absent from many others.[48] Considering the frequency with which they are excavated by historical archaeologists and the heavy reliance on cathartics as medical remedies, it seems likely that the care of these useful vessels was an important daily chore. However, it is difficult to know the conventions associated with their use. Jacob Wendell's privy was located in a corner of a detached barn, sixty-five feet from the back door of the house. For his family and for many others, gender, age, weather, pregnancy, stamina, health, and urgency must have influenced individual decisions. Abner Sanger's diary gives us two clues in this obscure area: on July 7, 1794, he purchased a "urine mug," and on November 19, 1778, he made a "shit house." Perhaps that was really the difference.

Household Routine

In addition to the indoor household chores, on farms there was additional daily work for women—milking to be done, hens to feed, and eggs to gather. All of this was in addition to the work that characterized weekly and seasonal routines and the productive year-round tasks of dairying, spinning, sewing, knitting, and specialized income-producing labor. The routines that encompassed all of this work were seldom written down or even described, yet they were fairly rigid. The nursery rhyme about "Monday washday" reflected common practice in New England as well as old.

Few New England diaries mention daily housework, even those that reveal a great deal about the patterns of weekly laundry and baking or the productive work of spinning, weaving, and sewing. The ordinary quality and repetitive nature of routine chores seem to have made them beneath any level of notice. No matter if the temperature indoors was near freezing or one was "almost sick with a headache," the work had to be done and was done. But to read the diaries of Sarah Bryant, Elizabeth Phelps, and others like them, one would think the beds were made, the table set, the water carried to the kitchen, and the wood added to the fire by fairies. The tasks were simply never mentioned.

Women like Elizabeth Phelps and Sarah Bryant were hands-on managers. Even though they enjoyed an elevated social status and some economic advantages, they organized the complicated work of their households and actively participated in most of it. When Silence Furguson came to help Elizabeth Phelps for two weeks in November 1797, the two women worked together. Elizabeth wrote to her daughter Betsy: "we have been hard at it I can tell you. made a cheese—churned—got dinner for between .20. & .30. persons, made between .20. & .30. mince pies."[49] In a more contemplative mood, Mrs. Phelps wrote again in 1802: "what is it material whether our time be spent in making cheese or making shirts,—it is apparently the dictate of providence I should do the business which is allotted for me, & may I not find as much communion with my savior, think of heaven as freely, & exercise as much love & benevolence to my fellow mortals (perhaps more kindness & pity) as when sitting in my parlour?"[50] A productive woman with high standards for herself and for those in her care, Elizabeth Phelps fulfilled the biblical image of a good housewife and the New England ideal.

Determining the day-to-day work schedule for such a person is not easy. Sarah Bryant's wonderfully detailed daily diary seems like an excellent record of the regularity of housework, but it is difficult to know if she recorded everything she did. Laundry, baking, sewing, and dairying are noted consistently, and there is some mention of food preparation; but more mundane tasks like lighting fires, washing dishes, caring for beds and chamber pots, dusting furniture, and setting tables are never mentioned. Since Mrs. Bryant had both daughters and hired help, it may well be that she never did any of these things herself, but that seems very unlikely, indeed. Perhaps she recorded a task only when it was part of a reciprocal work arrangement for which there was some value, when it was done by an employee, or when it was particularly difficult. It is not surprising that she recorded that she had "washed the floor" on June 11, 1798, for at the time she was eight months pregnant, and it could not have been an easy thing to do; the task is not mentioned again until June 13, 1799, and it seems unlikely that the floor was not washed for another whole year.

If it was only the worst jobs that were mentioned in Sarah Bryant's diary—the things that were done only once or twice a year—we can conclude that they were scouring pewter, washing floors, "cleaning up" or "cleaning out" rooms, making soap and candles, picking geese, scouring out the buttery, whitewashing, and the tasks associated with butchering. The unpleasant job of picking geese was nicely described by one local historian: "The women and girls of

Hadley, of families that owned geese, knew how to pick them. This was cruel and disagreeable work. They put on worn and faded garments, tied a handkerchief over their hair to keep it from the down, and drew a stocking over the head of each goose which they picked, to prevent its biting."[51]

The hardest tasks to study are those that would have resulted in a high standard of household cleanliness. Although Sarah Bryant never mentioned sweeping or mopping floors in her diary, she "spun a mop" every few months. She was the efficient kind of person who wouldn't have done this if she didn't need to, so she must have used the mops. What we don't know is how often she used them, in how many rooms, and whether she used them as dust mops or wet-mopped her floors. With doors opening directly from the unpaved dooryard and windows wide open in the summertime, dust swirled into the house on every current of air and mud was tracked in whenever it was wet outside. Downdrafts blew clouds of ashes from the fireplaces, and all sorts of chaff fell out of the firewood as it was carried into the house. Stray fibers and bits of dirt flew from the spinning wheel and the loom. Of course Sarah Bryant needed to clean her floors and dust her rooms regularly. These tasks were such a regular part of everyday life that she simply didn't mention them. Maybe nobody did.

Scrubbing and Scouring

Although it is nearly impossible to find out how often cleaning materials were used, we can patch together a picture of the kinds of equipment used by early–New England housewives to clean their homes—the strong soap, the scouring sand, the withy brooms, the corn brooms, the homemade mops made of woolen rags or yarn, and the stiff scrubbing brushes. Abner Sanger peeled birch saplings to make brooms for his sister Rhoda, and later for his wife.[52] Ruth Bascom bought two brooms from a peddler on November 7, 1810, and paid twenty-five cents for a corn broom on December 12, 1825. The Shakers invented a more efficient, flat broom and made it a commercial success. Clean white wooden floors were admirable, so much so that Harriet Beecher Stowe asserted in *Oldtown Folks* that grandmother's "white-sanded floor was always as clean as hands could make it."[53]

But how did they keep those floors so white? In the eighteenth century, and often in the early nineteenth century as well, the wood was usually unfinished—without paint, stain, wax, or any kind of sealer. Recalling one house where she used to call when she was a girl in New Hampshire in the 1830s, Susan Blunt was impressed that "it was so very clean, the chairs, table, floor and all the woodwork was unpainted and was kept white by being scoured with sand."[54]

Sand was not only used as an abrasive cleaning agent; a thin layer of clean sand was left on the clean floors and swept in ornamental patterns described as herringbones or a "remarkable combination of zig-zags."[55] This sand was strewn on freshly scrubbed floors to protect them by absorbing spilled grease, candle drips, and moisture that was tracked in from outside; it also continued to clean the surface of the wood through abrasion. Kitchen floors were usually scoured on Saturdays and then ornamented with a thick layer of clean white sand. In *Oldtown Folks,* Aunt Lois "finished the ablution of the floor," and then "took the dish of white sand to sand it."[56] Sarah Emery even recalled a kitchen floor on which the sand was spread so thick that she could pull a little boy "across the freshly sanded floor upon his tiny sled" when caring for him after he suffered a serious burn.[57]

Sand was used on floors in other rooms besides kitchens. Ellen Rollins recalled that in her childhood home in Wakefield, New Hampshire, between 1834 and 1844, there were two second-floor chambers with sand strewn on the floor—"a cheap, changeful covering, which at night I used to scrawl over with skeleton pictures, to be scattered in the morning."[58] When old New England houses are restored, sand is often found beneath the floorboards, even on the upper floors. Whether it was originally used for scouring the boards or was swept in ornamental patterns once a week is impossible to tell.

In the early nineteenth century, some people began to use paint to protect floorboards, especially in kitchens. At first, the most popular color was white, imitating the bleached, raw wood that had been the ideal for so long. Some fancy painters even ornamented floors with trompe l'oeil versions of the old-fashioned swirled sand. In other households, brightly patterned woolen carpets were laid over straw or newspapers and tacked down all around the edges. By the 1830s, inexpensive ingrain carpets were almost standard in New England middle-class parlors; Brussels carpets with looped pile were more expensive.

Walking through loose sand on the floors and cleaning carpets with a broom generated quantities of dust. Once the floors were cared for and the dust had time to settle, someone had to dust the woodwork and the furniture. When Lydia Maria Child summed up what she had done during the year 1864, she found that she had been away from home only five days, twice on overnight visits. In the course of the year she had filled the lamp 362 times, swept and dusted the sitting room and kitchen 350 times, and swept and dusted the chamber and stairs 40 times.[59] By the mid-nineteenth century, middle-class respectability demanded this level of daily household care, but we are left to wonder what Mary Lane, Elizabeth Phelps, or Sarah Bryant would have thought of it. There is no question that there would have been enough dirt to sweep out of their homes every day; they have not told us if they did it.

Spring Cleaning

Much of what we know about early housekeeping practices is derived from the prescriptive literature that began to circulate as advice books in the 1830s and 40s. The information these books contain is extensive and seems to combine clear outlines of current practice with an almost inexhaustible supply of handy household hints. These books were instrumental in spreading more uniform procedures and elevating housekeeping standards throughout the country. Some of the best of them were written by New Englanders and they offer a particularly useful window to an understanding of how things had been done for a long time.

One of the earliest of these books gives good information about spring cleaning. In *The House Book,* Miss Leslie tells us: "The usual custom in America is to have the house completely cleaned from top to bottom twice a year; late in the spring and early in the autumn. . . . It is a good rule not to commence house-cleaning in the spring until the trees are all in full leaf; but to begin it in the autumn as soon as the leaves become tinged with brown; having it entirely over before the 20th of September; at which time the equinoctial rains may be expected, fire will be necessary, and the house and furniture ought no longer to appear in the guise of summer."[60] But, the author continued, "at no season should house-cleaning be commenced when there is a prospect of bad weather."[61]

In most homes, all the women in a family pitched in to help with this exhausting task. On May 21, 1781, the versatile Abner Sanger "wait[ed] on Rhoda helping her scour the things in the house, pewter, and etc."[62] But hired help was at a premium during this busy season, and husbands often disappeared.[63] In early May 1828, Julia Evelina Smith recorded in her diary that she and her sisters were deep in the throes of spring cleaning. On the second, Julia took responsibility for doing some laundry, making butter, and scrubbing and cleaning the sink room, as well as making cakes, baking pudding and a loin of veal for dinner, and preparing the other family meals, while her mother and sisters whitewashed the dining room, the kitchen, and the third floor, moved the desk to the office, and made beer. On subsequent days they emptied other rooms, took up carpets and shook them, whitewashed walls, and replaced furniture. In August of the same year they gave the hall and entry two coats of whitewash and painted the woodwork.[64]

In larger towns and cities, where coal smoke and dirty streets created their own problems, some enterprising people made a profession of helping with heavy seasonal work. Upholsterers were particularly busy in the late spring, taking down one set of curtains and putting up another, putting up fresh blinds, installing slipcovers, taking up carpets, tacking down straw matting, and varnishing scuffed furniture. Most of this work was reversed in the fall.[65] In Salem, Massachusetts, William Reed advertised that in addition to his regular service as a furniture mover, he was available to wash windows, shake carpets, and clean gardens and cellars.[66]

The impossible ideal was a perfectly clean house. One late-nineteenth-century historian asserted that by Election Day—the first Thursday in May—in Hartford, "good housekeepers were expected to have finished their spring cleaning long before, and fire irons and brasses were papered and put away in the garrett."[67] Although it would be advantageous to have housecleaning finished before the press of spring and summer farm work, it would have been impractical to put away the andirons in early May. New England's spring weather is usually too cool for people to give up fires so soon. There is ample evidence in diaries that many women were still scrubbing at the end of May. On May 29, 1837, Pamela Brown recorded that she had "worked very hard all day whitewashing and cleaning the house"[68] and there were others like her.

No matter how hard a woman labored, or when she declared her housecleaning "finished," the work was never really done. Whether rooms were in active daily use or not, as soon as one was clean, dust began to accumulate, smoke curled through the air, and bugs flew in the window. No wonder women became more and more frustrated as standards of cleanliness rose and the ideal became even more elusive.

In prosperous households, spring and summer household chores included far more than the exhausting turning out of rooms, the thorough cleaning of walls and floors, and the scouring of pewter. As more and more luxurious household furnishings were used in the early nineteenth century, more and more care was needed to maintain them. Floors still needed to be scoured, but for those who could afford them, woolen carpets presented a special problem in summertime. Not only were they dusty and dirty, but they seemed hot to look at, and they certainly attracted moths. It was recommended that carpets be taken up in the spring, aired outdoors, and beaten thoroughly to remove dust, dirt, and moth eggs. Many people then rolled them up with tobacco or some other moth preventive;[69] others relaid their carpets and checked under them frequently to make certain that moths were not feasting on the underside.

The quest for cool surfaces and the fear of moths inspired many people to replace woolen carpets with straw matting or painted oilcloth. This practice had begun as early as the late eighteenth century. While en route to Braintree for the summer of 1791, Abigail Adams wrote ahead to her sister Mary Cranch requesting that her house be put in order. She was especially concerned about the parlor floor covering and said, "I think my dear sister that as it is coming Hot weather my oil cloth will do best for my parlour. I would wish to have it put down."[70] Even before the opening of the American trade with China in 1784, Chinese straw matting, commonly called "India matting," was used for floor coverings in summertime. In recalling the common practice of Boston households about 1828, Edward Everett Hale wrote that "carpets were always taken up and India mattings substituted in the living rooms."[71] Innumerable newspaper advertisements and merchant's account books confirm Hale's statement for urban houses, but there is little documentation for village homes or middling farmhouses before the 1860s. Catharine Beecher suggested using straw matting as floor covering in both parlors and chambers because it seemed very cool. Since chambers were "used most in Summer," she recommended that the straw carpets be permanent; it would be easy enough to lay a strip of wool carpet over the matting in winter.[72]

Bedding

Since feather beds were hot to sleep on, many families put them away for the summer, either in huge baskets in the attic or under the straw mattresses on which they would sleep for the next few months. When the temperature reached ninety-one degrees in East Windsor, Connecticut, on June 5, 1823, Thomas Robbins "took off" his feather bed.[73] In nearby Glastonbury, Julia Smith followed the same practice: "We put away our feather bed and we will sleep on a straw mattress—we put in a lot of straw."[74] Miss Beecher would have thoroughly approved, for she stated emphatically that "there is nothing more debilitating, than to sleep in warm weather, with a featherbed pressing round much of the greater part of the body."[75]

78. MAJOR REUBEN HUMPHREY, BY RICHARD BRUNTON, 1800. CONNECTICUT HISTORICAL SOCIETY, HARTFORD.

Festoon window curtains could be pulled up or lowered on a series of lines and pulleys to control light and air.

Feather-filled beds, pillows, and bolsters lasted for a very long time, but sometimes their ticking was soiled or the feathers became damp and musty. Both could be laundered on a warm day when there was not much of a breeze blowing. The feathers that escaped while the beds were being refilled were soon carried away by birds. In contrast to the longevity of feathers, straw and corn-husk mattress fillings had a tendency to become brittle over time and deteriorate with use. When new supplies of husks and straw became available in midsummer, good housekeepers emptied out the contents of their bedtickings, washed them thoroughly, and refilled them. It was advised that the husks be "gathered as soon as they are ripe, and on a clean dry day. The outer husks are rejected, and the soft, inner ones are collected and dried in the shade" or in a warm oven. Some people slit the husks before they were dried "with pins fixed through a potatoe; then take a common dull knife and scrape them until they curl"; others waited until the husks were dry and then cut off the hard ends that were attached to the cobs and drew the husks through a hatchel, or comb, to cut them into narrow strips. In either case, "the very cheapest ticking" could be used for husk mattresses, because there was "no down or dust to sift out." A husk mattress might last five years or more; straw became matted down more quickly.[76]

Winter or summer, beds were in disarray each morning, and bed making required more energy than the quick snap of a sheet and comforter over a taut fitted sheet and a boxed mattress that is often the standard procedure today. In 1843, Miss Leslie devoted three pages to instructions for making a bed, reminding women to begin by thoroughly airing the mattress and then smoothing it out, tucking in the bottom sheet firmly, plumping up the bolster and pillows, and then layering on the upper sheet and warm coverings.[77]

The fully enclosing bed curtains that were such a comfort in cold weather were sometimes taken down in summer, especially the foot curtains. If they were made of wool, the curtains were brushed thoroughly, sprinkled with black pepper or fine tobacco to ward off moths, wrapped in paper, and carefully

Proper and Improper Position to lie in Bed.

79. "Proper and Improper Position to Lie in Bed," in Jane Taylor, *Woulds't Know Thyself* (New York, 1858). Private collection.

This illustration appears in a health manual, and the accompanying text advocates sleeping in a prone position rather than being propped up on two pillows and a huge bolster.

laid away.[78] Apparently, many people left tester cloths, head cloths, and bed valances nailed in place for years, dusting them occasionally with a damp cloth. In the nineteenth century, when cotton fabrics became inexpensive, some people used a completely different set of bed hangings in summertime—often a tester cloth, valance, and matching ruffled counterpane of dimity, white muslin, or light chintz.[79]

Once the spring weather was really settled, on a day when drying conditions were ideal, blankets were washed outdoors, and some were packed away with tobacco leaves, camphor, or herbs to prevent moth infestations.[80] Some people simply folded the blankets and laid them under their mattresses, where the motion of the sleepers was sufficient to deter moths.[81] The lightweight summer bedcovers that were substituted were usually hemmed pieces of cotton or linen, sometimes with a binding or a fringe around three sides and a narrow hem at the head. Dimity was particularly favored for summer coverings, as early as the late eighteenth century. Miss Beecher advised that summer bed coverings be unlined, for otherwise they would be too warm; so it seems clear that these covers were not removed at night, except when it was really hot.[82]

Window curtains were fairly rare in eighteenth-century New England houses. When they were used, they served a utilitarian as well as an ornamental function, controlling light and air by being easily adjusted in length or drawn up and out of the way. In the nineteenth century, window curtains began to be more commonly used. Since they were made in complex styles of heavy fabric, they required more careful and regular cleaning. The stylish deep folds and heavy fringes were real dust catchers, and the popular white undercurtains were easily stained when water blew in around the windows. By 1830, it was considered normal practice to take down the heavy winter overcurtains during the summer to protect them from fading, as well as to create a lighter appearance.

Although heavily upholstered furniture was also rare before the 1830s, the cushioned easy chairs favored by the infirm and the elderly were usually upholstered in scratchy woolen fabrics. These same wools or woven horsehair fabrics were used as seat covers on some side chairs as well. Since both of these fabrics were expensive as well as uncomfortable in hot weather, loose cases or slipcovers of muslin, dimity, or linen were used as protective covers, sometimes on a year-round basis.

Summertime

Summertime brought an invasion of flying and crawling insects from which there was little defense. Few households used any kind of window screening before the middle of the nineteenth century, and both barnyards and carriage houses attracted flies, which soon found their way into the house. Although food was usually covered with protective cloths, flies were particularly annoying in the buttery, where they were attracted to the uncovered milk pans. Once they were attracted by food, flies swarmed and multiplied throughout the house. Since fly specks are highly corrosive and cause considerable damage to gilded and varnished surfaces, people tried to protect valuable paintings, frames, and looking glasses by covering them with gauze bags or by painting them with a boiled essence of leeks or onions, which was thought to repel flies.[83] "Green India Gauze" was advertised for this purpose in Boston in 1825.[84] In *Oldtown Folks,* Harriet Beecher Stowe described "a looking-glass in a gilt frame, with a row of little architectural balls on it; which . . . was always kept

80. CAPTAIN GEORGE BURNHAM HOUSE, MELROSE, MASSACHUSETTS, OIL ON CANVAS, ARTIST UNKNOWN, C. 1855. PRIVATELY OWNED.

In this summertime scene, light within the house has been controlled by exterior blinds, roller shades, and window curtains. There are no screens at the open windows.

shrouded in white muslin at all seasons of the year, on account of a tradition that flies might be expected to attack it for one or two weeks in the summer."[85] Mrs. Child offered a different solution: "Instead of covering up your glasses and pictures with muslin, cover the frames only with cheap yellow cambric, neatly put on. This looks better; leaves the glasses open for use and the pictures for ornament; and is an effectual barrier to dust as well as flies."[86]

Ants, of course, were another problem. Miss Beecher recommended pouring boiling water on them and then painting the places where "they resort, with corrosive sublimate" (mercury chloride, which, she cautioned, is "a deadly poison"). She also suggested putting the legs of sideboards and food safes in tin cups of water to inhibit the ascent of ants, completely disregarding the devastating effect this would have on the furniture.[87] Mrs. Child offered a safer solution for getting rid of red ants, which she termed "one of the worst plagues that can infest a house." She advised putting "a dish of cracked shagbarks [American walnuts] (of which they are more fond than anything else) in a closet." Mrs. Child assured her readers that the ants would soon gather "upon it in troops." Dumping the contents of the dish in the fire and then painting the cracks of the closet with corrosive sublimate would finish the job.[88] A correspondent for the *New England Farmer* tried this method "in a closet, and in a large cheese room" and agreed that the ants would "leave everything for the walnuts."[89]

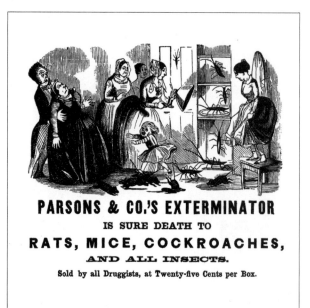

81. PARSONS & CO.'S EXTERMINATOR, ADVERTISING BROADSIDE, C. 1860. COURTESY AMERICAN ANTIQUARIAN SOCIETY.

Bedbugs are seldom mentioned in diaries, but they may well have been the impetus for Abner Sanger's actions on a very hot day in June 1794, when he took down his bedstead, carried it to the brook, soaked it, and scoured it.[90] Sarah Bryant "scalded bedsteads" on July 18, 1808, and June 18, 1810. Edward Jenner Carpenter, a cabinetmaker's apprentice in Greenfield, Massachusetts, left his bed one evening and slept at another house because the "bed bugs have got so thick we can't sleep here."[91]

Mosquitoes were an additional nuisance, especially at night. Some people tried to inhibit the gathering of mosquitoes by putting coals in an open chafing dish or burning a little brown sugar and smoking them out.[92] Thomas Fessenden, the editor of the *New England Farmer,* published "a cheap and effectual" solution to the problem of these "bold, blood-thirsty, and persevering" insects in 1826: "Make light frames of the size of the lower sashes of the windows of the bed chamber;

cover them with millinet, and place them in the lower sashes about 5 o'clock P.M. and shut the doors."[93] There is little evidence of the use of mosquito netting on beds in New England prior to the Civil War.

Once the fireplace had been emptied of ashes and the hearth thoroughly scoured, many people cleaned and polished the andirons and fire tools, wrapped them in old newspapers, and stored them in the garret or a shed chamber. Vases of ferns, evergreens, or flowers were placed in the empty opening during the summer, or else it was covered entirely by a decorative fireboard. If a fireboard was used, sometimes the andirons were left right on the hearth, protruding through slots in the fireboard. A fireboard effectively reduced the number of mosquitoes and other insects, or even birds, that might enter a house through an open, damperless chimney.

Fireboards might be perfectly plain, painted, or wallpapered to match the room in which they were used, or they might be embellished with a special wallpaper design or decorative painting of a landscape, a large vase of flowers, or a trompe l'oeil depiction of the hearth itself, complete with andirons, shovel, tongs, and wood. In 1841, Miss Beecher suggested that "handsome fire-boards can be made by nailing black foundation-muslin to a frame, the size of the fireplace, and then cutting out flowers from wall-paper, and pasting them on the muslin, according to the fancy."[94]

82. NORTH PARLOR OF DR. WHITRIDGE'S, TIVERTON, R.I., 1814, WATERCOLOR BY JOSEPH S. RUSSELL, C. 1848. OLD DARTMOUTH HISTORICAL SOCIETY, NEW BEDFORD, MASSACHUSETTS.

A summertime view with a bouquet and greenery in the cast-iron fire frame.

83. AN INCIDENT IN FOSTER, RHODE ISLAND, 1841, WOODCUT, IN ALBERT ALDEN PROOF BOOK. COURTESY AMERICAN ANTIQUARIAN SOCIETY.

A pro-temperance illustration showing terrified children hiding from their drunken father behind a fireboard.

Exterior blinds were a functional feature of many New England houses by at least the 1820s. They were made with widely spaced slats fixed in such a way that they shed rain to the outside when they were closed. During the summer months, they protected rooms and their furnishings from the heat and glare of the sun, while allowing air to circulate freely. So common was the practice of keeping blinds closed in the nineteenth century that the landscape architect Calvert Vaux recommended they be painted a dark color, in contrast to the siding, "for when the blinds are closed, which is generally the case, the house, except to a person very near it, will appear to be without any windows at all."[95] Blinds were closed because people were aware of the dangers of fading and wished to protect their expensive household furnishings. According to Miss Leslie, however, "There are families who condemn themselves to a perpetual twilight, by living in the dimness of closed shutters, to the great injury of their eyes. All this is endured to retard awhile the fading of furniture too showy for comfort. We have seen staircase-windows kept always shut and bolted, (so that visitors had to grope their way in darkness,) lest the small portion of stair-carpet just beneath the window should fade before the rest.[96]

In many households all these special summer procedures were reversed in the fall, after the flies had died and most of the harvest was completed but before cold weather really settled in. At the same time, the winter vegetables were being moved into the cellar and the attic, and the evenings were devoted to peeling apples to be preserved by drying or being made into applesauce. Windows needed to be washed, and if there were summer curtains, these needed to be taken down, washed, and put away, and replaced with the heavy winter sets. Fireplaces needed to be stripped of the fireboards or vases of greenery that had adorned them during the summer, while the hearths were cleaned of animal and vegetable matter that had fallen down the chimney during the summer, the fireplace furniture was polished, and fires were laid in anticipation of the first cold evening or chilly rainy day.[97] In 1796, Sarah Bryant "scoured the floor" on September 15, "washed the buttery" on the twenty-ninth, and within the next week whitewashed the bedrooms, kitchen, and west room. Once temperatures dipped below freezing inside the house, these chores became impossible.

No matter what internal sense of order governed the daily housekeeping

84. FIREBOARD, NORTH SUNDERLAND, MASSACHUSETTS, C. 1825. COURTESY OF THE SOCIETY FOR THE PRESERVATION OF NEW ENGLAND ANTIQUITIES. PHOTOGRAPH BY J. DAVID BOHL.

This trompe l'oeil painted fireboard shows the ideal summertime appearance of a hearth—swept and scrubbed clean, with polished brass finials on the andirons, tongs, and shovel.

routine, sometimes inspiration must have struck, or the temptations of fine weather inspired a change of plan. On September 29, 1829, Ruth Bascom confessed to her diary: "Mrs. Richardson came to wash but sewed all day covering our great rocking chair with green calico under Elvira's direction. I regulated some of my moveables, new lined Mr. Bascom's traveling trunk with blue paper & paste &c." Mrs. Richardson finally did the laundry on September 30 and October 1, returning on October 8, when she "finished the great chair covering."[98] Making a clean and colorful chair cover and pasting in a fresh trunk lining were

85. SOUTH PARLOUR OF ABM RUSSELL ESQ NEW BEDFORD, C. 1812, WATERCOLOR, BY JOSEPH S. RUSSELL, 1848. OLD DARTMOUTH HISTORICAL SOCIETY, NEW BEDFORD.

In the home of this prosperous Quaker family, the exterior blinds have been adjusted to control the strong winter light. With a coal fire burning on the grate, the room is warm enough to sustain potted plants on the window sill and for women to sit comfortably on the window seats. In all probability, the plants would have been moved away from the cold glass at night.

both more interesting projects, and less labor-intensive, than doing laundry, and it was important to have one's movables regulated. The laundry that Ruth Bascom and Mrs. Richardson postponed in the fall of 1829 was undoubtedly the hardest part of their weekly housework.

Laundry

Laundry was always a difficult task, especially for large families and for those caring for infants or the chronically ill. Some amount of laundry seems to have been done weekly in most households, even in severe weather. Family members dreaded laundry day, which was often the subject of jokes and satire focused on bad tempers, cold food, and exhausted women. If men and boys were advised to keep out of the house on laundry day, it was for good reason. Mondays were the favored days for this hard work, probably because women were relatively rested after the tranquility of the Sabbath, and they wished to complete the heaviest part of their work early in the week.

Sarah Bryant's diary records washing on an irregular schedule in the early years of her marriage, but as soon as she had a settled dwelling place, she "washed" almost every Monday or Tuesday and did some ironing almost every Saturday for forty-one years. Her brief diary entries underscore the ordinary quality of the work routine. Only after she was fifty-five years of age did she postpone the Monday task to Tuesday once when a January morning was "very cold."

In the best of weather, doing laundry meant a day outdoors carrying large quantities of water in heavy and awkward wooden containers, maintaining fires, and tiresome lifting, rubbing, and scrubbing. In wintertime, when laun-

86. DETAIL FROM "THE WASHING DAY," SHEET-MUSIC COVER, A. FIOT, LITHOGRAPH, PHILADELPHIA, C. 1835. COURTESY AMERICAN ANTIQUARIAN SOCIETY.

This laundry scene depicts three women using flatirons and a fourth using a goffering iron to finish ruffles.

87. "THE HUBBARD HOUSE," WATER-COLOR-AND-INK SKETCH BY EDWIN WHITEFIELD, CONCORD, MASSACHUSETTS, C. 1875. COURTESY OF THE SOCIETY FOR THE PRESERVATION OF NEW ENGLAND ANTIQUITIES.

This drawing clearly shows the common proximity of a dug well to the back doors of a house. Dish-water, laundry suds, and other slops were often thrown out the back door and contaminated water supplies. In the early nineteenth century, many similar wells were enclosed in sheds that were added to the rear of houses.

88. "AN OLD HOUSE," WATERCOLOR-AND-INK SKETCH, BY EDWIN WHITEFIELD, WETHERSFIELD, CONNECTICUT, C.1875. COURTESY OF THE SOCIETY FOR THE PRESERVATION OF NEW ENGLAND ANTIQUITIES.

A typical one-and-a-half-story house with a rain barrel at the back corner of the building.

dry was done inside, warm steam from the boiling water filled the room, but spilled water might still freeze on the floor, and drying was never accomplished easily. In the coldest weather, clothes put out to dry would freeze stiff, but a brisk wind caused most of the water to evaporate before they were brought in. On stormy days, many a New England kitchen must have featured a clothesline stretched in front of the fireplace and hung with garlands of drying diapers and wet stockings, a pile of stiffly frozen shirts and bedsheets, and the smell of wet warm wool. Still, laundry was done on rainy days and in glorious spring sunshine, in hot weather and cold. On December 16, 1835, Pamela Brown recorded her mother's industry: "It was one of the coldest days I ever knew. Mother washed."[99]

Laundry was the task most frequently delegated to hired help or to daughters, and some women performed this task as day laborers. In some households, teenaged daughters and adult women washed, starched, and ironed their own caps, collars, fancy aprons, and other "things," while help was hired for the heavy work. When help was unavailable, laundry was done by women who were doubled over with cramps or pregnant and were "almost sick with the headache" or "almost sick with a cold." Laundry was seldom postponed; Ruth Bascom and Mrs. Richardson's delay in 1829 was unusual.

Laundry was almost exclusively done by women, although men could be expected to provide the necessary equipment and to assist with carrying water, cutting firewood, and preparing a drying yard. Abner Sanger often helped his sister Rhoda on laundry day, setting up "bucking" facilities, "fetching water," cutting firewood and placing it near the door, and cutting and setting up the brush on which the clothes would be spread to dry.[100]

Enormous quantities of clean water were needed to ensure thoroughly clean and well-rinsed laundry. Reliable wells were not located at every city house or in every rural dooryard, and even in the nineteenth century very few homes had any source of indoor piped water or drainpipes. This meant carrying fifty gallons or more of water twice on washing day. Some families saved rainwater in wooden tubs or barrels for laundry. Both stored water and shallow wells were subject to freezing in extraordinary cold weather, and occasionally even piped water systems froze solid. When the water supply was reduced on laundry day, rinsing was impaired and some items might be set aside for a better day.

Despite the number of gallons of water needed for effective laundry washing, there is no reference to New England women washing in streams, as was customary in Wales and in some parts of Europe. One of the first New England missionary women, freshly arrived in Honolulu in 1828, was surprised to find the native women washing clothing successfully in a cold stream, and she expressed her concern that "the texture of fine fabrics suffers in the rough process,"[101] even though these were the very clothes that she had worn, without washing in fresh water, during the six-month sea voyage from the east coast.

It is hard to know how often garments were laundered under more normal circumstances, but it is clear that it was not every time something was worn. Although there was concern for an appearance of cleanliness, standards were markedly different from our own. Gowns, pantaloons, vests, and coats might be worn for months before they were cleaned. Even infants' clouts were not necessarily washed each time the baby wet them; many people simply hung them to dry and washed them only when they became soiled by excrement.

While visiting in Concord, Massachusetts, in 1829, Ruth Bascom tells us that "Mrs. Wentworth came & washed a great wash (28 pieces for Mr. B. & me) which hung up all night in the snow";[102] we do not know how long it had been since the last washday, but twenty-eight pieces of clothing seems to have been an unusually large number. In 1837, the *New England Farmer* carried an article that cautioned against letting dirty clothing and linen pile up in a corner until "a sufficient quantity is collected to form a washing,"[103] because it would be likely to absorb moisture and become moldy. In 1839, the author of *The Housekeeper's Book* agreed, stating: "It is a very bad plan to allow clothes to remain long dirty; in large families, three weeks should be the longest space between washes, for not only are the clothes injured, but more soap and labor are required to get them clean."[104] In households where laundry was done weekly, this was not a problem.

Travelers and people living away from home sometimes had their laundry done even less frequently. During his service in the Massachusetts legislature, Elihu Hoyt lived in boardinghouses and managed to have some of his laundry taken care of in Boston. Still, Hoyt regularly asked traveling friends and neighbors to carry to his wife, Hannah, in Deerfield small quantities of dirty shirts, waistcoats, pocket handkerchiefs, and stockings tied up in bundle handkerchiefs or packed in old meal bags together with the books, newspapers, textiles, clothing, and tea that he had purchased for his family or for neighbors. Hoyt sent his wife written notes indicating which garments he wished to have returned to him after they were washed.[105] The diaries of neither Elizabeth Porter Phelps nor Sarah Bryant indicate how their husbands had their laundry done while they served in the same legislature.

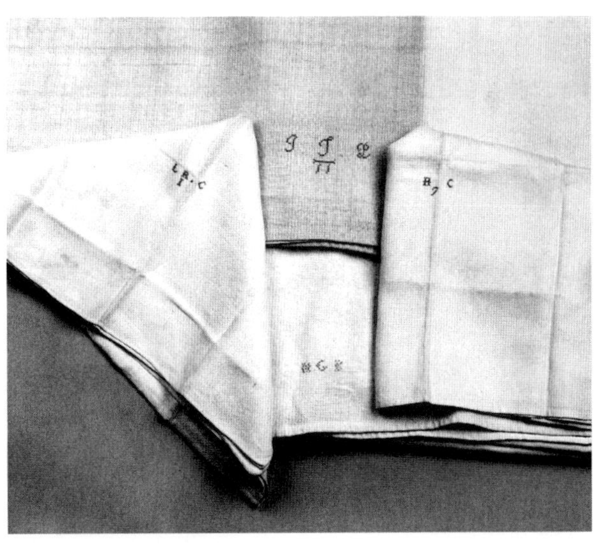

89. MARKED LINENS FROM THE THOMPSON FAMILY, NEW ENGLAND, LATE EIGHTEENTH AND EARLY NINETEENTH CENTURY. STRAWBERY BANKE. PHOTOGRAPH BY BRUCE ALEXANDER.

The numbers and symbols added below the owner's initials were signs of sets or clues to the date each piece was first placed in service.

Bed and table linens, handkerchiefs and stockings, men's shirts, women's shifts, aprons, and petticoats, and children's clothing formed the bulk of a normal weekly laundry. Since body linen—women's shifts, men's shirts, and the neck handkerchiefs of both sexes—was intended to protect outer garments from body odor and personal soil, it was washed more frequently than gowns, coats, vests, and pantaloons. Aprons were regularly worn by working men and women to protect their clothing from food and other external sources of soils and stains. Farmers and teamsters wore woolen frocks in winter and cotton or linen ones in summer to cover their coats and pantaloons and protect them from the dust and dirt that rubbed off animals or arose in the roads. Wearing a frock was proclaimed to leave "the clothes at the end of the week as clean almost as they were on Monday morning."[106]

Embroidered initials in counted cross-stitch or marking stitch provided a way to keep track of sets of linen that appeared identical. Sheets and pillowcases, tablecloths and napkins, handkerchiefs, women's shifts, and men's shirts were usually identified in this way, making ownership of body linen and sorting bed and table linen into sets after laundering a relatively easy matter.[107]

On washday, the cotton and linen pieces were usually rubbed with soap and rinsed, then boiled with more soap and rinsed again. Flannel undergarments, stockings, and other woolens were not boiled and had to be treated with care to avoid shrinkage and yellowing. Dark-colored calicoes were washed in lukewarm water and hung in the shade to avoid fading. Special stains were treated with fuller's earth, although it might have no visible effect. Ruth Bascom tried it once and thought it "brought little to pass."[108]

Silk or woolen gowns and fine muslin accessories, like caps and collars, were

90. DETAIL FROM ANOTHER VERSION OF "THE WASHING DAY," SHEET-MUSIC COVER, G. E. BLAKE, PHILADELPHIA, LITHOGRAPH C. 1835. COURTESY AMERICAN ANTIQUARIAN SOCIETY.

In this picture, the women are boiling, scrubbing, and wringing out laundry, but they are still plagued by a child.

not usually subjected to the rigors of boiling or long soaking. Both Julia Smith's and Ruth Bascom's diaries note their personal attention to some of these finer garments, while leaving the general washing and ironing to hired help.[109]

Successful laundry requires clean containers for carrying water, scrubbing the clothes with soap, and boiling them. A simple water bucket, a washtub, and a large kettle are the basic equipment, and this is all that Samuel Lane provided for each of his daughters. Broad smooth sticks, called washing sticks, were used to stir the clothes while boiling them and to lift them from hot water. Washtubs had to be kept wet so that they would not split or shrink and loose their hoops. All laundry equipment received hard use, and it did not necessarily last a long time. Although clean oak tubs were preferred for washing, improvisation was often necessary. On November 8, 1794, Abner Sanger "cut in two the cider barrel to make wash tubs of."[110] Since scrubbing and rinsing were more easily done if the tubs were raised to a convenient height, most people used wooden benches or wash-forms, whether they were working indoors or out. The bucking facilities that Sanger set up for his sister Rhoda in 1775 may simply have been raised tubs.[111]

Brass or copper kettles were considered best for boiling clothes, since they would not rust. Still, many people seem to have boiled their clothes in the same large iron kettles used for other chores such as making soap, scalding pigs, boiling applesauce, and evaporating maple syrup. In the nineteenth century, some prosperous and progressive people had large copper kettles set permanently in brickwork adjacent to the chimney in a scullery or summer kitchen for these same chores. Although conveniently located, they were not equipped with any piped water intake or drainage systems and were difficult to empty and to clean thoroughly.

After twenty years of finishing her entire washing in a single day, Sarah

Bryant seems to have adopted an even more time-consuming procedure. Beginning on June 7, 1819, during the summer months, the clothes were "steamed" on Monday and the washing "finished" on Tuesday. Although the diary carefully records these weekly activities for another sixteen years, there is never a clue as to how the process had changed. Most likely Mrs. Bryant had adopted the habit of bringing the most soiled clothes to a boil and soaking them overnight in soap suds before boiling them again and rinsing. This step may have avoided having to beat heavily soiled clothes with a stick to loosen the dirt before boiling them.

This procedure was the one recommended by Miss Catharine Beecher in her 1841 *Treatise on Domestic Economy.* Her book gives the most complete description of the sequential nature of New England laundry practice:

> Assort the clothes, and put the white ones to soak, the night before, in warm water. Do not allow *hot* water to be poured on them as it makes it more difficult to wash out the dirt. In assorting clothes, the flannels are to be put in one lot, the colored clothes in another, the coarser white clothes in a third, and the fine clothes in a fourth lot. Wash the fine clothes first, in suds; and throw them, when wrung, into another tub of suds. Then wash them in the second suds, turning them wrong side out. Then put them in the boiling bag, and let them boil, in strong soapsuds, for half an hour, (not more), and moving them about with the wash-stick to keep them from getting yellow in spots. Take them out of the boiling water into a tub, and rub the dirtiest spots. Then rinse them, throwing them, when wrung, into a tub of blueing-water. . . . Then wash the coarser white articles, in the same manner. Then wash the colored clothes. . . . Lastly wash the flannels.[112]

Reusing the water for darker and dirtier clothing saved labor, but some of Miss Beecher's recommendations created extra work. Still, there was not much that could be omitted if the task was to be done successfully.

Soap

Most laundry soap was made at home until well into the middle of the nineteenth century, and in some frugal households well into the twentieth. Soap was made each year in early spring, when the winter's accumulation of ashes could be used for lye and before the tallow from butchering and the grease from winter cooking turned rancid in warm weather. The best soap was the hard soap made by boiling tallow and lye and a small amount of quicklime, but

91. "HANGING THE LAUNDRY," C. 1810–15. DRAWING BY MICHEL FELICE CORNÈ. NEWPORT HISTORICAL SOCIETY.

This woman is hanging out wet laundry with a young child safely confined in a standing stool to prevent accidental scalding in the tubs of boiling water that were certainly nearby.

some families relied on boiling tallow or grease with the lye only until it appeared ropy and turned into a semiliquid, or "soft" soap. Hard soap was favored for laundry and soft soap for washing floors. Mrs. Child explained that soft soap "is so slippery, that it wastes a good deal in washing clothes."[113]

Lye, the strong alkali that was essential for soap making, was made by pouring water over clean wood ashes and some lime in a barrel and letting it drip through a hole near the bottom onto a special lyestone, which contained a groove that would channel the lye into a pail or a bucket. A key to success in soap making was the ability to judge the strength of the lye and to use an appropriate proportion of grease. Mrs. Child suggested that if the "lye will bear up an egg, or a potato, so that you can see a piece of the surface as big as a ninepence, it is just strong enough." She cautioned, however, that "if it sink below the top of the lye, it is too weak, and will never make soap; if it is buoyed up half way, the lye is too strong; and that is just as bad."[114]

Late in March 1782, Rhoda Sanger decided to make a quantity of soap. On the twenty-fifth her brother Abner helped her by putting up ashes, cutting and splitting wood, and carrying water. On the twenty-seventh, Abner brought more water for the soap, and their mother watched over the slow process of the soap boiling. On April 1, Abner made Rhoda a "little soap trough." Clearly, the task and the responsibility were Rhoda's, and it was she who prepared the grease, made and measured the lye, tended the fires, and preserved the finished product. Despite all this work, the Sangers may have run out of soap in seven months, for on November 20 Abner noted in his diary that he had fetched "home a pitcher of soap from Baker's."[115] The fact that this soap was carried in a pitcher indicates that it was soft soap, the kind that was most easily made but least economical to use.

Lye was sometimes added directly to the laundry tub to boost the efficiency of soap when the clothes were very greasy or badly soiled. In some households, stale urine was added to laundry, because the ammonia served as a whitening agent. Some people even added ashes to the wet linen and then ran water through the tub to strengthen the lye gradually as the linen became wet through. By 1841, Miss Beecher was describing the effectiveness of adding coarse washing soda to grated soap and boiling it to create "soda soap for washing";[116] others were adding the soda directly to the laundry tubs. Soda softened the water and eliminated the usual need for three or more separate sudsings.

In cities, tallow chandlers, who purchased fats from butchers and from private families, were also commercial soap boilers. With changes in typical cooking and heating fuels in urban areas toward the middle of the nineteenth century, more and more people relied on commercially available laundry soaps, for lye could not be made from coal ashes. Powdered lye, sold in small tins, was used by some city-dwelling women for soap making.

Since starch improved the appearance of household linens and clothing and also helped fabrics to resist soiling, many of the freshly washed clothes were dipped in starch just before they were hung or spread to dry, with care being taken to ensure that the fabric was evenly saturated. When the clothes were ironed, care needed to be taken to avoid scorching. Sarah Emery of Newburyport recalled that when she was a little girl she wore summer gowns and aprons "of blue checked home-made gingham, starched and ironed to a nice gloss."[117]

Many people simply spread the clean, wet laundry on the grass, on a hedge, or on brush that had been specially cut and placed in the drying yard. Things needed to be spread smoothly to reduce wrinkling and to ensure even bleaching by the sun. It was important to dry clothes in a protected grassy place, away from the dusty road or barnyard, and out of the prevailing wind. Careful placement of each item was necessary to keep it from snagging on twigs or blowing away. People wished to avoid the experience described by David Brown in 1791: "Came from the North East a Whirl Wind and took up Several Articles

92. DETAIL OF AN 1851 BILLHEAD FOR "NORTH AMERICAN ELECTRIC WASHING FLUID, . . . WARRANTED PERFECTLY HARMLESS IN ITS OPERATIONS, AND TO POSSESS DOUBLE THE POWER OF ANY THING OF THE KIND EVER DISCOVERED." 1851. COURTESY AMERICAN ANTIQUARIAN SOCIETY.

An up-to-date arrangement of laundry equipment, with a set kettle as well as loose tubs on a wash bench; the laundry has been hung on lines with pins instead of spread on the grass or on bushes to dry. The clock may have been included to suggest that using this product would save time.

that Mrs. Wheeler had washd and whirld them in the air, & Carried off Two Handkerchiefs and Several other small Articles."[118]

Some early clotheslines were made out of braided horsehair, but other types seem to have been available as well, such as the "5 dozen Clothes Lines, made of Manila Grass" that were advertised for sale at auction by J. L. Cunningham in Boston in January 1827.[119] If laundry was hung on a clothesline, clothespins or pegs were useful to hold it firmly in place. These were usually whittled by hand from hard wood. The production of clothespins was a simple task for old men, young boys, or anyone with basic woodworking skills. Still, it does not seem that their use was universal, for Catharine Beecher felt obliged to define

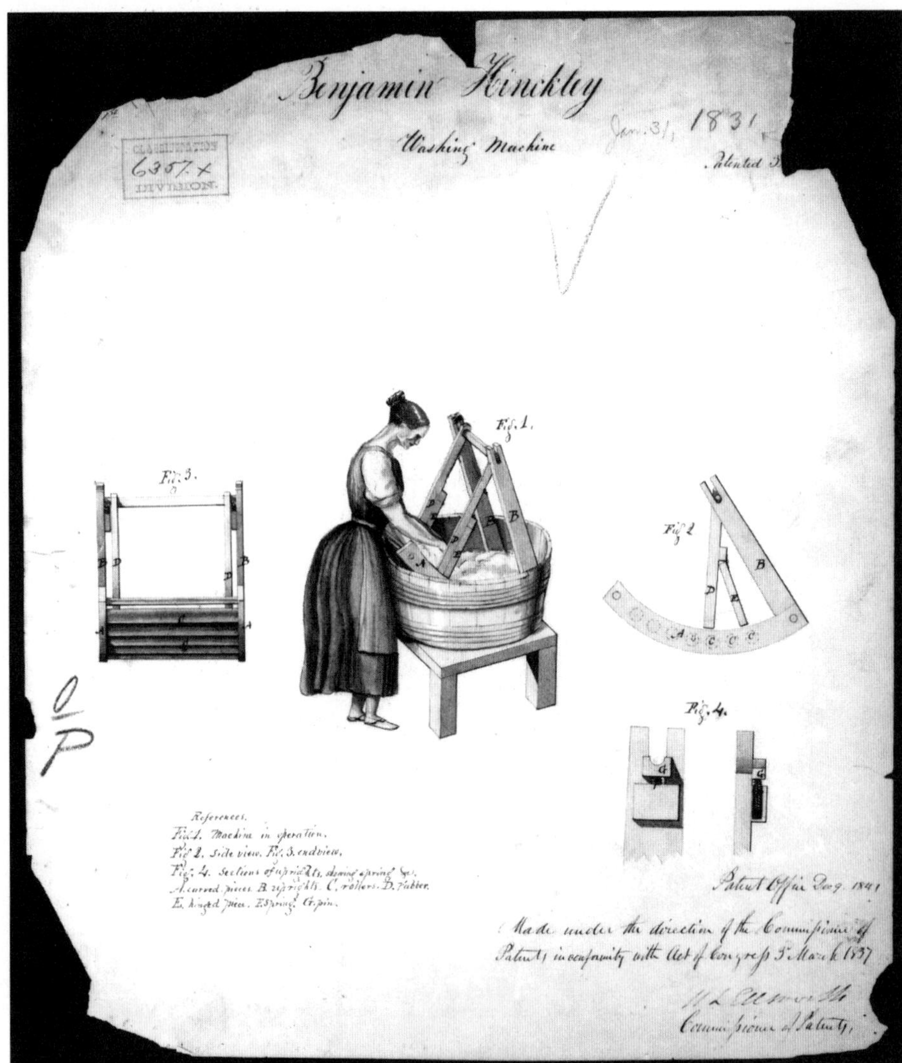

93. Reconstructed patent drawing for the washing machine registered on April 21, 1831, by Benjamin Hinckley of Fayette, Maine, December 9, 1841. National Archives Record Group No. 57, Patent Drawing No. 6357x.

Hinckley's design featured a spring-mounted agitator that held a series of rollers. It was sufficiently popular that the patent was reconstructed in 1841 following the destruction of the original in a Patent Office fire in 1836.

them as "cleft sticks" and to explain that they were used "to fasten clothes on the line"; and Mrs. Child cautioned those who used clotheslines never to leave them out "over night and [to] see that your clothes pins are all gathered into a basket."[120] Many people apparently still simply spread their laundry on brush or new-mown grass.

During cold or rainy weather, it was sometimes necessary to dry laundry indoors. When the temperature was below freezing, laundry would freeze solid in an unheated room. At such times, housewives might vary their weekly schedules to take advantage of unseasonable mild weather and to ease their tasks. Such a day was December 7, 1812, when Sarah Bryant noted "clear, pleasant, warm—washed—dried the cloaths out." If the laundry was spread out indoors in a room without a fire, it might take a very long time to dry. Mrs. Bryant's laundry took an entire week to dry during the rainy weeks of June 17 and August 27, 1831.

Some houses were equipped with folding wooden frames, called "clotheshorses," on which laundry might dry in cold or wet weather.[121] Sometimes these were used in the kitchen, but they also might be placed in the attic, where radiant heat from the chimneys would speed the drying process, and the clothes would not be dirtied by soot or cooking grease, nor be in the way of an active family. If left in a room with a fire burning, drying clothes could be damaged by sparks flying from the fireplace; if unattended, they could become a fire hazard.

94. SHOPPING FOR A WASHING MACHINE. WOODCUT, C. 1835. ALBERT ALDEN PROOF BOOK. COURTESY AMERICAN ANTIQUARIAN SOCIETY.

The principle of this washing machine is similar to that of a rotary butter churn; the pegs projecting into the main chamber would increase agitation when the drum was rotated.

Washing Machines

In an advertisement in the Barre *Gazette,* A. Hathaway noted: "Every washwoman seems to have an antipathy to the washing-day." To "make this day a pleasure rather than otherwise," he urged people to purchase one of Soule's Patent Washing Machines—"believed superior to any other." In the early decades of the nineteenth century, Soule and a host of other people patented various types of waterproof boxes, raised on legs, that either moved back and forth within a fixed framework or enclosed a series of rollers or paddles that could be turned to agitate the load. For a washing machine to be successful it was essential that the interior be finished smoothly, that there be ample agitation, that the box be large enough to accommodate an ample supply of water and a useful number of articles to be washed, and that there be some sort of drain.

Although these early machines saved a moderate amount of labor, they were far from ideal. The instructions for using Arnold's Patent Washing Machine indicate that the maximum load was six shirts or their equivalent and that good results could be expected only if all the badly soiled spots had been carefully rubbed with soap before the pieces were put into the machine.[122] Without hot and cold running water, a piped water supply, and power-assisted agitation and wringing, it is hard to imagine that any of these early patent washing machines really lightened the burdens of washday very much. Indeed, it seems that one of the only advantages of these machines was that young children could safely agitate the load, whereas it was dangerous for them to stand over a boiling tub of clothes with a laundry stick.

Ironing

Although Sarah Bryant's diary indicates regular early-in-the-week clothes washing throughout the year, her ironing seems to have been regularly postponed until Saturday, when other kitchen chores requiring steady fires—especially baking—were undertaken. Sometimes candle dipping was also done on ironing day.[123] In the Bryant household, ironing was not done every week. It was done less frequently in winter than in summer, probably because the woolen clothing worn in winter was less frequently laundered than the linen and cotton worn in summer.

95. CINDERELLA, WOODCUT, COOPERSTOWN, NEW YORK, 1824. PRIVATE COLLECTION.

Ironing was a chore that women happily delegated to servants. Here Cinderella is ironing a flat piece on a blanket spread on an ordinary table while her stepsisters are engaged in the more sedentary and ladylike occupation of sewing.

Ironing was most often done on a large table covered by an old blanket. Since there was always a danger of transferring soils or grease from the blanket or from a kitchen table onto the freshly laundered clothes, it is understandable that the authors of household advice books recommended special equipment. Mrs. Hale preferred "an ironing board, sheets and holders, . . . kept purposely for the ironing. A small board—two feet by fourteen inches wide, covered with old flannel and then with fine cotton, is handy to iron clothes on."[124] In *The Frugal Housewife,* Mrs. Child admonished women to "keep an old blanket and sheet on purpose for ironing, and on no account suffer any other to be used."[125]

An experienced woman could gauge the heat of her iron and knew what temperature range was appropriate for each type of fiber. Still, care was needed, espe-

96. "KITCHEN SETTEE TABLE," IN GERVASE WHEELER, *Rural Homes* (NEW YORK, 1851). OLD STURBRIDGE VILLAGE. NEGATIVE NUMBER B21892.

Wheeler recommended that a special settee-table be set aside for ironing, one made in such a way that the top could be kept folded up and the base used as a seat. The seat itself served as the top of a storage chest in which clothes and the ironing blanket could be stored safely. By folding the tabletop out of the way and providing a function for the base, the top was kept free of food and grease and reserved exclusively for ironing.

cially when ironing starched items, to avoid scorching and to attain a perfectly dry garment with a smooth finish.

There were two different types of irons: box irons, which contained a small charcoal fire and maintained their heat, and sadirons, or flatirons, which had to be returned to a trivet over coals or to the stove in order to be reheated. Working with these was greatly aided by having at least two irons, so that one could always be reheating while the other was in use. But even with two irons, the task was slow going. Elizabeth Porter Phelps was proud of her ironing skills and wrote to Betsy, "I must tell you what I Ironed in one hour or less—four stocks—1 muslin hankf—two caps for Juda—1 cap crown & border for myself."[126]

Judging the heat of an iron by holding it near the face or spitting on it was a matter of experience. Once the iron was heated the base was usually rubbed clean on an old cloth, and sometimes it was polished with a bit of candle wax before it was applied to the clean, damp cloth. To speed the task and perform fine work, specialized irons were available for fine ruffles or pleating. The nineteenth century saw an increasing variety of these.

No matter how bad the weather, it was agreed that clothing should not be put

97. *The Washing Day,* SHEET-MUSIC COVER FOR A COMIC BALLAD, LITHOGRAPH, PHILADELPHIA, C. 1835. COURTESY AMERICAN ANTIQUARIAN SOCIETY.

This shows laundry hung on lines with "cleft sticks" and the anxiety of a husband who feels neglected while his wife labors on laundry day.

away until it was thoroughly dry. Freshly ironed clothes were usually hung over the backs of chairs or the bars of a folding clotheshorse placed near the fireplace in order to assure that they were completely dry before being stored in chests or chests of drawers.[127] In 1829, Ruth Bascom expressed her annoyance when Mrs. Richardson went "home at night leaving many clothes wet" after working for two days to do "a fortnights wash for 7 of us" and tarrying overnight.[128]

For all the work involved in doing laundry, its never-ending quality, and the pure physical pleasure brought by having clean clothing and a freshly made bed, laundry is not one of those tasks that was described in detail by diarists or romanticized by those looking backward to the early days. Sarah Bryant's diary entries imply satisfaction at the completion of a rigorous task. "Washing done," she often wrote. In the late nineteenth century, laundry day was more apt to be described in satirical and humorous ways. The rigors of scrubbing, boiling, wringing, and ironing were still very much the same, if not intensified by higher standards of cleanliness and the increased quantities and more ornamental nature of clothing and furnishings after the industrialization of textile production, the increased use of cotton, and the invention of the sewing machine. People were not able to forget the rigors of the process, so they could only joke about it.

VI

Clean and Decent: A Family's Clothing

Although the rigors of washing day were a cause for humor, the piles of soiled and smelly clothing and bedding that went into the tubs were a serious matter. Clothing and bedding represented a significant investment for families at all economic levels. Those dirty shirts and petticoats, sheets and tablecloths, gowns and trousers, aprons and frocks, clouts and coolers, caps and stockings were made of costly materials and represented hours and hours of work. The style and color of counterpanes, gowns, and coats provided personal pleasure at the same time as they made significant fashion statements within the community. The larger inventory of bed and body linen helped to keep people clean and comfortable. The plain white sheets, shirts, shifts, and petticoats that formed the bulk of the weekly washing were designed to protect bed coverings and outer garments from "noxious effluvia" and body soil. In an era when few people ever washed their bodies entirely and hit the high spots only infrequently, clean linen was essential in protecting both beds and outer clothing from absorbing body odor. The coats, vests, and gowns themselves might be worn for many weeks, or even months, without any kind of cleaning. To protect these outer garments from exterior soil, farmers, teamsters, and some craftsmen wore long frocks or aprons; women wore aprons or the more encompassing coveralls called "tyers." Many women also changed their gowns in the afternoon, when the morning's hard physical work was over and they might go visiting or receive callers while performing more sedentary tasks. Indeed, women expected to do this. Elizabeth Phelps complained to Betsy that not only did she have no help on August 6, 1802, when she had "10 men to cook dinner for" and "heavy cheesemaking" to do, but "worse than that I never took off my morning cloaths till they were taken off to go to bed."[1]

A Quick Splash of Water

Regular bathing of the entire body was not a common practice in New England until well into the nineteenth century. Even after burning leaves "until almost smoked to death," on October 1, 1774, Abner Sanger only felt the need to "go to the brook and wash legs, hands, face and shoes."[2] In 1841, Miss Beecher noted that "to wash the face, feet, hands and neck is the extent of the ablutions practised by perhaps the majority of our people." However, she was certain that people in good health could take cold baths or shower baths "with entire safety and benefit," while those of more feeble constitution should be bathed in warm water. In both cases, after bathing, she felt that "the body should be rubbed with a brush or coarse towel, to remove the light scales of scarf-skin, which adhere to it, and also to promote a healthful excitement."[3]

The anonymous author of *The Mirror of the Graces* (1815) also had encouraged women to take baths but acknowledged that "the generality of English ladies seem to be ignorant of the use of any bath larger than a wash hand basin."[4] American women seem to have been equally ignorant. Anne Usher, the mistress of a small boarding school in Bristol, Rhode Island, wrote in June 1770

98. "Getting Dressed," in woodcut, c. 1840–45. Alexander Anderson Scrapbooks, Vol VIII, Print Collection, Miriam & Ira D. Wallach Division of Art, Prints and Photographs, The New York Public Library, Astor, Lenox and Tilden Foundations. This illustration was originally published in *The Pleasant Journey* (New Haven, 1845).

Dressing a child in a bedchamber, with a washstand placed directly on a carpet, without protection. This may have been a temporary arrangement, with the washstand brought to the center of the room for convenience; after the child was washed and dressed, the stand could be put back against the wall, the slops emptied, and the wet towels hung outdoors to dry. This would have been comfortable on a warm summer day with the window open; however, such a task was often moved to a warm kitchen in wintertime.

to eight-year-old Harriet Clark of Providence describing the rules of behavior that were enforced for all pupils. Harriet would be expected to rise at six o'clock, comb her hair, and wash her hands and arms. No other provisions for bathing were described, although there was a rule that indicated that the pupils must have bathed in the kitchen since they "were not to go into the kitchen except to wash."[5] Most Americans never even undressed completely, much less bathed the entire body at once.[6] The New England reformer William Alcott considered such neglect shameful and scorned those who "pass months, or even years, without washing the whole body once."[7]

Because she believed that the body exhaled waste matter through the pores during sleep, Catharine Beecher felt that it was important for children to "have the perspiration and other impurities which their exercise and sports have occasioned, removed from their bodies before going to bed." She commended parents who washed their children all over before putting them to bed, although she cautioned that it was dangerous to bathe within three hours of eating or immediately after severe exercise. To facilitate bathing, Miss Beecher suggested that "a *large tin wash-pan* should be kept for children, just large enough at bottom for them to stand in, and flaring outward, so as to be very broad at the top." This type of wash pan was lighter than a wooden tub and, being smaller at the bottom, required less water. It would also be more convenient, she asserted, because "a child can then be placed in it, standing, and washed with a sponge, without wetting the floor. It being small at the bottom, makes it better than a tub, as lighter, smaller, and not requiring so much water."[8]

In 1841, Miss Beecher recommended that separate bathing rooms equipped with access to plenty of hot water, a tub, and a drain be included in new house construction, and she joined Miss Leslie, Mrs. Farrar, and other authors in insisting that even "when families have no bathing establishment, every member should wash the whole person, on rising or going to bed, either in cold or warm water according to the constitution.[9] Apparently, she expected that this would usually be done in individual bedchambers, where the necessary amount of privacy could be assured, for she described "a washstand, bowl, pitcher, and tumbler, with a washbucket under the stand, to receive slops."[10] Although special washstands—tables with compartments designed to hold a basin, glass, and soap dish and a shelf for a pitcher or ewer of water—had been introduced by furniture makers in the mid-eighteenth century, they were not widely adopted for more than a generation, and Miss Beecher felt it necessary to offer a full description of their form and equipment. Each washstand was to be furnished

99. "THE MOST CONVENIENT MODE OF BATHING," IN JANE TAYLOR, *Woulds't Know Thyself* (NEW YORK, 1858). PRIVATE COLLECTION.

Jane Taylor recommended that people "should wash freely and rub with a coarse towel, the entire *body every day." She suggested that "in the morning, on leaving bed, [one should] step into an empty tub, and having placed a basin of water within reach, pour it on the body with the hands, or from a sponge, or a towel, rubbing the flesh at the same time. Continue this for a minute or two, then rub the whole surface vigorously, with a dry and coarse towel, till the body is all in a pleasant glow, then dress immediately." Taylor's recommendations do not include heating the water or using soap.*

with "a sponge or washcloth, and a small towel, for wiping the basin after using it. This should be hung on the washstand or towel-horse, for constant use. A soap-dish,[11] and a dish for toothbrushes, are neat and convenient, and each person should be furnished with two towels; one for the feet, and one for other purposes."[12] In addition, someone had to deliver water to the chamber, wipe up spilled water, pick up the wet towels, and remove the slops.

Of course, few households were organized according to Miss Beecher's ideal standards. Considering how often the temperature of a New England bedchamber was apt to be below freezing, it is no wonder her advice was often ignored. Sarah Emery recalled "the first wash stand I ever saw, a pretty triangular one of mahogany, a light graceful pattern to fit into a corner of a room" at the home of her newly married Aunt and Uncle Bartlett in Newburyport in 1796,[13] and washstands did become more common after that time. Still, even in the mid-nineteenth century, many people only gave their bodies an infrequent splash of cold water from a bucket near the back door. The simplest setup was that described by Hiram Munger of Chicopee Falls, Massachusetts, when he recalled an overnight visit from a preacher who "said he did not observe any accommodation for washing in his room," whereupon Munger "told him there was a good skillet out at the well and a towel behind the door."[14] Bathing in an old skillet was also something experienced by Mary Palmer while she was living with "a genuine New England farmer's family" in 1794 and found "the wash bowl was an iron skillet in which every member of the numerous family, father, mother and ten children (all who were old enough) performed their ablutions."[15] Similar arrangements are described in *Twice Married: A Story of Connecticut Life,* when "Joab finished dressing himself, hurried down to the back stoop, where, after filling an iron skillet with a pint of rain water from a hogshead at the corner, he laved his face and hands."[16]

Some sort of facilities for washing was standard in New England kitchens at all economic levels, although this was usually just a container of cold water and a towel near the back door, where it would be convenient to rinse the hands after returning from the barnyard or the privy. In summertime, the bucket might stand on a small bench near the door; in winter, it was kept close enough to the fire to keep it from freezing. William Davis recalled "a pewter ewer and bowl where I washed my hands when coming in from play" in a prosperous Plymouth, Massachusetts, household in the early nineteenth century,[17] but a wooden bucket was probably much more common. Washing up near the door made it easy for one to toss out the dirty water into the dooryard after one was finished. Frequently, a small looking glass was hung beside the door, for many men shaved in the kitchen, especially during cold weather. Even in the elegant Salem household of the Curwen family, there were facilities for bathing in the kitchen. When the antiquarian George Rea Curwen died in 1900, his will identified "the Canton China Washbowl and Water Jug which are in the washstand in the kitchen."[18]

As more and more people began to consider washstands an essential part of chamber furniture, some wealthy people had much more elaborate arrangements for bathing, even before the advocates of frequent bathing and cold-water baths began their written crusades. Bidets and tin bathtubs were available in Boston even in the late eighteenth century, and as early as 1806, Benjamin Evans, a tinplate worker who had a shop on Daniel Street in Portsmouth, New Hampshire, advertised that he had "BATHING TUBS. For Sale, or to let."[19] In 1791, Dr. Bentley described a "bathing room under the apartments of the nursery" in the elegant mansion house of the Honorable Mr. Jackson in Newbury, but he asserted that "house baths are very few indeed."[20] Although a special room for bathing, equipped with an English shower bath and running water, was constructed at Christopher Gore's country seat at Waltham, Massachusetts, in 1806, and both a shower bath and a "new English Water Closet, portable and never used," were offered at auction in Boston in 1823,[21] shower baths and tubs large enough to permit complete immersion of the body were rare indeed before 1850.

Not only did Miss Beecher feel that one should wash the entire body daily,

100. BATHING TUB MADE OF TINNED SHEET-IRON, BOSTON, C. 1842–57. COURTESY WINTERTHUR MUSEUM.

A tub of the type recommended by Catharine Beecher for its narrow base, which required a smaller amount of water. This example bears the label of Nathaniel Waterman, who sold "Superior Bathing Pans and Tubs" as well as "Patent Pneumatic Shower Baths" at his "Kitchen Furnishing Rooms, the place for all on the eve of housekeeping to procure every thing appertaining to the kitchen department, at the lowest prices, and of the best quality."

but she also asserted that body linen, or the "articles worn next to the skin should often be changed" and that "persons should not sleep in the article they wear next the skin through the day."[22] She did not go so far as to insist that nightclothes and undergarments be laundered after each wearing, however. For her, it was enough that they be aired in order to remove "much of the noxious effluvia received from the body by the clothing." Not surprisingly, she recommended that beds be thrown open and aired each morning for the same reason.[23]

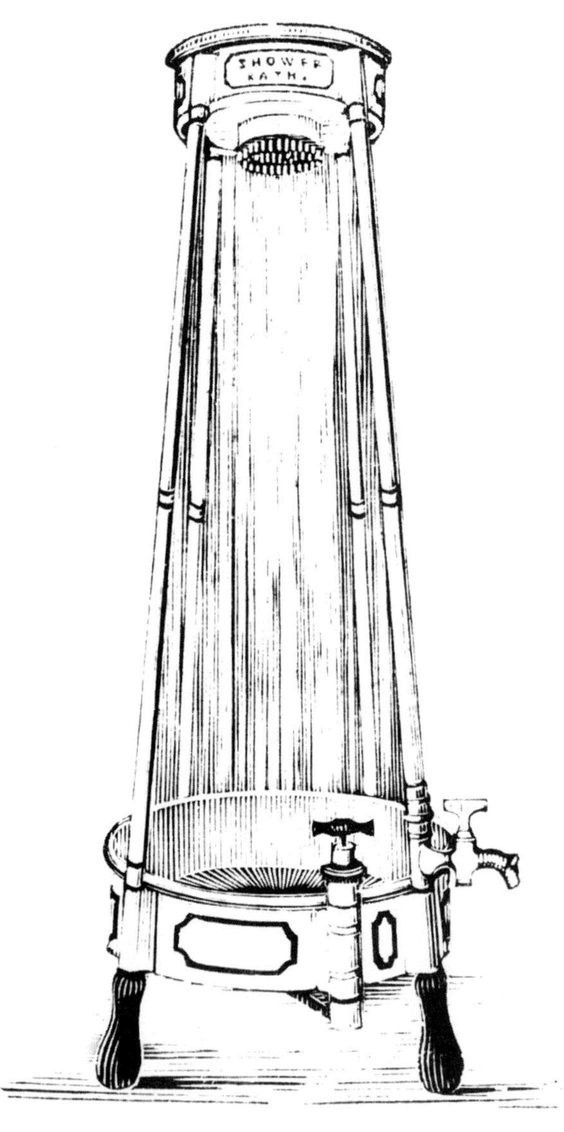

101. Shower bath, woodcut, apparently intended to be used in a metalworker's advertisement, c. 1840–45. Albert Alden proof book. Courtesy American Antiquarian Society.

Wardrobe Composition

It is usually difficult, if not impossible, to know how much clothing people owned at any given point in their lives, much less how often they changed it. Students of clothing have more often explored questions of fashion and the transmission of style, color preferences, and sources of fabrics. The early antiquarians preferred to sketch romantic pictures of hardy pioneers garbed in rough linen or woolen garments, which were the products of their own hard work and thrifty farms, or of bewigged merchants and their elegant ladies dressed in luxurious imported silks. Few of them saved or labeled everyday garments.

It is impossible to read an early–New England newspaper without being aware of the huge variety and quantity of imported textiles that were available. Thousands of yards of dozens of different kinds of goods with now-unfamiliar names were advertised almost every week. Warm and durable woolens, white linen shirting, blue-and-white checked linens, and colorful calicoes were all available at competitive prices from a very early date. As the industrial revolution transformed the British textile industry in the last half of the eighteenth century, both variety and quality increased. The nineteenth century saw rapid industrialization in New England, and, as will be shown in Chapter VII, fewer and fewer people relied on domestic production for even smaller percentages of their wardrobes.

Although many women were not directly involved in textile production, the construction and care of a family's clothing were time-consuming tasks for most of them. As household managers, wives were expected to plan, and usually to make, whatever clothing was to be worn by family members. They had to anticipate the needs of growing children, compensate for wear and tear, and make sure that everybody would be warm in wintertime. In order to do this, they had to make or acquire fabrics, select styles, develop and fit patterns, cut out garments, sew miles of fine seams, construct buttonholes, make and trim caps and bonnets, knit stockings and garters, employ specialized and supplemental help if needed, and supervise the work of others. All women and girls within the larger family were expected to help with sewing and knitting. Indeed, New England families came closer to being self-sufficient in terms of clothing production than they did in textile production. Almost no readymade garments were available other than shoes, boots, shawls, gloves, stockings, and men's hats. In the country towns, some women, like Ruth Bascom, specialized in bonnet making, but few families employed dressmakers or tailors on a large scale. Many of those who did relied on them only for cutting, fitting, and basting the bodices of women's gowns and habits or men's coats and pantaloons. They could sew the long seams themselves.

Sarah Bryant's diary illustrates the variety and quantity of the work involved in the preparation and production of a family wardrobe, and also the place of this work within the rhythm of a woman's everyday life. Six days a week, almost without fail, Mrs. Bryant sat down and picked up her needle to work on a garment for someone in the family—husband, parent, child, hired girl, farmworker, daughter-in-law, or grandchild. Once in a great while, she sewed for someone outside the family, usually as part of a reciprocal work arrangement, or for someone in special need. Over the course of a lifetime, she made literally hundreds of garments, and it must have been nice to have quiet work to do while sitting, and some projects that were small enough to be carried along

102. MRS. AMMI RUHAMAH ROBBINS, BY REUBEN MOULTHROP, 1812. DETROIT INSTITUTE OF ARTS. GIFT OF MR. AND MRS. HAROLD R. BOYER AND MR. AND MRS. FREDERICK M. ALGER, JR.

The mother of the diarist Thomas Robbins is shown with her knitting. The fine steel pins she is using were probably thinner than a modern 0000 knitting needle. Being made of steel, they developed rust spots, which made it difficult to slip the work along the pins or from one pin to the other easily.

when going visiting in the afternoon. Sewing was painstaking and required good light as well as close attention. The evening hours were better devoted to knitting.

Ruth Henshaw Bascom's diary depicts a different pattern of sewing and clothing production over a lifetime. What had been a normal amount of family sewing changed after her first husband died and intensified after her marriage to Mr. Bascom, as she made clothing, made and trimmed bonnets, and made all kinds of mourning garments for her neighbors. Late in June 1810, after an especially busy spring, Mrs. Bascom noted in her diary that she "rose early & set up late to work for others because we have no milliner in town."[24] As a minister's wife and sometime schoolteacher, she seems to have been reluctant to identify herself as a professional milliner, yet this was obviously an important source of income to her in these years. Later in life, when she was able to generate some income from her work as a profile artist, Mrs. Bascom patronized dressmakers and milliners herself. In April 1829, she went to Boston and "called at Col Watson's daughter Susan, 365 Washington st, [and] engaged her to fit a circassian cloth riding habit." Mrs. Bascom bought nine yards of fabric, lining, buttons, and other materials for the habit at other shops and paid Miss Watson "$2-40 cts for making—very cheap for Boston!"[25] A month later she returned to Boston and stopped twice at "Miss Watsons (the mantua maker's)" to have a green gown fitted.[26] Shopping seems to have been a ritual for Mrs. Bascom whenever she visited Boston. She enjoyed going to the stores, even if she didn't purchase much, as on October 9, 1830, when she "went into 20 stores & bought only 4 yds Cap ribbon."[27]

Sewing

All young girls were taught to sew, and their work was supervised by their mothers, aunts, and grandmothers. Plain sewing and marking* were also a standard part of the curriculum in girls' schools, where no one could begin an

* Embroidering letters of the alphabet in counted cross-stitch, practiced and exhibited by schoolgirls on samplers, utilized by mature women in personalizing household and personal linen.

ornamental embroidery project until she had demonstrated her proficiency with completed shirts and a sampler.

Some district-school teachers found that they were taken advantage of by busy mothers, and one late-nineteenth-century author described what might happen. "Sewing was one of the branches to be taught, and I soon learned it was an adroit way for the mothers to get the family sewing done. Small children would appear, boys as well as girls, with difficult parts of dresses to be made, also trousers both large and small. Of course, the teacher was expected to know all kinds of sewing, and little boys could not put in pockets or make buttonholes, and that was a way to get the work done by the teacher. One day my table was loaded with fourteen pairs of trousers! I took garments home and worked evenings at them, instead of doing my own sewing. I understand they are sorry I will not teach longer."[28]

103. FAMILY GROUP. WOODCUT, ALEXANDER ANDERSON SCRAPBOOKS, VOL. VIII, PRINT COLLECTION, MIRIAM & IRA D. WALLACH DIVISION OF ART, PRINTS AND PHOTOGRAPHS, THE NEW YORK PUBLIC LIBRARY, ASTOR, LENOX AND TILDEN FOUNDATIONS.

A woman is sewing and teaching a young girl to sew, while another girl reads, perhaps aloud.

Whether the work was done in school or at home, young women were proud of the shirts they stitched for their fathers and brothers. Elizabeth Phelps had stitched shirts for her brother Charles while he was in Boston. She wrote to him: "Mr. Hopkins is so obliging as to take charge of two shirts, your finest . . . they are not wash'd for we had to finish making them this morning—we have made up all your fine Holland and cambric—& sometime if you will get some more we will make them up for you—we have not made your others but shall soon and send them by the first safe opportunity." Charles must have sent more fabric, for the following April, Betsy wrote again: "As to your shirts, you shall have them as soon as possible—we shall go immediately to work upon them." By May 19, she could write: "Your shirts are ready—we wait for an opportunity to send them." On the thirtieth, she packed them up and tucked in a brief note: "I have made your shirts, with my own hand—& send them by Ma."[29]

In her diary, Sarah Bryant usually specified the name of the person for whom each garment was made; rarely is the kind of fabric identified or its source indicated. Some fabrics were purchased from local storekeepers, but cloth for coats, pantaloons, shirts, aprons, tyers, and winter gowns was woven within the family. Whenever Mrs. Bryant traveled outside Cummington, especially when she went to Northampton or Boston, she brought back fabrics, trimmings, or small articles of clothing. Peter Bryant sometimes brought fabrics when he returned from an urban area, and William Cullen Bryant sometimes sent his mother gifts of fabric from New York after he moved there. When Sarah Bryant traveled to visit her brother the Reverend Ebenezer Snell and his family in Brookfield, Massachusetts, she usually "went a shopping," taking advantage of the momentary lull in her household work to select fabrics and sewing supplies at the local store or at the larger number of shops in Northampton, where she often spent a night before returning home.

When women visited cities, especially Boston, they were careful to observe new styles and to conform as much as possible, buying new accessories and fabrics, and often a new gown, bonnet, or other garment that would serve at home as a pattern for many more. In the eighteenth century, teenaged daughters of prosperous rural families were often sent to spend a winter or two living with relatives or friends in Boston in order to learn manners and polite accomplishments such as drawing, embroidery, music, dancing, and French. Before her marriage, Sarah Emery probably traveled all of six miles, to Newburyport, in order to make her "usual winter visit in town,"[30] a change of residence that afforded her the opportunity of long visits with friends and relatives, becoming familiar with the goods in stores, observing fashionable clothing and furnishings, and attending evening parties and balls without having to travel a long distance late at night in order to get home. This practice continued into the nineteenth century and was often augmented by attendance at a young ladies' academy. Whether living with a family or at a boarding school, young women were eager to conform to urban fashions, and their letters home are laced with requests for spending money and new clothes.[31]

Visiting Boston in the summer of 1797, Betsy Phelps wrote hurriedly to her mother: "I want those silk stockings my brother left at home for me—they are very much worn now by the ladies."[32] Betsy and other fortunate young women like her wrote vivid letters describing the new styles the saw in cities. They also spent what money they had available and brought the concepts and details of new styles home with them. After Betsy Phelps spent some time in Boston in 1797, she attended meeting at Hadley wearing a new fashion and wrote to Charles: "Our good folks appear'd glad to have me return again, my *pudding* or neck cloth, was not dislik'd tho' ma said I should frighten some out of the house of worship—however I believe they withstood the shock—for I heard of no disturbance."[33] A few years later, Mrs. John Inness Clark of Providence was probably relieved by a note in a letter she received from one of her daughters, who was visiting in New York City: "Pray tell Aunt Ward that there are no new fashions—we have had our muslins made as we have had gowns for these two years past."[34] However, Lydia Trumbull of Lebanon, Connecticut, who was also visiting in New York in 1801, hadn't been able to resist buying new gowns. She wrote to her father: "I hope you will think it moderate, tho I was almost frightened at it; we have purchased us some new dresses today, as we thought they were quite necessary—we don't wish to appear as some of the young ladies we meet with [but] to dress handsomely and so as your friends would not be ashamed of us."[35] We can be sure that once those new gowns appeared in Lebanon, dressmakers of all skill levels were eager to copy them.

Sources of Fashion

People were well aware that rural styles were not as advanced as those in Boston or New York, and those who went too far in adopting the *ton* were apt to be regarded as singular. Although Betsy Phelps dared to wear her pudding neckcloth in Hadley, she knew that as long as she stayed in the country, she could avoid spending money for a hat that would be fashionable in Boston. She wrote to her brother Charles and told him that "a cheaper one would answer as well as any here in the country—and if I should ever visit Boston again—I should want a good one."[36] Knowing that Boston fashion would change, she wisely decided to defer her purchase until her next visit to town.

Keeping up with fashion was expensive and was considered by many to be an extraordinary self-indulgence. New silhouettes of gowns and styles of trimming bonnets moved most quickly among those who could afford to pay for them, but some people couldn't afford to respond to any kind of change, and those who were poorest and most isolated may not even have been aware of it. Abner Sanger had no hesitation about wearing secondhand clothing[37] and durable sheepskin breeches, moccasins, and leather mittens. His sister Rhoda could not possibly have participated in anything that would today be considered trendy, yet when it came time for her to have a new bonnet or gown, one can be sure that years of observation had paid off, and she was able to select a more contemporary style than that of the one she was relegating to next best. Those who attended meeting on Sundays had an opportunity to view each new gown and ribbon; visitors' clothing was carefully scrutinized. At any Sunday gathering one could probably have seen clothing made over a very long time.

104. RURAL SCENE, WATERCOLOR, NEW ENGLAND, C. 1810. NEW HAMPSHIRE HISTORICAL SOCIETY.

Contrasts in taste and fashion are shown, with a young couple and children dressed in the height of fashion and an older woman in the cottage doorway dressed in rural work clothing of indeterminate late-eighteenth-century style.

Thirty-year-old cloaks and greatcoats, twenty-year-old silk gowns that had been taken apart and turned, ten-year-old bonnets with new linings and trimmings all came together with the bride's new finery and the widow's solemn black. Elderly men were apt to be conservative in dress, a few wearing cocked hats and knee breeches even as late as 1825. Sarah Emery described the appearance of age differences among the women in a congregation as they entered the meeting house on a Sunday, picturing the "elderly women in close, black silk bonnets, and thick silks, or bright chintzes" with demure "Sabba'day faces," while "more youthful matrons and maidens glided in, radiant in lighter silks, white muslins or cambric calicoes, and silk hats of various hues, gaily trimmed with ribbons, flowers or long waving plumes."[38]

The late-nineteenth-century antiquarians were aware of the longevity of some of these garments, seeing them as symbols of New England frugality and individual high-mindedness. According to one of them, "topcoats, cloaks, and caps defied fashion, and apparently outlasted their wearers. The outer garments of most old men were characteristic in form and color, and like their wives, were taken for better or worse until death part them." A good example of this is Sarah Bryant's own scarlet cloak, or riding hood, which she first cut out in 1797. Although she added a satin cloak to her wardrobe the next year and acquired greatcoats in both 1799 and 1808 and a woolen habit in the cold year of 1816, she made alterations to her old scarlet cloak in 1819 and repairs to it the following year. Apparently, she gave up trying to make it presentable in 1825, for in that year she noted that she had made a gown out of her red riding hood, and she had had no other since the first one she had made, nearly thirty years before. The broadcloth that was usually used for riding hoods was so tightly felted that it would not fray, and these garments were not even hemmed. Because they were so durable, many of these scarlet cloaks survived to be labeled by antiquarians and displayed in "New England Kitchens."[39]

As in any society, young people were the most easily influenced by new fashions, and older people who paid too much attention to such things were often ridiculed.[40] This was particularly the case with the rage for thin white muslin gowns in the neoclassical, or "Grecian," style, which so inflamed New England ministers. Although Timothy Dwight stressed that these gowns were suitable only for slender young women, he felt that even young ladies being "dressed *à la Grecque* in a New England winter violates good sense, correct taste, sound morals and the duty of self preservation."[41]

Young men were not immune from the dictates of fashion, either. When William Cullen Bryant returned from Williams College in 1811, his mother Sarah made an overcoat for him before he left home to study law with Judge Samuel Howe in Worthington, Massachusetts. The young man apparently had some interest in the appearance of his clothing, for he wrote to his father in 1815: "It would be convenient for me to have an additional pair of thin pantaloons this summer—If my mother should think proper to send down a pair by you next June I should like to have them middling large—and made upon the tight knee and bell-muzzle plan."[42] His brother Rush was even more concerned that his mother in rural Cummington might not know what a young man had in mind, and he persuaded Cullen to write to their mother: "Peter [Rush] seems to think that he must have a cloak but wishes that the plaid may not be bought till he comes home, as he would like a voice in the choosing of it. It took nine yards for my cloak but it is made very full. —He likewise wishes me to say that he will need another pair of pantaloons this winter."[43]

Peter Rush Bryant was not the only young person who found fault with clothing made by a parent at home. Anne Jean Lyman's mother sent a strong letter to her daughter while she was attending George Emerson's school in Boston in 1829: "My dear Anne Jean,—I was sorry the cloak did not suit you any better, but it was made like the one from New York which we supposed to be the height of fashion. . . . Your cloak was made, with my assistance, for forty cents, which could not have been done in Boston under five dollars. It is the multiplication of such little expenses that in the aggregate make large sums. Now, the dyeing and fixing of your merino will be all the expense of a new dress, if you carry it to a mantua-maker in Boston; but if you will describe how you wish it to differ from your other gowns, I will attend strictly to your orders. You said nothing about the worked collar, but I hope you have got it and it suited you better than the cloak did. I moreover hope you will live to see what I probably shall not—a millennial existence, one in which there will be no sorrow about *clothes.*"[44]

Basic Garments

New England probate inventories seldom include detailed lists of clothing, yet those wardrobes which were recorded indicate that very few people had large numbers of any kind of garment. Women seldom owned more than four or five gowns and petticoats at a time; men usually owned a few coats and pairs of breeches or pantaloons, a few vests, and perhaps as many as half a dozen shirts. Both owned a few pairs of stockings—perhaps half a dozen; one or two pairs of shoes and boots; and a hat or bonnet. Of course, there were wealthy people who owned much more; there were also desperately poor people who owned only the clothes on their backs. Nobody changed all of their clothes daily.

Layers of clothing in natural fibers helped to keep people of all ages warm in cold weather. In both the eighteenth and the early nineteenth centuries, women wore a loose-fitting knee-length underdress called a shift as well as a petticoat under a gown. Stays were worn with fashionable clothing, but they were impractical for daily work. Expensive and inexpensive gowns differed primarily in the matter of the cost of the fabric from which they were made rather than in line or style, although some women preferred to wear hip-length short gowns over an exposed petticoat for daily work. In cut, construction, and fabric, women's shifts resembled men's shirts, although with short sleeves. Linen was standard for both until the 1830s, when cotton began to be more commonly used. In cold weather both sexes might wear fleecy woolen undervests or long flannel drawers for months at a time, although these were apparently not common. Woolen or linen stockings and stout leather shoes were everyday wear.

105. GROUP OF WOMEN CUTTING AND FITTING DRESSES, WOODCUT, C. 1845. ALEXANDER ANDERSON SCRAPBOOKS, VOL. I, PRINT COLLECTION, MIRIAM & IRA D. WALLACH DIVISION OF ART, PRINTS AND PHOTOGRAPHS, THE NEW YORK PUBLIC LIBRARY, ASTOR, LENOX AND TILDEN FOUNDATIONS.

Everyday gowns, coats, and trousers were made in practical dark colors, while white was favored for undergarments and stockings. Silk or woolen gowns, suits, and stockings were worn for best by both men and women; the uppers of women's dress shoes were also silk. Both men and women wore some kind of neckwear—usually large linen handkerchiefs for every day, but sheer muslin handkerchiefs, fichus, and collars were as fashionable for women as silk stocks were for men. Outdoors, cloaks were worn by many women and some men; others wore heavy woolen greatcoats. Everyone wore mittens or gloves and some kind of head covering when outdoors. At night, many people did not undress completely but wore their shirts or shifts to bed with wool stockings and nightcaps in wintertime to preserve warmth in the head and extremities.

Although Sarah Bryant's diary contains a remarkably detailed list of her sewing projects, it is not possible to develop an accurate inventory of the number of garments owned by each adult and child in the family, because some of them may have been sewn by Sarah's mother, a hired girl, a daughter, or a daughter-in law. Without question, Sarah Bryant coordinated the fabric selection, pattern making, and sewing efforts of all of these people; she also did much of the cutting out of clothing, as well as a great deal of the actual sewing. Still, this diary record of her own work gives us an unusual picture of wardrobe composition for each member of the family.

Perhaps most interesting to the modern reader is the relatively small number of garments made each year for each individual. Every garment was clearly intended to be worn for a long time; the diary contains frequent references to mending or altering clothing for adults as well as for children. At this time, women's and children's clothing was cut generously and made so that the size could be adjusted with tapes and drawstrings, tucks and bastings. Women who were pregnant or nursing babies did not have to have special garments, but adjusted the waistlines of their gowns, let out the drawstrings of their petticoats, adjusted a handkerchief over their bosom, and pinned it all together with long, strong, common pins. Sewing manuals suggest that only two sizes of shirt would be needed for a baby's first nine months of life; the smaller one was intended to fit for only six weeks. Many other garments for children were intended to be worn for several years and were made with broad bodices gathered on drawstrings and generous tucks and hems that could be let down as a child grew. People who were dressed in this way certainly lacked uniformity in the height of their hemlines and the bulkiness of their silhouette.

Even in years of relative prosperity, Sarah Bryant's own wardrobe was small by modern standards. In 1801, the young mother of three children acquired three new shirts; one half robe; two silk gowns, one of them made of Italian striped silk; two short gowns, one of them calico; and one worsted skirt, or petticoat, to wear with the short gowns. She also acquired a satin cloak, a muslin shawl, a spencer, and a tippet, as well as a sable muff, a black silk handkerchief, a pair of gloves, a fur cap, another cap, a white bonnet, two pairs of shoes, and four pairs of stockings, one of them cotton. This lavishness can be compared with 1820, the year her husband died, when her total clothing acquisitions were confined to a homespun plaid wool gown, a calico gown, a pelisse, a mourning bonnet, one pair of stockings, and the repair of her shoes.

When Peter Bryant died, his will directed that his new drab greatcoat be given to his eldest son, Austin; his blue cloak to his second son, William Cullen; his best hat to Peter Rush; and his second-best hat to Cyrus. The appraisers of his estate listed the value of his clothing, singling out a cloak valued at eighteen dollars, a coat valued at twelve dollars, a greatcoat valued at fourteen dollars, and a watch valued at eighteen dollars; the remainder, including the two hats, was listed simply as "Sundry other articles of clothing" worth seventy-five dollars.[45] According to his wife's diary, his new coat was four years old, having been made in 1816. Prior to that, he had not had a new greatcoat since 1799, although it had been altered in 1804.[46]

Dr. Bryant's wife's diary gives much more information about the composition of his wardrobe than does his probate file. She made him an average of five new shirts each year, along with two to four pairs of trousers or pantaloons, a coat, and a jacket or two. She also made him a pair of mittens and one or two pairs of new stockings annually. Although he wore small clothes, or knee breeches, until at least 1806, he never had a new pair after that time. The diary reveals that Peter Bryant wore both drawers and underwaistcoats, the latter made of flannel, especially as his consumption worsened in 1818 and 1819. Five years after Peter Bryant's death, his widow made over his blue wool coat for their eighteen-year-old-son John. This may have been anticipated, for Dr. Bryant's will specified that all the residue of his wearing apparel be given to Sarah "to be distributed among his 3 youngest sons."

As babies, the Bryant children were dressed alike in shirts, slips, coolers,[47] covers, frocks, gowns, and petticoats. Austin had his first coat and trousers at twenty-eight months of age, Cullen at thirty-one months, and Cyrus at twenty-nine months; presumably, these dates coincided with successful toilet training. Throughout their childhood, their mother made most of their clothing, including stockings, mittens, and some shoes. She usually made one or two shirts and pairs of trousers for each boy and two or three gowns, petticoats, and tyers and one bonnet for each girl. With a family of seven growing children, clothing was passed along, mended, and altered to fit whoever was closest in size.

Clothing for Special Occasions

Throughout New England, distinctive garments were made for special occasions, such as enrollment in the militia, membership in a masonic lodge, participation in an exhibition at school, weddings, and funerals. While wedding clothing and graduation gowns were intended to be used for best for many years to come, militia coats and hats, masonic aprons, and other distinctive uniforms were restricted in their use.

When someone died, it was unusual for him or her to be buried in everyday garb, and neighbors stitched special grave clothes or a shroud to dress the body for burial. When one of a neighbor's twins died in 1813, Ruth Bascom "prepared a little suit and dressed it for the last time and returned home at tea." Three days later, she was called again to the same house and "prepared some clothes for Mr. Whiting's 2d infant who died at 10—went over there, assisted in laying it out, returned at 1 PM. and made Lucy Whiting [the children's mother] a mourning bonnet."[48]

Ruth Bascom's special skill in preparing mourning garments was recognized even before her first husband, Dr. Miles, died in 1805. After Mrs. Adams died of consumption on June 20 of that year, Ruth "went a shopping with Mrs. Moore and purchased materials for bonnet, gowns, mitts &c for Mr. Adams children—cut out vandykes &c—Betsy Denney assisted in sewing for them at

106. *Memorial to Shuabel Abbe*, EMBROIDERY, WINDHAM, CONNECTICUT, C. 1804–10. PHOTOGRAPH BY RICHARD MERRILL. COURTESY OF THE SOCIETY FOR THE PRESERVATION OF NEW ENGLAND ANTIQUITIES.

Worked by a young woman in memory of her father, this picture depicts members of his family in their distinctive black mourning clothes.

Dr. Flints." She continued working on the bonnets with four other women all the next day, and she "sew'd till after dinner on bonnets, &c." before the one o'clock funeral itself. On August 5 she worked with more than four other women on "mourning clothes for Wm Dennys family; their child died this morning at 1 oClock of the disentery, aged 20 months." The next day they "sewed and at 3 finished all the things—4 gowns, five bonnets, four scarfs, 2 pr mitts, &c."[49] Sometimes Ruth stayed up very late at night in order to finish mourning clothes for other people.[50] However, not everyone had new mourning clothes for a funeral. When a child of the Basset family died in June 1813, "the family concluded to borrow their mourning." Still, there was sewing to do. Mrs. Bascom made a new wreath for one of the bonnets, and a neighbor made alterations to fit a mourning gown.[51] Mrs. Bascom herself wore borrowed mourning garments to attend the funeral of her husband's brother when he died unexpectedly on March 7, 1814, and was buried the same day.[52] At this time, it was generally recognized as important for people to be furnished with the distinctive clothing that symbolized their grief and loss. These black garments were worn both at the funeral and at the regular Sunday meeting the following week. Mrs. Bascom's diary contains many notices of people attending meeting in family groups "as mourners." How long they wore mourning garments afterward is not well documented, although Ruth herself observed the tradition that widows wear mostly black for at least a year. When George Washington died in 1799, some women in Boston dressed in mourning "as much as if for a relation, some entirely in black, but now [a month later] many wear only a ribbon with a line painted on it.[53]

Even when she was in mourning for her first husband, Ruth did not lose interest in fashion. She visited Sally Lynde while on a trip to Boston in December 1805 and had Sally help her make a bonnet, a black silk spencer trimmed with velvet, new trimming for a plum-colored lutestring pelisse, and full sleeves for a black silk gown. She was still wearing black when she was published to Mr. Bascom less than a year after Dr. Miles had died.[54] Later, when Mr. Bascom's brother-in-law died, she made herself a black silk dress and bonnet out of old ones in her possession.[55]

Mending

Thrifty New Englanders kept their clothing in good repair and extended its longevity with finely sewn seams and durable fabrics. It was not at all unusual to cut apart garments that had outlived their usefulness and to restyle them or make them over for another family member. This was, of course, most commonly done when adult clothing was cut down for children, but both silk and woolen garments could be carefully taken apart, cleaned, and the pieces turned over and stitched back together again. With the unfaded side turned out and worn spots concealed, a dress, coat, or vest would be good for many more years.

Even though garments were not laundered every time they were worn, washing, ironing, and mending were considered part of the regular weekly ritual of clothing care. On Saturdays, the clothes that passed over the ironing board were carefully examined, and those that needed repair were set aside for mending or patching, which were done promptly. Sarah Bryant's diary entries for Saturdays almost always indicate that she mended as well as ironed on that day. After the hard work of ironing, which Sarah usually combined with baking, it must have been a satisfying pleasure to sit comfortably in a chair and work through a basket of mending, having all in order at the close of the week.

Women kept supplies of patches and mending yarn readily available. Catharine Beecher suggested that patches be sorted by color and kept in bags in a closet, rather than jumbled together in the sewing basket. Stockings might be darned with new yarn, but some were repaired with yarn unraveled from stockings that were worn beyond repair. Some women wove extra yarn into the toes and heels of stockings to prolong their wear, and some even lined the heels of their stockings with pieces of old calico. Since the feet of stockings wear out more quickly than the legs, new feet could be knitted and joined to old stocking legs. Anything that could be done to extend the life of the stockings was worth a try. In a large household, there were always stockings to mend; on August 6, 1802, Elizabeth Phelps wrote to her daughter Betsy: "There is now more than 15 or 20 pair of stockings to mend."[56]

Soon after she set up housekeeping in Litchfield, Connecticut, Betsy Phelps Huntington found herself faced with a big backlog of all kinds of mending to be done. She wrote to her mother: "I have been mending old waistcoats and stockings all this week—have been at work all this day upon a sattin waist-coat, which Mr H will wear on his journey." She wrote again on Friday: "Today I

107. "LADIES SEWING BIRDS," ADVERTISING BROADSIDE OF C. E. STEARNS, MIDDLETOWN, CONNECTICUT, 1851. CONNECTICUT HISTORICAL SOCIETY, HARTFORD.

Companionable sewing at a parlor table strewn with shears, sections of a bodice pattern, and other equipment. The broadside promotes the use of "Ladies Sewing Birds" as "useful articles" that could be clamped to a tabletop. By securing in the beak of the bird one end of a piece of fabric that was to be hemmed and thus creating tension with the sewing bird rather than the fingers, a seamstress could sew much more rapidly. The device is here advertised as a boon to health as well, for its use would enable a person to sit up straight while sewing rather than bending over and holding the work against her knees.

have been mending again—and think I have nearly finished. . . . I have all John's summer cloaths to make—three shirts for my husband—besides some mending, and preparation for myself." The following Monday, she was still at it: "I have been mending and must now cut out my husband's shirts."[57]

Betsy had discovered something that was part of the endless routine for all women—patching, sewing, knitting, and darning. Perhaps because this aspect of women's work did not change significantly in the mid-nineteenth century, it is one that was not romanticized by those looking back at the "olden times."[58] When they thought about earlier times, they envisioned the homespun-clad woman at her spinning wheel or the gentleman in his closely fitted broadcloth coat. They preferred to ignore the overflowing mending baskets and those sociable afternoons when women sewed for hours to make or mend clothing for their families. They neglected to identify the work of professional milliners and tailors while they labeled the wedding gowns, beribboned bonnets, and the tiniest baby clothes with the names of their original owners. They ignored the ill-fitting and bad-smelling garments, the worn aprons and the moth-eaten woolen trousers, the stained nankeen trousers of little boys, and the little girls' tumbled calico frocks with worn-out pockets, consigning many of them to the ragbag, whence they emerged as quilts or carpets. They forgot that all of the new styles and many of the fabrics had originated in England, and that fashion had bred envy and symbolized grief as well as joy.

VII

Toward Our Mutual Support

On a busy August Saturday in 1824, Sarah Bryant "scoured more than a hundred skeins of yarn—colored with smart weed some mixed yarn for filling to a piece—made five gallons of currant wine—churned."[1] Relieved of some of the direct responsibility for household management by living with her son and daughter-in-law, and apparently almost untouched by the industrialization of the textile industry which was accelerating at that very moment, the fifty-six-year-old widow continued to utilize her own skills and the products of the family farm in a productive way. It really did not matter to her what would become of the butter, who would drink the currant wine, or how the finished cloth would be used. In the thrifty world she knew, it was essential that not a thing or a moment be wasted. She—and others like her, both then and now—believed that every thing and every minute could be turned to some kind of advantage by frugal and industrious people. Sarah Bryant's labor enhanced her life by earning her cash or store credits, by creating products for direct exchange with neighbors, or by making it possible for her to step into a warm and colorful new winter gown, sip a flavorful homemade wine, or spread her butter thickly on a piece of freshly baked bread. She was gratified by the knowledge that her labor contributed to the support of her family, whether directly or indirectly, and that it could also permit her to be charitable with her neighbors if the need arose or to be hospitable if someone came to visit.

The work accomplished by the individual members of the Bryant household contributed to the well-being of all of them. Much of it was directly related to providing food, clothing, heat, and light, yet the family was not self-sufficient, nor were any of their neighbors. Even families that were considered successful did not totally provide for themselves. Few owned enough land, tools, or raw materials, or controlled enough labor, to be completely self-sufficient. The most prosperous people in any New England town were the most highly specialized in terms of production and the most heavily involved in the extensive and complex interchange of goods and services that made possible the relative self-sufficiency of the village.[2] In contrast, some New Englanders lived in neighborhoods referred to as "hardscrabble," "Podunk," or "two-penny parish"—places where people lived in decidedly substandard housing, struggled to scratch a living from infertile rocky soil, earned some supplemental income from a string of odd jobs, and subsisted on a diet notably lacking in vitamins and protein. As wealth increased, so did the standard of living, with its expectation of imported textiles, foodstuffs, cups and saucers, brass candlesticks, forks, and drinking glasses, and its more complicated social rituals.

Economic relationships within a community were based on complex credit systems more often than on the direct exchange of goods or money. People with particular talents needed to exchange their specialized work with others in order to make certain that their families were provided with what they needed. A good example of this is shown in the eighteenth-century account book of Asa Talcott of Glastonbury, Connecticut, which documents the wide range of goods and services that were accepted as payment for his work as a tailor. At the same time, the account book makes it clear that, like 95 percent of New Englanders who lived in country towns, Talcott engaged in small-scale farming as well as a profession—in his case, tailoring—and that his work provided supplies and essential equipment repairs for his wife's work as both a seamstress and a traditional housewife. Talcott took credits in food (some wheat, pork and beef, many bushels of Indian corn, pecks of beans, and pounds of salmon, molasses, and salt) and beverages (rum and brandy), labor (plowing, sledding, driving animals, cutting wood, dressing flax, roping onions, carting wood and dung, fence work, painting, making a coffin and digging a grave, and the unspecified work of men, boys, and teams of oxen), transportation (ferriage across the Connecticut River and the use of other people's vehicles and horses), farm supplies (apple trees, hooks, boards, nails, seeds, hog rings, and pasturage), repairs (harness mending, cooperage, fixing a chimney, bottoming chairs), specialized services (sheathing a bayonet, hairdressing and cutting, butchering, blacksmithing, taking an inventory and distributing an estate, drawing a tooth, "bleeding Mrs. Talcott," building shelves in the tailor shop, crowning chairs, making a ferrule for a walking stick, grinding corn, and replacing the handle on a pint cup, altering a gunlock, mending a porringer, setting a razor, rimming and bailing a skillet, mending a spur, repairing shoes and boots), housekeeping supplies (scouring sand, soap), and household furnishings (tea dishes, a brass skimmer, and a chafendish), as well as goods and services more directly related to the tailoring business (carding wool; scouring, pressing and coloring cloth; dressing flax, weaving, and washing; coloring Talcott's own hat; brass buckles; yards of cloth; and repairing and sharpening buttonhole cutters).

In 1774, Asa Talcott remade an old coat for Phineas Grosvenor and provided the necessary buckram and thread for a job that was worth twelve shillings. In payment, Talcott agreed to give three shillings' credit for "a puppy dog" that he had received from Grosvenor six months previously, and he waited a year and a half before receiving the cash payment of nine shillings with which he balanced the account.[3] As a skilled tailor, Asa Talcott cut and made coats, greatcoats, pantaloons, and vests for neighboring men. His primary tools were pins and needles, scissors, buttonhole cutters, and a tailor's goose, or large iron. Occasionally he made clothing for motherless children and tailored habits and cloaks for women. Less than half of his work as a tailor was devoted to making new garments, though. A large percentage of his time was spent in cutting and fitting garments that were then sewn and finished in their owners' homes, and in cutting apart, turning over the fabric, and resewing or resizing old clothing to extend its period of usefulness. When there was no tailoring to be done, he tended his own fields, chopped his own wood, or worked for his neighbors in exchange for their services, for credits, or for cash. Only occasionally did he credit his wife for help in the tailoring business, sewing seams or covering buttons. She had plenty of her own work to do.

Talcott's exchange of his specialized skills as a tailor is typical of that of many essential members of rural communities. Potters, butchers, millers, and clothiers found their services in seasonal demand; those who depended on water power to operate their mills could not work when the streams were frozen or when there was a serious drought. Surveyors, blacksmiths, coopers, tanners, and carpenters worked when there was a need for their services; everyone, usually even ministers, lawyers, and doctors, worked at woodcutting, maple sugaring, haying, sowing, and harvesting.

Asa Talcott provided his wife with raw materials, equipment, and repairs to the equipment for her basic work. Like most women, her work was focused on food, clothing, and care of the house and family, but much of this, too, was tied to agricultural productivity and the changing seasons, and it had measurable value in the rural economy. In every community a complex web of exchanges of goods and services maximized skills and raw materials at the same time that it enriched the lives of individuals. Women contributed to the household economy by producing goods for domestic consumption and for credit; some of them also sought employment outside the home. In 1762, Samuel Lane noted the effects of diminished agricultural production on families in Stratham, New Hampshire: "Poor women . . . by reason of the uncommon scarcity of flax & wool . . . cannot get Employ; . . . those that are able and willing to work for their Living are obliged to be Idle, and Consequently had no income to support themselves withal."[4] Some women were employed by the day, supplementing regular help in prosperous families or pitching in when another woman became ill and assisting with laundry, spinning, nursing, and general housework. Other women provided more specialized services, such as tailoring, millinery, midwifery, or weaving. Throughout her lifetime, Elizabeth Phelps hired women to assist with these and other specific chores. Some of them were close neighbors; others came from nearby Hadley or from Hatfield and Northampton, on the other side of the Connecticut River.

Sometimes complex work exchanges took place between family units rather than between individuals. Ebenezer Parkman noted this kind of interchange in his diary on February 12, 1779, when "Mr. Thos. Warrin & Stephen Maynard cutt up part of ye woodpile today to pay Mrs. Parkman for knitting for ye latter of ym. They dined. They work till evening."[5] In these relationships as well as within each individual household, the worlds of men and women overlapped in both house and barn, dooryard and woodlot, kitchen garden and broad field. Sarah Bryant was involved in this kind of complex economic exchange throughout her life. On January 11, 1832, when she was sixty-five years old, she began to sew a spencer for Latimer Briggs. The next day, Mr. Briggs "came to thresh wheat," and the following day "to work." On the fourteenth, Sarah Bryant "finished a spencer for Latimer Briggs."[6]

Many of the financial records of this kind of work were kept by men in complex double-entry account books. In a nearly cashless society, the financial value of goods and services was carefully calculated and accounted for in order to make certain that people were treated fairly. Accounts sometimes ran for months or years before being settled, although they were usually balanced at least once a year, often on January 1. The exchanges of goods and services between women were less frequently accounted for in such formal ways, but they were no less valuable. A few women kept records in diaries or account books; for many the entire system was based on memory and trust. Because very little of the women's work is documented in traditional written sources, it has remained invisible to historians; this has contributed to the concept of household self-sufficiency and the idealization of the productive housewife.

Some women left their own homes to provide important services to others—nursing, delivering babies, washing and ironing clothes, and cleaning houses. At home, most women's productive "earning work"[7] was related to dairying, textile production, dressmaking, or millinery, but even in the eighteenth century, some women made money by stitching shoe uppers or covering buttons, like Mrs. Talcott. In the early nineteenth century, New England women and girls made straw braid, bonnets, or palm-leaf hats; wove carpets; and stitched shoes. Ruth Bascom worked as a milliner for nearly twenty years before she began her active career as a profile artist, and, like many women, she was always able to turn to her needle for employment if necessary. All of these activities were valuable to those who were able to use them to earn things they wanted or needed, but none appealed to the nineteenth-century idealist more than domestic textile production.

Homespun

Despite the reality of messy straw braiding and smelly cheesemaking in many New England kitchens, the popular idea of a New England household as a bustling hive of domestic production usually centers on a bountiful table, a warm hearth, and continuous spinning. Francis Underwood painted a perfect picture of a house in *Quabbin,* where "the most notable objects in the long kitchen were the spinning-wheels—a small one for flax, getting out of use more than sixty years ago, and a large one for wool, which was often seen down [perhaps] to 1850. . . . A pot of blue dye (fortunately covered) stood in the corner of the fireplace. This departed with the spinning wheels."[8] Certainly no image of the New England home is more powerful than that conjured up by the sight of a spinning wheel. In literature and fine art, in high-style domestic interiors and historic house museums, spinning and the spinning wheel have been seen as an essential expression of the New England woman's devotion to her home and family, and as suggestive of self-sufficiency. The monotonous thump of the loom in a chilly shed chamber and the laborious and messy preparation of flax and woolen fibers, although both real and necessary, were far less appealing.

Recalling her girlhood in the 1770s in a small-town parsonage, seventy-year-

108. WOMAN SPINNING BY A FIRE, POSED BY C. ALICE BAKER AND PHOTOGRAPHED BY EMMA COLEMAN IN THE NIMS HOUSE, DEERFIELD, BETWEEN 1892 AND 1909. COURTESY OF THE SOCIETY FOR THE PRESERVATION OF NEW ENGLAND ANTIQUITIES.

This picture was published in George Sheldon's The Little Brown House on the Albany Road *(Deerfield, 1915), with the caption, "From the flax taken in barter for the products of David's labor, she spun and twisted the honest thread with which his seams were closed; and while her foot pressed the treadle, and her busy fingers gauged and guided the slender thread her buzzing wheel sang a lullaby."*

old Eliza Buckminster Lee wrote in 1838: "All the linen and cotton for the use of the family were spun in the house. The weaving was done by poor women of the village."[9] In a history of Antrim, New Hampshire, published in 1877, W. R. Cochrane tells us: "For many years, almost every article worn by man or woman, young or old, in this town, was spun, woven, colored and made here. Every woman knew how to do every part. Men had their whole suits of 'striped cloth' and these were worn to church and everywhere else. In later days, they took the plain white woolen cloth to the 'fulling mill' and had it 'dressed' for 'nice suits,' either blue or black, or what the old folks called 'blue-black.' Blankets and table-cloths were always made at home, and were taken as tests of the woman's skill. The maiden manufactured her own 'outfit,' as it was called; and her 'intended,' as they named the happy creature, had ample chance to judge her work beforehand. Every woman in this town had her 'patch of growing flax,' which she cultivated herself. From this they made strong and beautiful linens, of many styles."[10] Cochrane's account, for all its rich detail, is typical of those of many town historians,[11] who did not realize the actual scarcity of raw materials and equipment, oversimplified the production process, attributed technical skills to too many people, and romanticized what was already known as "the age of homespun."[12]

Despite these rosy descriptions, New England's domestic textile production was neither universal nor all-encompassing. The successful British mercantile policy had been designed to discourage the development of commercial textile production in the colonies and to support British imports. Some Colonial New England farms produced high-quality linens and coarse woolen cloth for their own use. Professional weavers and clothiers could produce more highly finished goods, but there were few of them. In the Colonial period, perhaps half of all households owned spinning wheels, and in some areas fewer than 10 percent owned looms, raised sheep, or cultivated flax.[13] In settled farming areas in the Connecticut Valley and in some parts of Worcester and Essex counties in Massachusetts, a higher percentage of the population was actively engaged in textile production; but in many farmhouses there was only a single great wheel on which the wool from a small flock of thin sheep was spun for stocking yarn.

Domestic textile production in New England centered on bed and table linen; linen for shirts, shifts, petticoats, aprons, and summer pantaloons; coarse woolens for work clothing for men and boys; and a variety of linen and woolen garments for infants and young children. During both the American Revolution and the War of 1812, homespun textiles were associated with domestic necessity and patriotism, as the idea of American independence was merged with self-sufficiency. In the more successful farming areas, textile production increased during the years after the Revolution, when patriotic sentiment combined with economic necessity; self-sufficiency was often expressed as a goal. The *Massachusetts Spy* printed "A New Year's Gift," or wish, in 1789 that "the exertions of almost every member of the community yield the most lively prospect of the future greatness of this rising empire. Our young women grow less ashamed of putting forth their hands to the distaff, and our young men to the plough."[14] Shortly thereafter, the local reporters who responded to Alexander Hamilton's survey of American manufactures described the state of local production. William Hillhouse reported that in Montville, a town in New London County, "the Familys make plain Cloth, Bearskin, thin Cloth & Linnen for Family Use, they also make Check[d] flanning [flannel] & Tow Cloth, which the Women Barter with the Storekeepers for Calicoes, Muslins and other Female Clothing and ornaments." Hillhouse wished to encourage the expansion of domestic textile production and suggested that "the Good People in their Patriotism to Eat and Make away with as much Lamb and Mutton Sheep as possible instead of other Meat, which would make such Demand for Sheep as would induce the raising them, for it is a Well None fact, that the Wool that is Shorn from Sheep is no Compensation to the Farmer for keeping them."[15] New England's native sheep produced a meager fleece, and considerable attention was given in the early national period to improving wool production by introducing merino sheep and practicing selective breeding. Carding mills to process wool were erected in many country towns, and premiums for high-quality textiles were offered at agricultural fairs. Spinning-wheel makers conducted successful businesses and advertised their products. Among families in Hampshire County, Massachusetts, who had owned almost twice as many looms as those in other Massachusetts counties before the Revolution, the number increased to 19 percent during the years 1780–1820.[16]

On September 3, 1788, the editor of the Hampshire *Gazette,* in Northampton, Massachusetts, printed a long letter to the editor purported to be from "A Farmer" and titled "Cause of Hard Times." This is a diatribe against the evils of conspicuous consumption and a virtual hymn to Jeffersonian politics, dutiful women, and absolute self-sufficiency. The alleged author was a farmer who described the financial ruin that had fallen upon him as a result of the extravagance and folly of his wife and daughters. The farmer claimed that "nothing to wear, eat or drink was ever purchased" and that they "never spent more than ten dollars a year, which was for salt, nails, and the like." He claimed that when his first daughter was to be married, she "had been a working dutiful girl, and therefore I fitted her out well and to her mind; for I told her to take of the best of my wool and flax, and to spin herself some gowns, [petti]coats, stockings, and shifts: nay I suffered her to buy some cotton, and make into sheets, as I was determined to do well by her." Things changed for the second girl, however, and his wife persuaded him to give her some money, which she spent on "a calimanco petticoat, a set of stone tea-cups, half a dozen pewter tea-spoons, and a tea kettle, things that never were seen in my house before." Things went even further for the third daughter, who had "a silken gown, silk for a cloak, looking glass, china tea-geer, and a hundred other things." To the farmer's disgust, large quantities of clothing were purchased, and "the wheel goes only for exchanging our substantial cloth of flax and wool for gauze, ribbands, silk, tea, sugar, &c." The farmer selected imported textiles, tea, and tea equipage as symbols of economic decline. For him, these were things that wasted time and money, and he declared "the tea kettle shall be sold" so that his wife and daughters could revert to their former thrifty habits. Most important, the entire family would be dressed in homespun flax and wool; nothing was to be purchased to feed vanity or idleness. In celebrating self-sufficiency and rural virtue, the author of this charming little tale admired and described a world that did not really exist in New England at the time he wrote, and probably never did.[17]

Looking back over a lifetime to 1801, when she was finally able to set up her household in Brattleboro, Vermont, Mary Palmer Tyler asserted that she had been quick to establish domestic textile manufacturing.

> All this time my . . . spinning wheels were busily attended, . . . by myself, with the assistance of one and at times two girls. Our sheep furnished wool, and we raised flax. I spun all the thread I used for years, whitening some, and coloring some, and some keeping flax color. I hired a girl to spin what I wanted wove, and the tow also, with which we made cloth for sheets and common table linen. Mrs. Peck could weave very nice diaper, which we bleached at home. After she left us, Mrs. Fisher did my weaving, but having to give nine pence a yard for the weaving, I suggested to your father the expediency of getting a loom, and having our flax and wool wove in the house. Ever ready to comply with my wishes, he got one immediately, and for twelve or fifteen years we made the children's clothes summer and winter for common wear.[18]

Many homespun woolen goods were used in the coarse state in which they came from the loom, making them easily identifiable, and unfashionable in certain circles. Still, they were warm and serviceable for children's winter clothing, men's work pantaloons, everyday winter petticoats, and other simple garments; but there is little evidence of even the poorest people dressing exclusively in homespun flax or wool. The 1785 probate inventory of Joseph Barnard of Deerfield, Massachusetts, included a homespun coat and vest, but very few of his neighbors owned even one similar garment. Practicality and economic necessity dictated the patterns of use of these fabrics in rural families. One woman wrote, "I can assure you that my children are now warmly clad in the fleeces our sheep wore last winter; and, though a homespun frock on the baby scandalized his Aunt Catherine, he wears one every day and finds no fault with it."[19] Beginning in the 1770s and continuing even to the present day, those who have honored or sought self-sufficiency admire the thrift and virtue of those who wear homespun, but pejorative attitudes persist among fashionable people.

Imported Textiles

A quick look at any general merchant's account book or the advertisements in an early newspaper reveals at once the huge quantity and tremendous variety of textiles imported from Britain during the Colonial period. Long lists of fine broadcloth, shalloon, tammy, harrateen, kersey, and other woolen yard goods, as well as blankets, silks, velvets, and corduroy; damask woven, plain, and checked linens; and block- and plate-printed, striped, checked, or plain cottons of all kinds were readily available in city and country. With independence, French prints and Italian silks, Russian linens, Indian cottons, and Chinese silks and coarse cottons called nankeen were added to the offerings; and soon the impact of the industrial revolution was reflected in lower prices, more interesting printed designs, and an even greater variety of British goods.

Homespun and locally woven fabrics could not compare with the fine quality of these imported textiles. Even in homes where large quantities of fabrics were spun and woven, imported fabrics of finer quality, richer color, and more interesting design were purchased for women's gowns, men's and boy's coats, bedding, and upholstery. This is well documented in family textile collections preserved in both local historical societies and larger museums of art and history, as well as in household accounts. The collections of textiles from the Robbins family that Ellen Stone gave to the Society for the Preservation of New England Antiquities; the Wilbur family textiles from Swansea, Massachusetts, which are now at Old Sturbridge Village; and the Copp family textiles from Stonington, Connecticut, at the National Museum of American History[20] all contain a wide variety of bed and table linens, towels, children's clothing, shifts, shirts, blankets, and checks made on home looms, as well as colorful quilts made of samples of the imported harrateens, plate-printed furnishing fabrics, and block-printed cotton dress goods once used in these families.

Imported sheeting, shirting, blanketing, and checks were often similar in quality to those that could be produced at home, yet for people with cash or ready credit, there was often a price advantage to the imported goods. Elihu Hoyt described such a case in a letter to his wife, Hannah, in Deerfield, written from Boston on January 25, 1805, in response to her request that he purchase some indigo: "I recollect you wished to have me get some Indigo to make a short piece of check—if you want but a few yards I think I can get it here better than to trouble yourself to make it, there is different kinds both linnen & Cotton—some coarse & some very fine of all widths—if you should think it better to get what little you want here, send me an account of quantity & quality, width, etc."[21]

Domestic Textiles

Some households produced finished yard goods for sale even during the Colonial period, but there was a tremendous increase in this kind of production in the early years of the new nation. Plain and checked linens, tow cloth, sacking and bagging, rough woolens, and flannels were woven for sale or store credits. Storekeepers specified in their advertisements the quality or quantity of the goods they wanted, in addition to the type: "home-made Flannel . . . of good quality and full yard wide"; "whitened Tow Cloth"; "2000 yards of check'd and white FLANNEL"; "real good Linen Stripes and Checks, 4-4 brown or well bleach'd Tow Cloths, Diapers and Bed Ticks"; "500 Meal Bags, twenty two inches wide, thirty six inches long, ALSO, 100 Meal Bags, of the common size"; "100 good Corn BAGGS"; "Homespun Check Linen"; and "3000 yards CHECK'D WOOLLEN SHIRTING, made in the following manner, 3-4ths wedth—half-blue, and 4-4ths check" were among those called for in the Connecticut *Courant,* the Massachusetts *Spy,* and the Hampshire *Gazette* between 1787 and 1809. William Porter of Hadley, Massachusetts, placed an ad in the Hampshire *Gazette* on December 9, 1801, noting that he "thanks those that have favored him with their custom the year past, and still wishes to encourage the Industrious Females, by receiving Check'd Flannel, do. Linnen, Bedticks, Brown and White Tow Cloth, Fulled Cloth and Meal Bags in Exchange."

109. BLACK GLAZED REDWARE PITCHER, ENGLAND, C. 1770. OLD STURBRIDGE VILLAGE. NEGATIVE NUMBER B17226.

This pitcher was given to Olive Sargent, of Brattleboro, Vermont, in exchange for several days of weaving. Tradition tells us that she was so disgusted to receive so little reward for her work that she almost smashed the pitcher right then and there.

Even though these were fairly basic materials requiring little weaving skill, apparently some goods offered for sale were not up to standard. A long letter in the Hampshire *Gazette* published on September 20, 1790, listed criteria for woolen cloth that would compete with imported goods and thus command the best price. It was recommended that the cloth be woven five quarters (forty-eight inches, or one and a quarter yards) wide, with firm selvages of ten or twelve threads on each side, and that the pieces be at least thirty yards in length. The author urged that attention be given to sorting fleece so that the finished woolen goods would be even in texture after they were fulled, and that only white flannels be woven for market. He further cautioned that "people are apt to think, because they wear checkered or striped cloth themselves, that the same will suit best in the market. This is a mistake. None but white is worn in the large towns, and none but white is ever imported." This good advice came almost too late, for the impending technological revolution in textile making soon rendered large-scale home manufacture obsolete. After 1800, there were fewer calls for linen yard goods or flannels and more for knitted mittens and stockings, indicating a decline in local weaving for credit and a continuation of spinning and knitting as a means of processing home-grown wool. In some places, domestic weaving for credit continued for a few decades; a textile worker in a factory at Lowell recalled in 1845 that before she left home, she and her sisters "had to make tow and linen cloth to purchase our white dresses and summer bonnets."[22]

As competition from factory production increased, skilled weavers were recruited to participate in the outwork system, weaving factory-spun cotton yarns on home looms for commercial production. Other weavers turned their attention to carpet making, again using woolen or factory-spun cotton warps and locally spun and colored woolen or rag wefts. Some continued in the old way, weaving coarse kerseys and tow cloth to contribute to a meager income. Still others, in prosperous families, free from the demands of the marketplace, experimented with much more complex weaving patterns, and some of the most beautiful hand-woven textiles from New England households date from this period.

The Annual Cycle of Work

Textile production is labor-intensive and messy, and demands bulky equipment and a large amount of space. Because the process is time-consuming, it has an impact on the household throughout the entire year. In households where both flax and wool were raised, the process began with washing and shearing sheep in the spring. Scouring and carding were necessary before the wool could be spun, and there were few mills with carding machines available before 1800. Usually the new wool was put aside in large bags during extraordinarily hot weather and the busy summer months. On August 29, 1791, Ruth Henshaw recorded the beginning of a long process: "I began our wool by breaking 3 or 4 pounds"; in December, she was still carding and spinning wool.[23] Weaving woolen cloth began sometime in the fall and usually continued until it had all been woven or work was halted by severely cold weather in the weaving room. Flax was harvested in summertime, soaked or retted to loosen the long linen fibers within each stalk, then set aside to dry. In most households the wool was spun and processed first, and the linen spun in late winter. Then, "as soon as the spring weather would permit weaving without a fire, the looms in the back chamber were set in motion, weaving the next season's linen."[24]

No active loom or spinning wheel existed without quantities of hatcheled and combed flax, bags of fleece, rolls of carded wool, or piles of imported cotton being stored in the same house. Whether kept in bags, in baskets, or in loose piles on the floor, the fibers generated dust, attracted insects, and gave off bits of chaff, small sticks, and bits of dirt. Wool gave off its own distinctive odor, especially in damp weather. Since unprocessed flax was a fire hazard as well, the bulk of a season's production was usually kept in an unheated room—a shed or garret—and smaller quantities were brought forth as needed. Many people spread undressed flax before the fireplace to dry, sometimes with disastrous results; and newspaper editors cautioned families against this "too frequent practice."[25]

In some houses a separate room was set aside for spinning, but often the work was done in the kitchen. Spinning wheels were considered standard kitchen furnishings in the re-creations of New England kitchens, beginning with the birthplace of Dr. Franklin in Boston in 1858 (fig. 16). Spinning wheels are light in weight, especially small foot-wheels, and it was easy enough to move them to a warm spot by the fire, out onto a cool piazza, or out into the dooryard. The great wheel, or walking-wheel, is a different matter. Although such a wheel is not heavy, its large size makes it difficult to move alone or without disassembly. In use, a great wheel requires open floor space, for the rhythm of spinning required "a free movement of the arms" and involved a "long, gliding step, advancing and retreating." In *Quabbin,* Francis Underwood rhapsodized:

> Look at her. She is leaning forward, lightly poised upon the toe of the left foot. With her left hand she picks up by the end a long slender roll of soft wool, and deftly winds the fibres upon the point of the steel spindle before her. Now holding it an instant with thumb and finger, she gives a gentle motion to the wheel with the wooden finger which she holds in her right hand. Meanwhile, with her left hand she seizes the roll of wool at a little distance from the spindle, measuring with practised eye the length that will be required for one drawing. Then, while the hum of the wheel rises to a sound like the echo of wind in a storm, backwards she steps, one, two, three, holding high the long yarn as it twists and quivers. Then, suddenly reversing the wheel, she glides forward with a long, even stride, and lets the yarn wind upon the swift spindle.[26]

110. FAMILY GROUP WITH YOUNG GIRL SPINNING AT THE FIRESIDE IN THE EVENING, WOODCUT, ALEXANDER ANDERSON SCRAPBOOKS, VOL. VIII, PRINT COLLECTION, MIRIAM & IRA D. WALLACH DIVISION OF ART, PRINTS AND PHOTOGRAPHS, THE NEW YORK PUBLIC LIBRARY, ASTOR, LENOX AND TILDEN FOUNDATIONS.

Spinning flax was a more sociable activity than spinning wool or weaving. The equipment was fairly small, and the work could be done while seated. In contrast, spinning at the wool wheel, or "walking-wheel," required a space of at least thirty-six square feet; a woman could walk three or four miles in the course of a day's wool spinning.

Spinning is also noisy, and the hum of the wheel that was romanticized in the late nineteenth century could be very annoying indeed. In Rowley, Massachusetts, in 1747, a woman named Joanna Dresser had trouble with tenants who were annoyed by her spinning and compared the sound to that of a drum.[27]

Spinning was often the task of young women, and many of their journals document the long hours and the repetitive nature of the task. Elizabeth Fuller, the daughter of a Princeton, Massachusetts, minister, kept a daily diary for a few years, beginning in 1791, when she was fourteen years old. Six days a week, Elizabeth's primary work during this period was textile-related. She spun linen warp, tow filling, wool warp and filling for cloaks, and linen for a loom harness, as well as weaving the wool for cloaks, winter gowns, linen shirting, blue worsted, rag coverlids, and several pieces of unspecified linen and wool. Although there was a certain satisfaction in each finished project, this work was tedious and boring. After spinning tow daily from January 23 until February 9, 1792, Elizabeth commented: "I should think I might have spun up all the Swingling tow in America by this time." On May 3 of the same year, after weaving thirty-one and a half yards of linen in six days, Elizabeth expressed a hope that she had finished her weaving for the year, for she had woven one hundred and forty yards since March 9. Her hope was unfounded; she wove an additional piece of thirty-six yards before expressing the sentiment "Welcome sweet Liberty, once more to me" on June 1. By early July she was breaking some of the new season's wool for a coat for her father, and the round of work began again.[28] Ruth Henshaw of Leicester, Massachusetts, spun cotton, wool, and flax during the 1790s for her mother and her aunt, and indicated in her diary that she made different-textured threads for warp and filling (weft). Ruth also happily participated in neighborhood spinning "frolicks," where after the work was done she "met 16 or 18 Gentlemen & Ladies . . . spent a very agreeable evening, din'd &c."[29]

In their 1875 history of Northfield, Massachusetts, Josiah Temple and George Sheldon affirm that producing four skeins of woolen yarn was considered an ordinary day's work "when the spinner carded her own wool," but that "after the introduction of carding machines, she could as easily spin 6 skeins. Two skeins of linen thread was a large day's work."[30] Actually, many women were much more productive. In 1815, "Miss Polly Sweet, daughter of Mr. David Sweet, of Pompey, spun on a common wheel . . . between the hours of four A.M. and seven P.M. *fourteen* skeins of common woolen yarn."[31]

As spinning progressed, the finished threads were wound into skeins on bulky reels in order for the threads to be measured. The room was "hung all around with skeins of linen and woollen yarn"[32] as the spinners completed their task. In December 1791, Ruth Henshaw recorded that she had carded and her mother had spun forty-two skeins of wool in four days.[33] Six years later, she spun one hundred skeins of linen in four weeks.[34] While spinning linen and tow in that same winter of 1797, Sarah Bryant kept a steady pace, producing four skeins, or thirty knots, per day for sixty days, with the exceptions of one five-day period and of course, Sundays. The pace was not even slackened on February 4, when Sarah was "almost sick with a cold."[35] Depending on the supply of raw materials, a season's production could range from several dozen to several hundred tidy skeins, each measuring sixteen hundred yards.

Not all of this was woven in the household in which it was produced. The Henshaws, the Fullers, and the Bryants were among the small percentage of families that owned looms and other weaving equipment. Typical New England looms are tall wooden frames that occupy at least sixty-four square feet of floor space, and most require a ceiling height of at least six and a half feet as well. Since they were heavy and cumbersome affairs, patience was required to maintain the consistent fine adjustment that would produce quality cloth. Setting up a piece of fabric on a loom required special spooling and warping equipment, itself heavy and bulky. Not every family that owned a loom had these more specialized items, and people often used a neighbor's warping bars or spools. Elizabeth Fuller usually went to "Mrs. Mirick's" to warp her pieces. Twice she had help from Mrs. Garfield with drawing in a piece or making a harness for the loom.[36]

Because of their size, looms were usually set up in large, unfinished (and therefore unheated) spaces, often the large attic of the main house, but sometimes a shed attic or an unused chamber. Some professional weavers worked in ell rooms or dedicated small buildings known as "shops," where the equipment could be set up permanently.

Weaving requires reeds in a variety of sizes, spare harnesses and heddles, shuttles, quills and a quilling wheel with which to wind them, a reed hook, paper patterns, scissors and an assortment of needles, weights, and pieces of string with which to repair broken threads, splice in new colors, and tie new heddles. Highly skilled weavers also made use of temples and other specialized equipment to control fabric width and texture. All of this equipment, together with the filling threads themselves, needed to be kept within reach of the weaver's bench. Good light was also a necessity.

Once the cloth was woven it required finishing, and although fine woolens were often carried to a fulling mill or a clothier's shop to be dyed and finished, blankets, some coarse woolens, and all linen was finished at home. Whether one colored raw fleece, spun yarns, or finished yard goods, dyeing required the storage of poisonous mordants, papery onion skins, crumbling leaves, pieces of bark, and more expensive imported dyestuffs, maintaining a smelly indigo pot and quantities of stale urine, ample supplies of water, and large, clean kettles. Freshly woven linens were laid out to bleach in the sun—a process that was repeated for many days and required frequent dampening of the cloth while protecting it from being drenched by sudden rainstorms and from wandering dogs, pigs, and chickens, and cleansing it of spots caused by insects, bird droppings, and dirt kicked up by passers-by.[37]

Sarah Emery's childhood home was equipped for domestic textile production, and she described the center of all this work as a "back chamber—the large one under the long sloping back roof—[which] was set apart for manufacturing purposes. Here the chief part of the clothing and other household goods for the family were spun and woven. The apartment was conveniently fitted up with looms, woolen, linen and spooling wheels, swifts, reels, cards and warping bars."[38] Household inventories make it quite clear that not every New England farmhouse was so well supplied, and many depended on the use of their neighbors' equipment or purchased textiles to outfit their families.

When Peter Bryant died in 1820, the appraisers of his estate found three large and small wheels, as well as a "Loom and Slaies" among the agricultural equipment.[39] His wife's detailed diary gives us a very clear picture of the way in which these tools were used, as well as the quantity of textile production. Analysis of her daily entries reveals seasonal patterns, as well as changes in her work habits and production over a lifetime. From other sources, we can affirm that her story was typical of many women in prosperous households in the years between the American Revolution and the initial impact of the industrial revolution. This is the kind of life that became idealized as the homespun myth developed, and it demonstrates vividly how the apex of domestic production coincided with the firm establishment of industrialization.

On the Bryant farm, linen and tow were processed in the spring, and wool was processed in the fall and early winter. Each season's production of wool and flax was turned into finished yard goods before twelve months had gone by. On November 14, 1820, Sarah noted that she had "warpt a piece for flannel—it's the last woolen piece we have to weave." Martha, a hired girl, drew in the piece the next day, and just four days later, on Monday, "Martha finished weaving the wool." Weaving was sometimes hampered by extraordinary cold weather, as Sarah noted on December 24, 1831: "wove on the plaid—have not wove any for two weeks . . . very cold so that I could not weave." Toward the end of December or in early January, the year's weaving was usually finished: "Got out my piece of blue, the last for this season," Sarah wrote on December 25, 1827. But soon, no later than February or early March, flax preparation and linen spinning began again, and in the first warm days of May it would be time to wash and shear the sheep.

As a married woman with two young children, Sarah Bryant spun linen six days a week from January 1 to April 27, 1797, toward the end of this time producing four skeins a day at a steady pace. This work completed, she then spooled, warped, and wove pieces averaging thirty-four yards in length until June 26. After taking a break to teach school from June 26 to mid-September, on the fifteenth she began again by drawing in a piece and weaving it off. During these years the diary seldom mentions the composition or intended use of each woven "piece," specifying only shirting, handkerchiefs, diaper, twenty yards of tape, and a horse blanket before 1800. After 1800, when her husband's medical practice became more successful, Sarah Bryant began to rely on hired girls to do more of the work of textile production, although she always spooled and warped the pieces to be woven and continued to do some spinning. She owned her own spooling and warping equipment and often assisted neighbors in their use of it. Sometimes, however, she spooled her own warps at other houses, perhaps because of their extraordinary complexity or size, or because her own equipment was being used by others. Wool was carded by machine at a mill in Chesterfield after 1800 and locally at Mr. Derias Ford's mill from 1816 until it was destroyed by fire on October 23, 1823. Sarah Bryant acquired a new loom in 1805, and she occasionally wove for others, including her mother, her sister-in-law, the minister's wife, and a few neighbors. Rarely, a neighbor used the Bryant loom for her own work. Sarah's daughters began to help with the spinning when they reached the age of eleven, but the spinning by hired girls continued with some intensity until 1820.

During these years, fabrics woven on the Bryant farm included cotton, linen, and flannel sheeting, dimity, cheesecloth, table linen, checked linen, shirting (both linen and flannel), a carpet, and a rag coverlet. They also wove kersey for a loose coat and unspecified amounts of woolen and worsted, which were finished at a clothier's. Fabrics were woven for short gowns; boys' trousers; common pantaloons; aprons; woolen and linen tyers; pocket, common, and bundle handkerchiefs; pillowcases; and bags; but the diary does not identify either the fibers or the colors of any of these.

Fabric for tyers (long aprons with attached bibs) was once made with madder-and-white stripes; woolen quilt linings were usually dyed yellow. Dyestuffs used in the Bryant family included locally gathered peach leaves, goldenrod, butternut bark, smartweed, and hemlock, while "annetto," copperas, and madder were purchased. The diary mentions production of blue, so indigo must also have been purchased. Dyes were used for linings and knitting yarn as well as for yard goods and recoloring old clothing.

During the 1820s, Austin Bryant engaged in a number of schemes to improve the profitability of the family farm. One result of this was a dramatic increase in flax production. In 1821, they had thirty-six and three-quarter pounds of flax to process; by 1834, they had over one hundred pounds.

In the 1820s, with her eldest son in charge of the farm and no husband or young children to care for, Sarah Bryant spent much more time weaving than she had earlier in her life. On July 14, 1820, they moved the loom into the room that had been Peter Bryant's medical office, and within the week Sarah drew in "a piece for Adeline striped blue and white for trowsers."[40] During the summer of 1820, Sarah Bryant and a hired girl wove bedticks, shirting, dimity, flannel and "fine flannel," bags, cheesecloth, and fabric for trousers, before the loom was "taken down and carried to the chamber" on September 6. During November and December, Sarah Bryant wove a piece of blue cloth for a coat for herself. Interrupted frequently by other tasks, she finally finished it on December 13, commenting in her diary that it "has been in for a long time." In the fall of 1823, a flurry of dyeing "mixed yarn with golden rod," "green," "yellow," "red with madder," and "coloring with peach leaves" preceded something new: "homespun plaid is my gown." This gown was woven in November, and after the first yard was completed, Sarah recorded with some satisfaction, "I like my plaid much."[41] Sarah finished the weaving on December 4 and cut out the gown on January 8; her daughter Louisa stitched it for her in three days.

During the next few years both Sarah Bryant and her daughters had a number of homespun gowns, probably reflecting straitened economic circumstances after Peter Bryant's death, as well as their pleasure in experimenting with color and design. Plaids were undoubtedly more interesting and satisfying to weave than plain white sheeting or shirting. The challenge of producing compatible colors with natural dyestuffs and developing a pleasing pattern, and the steady pleasure of watching the colorful pattern emerge on the loom, clearly appealed to Sarah Bryant.

The new emphasis on weaving in Sarah Bryant's life during the 1820s is reflected in the seasonal relocation of the loom to the office in summer and to her chamber in winter, and by an increasing number of diary entries which indicate that Sarah was actually doing the weaving herself. During this period the diary also begins to record more detail about the set of the loom—"a thirty four reed,"[42] "a thirty two for shirts"[43]—and records the undertaking of many more complex projects. In 1828, Sarah Bryant proudly recorded that she had begun weaving table linen in "double diamonds" with eight wings (harnesses) on the loom. Late in the summer she wove table linen in a damask pattern. In 1833, her ambition got ahead of her, and she tried a "12 wing damask" in a number 60 reed, but she couldn't get it to work and eventually cut it out of the loom and reverted to her practiced eight-wing pattern.

Unfortunately, just as Sarah Bryant was beginning to experiment with complex color and design, her family fortunes diminished, and she was forced to weave coarser goods for the sake of the income they could generate. She began to do weaving for her neighbors, especially warp-striped carpets, and made both bags and flannel in pieces of up to forty-five yards to sell. On November 1, 1830, she recorded that she "went to Greenfield a shopping—carried some flannel—bought some shawls, Adeline silk levantine for a gown & numerous other articles." On December 17, Austin sold their forty-five-yard piece of fine flannel to Mr. Hubbard, and in November 1832 she struggled over a seventeen-yard piece of flannel that she described as "very tender" and not easy to weave; on the twenty-third she got it out of the loom, and Adeline immediately carried it to Mr. Mitchell's store and got some dark calico to make gowns for herself and Louisa. Although Austin "sold His wool"—one hundred ninety pounds in June 1834—Sarah continued weaving, both for the family and for sale, right up until March 20, 1835. On the twenty-first they "took down the loom"; four days later, she departed for what would be her last visit to her brother and his family in Brookfield, and in May the entire family moved to Illinois. Her final weaving projects in Massachusetts were things that would be easily portable—towels, bags, and suspenders.

Sarah Bryant's textile work in the 1820s and early 1830s may be seen as typical of that done on many prosperous New England farms during those decades. The lists of awards that were made at the agricultural fairs at the county and state level document the range of that work, including woolen and linen yard goods, blankets, coverlets, pattern-woven table linens, and a variety of other hand-woven textiles. Those who exhibited at the fairs were usually the same people who raised merino sheep for their improved fleece and planted mulberry trees and experimented with silk culture. Even Austin Bryant planted mulberry trees in 1833! After reeling nine skeins of silk from seventy-four cocoons that year, he and his mother visited the local expert, Deacon Cobb, to observe silk reeling. Never willing to leave a project unfinished, Sarah Bryant spent part of April 21 and 22, 1835, "reeling my silk" so it could be taken with her to Illinois when the family moved, a few weeks later.

It is perhaps ironic that the success of these efforts at household textile production came just at the time when the inexpensive products of the new textile factories would make domestic production uneconomical. Many people, like the Bryants, left their hill farms for promising opportunities in Ohio, Indiana, or Illinois. Neighboring daughters and some whole families entered the new mills as operatives. Stores offered hundreds of yards of brightly printed calicoes and inexpensive cotton sheeting and shirting. On thousands of New England farms the looms fell silent, except for the occasional production of a blanket or a rag carpet; the spinning wheel was used exclusively for stocking yarn. Soon the looms were shrouded in dust and the spinning wheels retired to a corner of the attic; as early as 1820, the conservative agricultural press decried the passing of domestic textile production, predicted the growth of idleness and even immorality among young women, and began to enshrine the spinning wheel as an icon of an imaginary past. In 1830, the editor of the *New England Farmer* reprinted a notice from the *Massachusetts Spy* honoring "A good day's work" produced at Shutesbury, Massachusetts, on September 29, when "Mrs. Bogue, on the anniversary of her birth day at the completion of her ninety fifth year, spun fifty four knots of woollen yarn, of a superior quality." The *Spy* enthused, "Such women were our mothers! How many of the younger portion of their descendants at the present day can equal this performance?"[44] Probably many of them could, but the need to do so was diminishing. Fewer farmers were growing flax, and the stores were filled with colorful calicoes and inexpensive cotton shirting and sheeting. In the face of these powerful changes, people clung to the old values even as the world was changing around them, idealizing a kind of self-sufficiency that had never really existed.

VIII

A Comfortable Sufficiency: Food and the New England Kitchen

ANTICIPATING A VISIT FROM HIS SISTER, FILANIA, AND HER HUSBAND, Consider Dickinson, of Deerfield, the household of Samuel Field in Conway, Massachusetts, was in a tizzy on a Saturday morning in September 1794. There was no shortening on hand for making piecrusts, and "Before breakfast, Tirzah was sent off to Mr. Roots with a Box to get a Pound of Hogs Lard—in order to make a great *Batch* of Apple Pies, and they were to be made, if possible, exactly to the *Deerfield Taste.*" It turned out that the Fields were not the only ones out of lard at that time of year, and Tirzah returned empty-handed, not only from the Roots but from the Boltwoods as well. Samuel himself went to the store and came back empty-handed. Apparently, no lard was to be had any closer than Deerfield itself, and there was no time to go there to fetch it and return "before the Oven would be cold," so Mrs. Field set about to "do the best she could—went directly about making a *Forty Acre**—raised the crust—and Shortened it with Cream and to have it better than common ordered the apples to be pared."

The eagerly awaited Dickinsons never appeared, much to the dismay of all the family in Conway, and Samuel soon wrote to his sister describing what they had done to welcome her in addition to pie making: "a Skillet of Pork & Beans was lodged in the Oven for the purpose—we had provided ourselves with a store of fresh Beef, for your entertainment—A parcel of exceeding good Beef tripe was brought nearly a Mile, and waited your Arrival—well cooked—altho we were in the midst of pickling for the Winter—yet a number of Cucumbers

* If not a description of the size of this pie, perhaps this is a reference to the origin of the recipe. "Forty Acres" is the name of the extensive Phelps farm in nearby Hadley.

were left on the Vines, to be dressed for Supper, to add a Relish to the Entertainment—A number of Watermelons kept for the Business—a fine large one over ripened and was since hardly worth eating." The Fields had obviously gone to a great deal of trouble and expense to honor their expected guests, going far afield to find appropriate ingredients and fresh meat, preparing a meal that featured several kinds of meats, pies "better than common," and seasonal delicacies. It is not surprising that Samuel wrote to tell his sister that they felt they had not been "quite fairly dealt by" at the same time that he sought an explanation of her nonappearance. For historians, Samuel's letter at once addresses the questions of limited supply, neighborly food exchanges, food preservation, technology, local tradition, seasonality, unexpected company, and the time-honored tradition of honoring guests with special foods.[1]

Popular images of early–New England tables are replete with the idea of wholesomeness and bounty, but recent scholarship has shown that the diet of most people was unvaried throughout much of the year and that it was both high in saturated fats and lacking in essential vitamins. Heavily salted meat and fish were the primary sources of animal protein, and it was common practice to boil vegetables for an hour before serving them.

The basic components of the eighteenth-century New England diet are included in the lists of food that were added to wills by occasional considerate husbands wishing to assure their widow's support, yet even these lists raise as many questions as they answer. Consider, for example, the bequest made by Samuel Denney of Georgetown, Maine, in 1772: "I give unto my loving wife Catherin Denny fower good milch cows . . . ten sheep . . . [and] all the provision that may be in the hous of meal pork bief flower butter chese talu candels molases shuger cofey tea rise spises chocolet corn and other grain . . . towards her comfortable support."[2] This is an unusually detailed list for Maine at the time, yet from Denney's will alone we can know nothing about the actual quantities of food, where they came from, what facilities and equipment were available for food storage or cooking, or how Catherine was to get along once all the food in the house had been eaten. The 1797 will of Richard Adams is far more informative, and must have been more encouraging to the widow as well, for it specified that she have "One good Cow to Be kept both Summer & Winter, Fire wood brot to her Door & Cut fit for the Chimney during her Life, Fifteen Bushels of Bread Corn of different kinds annually, . . . [and] a Sufficient annual supply of Potatoes & other kinds of Same & Vegetables & of Tea Coffee & Sweetening & other necessaries" provided by her husband's executors.[3] For any woman, converting perishable resources such as these into a "comfortable support" and maintaining adequate supplies throughout the year required energy as well as experience in both housewifery and husbandry—the technical and managerial skills that were characteristic of a good housewife.

Fireplace Cooking

The massive fireplace that was the center of the New England kitchen has been thoroughly romanticized. Samuel Goodrich described the building of the morning fire as "a real architectural achievement . . . always begun by daybreak. There was first a back-log, from fifteen to four and twenty inches in diameter and five feet long, imbedded in the ashes; then came a top log; then a forestick; then a middle stick, and then a heap of kindlings, reaching from the bowels down to the bottom. A-top of all was a pyramid of smaller fragments, artfully adjusted, with spaces for the blaze."[4] Harriet Beecher Stowe built on

III. A KITCHEN HEARTH, PHOTOGRAPH BY EMMA COLEMAN, DEERFIELD, C. 1883–86. COURTESY OF THE SOCIETY FOR THE PRESERVATION OF NEW ENGLAND ANTIQUITIES.

A photograph featuring objects selected to epitomize the idealized New England kitchen hearth: a huge backlog and forestick on the andirons, cooking pots and kettles, a spinning wheel, sociable pipes, and a Bible.

Goodrich's description in *Oldtown Folks,* agreeing that a good kitchen fire "was built up on architectural principles."[5]

The blazing backlog may have been the magnet that drew a family together on cold days, but the capacious hearth itself was very useful indeed. Although some pots and kettles were hung directly over a carefully tended and moderate fire, no delicate cooking was successfully accomplished over a big blaze. Small beds of glowing coals, built as needed at various places on the hearth, provided more steady, controllable heat for cooking in footed pots and skillets or in flat-bottomed vessels set carefully on trivets. Yet the images of blazing fires that seem so romantic may have been based in reality. By the 1840s, cookbook authors who addressed the management of fire condemned huge fires as wasteful and suggested that a woman could manage the cooking, save fuel, keep the kitchen cooler in summertime, and reduce her own work by hanging pots low over the fire and cooking with only a few embers. They were right, of course; but is it possible that there were women who preferred the bigger fire? It is certainly simpler to boil meat and vegetables together in a single kettle for a long time than to work closely at floor level with more specialized equipment.

Most cooking fireplaces were equipped with some kind of suspension system for large pots and kettles. This was either a green log, called a lug pole, which was mounted high in the throat of the chimney and from which the pots and kettles were suspended on long hooks or trammels, or an iron crane that could be swung out toward the room in order to inspect the contents of the pots and kettles, to add something, or to serve from them. By raising and lowering pots to adjust the distance between them and the fire, or by moving the crane forward into the room, cooking temperatures could be adjusted.

For fireplace cooking, Miss Beecher preferred ironware and recommended "a nest of iron pots, of different sizes . . . , a long iron fork, to take out articles from boiling water; an iron hook, with a handle, to lift pots from the crane; a large and small gridiron, with grooved bars, and a trench to catch the grease; a Dutch oven called, also, a bakepan; two skillets, of different sizes, and a spider, or flat skillet, for frying; a griddle, a waffle iron, tin and iron bake and bread pans; two ladles, of different sizes; a skimmer; iron skewers; a toasting iron; two tea kettles, one small and one large one; two brass kettles, of different sizes, for soap boiling, etc. Iron kettles, lined with porcelain, are better for preserves."[6] The list, in fact, is not significantly different from that of the ironware provided by Samuel Lane for his daughters in the second half of the eighteenth century. Only the porcelain-lined preserving kettles were newly available when Miss Beecher was writing in 1841.

Although this great variety of ironware would have been useful, it is clear that some people went to housekeeping with only a small kettle, a spider, and a long-handled spoon. Abner Sanger borrowed pots and kettles for butchering and maple sugaring, as well as for his mother and sister whenever they undertook large-scale projects such as soap making. If repairs were needed, a man interrupted his other work to take a pot or a kettle to the blacksmith. In 1781, Sanger visited a blacksmith "with pot to mend . . . tend on McCoy while he puts a rivet in our pot."[7] Although cast iron cracked and sometimes needed to be patched or riveted, and pots with broken handles could be fitted with new bails, seldom was a piece so badly broken that it needed to be replaced.

Mainstays of the New England Diet

The food served up from these pots and kettles was the inspiration for nostalgia once circumstances changed for many people in the late nineteenth century. Seeking to describe the heartiness of rural New England foodways in *Quabbin,* Francis Underwood described a man who began each morning with a preliminary nip of hard cider, followed by "a substantial breakfast. This might be of ham and eggs, or of salt fish prepared with cream, or of bean porridge (for which a ham bone furnished the stock), or of cold corned beef, with hot potatoes, and usually hot bread (called 'biscuits') resembling muffins; and with sauces, pickles, and other provocatives in plenty."[8] Like many late-nineteenth-century fictional accounts of New England life, here Underwood has condensed many experiences, making everyday experience seem richer and more varied than it was for most people. Harriet Beecher Stowe did the same thing in *Oldtown Folks,* having a character say, "I can inform all whom it may concern that rye and Indian bread, smoking hot, on a cold winter morning, together with savory sausages, pork, and beans, formed a breakfast fit for a king, if the king had earned it by getting up in a cold room, washing in ice-water, tumbling through snow drifts, and foddering cattle."[9]

In the family of Judge Lyman in Northampton, Massachusetts, in the early nineteenth century, it was remembered that "the breakfast was always simple but abundant,—tea and coffee, broiled fish or steak, bread, and some kind of pudding for the children, to be eaten with milk or cream."[10]

Abner Sanger's late-eighteenth-century diary documents a few much simpler meals, such as a "breakfast of bread and milk at Dr. Pomeroy's,"[11] but Sanger's meals were usually not worth mentioning. His diary includes many

112. "Dining room of Dr. Whitridge as it was in the winter 1814–15. Breakfast time (pot-apple pie)," watercolor, by Joseph S. Russell, c. 1848. Old Dartmouth Historical Society/New Bedford Whaling Museum, New Bedford, Massachusetts.

The interior of a home in Tiverton, Rhode Island, with a man reading the Bible beside a fire that had been lighted in the fire frame before breakfast. Even for this simple meal, a tablecloth has been spread, and the coffee service is arranged on a waiter, or tray.

references to the difficulties and concerns of producing and preserving food, but there were only few occasions when he described a menu, such as that of December 12, 1774, when his mother served a dinner "of meat and onions." In old age, Sanger was content with two meals a day of bread and milk or hasty pudding and milk. By the time he was eighty-two he had given up eating "fat, meat or butter";[12] apparently, he never considered fruits or vegetables.

Sanger was not the only person for whom food was relatively unimportant. The hardworking George Boyd of Portsmouth described his daily schedule in a letter in 1773, saying, "up at daylight in the morning & never in the house only to breakfast & Dine which Seldom takes me more than fifteen minutes for either." For him, dinner was something to rush through in order to get back to work—the kind of attention to meals that was admired by the "farmer" who praised self-sufficiency in 1788. In his long diatribe about the evils of extravagance, he described breakfast, "which used to take ten minutes, when we were satisfied with milk or pottage made out of it, [and] now takes my whole family an hour at tea or coffee."[13]

In prosperous families in the eighteenth century, the midday dinner was a hot meal that was usually composed of two courses, one of abundant meats followed by another of a starchy pudding, a pie, or a rich variety of sweets. No matter how warm the weather, a hot meal was required. Sarah Emery recalled that in Newbury, dinner "was on the table punctually at twelve o'clock. In the hot weather we usually had boiled salted meat and vegetables, and, if it was baking day, a custard or a pudding."[14] Ruth Bascom didn't mind eating a hot dinner on a hot day, but after eight hot days in a row in late July 1830, she hired a girl to cook for her, noting in her diary, "the cooking of meat & vegetables these sultry days being repugnant to my inclination if not to my health."[15] While Betsy Phelps was visiting friends in Boston in late August 1797, she wrote to her mother in Hadley: "now I fancy you are eating dinner assembled round that *jovial table*—partaking of a wholesome repast—it makes my mouth water—as the saying is, to think of it—good *fatt meat*—with *green sauce* is too *delicious*." Three months after her marriage in 1801, Betsy was writing of much simpler fare: "after nine we had our supper, which consisted of *cyder-soup*—or toast and cyder—a dish which my husband is particularly fond of." On arrival at home in Litchfield after a Thanksgiving visit, Betsy and her husband enjoyed an "excellent dinner" of tongue and bread, which had been packed by her mother and carried all the way from Hadley.[16]

Many authors of reminiscences concurred with Caroline King, who remembered her father saying that in his own Salem boyhood, pudding had been served as a first course to stay the appetite.[17] In early-nineteenth-century Northampton, Mrs. Lyman may have been serving more vegetables and simpler deserts. Her daughter recalled that "at one o'clock came dinner; always a large joint, roast or boiled, with plenty of vegetables and a few condiments—for she thought them unwholesome,—good bread and butter, and a plain pudding or pie."[18]

113. "DINING ROOM OF ABM RUSSELL NEW BEDFORD," C. 1812, BY JOSEPH S. RUSSELL, C. 1848. OLD DARTMOUTH HISTORICAL SOCIETY, NEW BEDFORD, MASSACHUSETTS.

Another of Russell's retrospective views showing life as it was in the artist's youth. The family has gathered for dinner, probably in the early afternoon. Most of the food has been placed on the table, with the vegetables in covered serving dishes. The roasted meat has been placed in front of the older man for him to do the carving. A black serving woman is carrying in another covered dish of food.
In Abraham Russell, Sr.'s, probate inventory, taken in 1837, this room contained a dining table, a tea table, six chairs, and a refrigerator—perhaps the large chest shown under the window. A second room was also furnished for dining, with another dining table, a sideboard, a dozen chairs, and a looking glass.

114. FAMILY DINNER, WOODCUT, IN *Good Girl's Soliloquy* (NEW YORK, n.d.). PRIVATE COLLECTION.

Dinner has been served in one large pewter dish; there may be cider in the pitcher, but it is unclear whether the family will share the tumbler or only one will partake. They will probably eat directly from the broad knife blades, pushing the food with two-tined forks. There are no tea or coffee cups on the table; these beverages were not usually served at dinnertime. Illustrations in juvenile books depicted familiar situations in order to encourage children to identify with the context of the lesson being taught.

Although ceramic dinner services began to appear on the tables of the wealthy in the late eighteenth century, many of these dinners were brought to the table in a single large pewter serving dish and dished out on pewter as well. Susan Blunt recalled a "large one that was used when the family had a boiled dinner. In the center they would place a great peice of corned beef, another of pork, and all around the edges would be placed all the vegitables. They would always have a bag of beans boiled at the same time as a side dish." These great pewter dishes and rows of matching eight- or ten-inch plates were usually stored and displayed at once on long open shelves in the kitchen of the type described by Susan Blunt as "an old fashioned dresser, that was built [along] and nearly covered on [one] side of the kitchen."[19] There they were handy for food service, and if they were scoured regularly with coarse sand, their shiny surfaces increased the level of illumination in the kitchen by reflecting ambient light. Although the rows of pewter plates were a dominant feature of the kitchen dresser, its ranks of open shelves also provided convenient storage for all kinds of kitchen equipment and tableware, as well as a spot on which to put something down temporarily. Usually the top shelf was the only one made wide enough for the largest pewter dishes, but its relative security made it a good place to put something precious for safekeeping as well. Not much could dislodge something stored on a high shelf, but natural disasters did occur occasionally. One young man noted in his diary in 1791: "This Evening there was an Earth Quake which shook Dadda's house so much that the Pewter and Earthen Vessels that Stood on the Shelves Made Considerable of a Rumbleing."[20]

Samuel Lane's daughters had been supplied with quantities of pewter plates for meal service; however, food in their homes must have been eaten from knife blades or with spoons, for none of them had table forks. The New England customs of eating with a knife and presenting an entire meal on a single serving platter were scorned by prosperous city dwellers and commented upon by European travelers. These practices were gradually abandoned in the nineteenth century in response to changing standards of gentility and the increasing availability of inexpensive cutlery and ceramic tablewares.

In the nineteenth century, city dwellers noted that country people clung to the custom of dining in the middle of the day and having a lighter meal, called supper or tea, between five and six o'clock in the evening. At nine o'clock, Sarah Emery's mother offered an additional snack of "Bowls of bread and milk . . . for those who wished the refreshment."[21] On a Saturday evening in November 1796, Elizabeth Phelps had supper before picking up her pen to write to Betsy: "Having just eat about a quart of hasty-pudding & milk, I feel lazy eno' to write and tell you how I feel for you."[22] Well into the nineteenth century, simple suppers of bread and milk; toast, cheese, and cider; a slice of pie; or a dish of hasty pudding and milk seem to have been standard country fare. In many families this meal was served after the men's outdoor work was finished; in others, it was served at five o'clock, giving the women a chance to take care of the dishes before the milk came in to be strained.[23] Underwood wrote of young men visiting Quabbin who soon learned that the difference between dinner and tea might be one of no more than nomenclature, and he noted that in the country town, "dinner parties are seldom given; principally because everybody dines in the middle of the day. But a tea, with a reinforcement of steaks, chickens, and oysters, is not a bad substitute for a dinner."[24]

No matter what a meal was called or when it was served, standard fare among rural families was indeed simple. Asa Sheldon of Wilmington, Massa-

115. DRESSER, COFFIN HOUSE, NEWBURY, MASSACHUSETTS. COURTESY OF THE SOCIETY FOR THE PRESERVATION OF NEW ENGLAND ANTIQUITIES. PHOTOGRAPH BY ARTHUR HASKELL.

"I remember distinctly the great fireplace in the kitchen, which was the room back of the 'sitting room,' and opening into it. . . . At the right as you entered was the Dresser, with its shelves well filled with very bright pewter platters, plates and 'porringers'—an article of housekeeping quite gone out, I believe." (From a letter written in 1901 by Caleb Huse [b. 1831] and published in "The Coffin House in the Early Nineteenth Century," Old Time New England 27 *[October, 1936]: 2, 70.)*

116. FAMILY TEA OR SUPPER IN SUMMERTIME, WOODCUT, C. 1820. ALEXANDER ANDERSON SCRAPBOOKS, VOL. VII, PRINT COLLECTION, MIRIAM & IRA D. WALLACH DIVISION OF ART, PRINTS AND PHOTOGRAPHS, THE NEW YORK PUBLIC LIBRARY, ASTOR, LENOX AND TILDEN FOUNDATIONS.

This family is using handleless cups, or tea bowls, but the boy is not drinking from his saucer. All of the equipment for serving tea has been assembled on a waiter to protect the tabletop from spills.

chusetts, recalled the diet of poor farm families being based on meat, grain, and dairy products, and this is well documented in the diary of Abner Sanger of Keene, New Hampshire. For such families, both breakfast and supper were usually brown bread and milk in summertime, while bean broth or cider were substituted in wintertime, when milk was unavailable. The midday meal centered on meat or cheese—again, depending on the season.

Lyndon Freeman of Sturbridge, Massachusetts, recalled the staples of a rural diet in the first decades of the nineteenth century: "At the setting in of winter every farmer was presumed to have at least a pork and beef of sufficient quantity. The larder was well supplied with butter, cheese, applesauce, pickels, sausages, souse, etc. Their dinner commonly consisted of boiled pork or beef or both, potatoes, cabbage, beets, carrots, etc. These were all served on a large pewter platter placed in the centre of the table. A *mug* of cider was upon the table never forgotten of as all drank as freely as we do of water today. The meat and sauce left of the dinner were hash-up for breakfast the next morning. The supper was usually brown bread and milk for all."[25]

Country people observed real differences when they had an opportunity to dine with wealthy city dwellers. While in Boston to attend the General Court, Elihu Hoyt of Deerfield reported to his wife: "I dined yesterday with The Hon. Mr. Otis in C° with a quorum of The Senate, we had a most splendid entertainment, this day dined at Govr. Phillips in the Deacons usual good style, we had plenty of green peas at both tables, but believe me, I had much rather have dined at Deerfield in our common pork and cabbage style."[26]

In cities like Boston, Portsmouth, Hartford, Worcester, Newburyport, and Salem, men left their work and went home for the midday dinner, which was usually served at one o'clock. Taking notice of a young man who drowned unobserved in Salem harbor at one o'clock in the afternoon, William Bentley commented: "So uniform is the hour of dining that not a person saw the accident which must have been within sight of all our wharves where thousands are busy at the usual hours of labor. Proof of our present habits."[27]

Many people believed that it was wrong to light a cooking fire and prepare a hot dinner on Sundays. For those who attended both morning and afternoon services and lived relatively near the meeting house, there was time to hurry home for a cold dinner. Those who lived too far away to rush home for something to eat either repaired to a nearby tavern or brought food from home and ate it outdoors, in their carriages, or even in the meeting house itself, if the weather was bad.[28] Sunday was a trying day for a minister's wife, who was expected to entertain visiting clergymen and other dignitaries during the nooning. On very cold or rainy days, she might find dozens of people camped out in her parlor or kitchen, eating cold pies or bread and cheese and hoping for a cup of hot tea.

Food as a Medium of Exchange

In the eighteenth century, and even into the first decades of the nineteenth, farm produce was a medium of exchange within rural communities. With 95 percent of the population engaged at some level in farm production, families exchanged beef, pork, mutton, veal, butter, cheese, and grains for the specialized or general labor of their neighbors or for store credits. Fish, potatoes, turnips, butter, beef, veal, and pork were used as credits for drinks of rum at William Jones's tavern in Rye, New Hampshire, between 1761 and 1800.[29] Few farmers raised all the food needed for their families and livestock, but neighborhood exchanges and village stores could supply most of whatever else was needed. Like many ministers, the Reverend Jonathan Fisher of Blue Hill, Maine, farmed his own fields and received contributions of all sorts of farm produce from his parishioners; still, he needed to purchase things at a nearby store. In August 1810, these purchases included eggs, potatoes, turnips, beef, halibut, shad, cheese, vinegar, and rum.[30] The Bryant family in Cummington relied on their own farm produce for their primary food supply. They purchased tea, coffee, sugar, molasses, salt, spices, and an occasional barrel of flour from local storekeepers, using butter and cheese for the majority of their store credits. The familiarity of this kind of exchange was confirmed by Francis Underwood in *Quabbin,* in a description of country people "bound for the store. In the box behind the seat, they have a basket of eggs, a 'four-meal' cheese, and a firkin of butter, to be exchanged for tea, molasses and other 'boughten' goods."[31]

Unlike productive farm families, urban New Englanders usually did not keep large quantities of food on hand, relying instead on bakers, grocers, and commercial markets, where imported foodstuffs and supplies from nearby

117. "ABOUT GROCERIES," IN *Peter Parley's First Book of Arithmetic* (1834). PHOTOGRAPH BY BILL FINNEY. COURTESY OF THE SOCIETY FOR THE PRESERVATION OF NEW ENGLAND ANTIQUITIES.

The illustration "represents one boy drawing molasses, and another measuring salt," the most important groceries. The text continues to explain that "these articles together with sugar, tea, coffee, nutmegs, pepper, allspice, cinnamon, cloves, and many other things are called groceries."

farming communities were offered for sale. Even in the eighteenth century there was considerable coastal trade in food, in addition to importation from Europe and the West Indies. In the first issues of the New Hampshire *Gazette* in 1756 and 1757, merchants advertised "Rhode Island Cheese," "PEPPER, Nutmegs, Cinnamon, Cloves and Mace. Choice Philadelphia FLOUR, and Connecticut Pork by the Barrel," "Virginia Corn, Wheat and Oats."[32] Merchants in coastal cities and country towns alike sold these goods, as well as Cheshire and Gloucester cheese, Irish butter, molasses, tea, coffee, chocolate, salt, sugar, beef, pork, vinegar, rice, raisins, figs, currants, limes, almonds, olive oil, anchovies, and spices, along with rum, gin, brandy, and wine; oranges and lemons were available in the spring and early summer.[33] Country people brought beef, veal, mutton, pork, hams, and bacon, as well as fruits, vegetables, and grains, into the large towns to sell, long before there were established markets. Some city dwellers kept cows or pigs and tended kitchen gardens, if land was available. In most cases, the cows were taken daily to a community pasture or to rented grassland.[34] Wealthy merchants sometimes owned tenant farms in nearby communties where crops and animals were raised for sale as well as for the owner's table.

In urban markets, meat, poultry, and fish were regularly offered for sale by

118. TRADE CARD OF WILLIAM B. BRADFORD, JR., WHOLESALE & RETAIL GROCER, BOSTON, C. 1820. COURTESY AMERICAN ANTIQUARIAN SOCIETY.

This advertisement illustrates both sources and distribution patterns of basic groceries.

people who rented stalls by the year. In Portsmouth, New Hampshire, stalls outside the market were reserved for "the free use of transient country people," who came to town on an irregular basis, bringing a variety of surplus farm produce to be sold. These markets were open Monday through Saturday, with the exception of Thanksgiving day and fast days; on Saturdays and the afternoons before Thanksgiving and fast days, the markets were kept open until eight o'clock in the evening.[35] Severe cold weather could interfere with deliveries from the countryside and drive up the food prices in cities. Samuel Larkin was concerned about this in February 1839, writing in his diary: "This month commences with Snow—there has not however much fallen it would be very desirable to have enough to make good sledding—in order that the people from the Country may bring their produce to market—provisions of all kinds is high—Butter scarce—I paid 23 Cents per lb."[36]

Food Preservation and Storage

Caroline King tells us:

> In those days people bought things in large quantities. I do not know whether it was for economy or to save trouble. In our store closet there were cranberries by the bushel, kept in their place on the floor . . . barrels of sugar both white and of a moist dark brown sugar, which I never see now, but was always thought to give an especial richness to coffee. . . . There were chests of green and black tea . . . bags of Java and Mocha coffee . . . strange long-tailed pottery olive jars that would not stand upright, boxes of great purple Malaga raisins, drums of figs, casks of grapes packed in sawdust as light as a feather which we were told was from the cork tree; and jugs of molasses. . . . Then there was my especial delight, the row of tall conical shaped pyramids of loaf sugar which always looked to me like a party of masqueraders cloaked and hooded in long purple dominos, while their bright-colored labels fastened with little bows of red ribbon formed gay aprons for the group.

She also tells of "locked cupboards for the queer old demijohns which held brandy and wine and cherry brandy, and broad shelves with rows of preserves and pretty china ginger jars, and the quaint bottles which held tamarinds. I remember the flavourous smell which floated out from it as my mother unlocked the door, when I was allowed to visit it with her."[37]

However, if this kind of store closet ever existed, it was only among the most wealthy urban families. The evidence of family account books corroborated by those of city and country storekeepers indicates that much smaller purchases were the norm. Sarah Emery described her father's one-time purchase of a large quantity of flour, but cautioned readers: "It must be remembered that the family flour barrel had not then come into vogue. Wheat was raised upon the farm, or bought and ground by the bushel . . . Indian meal and rye, especially rye, were the staples for daily use in most households . . . wheat flour was somewhat of a luxury; a housekeeper felt rich with a bushel or two on hand, and it was made to last a long time."[38] Poorer people usually had only a tiny amount of food on hand at a time. There were some advantages to this, for one did not have to worry about spoilage. Nineteenth-century cookbook authors advised housekeepers to turn over the flour barrel on a regular basis and to inspect it carefully to avoid insect infestation or spoilage from mold growth.

In early December 1780, Abner Sanger was obliged to buy a peck of wheat in order to provide flour for family baking. Normally, he had husked corn, which could be ground into meal and stored in an upstairs chamber, but at the end of January 1782, the Sanger household ran low on Indian meal. Abner wrote: "I come home and shell out some corn, viz. ½ bushel, the last I have, and carry it to mill and borrow one pint of corn, have it all ground."[39] The Sanger household had to borrow from a neighbor when they were unable to get their meal ground on February 23, 1775; two days later, they were able to repay their neighbor and replenish their own supply. This was not an unusual occurrence at all; during the years covered by Abner Sanger's journal, rye and Indian meal were frequently borrowed from or lent to neighbors, and measured in "great basins," "quarts," a "3 pint basin," a "pudding-panful," a "peck," "a brown earthen quart bowl (6 times)," and "my gallon bowl."[40] Even if one had a supply of grain to be ground, no grinding could occur if the water-powered gristmill had been stopped by freezing weather, severe drought, or flood damage. Sarah Bryant summarized that problem in the fall of 1833: "Can get no grinding near."[41]

Baking

In order to make raised bread or cake, it was necessary to have a supply of yeast, as well as some kind of meal or flour. Yeast could be made in a few days, but the "emptyings," or dregs, from a keg or barrel of beer could also serve this purpose. Emptyings were often solicited from neighbors, if there were none on hand.[42]

Sarah Bryant baked at least once a week, often combining this task with either washing or ironing, which required keeping a fire and remaining in or near the kitchen. This is in sharp contrast to the suggestions given by the authors of household advice books, who urged women to separate these arduous jobs. Mrs. Bryant's baking could take place early or late in the day; on January 7, 1808, she recorded in her diary that she had "baked before sunrise," while on October 17, 1814, she "baked pies in the evening."

119. BREAD MAKING, IN *Marmaduke Multiply* (BOSTON, 1845). COURTESY OF THE SOCIETY FOR THE PRESERVATION OF NEW ENGLAND ANTIQUITIES.

Here a woman is kneading bread while the brick oven is heating. The crookneck squash have been hung high against the ceiling for safe dry storage out of the reach of rodents. The huge blaze in the fireplace seems to be overstated, but the artist has shown the long-handled slice, or peel, which would be needed to place loaves of bread in and remove them from the oven.

Mrs. Bryant's diary entries often consist simply of "Baked," implying that there was a regularity to the task that stimulated no further description. The bulk of the baking she did describe was of bread and pies, the latter sometimes further described as egg, minced, chicken (or "chicking"), apple, pumpkin, or squash; it is unclear whether the "grate apple pie" baked on December 11, 1817, was made of grated apples or was unusually large. Gingerbread, sweet cake, pound cake, "bisquit," plain and apple custard, and squash pudding were also baked from time to time. As early as 1808, Mrs. Bryant's diary includes an occasional reference to "white bread," suggesting that at least some of the wheat grown on the Bryant farm was ground into flour for their own use. Usually meats were roasted in front of an open flame, but on August 20, 1808, the same day that white bread was mentioned for the first time in the diary, the meat was "baked." Foot pies were usually made in conjunction with any butchering, after the hired girl had "cleaned the creature's feet."

Although any of these things could be baked on the hearth in a Dutch oven, the regularity and quantity of Sarah Bryant's baking implies that she had access to a brick oven constructed as an integral part of the kitchen fireplace. The average oven in a New England kitchen fireplace was about forty inches deep, large enough to hold the ten or twelve pie plates that one cookbook author, Mrs. Cornelius, felt were enough to last a week "for a family of medium size."[43] An oven like this used radiant heat that had been absorbed from a fire built directly inside it. Up to two hours were required to heat the oven, depending on the dryness and the species of wood used. Once the fire had burned down to hot coals, the oven was emptied, and sometimes swept out with a damp broom. Most oven doors were left open while the bricks were being heated, the smoke escaping up a flue directly in front of the opening. Once the food had been placed in the oven, a solid wooden or metal door was shoved into the opening to retain the heat.[44] Beginning in the 1820s, cast-iron oven doors were made with adjustable baffles, which permitted some control of the amount of oxygen entering the burning oven or the amount of heat escaping during baking.

Some cooks put their hands into the oven to test the temperature, and others threw handfuls of flour into the oven, judging the relative temperature by the speed at which the flour browned. The author of an 1848 cookbook suggested that an oven built with sufficient heat-retention qualities could serve for five successive loads of food without reheating: "the bread first—then the puddings—afterward pastry—then cake and gingerbread—and lastly, custards, which, if made with boiled milk and put into the oven hot, and allowed to stand a considerable time, will bake sufficiently with a very slight heat."[45]

One baking day each week seems to have been the norm in most families, although in poor households or newly settled areas, not everyone had an oven. In Augusta, Maine, in the 1780s, people came to Martha Ballard's house to bake their own bread and pies.[46] In houses without bake ovens, or between regular baking days, housewives used Dutch ovens for quick breads, pies, and cakes. These shallow kettles stood over the coals on three legs and were fitted with a deep lid into which glowing coals could be piled to provide even heat above as well as below the dish being baked.

Normally, Sarah Bryant heated her oven only once for each baking day, but as her family expanded in the 1820s, this changed. On October 30, 1826, she had to "heat the oven twice" in order to bake a sufficient quantity of "bread and pies," and during the winter of 1827–28 she often had to "heat the oven three times."[47] Her usual diary entries in the day or two before Thanksgiving indicate simply that she "baked pies"; the diary gives no indication of baking an unusual quantity. On November 4, 1797, Elizabeth Porter Phelps was able to make "between .20. & .30. mince pies,"[48] but there was more than one oven in her house, and she may have heated at least one of them more than once.

In using a brick oven, the length of time required for baking depended upon the temperature of the oven and the quantity and type of food being cooked. Meat pies needed a hotter fire than fruit pies or delicate custards, while the residual heat of the oven was all that was needed for pots of beans, which were left in the oven overnight.

Sarah Bryant usually baked on Saturday. Mrs. Hale recommended that "when baking is done twice a week, Wednesdays and Saturdays should be chosen; if only once a week, Saturday is the best, because it allows for preparation for the Sunday dinner—a pudding can be baked—and meat, too, if the family have a real desire of keeping the day for that which it was evidently intended, rest for worldly care, as well as for moral and religious improvement."[49]

The regular use of a brick oven could damage the bricks or mortar, and it was important to have repairs made promptly to avoid the danger of fire spreading from cracks in the oven to the frame of the house or the back side of sheathed walls. Families had to rely on quick breads or improvise in order to avoid an interruption in their bread supply when their oven was damaged. On September 11, 1819, Sarah Bryant noted that "Mr. Gardner built our oven anew"; two days later, while the mortar was curing, Mrs. Bryant "went to Mr. Briggses & baked in their oven."[50]

120. "ABOUT A BAKER'S SHOP," IN *Peter Parley's First Book of Arithmetic* (NEW YORK, 1834). PHOTOGRAPH BY BILL FINNEY. COURTESY OF THE SOCIETY FOR THE PRESERVATION OF NEW ENGLAND ANTIQUITIES.

Another arithmetic lesson, illustrated by an urban baker's shop, where "bread, gingerbread, cakes, biscuit, &c." are displayed in the window. The lesson makes it clear that "in small country towns people generally bake their own bread," while city dwellers enjoy the convenience and greater variety afforded by commercial bakeries.

City dwellers relied on commercial bakers for breads, beans, and pies, and professional confectioners offered more exotic desserts. As early as 1810, a French pastry maker, M. Labatut, opened a confectionery shop in Portsmouth, where he offered "the best Jelly of all kinds. Wedding Cake, and refreshments in general."[51] Peter Pailhes advertised in Boston that he had fixed up several chambers "in the neatest style, for the accommodation of Ladies and Gentlemen," where he offered "a large assortment of Refreshments—viz. CREAMS of great variety—made by one of the best workmen of Europe, in all kinds of shapes—in imitation of Pyramids, Musk and Water Melons and other kinds of fruits." Pailhes's creams could be enjoyed in combination with "lemon, orgeat, capiliaire, groseille, framboise or vinaigre syrups," or accompanied by a selection of cordials, pastries, and other confectionery, all "calculated to promote health during the summer season."[52] In Salem, John Remond was also a professional caterer, having headquarters in Hamilton Hall. His wife Nancy worked with him and was well known for her fine baking. In 1849, she advertised "Cakes of various kinds made to order, at short notice, among which are Wedding, Plum, Pound, White, Bride, Currant, Taylor, Sponge, Compositions, elections, etc."[53]

Dairying

On farms, dairying was usually women's work. Even though she had hired girls to handle the actual milking, Elizabeth Phelps referred to herself as "the old dairymaid" when writing to Betsy in 1810: "Tomorrow I shall have churning and cheese."[54] In October 1813, the sixty-five-year-old Mrs. Phelps

121. BUTTER MAKING WITH BOTH A ROTARY CHURN AND THE TRADITIONAL UPRIGHT CHURN AND DASHER, WOODCUT, C. 1820, ALEXANDER ANDERSON SCRAPBOOKS, VOL. I, PRINT COLLECTION, MIRIAM & IRA D. WALLACH DIVISION OF ART, PRINTS AND PHOTOGRAPHS, THE NEW YORK PUBLIC LIBRARY, ASTOR, LENOX AND TILDEN FOUNDATIONS.

A single broad milk pan is on the shelf above the wooden milk pail, although the amount of cream that would rise in just one milk pan would not be enough to make into butter in such large churns.

was making three cheeses a week. Dr. Peter Bryant had such confidence in his wife's skill at handling this aspect of the household economy that in his will he bequeathed the dairy operation solely "to the discretion and good management of my beloved wife, Sarah."[55]

Both women's diaries contain abundant documentation of the work involved in managing a dairy: weaning calves, selling veal, hiring girls to do the milking, supervising their work to be sure the cows were well stripped of milk, straining milk, scrubbing and scalding milk pails, washing the milk pans and straining cloths, setting milk for butter or cheese, skimming cream, churning, working butter, exchanging milk, making cheese, and cleaning out the buttery at the beginning and end of each season. Sarah Emery described the routine:

> In those summer days, when my recollection first opens, mother and aunt Sarah rose in the early dawn, and taking the well-scoured wooden pails from the bench by the back door, repaired to the cow yard behind the barn. We owned six cows; my grandmother four. Having milked the ten cows, the milk was strained, the fires built, and breakfast prepared. . . . The milk being from the ten cows, my mother made cheese four days, Aunt Sarah having the milk the remainder of the week. In this way, good-sized cheeses were obtained. The curd having been broken into the basket, the dishes were washed, and unless there was washing or other extra work, the house was righted. By the time this was done, the curd was ready for the [cheese] press. . . . After dinner the cheeses were turned and rubbed.[56]

The work was relentless, for the cows had to be milked twice daily, and all the milk used. Elizabeth Phelps felt the strength of this obligation on a June Saturday in 1801: "about .3. in the morning I wak'd with the sick headach, grew worse, puk'd a number of times—but knew I must get up, which I did towards .6.—skim'd my milk, being oblig'd to stop, go to the door & puke a number of times—but at last got my cheese set, could do no more, took to my bed."[57]

Butter making and cheesemaking in the Bryant family were both for family use and to bring in some cash in the decade after Peter Bryant's death. Sarah seldom noted the quantities of butter she churned; when she did, they were relatively small, such as the two pounds she made on April 10, 1817. During hot weather, when milk production was at its greatest, and butter could not be preserved safely, the excess milk was turned into cheeses of various sorts.

Cheesemaking usually began in a small way in June, when the cows had freshened and "new milk cheese" was made in addition to butter.[58] Sometime during the latter part of June, Sarah Bryant began to "exchange" milk with her neighbor, Mrs. Briggs, a process that continued until near the end of September, when the weather was again cool enough for butter making. The exchange of milk was a common practice by which families with only a small number of cows pooled their resources to ensure that each would have enough milk to make good-sized cheeses on an agreed-upon number of days per week.[59] Ruth Bascom began an agreement like this on a Saturday in late July 1810, when "Mrs. Hastings sent up her milk by Nabby & Charlott. Lucinda Baker brought theirs over, to exchange milk, to make larger cheeses." On Monday, Ruth "made the first cheese" since she had begun housekeeping, four years previously; that evening she sent her milk to Mrs. Hastings; on August 3 she made her second cheese; and on the fourteenth her "fifth and last cheese."[60]

122. BUTTERY, COFFIN HOUSE, NEWBURY, MASSACHUSETTS. COURTESY OF THE SOCIETY FOR THE PRESERVATION OF NEW ENGLAND ANTIQUITIES. PHOTOGRAPHED BY ARTHUR HASKELL.

Caleb Huse recalled this as "the dairy-room, always as clean and sweet as possible" (Old Time New England, *p. 71). The buttery's shallow shelves were designed to hold large earthenware milk pans, in which cream was set to rise after each milking. In this room, the cream was skimmed from the milk and the cheeses were made. Located on the north side of the house, it was always a cool room.*

Sarah Bryant sometimes used sage to flavor a new-milk cheese, but there is no other indication of flavoring cheeses given in her diary. She frequently made "four meal" cheese, which was less rich than the cheese described by Sarah Emery as a "two meal cheese," made with "one milking of new milk and one of skimmed to the cheese," while the cream of the second milking was set aside for butter.[61] Sarah Bryant's economical "four meal cheese" was made of 75 percent skimmed milk.

Butter making and cheesemaking had to be done in a cool room located near the water supply and the cow barn. Such a room was often called the "buttery." As dedicated spaces for domestic work were added to New England farmhouses in the middle of the nineteenth century, and butter making and cheesemaking rose in commercial importance, special rooms for dairying became a high priority. Thomas Walter Ward, Jr., described a makeshift situation in a Massachusetts farmhouse that was going into commercial butter making and cheesemaking in a big way in 1847: "We have for the present turned the bedroom or the south room so-called into a dairy room. It is much more convenient than the old 'cheese room.' And better than the cellar, and with 70 to 80 pans of milk looks rather imposing. We make more than 80 pounds of butter a week."[62] Francis Underwood described such a space, where "adjoining the kitchen, and

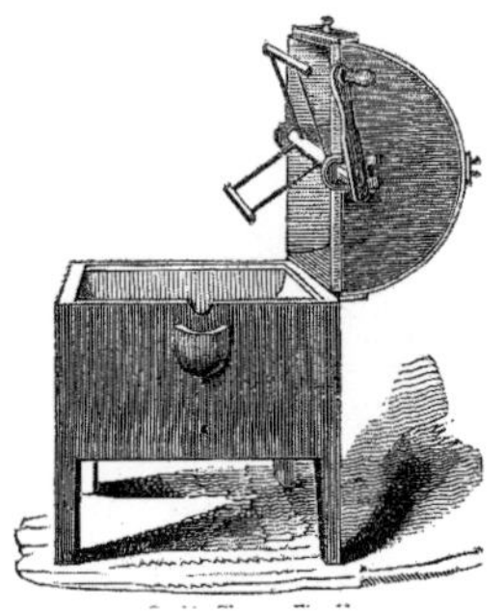

123. GAULT'S CHURN, ILLUSTRATION IN CHARLES A. GOODRICH, *The Family Encyclopedia, or Compendium of Useful Knowledge* (HARTFORD, 1850). PRIVATE COLLECTION.

This churn was "a celebrated article, and by some, even preferred to any other kind. The cut represents the top or upper half lifted up to receive the cream or discharge the butter." Technical improvements in butter-making and cheesemaking equipment accompanied increasing emphasis on market production on some New England dairy farms in the 1840s.

124. BUTTERY WITH NEARLY ONE HUNDRED CHEESES, WOODCUT, C. 1810–30. ALEXANDER ANDERSON SCRAPBOOKS, VOL. I, PRINT COLLECTION, MIRIAM & IRA D. WALLACH DIVISION OF ART, PRINTS AND PHOTOGRAPHS, THE NEW YORK PUBLIC LIBRARY, ASTOR, LENOX AND TILDEN FOUNDATIONS.

Successful cheesemaking required careful attention. In her Reminiscences of a Nonagenarian, *Sarah Emery casually described a daily task: "After dinner the cheeses were turned and rubbed" (page 7).*

generally in an addition, or lean-to, were the cheese press and tubs, diffusing in mild weather the faintly sour odor of whey. There, too, were shelves, on which lay ripening cheeses, turned daily, and polished with butter and red annatto by diligent hands."[63] Sarah Bryant carefully scrubbed her buttery each autumn after the weather turned cold and milk began to freeze on the open shelves, and the family supply of cheeses had been carried to the cellar for winter storage.

During the early years of her widowhood, Sarah Bryant applied her energy and management skills to producing cheese for sale, with considerable success. On October 1, 1822, she noted that she had "sold 302 lbs. of cheese to a Mr. Loud of Abington." Three years later, on September 29, "Mr. Globe carried away six hundred pounds of cheese at six cents per lb." Having been paid only thirty-six dollars for making six hundred pounds of cheese, Mrs. Bryant's only comment in her diary was, "Washed out the buttery."[64]

Meat

Although the New England diet relied heavily on meat, fresh meat was in limited supply in rural kitchens. Underwood rightly tells us that "in ancient times few farmers had regular supplies of fresh meat. Except at the autumnal pig-killing, or at the slaughter of a lamb in the spring, or very rarely in winter of a steer, their tables were furnished with salted beef and pork from their own cellar, and with dried salt fish. To allay the irritation caused by such viands, many vegetables were used; but the main dependence was pickled peppers and 'cowcumbers,'—a dangerous indulgence, one would think,—and applesauce."[65]

Farmers who kept large flocks of sheep could supply their own families or their neighbors with "fresh meat in any emergency."[66] Because sheep were relatively small animals, the fresh mutton or lamb could be consumed within a few families before it spoiled. During the late-fall butchering time, one could expect one's neighbors to have fresh meat and to be willing to sell or to "lend" useful quantities with the expectation of being paid back when one butchered an animal of one's own. Seeking fresh beef on the evening of November 27, 1782, Abner Sanger went "up to Abijah Wilder's for beef. There is none. Then to Ichabod Fisher's and borrow a few pounds."

When a family killed a cow, a sheep, or a pig, there was a huge amount of work to be done in both the barnyard and the kitchen. "You remember it used to take all the week to get thro' with all matters," Elizabeth Phelps reminded Betsy in 1805.[67] Huge tubs or kettles for scalding, storage containers, sharp knives, and plenty of salt were needed; the Sangers had to borrow kettles and tubs for salting meat on many occasions. Steelyards were useful in order to repay the exact amount of meat a family had "borrowed" from its neighbors, and Abner Sanger usually borrowed those when he was butchering as well.

The Phelps and Bryant families, like many others, usually did their butchering in late November or early December, after Thanksgiving and when cold weather could be relied on to help preserve the meat. The women's work included cleaning tripe, trying out tallow or hog's lard, utilizing the animal's head and feet for making headcheese or baking foot pies, and cleaning "the guts."[68] Sausage making was a high priority in the first days after butchering; one night in 1812, a weary Ruth Bascom noted in her diary: "I prepared meat for Sausages after midnight."[69] Some meat was frozen for winter use; hams were salted down in anticipation of smoking in late winter; some meat was exchanged with neighbors; and most of that which was to be preserved for family consumption was salted down in large barrels in the cellar. Meat that was to be frozen was stored in the attic or in an unheated lean-to or chamber. Relying on natural freezing required close attention and quick action if the outdoor temperature rose above thirty-two degrees, as it often did during a January

125. COVER, *Fisher's Improved House-Keeper's Almanac and Family Receipt Book* (PHILADELPHIA, 1858). COURTESY OF THE SOCIETY FOR THE PRESERVATION OF NEW ENGLAND ANTIQUITIES.

The bounty of the New England kitchen is here symbolized by an extraordinary quantity and variety of meat and fish rather than by fresh vegetables or pastry.

thaw. On January 10, 1831, Sarah Bryant had such a situation to cope with: "Very warm—meat thawed out."

Having no pig to slaughter, Betsy Phelps Huntington purchased a large quantity of fresh pork after her family consumed the fresh meat that had been carried back from her parents' large farm in Hadley after a Thanksgiving visit there in December 1801. Betsy expected a large number of guests at her table, for she was obliged to entertain the judges of the county court, which was then sitting in Litchfield. She wrote to her mother describing the meal: "For them we had a Hadley supper at the table—sausages (cakes which I make of the pork we had sent in after our return), toast, bread & butter, cake, etc." She added: "Tomorrow I make mince pies."[70]

On farms, chickens and fowls could be killed at any time for pies or for roasting; turkeys and an occasional goose were usually roasted. For market-dependent families in urban areas, butchers offered cuts of fresh beef, pork, and mutton nearly all year, but poultry was not always available, for it was difficult to transport large quantities of live fowl long distances in extraordinarily hot or cold weather. Poultry was usually available in the Boston markets in the fall; in smaller cities like Worcester, Portsmouth, and Salem it was available more often. An unusual situation occurred in Salem in February 1810, when, according to Dr. Bentley, "10 hundred weight of turkies & fowls [were] brought into our market by one farmer this day. They had been preserved in Snow."[71] Still, roast fowl was considered such a treat that in 1818, Bentley called it "the greatest luxury of New England."[72]

In heavily forested areas, there was wild game to be caught, and venison was popular. Wild animals posed some danger to domestic animals, and as late as 1794, Abner Sanger recorded a meal of "wolf-killed mutton" in Keene, New Hampshire.[73] Martha Ballard occasionally cooked rabbits for dinner in Augusta, Maine, but there is only one reference in Sarah Bryant's diary to any kind of wild meat: on October 4, 1831, the family "had a raccoon for dinner." By the 1840s, Massachusetts regulated the hunting of wild birds and game, including partridges, quails, woodcock, snipe, capon, robins, grouse, plovers, curlews, dough birds, chicken-birds, and deer, suggesting that the hunting of these species was becoming both dangerous and excessive, and resulting in some control of at least the market supply of wild game.[74]

Salted meats were usually fried, but fresh meats were hung from a roasting string in front of a fire for cooking, unless a family owned a spit and kitchen andirons equipped with hooks to support it. Particularly affluent families and many tavern keepers owned jacks with geared mechanisms that turned spits continuously and ensured even browning. About the turn of the century, shiny tin reflecting ovens of the type now often known as "tin kitchens" were more readily available; these were equipped with a spit that could be fixed at regular intervals around a 360-degree axis, making it possible to direct heat where it was most needed and to avoid singeing wing tips and other tender areas when roasting. Sarah Emery first saw one of these ovens in 1796, while visiting in Newburyport her newly married Aunt Bartlett, in whose kitchen some recently "invented implements for housekeeping were displayed, among which was a tin rooster [*sic*]. . . . This new 'tin kitchen,' Aunt Betsy displayed as a rare implement of great value to the culinary art." Remembering this innovation stimulated Sarah Emery to describe how meats were usually cooked in the eighteenth century, when "heretofore our meat and poultry had been baked in the brick oven, or roasted on a spit, resting on brackets, fastened for that purpose to the high, iron andirons, common to every kitchen. Sometimes a turkey or a goose was depended before the fire by a strong string hitched to a nail in the ceiling."[75]

Fish

The New England diet included fish of various kinds as well as meats. In coastal towns, fresh fish, eels, and shellfish such as clams, lobsters, and oysters were boiled, baked, or made into chowders, which were an important part of the diet during most of the year. In Salem, William Bentley occasionally noted shortages based on extraordinary weather conditions or market demand. In February 1805, he wrote: "The thaw continues but not as yesterday, & our fish market again supplied with fish at 4 cts. a lb. For some time past fish was not to be had, from the severe weather, & from the very high price in Boston."[76] Bentley also noted his concern that excessive cold weather drove eels into hiding places and made it hard for poor people, who depended on them for food, and wrote of his appreciation of seasonally available fish, particularly mackerel, bass, smelts, and salmon.

In Plymouth, Massachusetts, William Davis recalled at the end of the nineteenth century that "short, thick fish were selected for the table, and every Saturday [four of] these were served with a napkin above and below, the upper one being removed to the kitchen, and the middle one eaten, while the other two supplied minced fish for Sunday's breakfast, and the Monday washing day dinner. A slice of dunfish cut up with potatoes, beets, carrot and onions, well covered with pork scraps and sweet oil, judiciously peppered, makes a dinner, which, with the white salt fish of today it is impossible to prepare. Fish balls were not in vogue in my early days, but gradually took the place of mince fish, especially Sunday morning."[77] In the King family of Salem, a similar dish was standard fare for the Saturday dinner, where "the legitimate way of enjoying all these good things was to mix them together, making your plate look like a painter's pallet [*sic*] with the various colors of the vegetables, the whole amalgamated and softened by the pale yellow of the egg sauce," which was the traditional Salem addition to this menu.[78]

Families living far from the sea purchased salt cod and mackerel in small quantities at local stores or by the barrelful from regional merchants. In cold weather, country storekeepers might have some fresh fish available, and occasionally a friend or relative visiting from a coastal town might bring fresh fish. The Bryants enjoyed fresh cod for dinner in Cummington on December 26, 1807, the day after a friend arrived from Bridgewater. Elihu Hoyt made arrangements for fresh fish to be delivered to his wife in Deerfield in early March 1826, saying in a letter to her from Boston: "I suppose you will be in want of something fresh if you have not killed the hog."[79]

Even freshwater fish were salted for storage, if they were caught in sufficient quantities to make it seem worthwhile. Abner Sanger and his brother El spent a Sunday afternoon in late May 1775 fixing and salting thirty shad that El had caught near the "Falls."[80]

Vegetables

Root vegetables, squashes, cabbages, peas, and beans were grown for winter storage as well as to be eaten fresh. Vegetables of any kind might be referred to generically as "sauce," whether they were cooked to mush or served raw. Abner Sanger planted string beans and potatoes "for mother to eat" on May 20, 1776; during the 1790s he grew potatoes, parsnips, pumpkins, turnips, beans, peas, cabbages, and carrots for his own family. All of these except the peas were stored for winter in the cellar. In October 1774, Abner fixed "a place in the cellar to put sauce in to keep it from freezing," and several times he helped neighbors "secure sauce in their potato tomb" or "potato hole."[81]

Sarah Bryant kept a kitchen garden and expected her sons to help with soil preparation, sowing, and weeding when they were young. At various times, her diary mentions green peas, corn, string beans, onions, green squash, cabbages, and potatoes. Most of these were grown in quantities large enough for winter storage as well as summer consumption. Still, there was delight in the first fresh produce after a long winter, as when, on May 9, 1809, Mrs. Bryant "boiled some greens." On July 27, 1819, she served "some cowcumbers for breakfast," but during the unusually cold summer of 1816—sometimes referred to in New England as "the year without a summer"—the cucumbers were very late. On Wednesday, August 21, the Bryants "had a mess of cucumbers last Monday the first we have had this summer" and the same day suffered from "frost at night which killed vines in low lands and some corn."

Slices of apple and pumpkin were dried in the fall to be reconstituted later for pies. Abner Sanger preserved pumpkin in several ways—by cutting it up and drying the pieces, by brewing it, and by grinding it up and extracting the juice in a cider mill.[82] Even Elizabeth Phelps's husband, Charles, sometimes participated in this important task. She explained the reasons to Betsy: "Our folks are all hands about pareing pumpkin.—father and all, . . . Prince you know takes himself off soon after supper [and] it becomes necessary for the Esqr to lend his aid that there may be good stewed pumpkin sauce . . . and a scrap for next winter."[83]

Peas and beans were dried and shelled for winter storage, while bunches of herbs, peppers, whole winter squashes, ears of seed corn, and some other vegetables were hung to dry near the kitchen fire. Despite the fact that most of these foods were soon moved to drier, darker places for actual storage, these picturesque activities created the kind of image that has come to symbolize the bounty and self-sufficiency of a New England farm. In our own time they have become a formula for decorating a country kitchen. Underwood's vivid description of the farmhouse kitchen in fall in *Quabbin* was copied in more than one New England town history: "The kitchen was adorned in autumn with festoons of dried apples and red peppers, bunches of ears of seed corn, dried bouquets of sage, savory, mint, and other herbs; and about the fireplace in racks set against the walls, hung crookneck squashes."[84]

Considering the year-round activity, the amount of ambient grease, and the occasional high humidity of a kitchen, Samuel Goodrich's recollection of food storage in the attic was perhaps more accurate: "The garret, which was of huge dimensions, . . . displayed a labyrinth of dried pumpkins, peaches and apples hung in festoons upon the rafters, amid bunches of summer savory, boneset, fennel, and other herbs."[85]

Reflecting the tremendous importance farm families placed on the production and preservation of an adequate supply of food, Sarah Bryant gives far more attention in her diary to food processing and preservation than to the daily work of cooking or the details of the menu. Clearly, her long-term concerns were to assure her family an adequate supply and not to waste anything. At the end of each December, she often commented on the successes and failures of the agricultural season and the health of the community in general. The entry for 1808 is typical: "The season has been fruitful very good for Dairy hay quite plenty, fruit aplenty as common in these parts but scarce in the lower towns."[86] Many men's diaries contain similar summaries of the agricultural year. Each year Samuel Lane noted the effects of drought or evidence of unusual productivity, as in 1762: "What is further remarkable: we have a vast help this fall, by a very Unusual great Quantity of Acorns and Nuts; by which More good Pork is fatted this fall, than was fatted by Corn last fall; and but little Corn is given to Swine this fall. And many people gather'd abundance, to keep their Swine on in the winter, which is a great Saving to Corn."[87]

Maple Sugaring

In late winter, both Abner Sanger and Sarah Bryant described tapping maple trees, making sugar troughs, cutting firewood, and sledding kettles and other equipment to the woods, and noted the extent of the sap run and the quantities of sugar produced. The production of maple sap and sugar was an important and time-consuming business; many times, Sanger and his brother worked for days without stopping. On March 28, 1775, after working around the clock for two days, Abner seems to have lost track of time. His journal records "a very good sap day. Fair, clear and pleasant. I help him [El] gather and boil sap all day and I think all night too." When Austin Bryant began his efforts to improve the profitability of the family farm in the late 1820s, he made additional sap troughs, borrowed extra kettles, boiled large quantities of sap, and set out new maple trees. Most of the work was done in the woods, and although occasionally they "sugared off in the house,"[88] this seems to have been unusual. After all the hard work was done, sharing the fresh sweet was a welcome treat;

on April 3, 1830, "the family went to Mr. Briggs to eat sugar."[89] In the spring of 1844, Edward Jenner Carpenter left his apprenticeship in a Greenfield, Massachusetts, furniture shop and went to his uncle's home in nearby Bernardston and "ate maple sugar till it did not taste good." Even after this indulgence, the next day he went back for more, brought back some syrup, "& sugared it off & made 8 little cakes to carry home with me."[90]

126. WOMEN VISITING A MAPLE-SUGAR CAMP IN THE WOODS, WOODCUT, C. 1820. ALEXANDER ANDERSON SCRAPBOOKS, VOL. I, PRINT COLLECTION, MIRIAM & IRA D. WALLACH DIVISION OF ART, PRINTS AND PHOTOGRAPHS, THE NEW YORK PUBLIC LIBRARY, ASTOR, LENOX AND TILDEN FOUNDATIONS.

Springtime

As the season advanced, Sarah Bryant's diary records the fruitfulness of animals as well as changes in the growth of plants. On February 21, 1833, she noted, "hens begin to lay"; and in late May or June of many years she observed the swarming of bees. Mrs. Bryant often noted the date of the first blooming of plums, apples, peaches, and cherries in the orchard, and she worried over the threat of late frost during the blooming season. Her diary records the first sowing of grains and garden vegetables, and she took satisfaction in recording the date when the first peas and cucumbers were gathered in the garden. The year 1805 must have had an exceptionally cold spring, for on June 11 they experienced "frost at night which killed the cucumber vines." Nothing, however, could compare with 1816 when a combination of snow in June, and cold nights and drought in July and August comprised a season referred to by many as the year without a summer.

Fruits

Ruth Bascom bought berries picked by young neighbor girls, and Sarah Bryant's diary describes eating or picking strawberries, raspberries, blackberries, and thimbleberries, none of which appear to have been cultivated. The Bryant family did grow currants, which were used in 1818 to make wine, and they obtained quinces from an unidentified source for "quince sauce." The ripening of peaches and watermelons provided many people with an excuse for hospitality or visiting. In 1832, Thomas Robbins enjoyed such an occasion: "At evening eat watermelons at Mr. Tudor's, with Mr. and Mrs. Lee."[91] Ruth Henshaw Bascom and Elizabeth Porter Phelps also described going to friends' homes to eat these special summer fruits.[92] Betsy Phelps had imagined that her mother would enjoy a dessert of "a fine watermelon—at the end of the entry or perhaps in your bedroom."[93] Although she and her husband did not raise their own melons, Ruth Bascom was able to treat her neighbors to this delicacy in August when she sent "a piece of our great Savannah Watermelon, which we received 2 or 3 weeks ago cut today & distributed a part to our neighbors."[94] The Reverend Jonathan Fisher enjoyed the challenge of growing both muskmelons and watermelons way down East in Blue Hill, Maine. In 1826, he raised a particularly large number of melons, one of which was "in length 12 in., in girth 23 in., and in weight 8 lbs." Fisher exulted in his diary: "I am unconscionably fond of melons, and I have enjoyed eating them, with, I trust, thanks to God for his great bounty. We gathered and ate the last of this large crop on the 30th day of September with some friends invited in for the occasion."[95]

Although cookbooks are full of recipes for fruit preserves and jams, some housewives felt that these were too rich and contained too much expensive sugar for regular family use. In Sarah Bryant's diary there are only a few references to preserving berries as jam or jelly, usually for strawberry preserves. In 1831, William Cullen Bryant's wife, Frances, gathered berries for jelly, but it is unclear from the diary whether she did this every year or not. It could have been a bid for attention, or a romantic rural adventure for the well-to-do urban daughter-in-law.

Apples were stored whole and used for cider, applesauce, and pies. It was always a triumph to preserve some good, sound apples until spring or early summer, when the first of the new crop would be ready for picking. Thomas Robbins exulted in his diary that year-old apples were still sound on both July 5, 1833, and June 21, 1834,[96] and he annually described his pleasure in freezing hard cider, reducing it in volume by removing the ice, and bottling the stronger beverage. Anticipating good crops of apples, the Bryants often hired a cooper to repair and hoop barrels sometime in September or early October. On the Bryant farm, apple picking usually occupied the men for a week in mid-October, after which some barrels of whole apples were stored in the cellar and others were carried to the cider mill.

Making barrels of applesauce for winter storage was a time-consuming kitchen project in November, which began with several days and evenings devoted to paring and cutting apples and to boiling cider for "cider molasses," the sticky, sweet syrup that was the basis for applesauce. After boiling both the cider and the sauce, securing a good quantity, and restoring order in the kitchen, Sarah Bryant often recorded her satisfaction: "Finished making the sauce—washed up the kitchen," she wrote on October 29, 1814; and "made three kettles of applesauce & *finished*" on November 16, 1820. Betsy Huntington agreed: "My business has been making applesauce—a tedious job . . . tho I have so many blisters on my hand they are quite troublesome."[97] Betsy had been peeling apples and quinces in the lower kitchen with the help of her "boy and girl," but the job was still not done. The next day, her husband wrote to his new brother-in-law in Boston describing the ongoing project: "I do not know but you are indebted for this letter to a piece of business with which I presume in your family you are not much conversant, but which is much in fashion with us country folks, once a year. Without much circumlocution, then, I must tell you that Eliza, poor girl, is making quince sauce. She has been at it all day, & when I tell you she is going to make two tubs full, you will easily conceive of her having business enough without writing just now & she told me if I would go & write to you, that I need not pare apples."[98]

Making applesauce with quinces was described by Francis Underwood in *Quabbin:* "This latter preserve was wholesome and appetizing, but is now seldom seen; perhaps on account of the scarcity of cleanly made and unfermented cider. The cider was boiled down almost to sirup, and pared and cored apples, with a few quinces for flavor, were slightly cooked in it, after which the mass was poured into a clean barrel, and kept in a cool place."[99]

Receipts and Cookbooks

Heating a brick oven and regulating a fire; making cider applesauce and chowders; baking pies, beans, and bread; chopping meat for sausages; producing a capital chicken pie—these are traditional New England ways of cooking, which young women learned directly from their mothers, sisters, neighbors, female relatives, and other mentors. Cookbooks were almost unknown in eighteenth-century New England households. The traditional fare of boiled or baked meats, beans, pies, breads, and puddings required little in the way of careful measuring or subtlety in flavoring. Still, some cooks were renowned for certain dishes and were asked to share their secrets. Patient tutelage was usually far more successful than written receipts, as the need for exact measurement was not generally understood. Inexperienced cooks might never duplicate the results, especially in baking, as directions calling for a handful of this and a mite of that, mixed until just right, and baked in a hot oven were hard

127. KITCHEN FIREPLACE, IN ESTHER A. HOWLAND, *The New England Economical Housekeeper* (WORCESTER, 1845). WORCESTER HISTORICAL MUSEUM.

A well-regulated kitchen, with a clock and two separate worktables. Here, meat was still cooked in a tin kitchen and in a large pot on the crane, rather than in a stove.

to judge, and leavening agents were inconsistent in their results. Experienced cooks who were unused to written receipts sometimes made serious mistakes when trying to write down a procedure that was second nature to them. When Mrs. Bryant included a receipt for gingerbread at the end of her diary for 1825, she left out two essential ingredients, flour and ginger. She wrote:

> To make ginger bread
> half pint molasses
> half a pint of cream
> a tablespoon full of pearl ash
> alum a piece half as big as a
> wallnut dissolved in water[100]

Most cookbooks sold by eighteenth-century New England booksellers were English texts that were usually addressed to the upper classes, relied on large staffs of professional kitchen workers, and utilized expensive ingredients. Some of these were republished in America, but few had more than a brief appendix containing information designed for American situations. Amelia Simmons's 1796 *American Cookery* is the first cookbook said to have been entirely written by an American author. Some of the receipts were particularly suited to American ingredients. Pumpkin pie, winter-squash pudding, and spruce beer were featured as well as "Johnny Cake," "Indian Slapjacks," and three versions of Indian pudding, all of which were based on cornmeal. *American Cookery* was the first cookbook to recommend pearlash (potassium carbonate) as a leavening agent in baking, making it possible to produce gingerbread and cookies that were light in texture without relying on yeast or beaten egg whites. The book was so popular that a second edition—which included receipts for "election cake" and "independence cake"—was published just four years after the first.

American Cookery was only the first of a large number of cookbooks that were published in the first half of the nineteenth century to meet the growing demand for more system in household management and greater variety in diet. Many of these were based on Amelia Simmons's text and format, although her name appears nowhere in them. Other authors developed cookbooks adapted to the cuisine of particular regions of the country. Typical was *The Virginia Housewife* by Mrs. Mary Randolph, which began with a text, "Method Is the Soul of Management," very much like a minister preaching a sermon. Mrs. Randolph's 1828 book, with all its recipes and tart advice, was reprinted in an

1831 stereotype edition, which had some circulation even in New England. One copy, used in a New Hampshire family, has this poignant inscription written inside the cover: "This was my mother's first cook-book. She sent to town by my father. He bought one of the only kind they had. Mother was so disappointed, she cried. My mother became a very nice cook, although she did not use the Virginia Housewife. Ma's next cook book was by Mrs. Child."

"Mrs. Child" was Lydia Maria Child, the author of *The American Frugal Housewife,* a book of practical household advice, remedies, and receipts so popular that by 1830, more than four thousand copies had been sold, and it, too, was offered in a stereotype edition.[101] Mrs. Child's receipts and suggestions for food preservation were designed to systematize "common cooking" and to help women avoid waste. *The American Frugal Housewife* began with a long and detailed series of household hints titled "Odd Scraps for the Economical"—a practical text that was also printed as a broadside titled "Domestic Economy," with instructions that it be "hung like a map."[102] Lydia Maria Child, like Eliza Leslie, Catherine Beecher, and so many others who would come after them, sought to introduce regularity and economy into kitchens that already knew the virtues of both.

Cookstoves

Despite the fact that there were more than 550 patents issued for cookstoves between the years 1820 and 1850, most authors of cookbooks, even Catherine Beecher, assumed that cooking would continue to be done on a fireplace with an iron crane, and baking done in a brick oven or on the hearth. The new cookstoves were widely available throughout New England, and many people rejoiced in their advantages at the same time as they struggled with their disadvantages. The new devices were said to be both more convenient to use and more efficient in their consumption of wood. Their raised cooking surfaces reduced the amount of bending and heavy lifting required for cooking and made it easier to maintain a constant supply of clean hot water. Most of the stoves used smaller pieces of wood, but they all needed much more tending than an open fireplace in order for the heat under the pots to be controlled and an even oven temperature maintained. Most of the ovens were considered tiny by people who were used to doing a week's baking at a time. Although stoves confined smoke and flying ash, they had to be emptied of both soot and ashes frequently. Hot coals lurking in the bucket of recently removed ashes were a

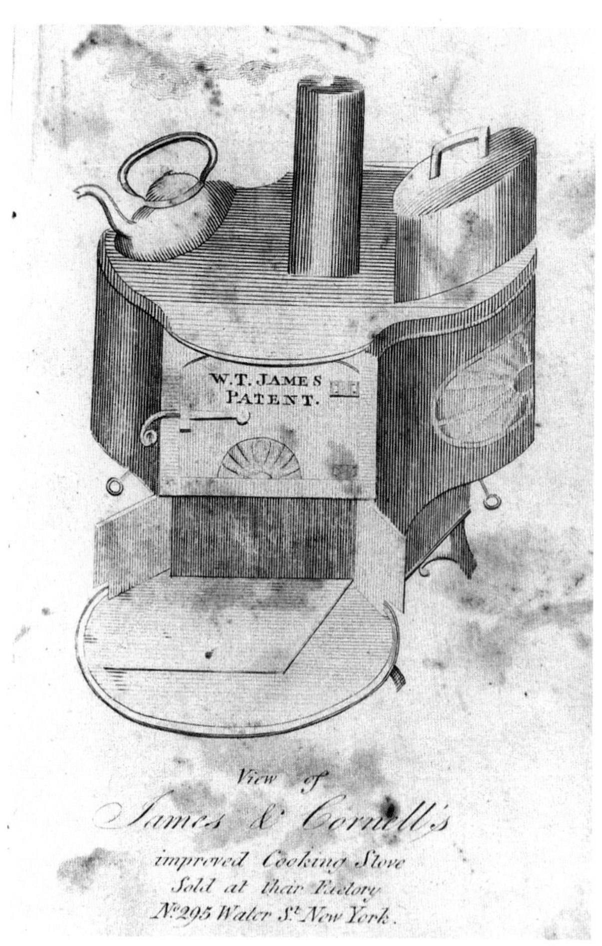
W.T. JAMES
PATENT.
View of
James & Cornell's
improved Cooking Stove
Sold at their Factory
No. 295 Water St. New York.

128. JAMES'S STOVE, IN *The Experienced American Housekeeper, or Domestic Cookery; Formed on Principles of Economy for the Use of Private Families* (NEW YORK, 1823). PORTSMOUTH ATHENAEUM.

serious fire hazard, especially if it was a wooden bucket. Every six months or so it was necessary to take down the stovepipe and clean it thoroughly. Many preferred the old ways.

The first successful cookstove in America was patented by William T. James on April 26, 1815,[103] and manufactured by the firm of James and Cornell of Troy, New York. James's stoves were advertised widely, even in small cities like Keene, New Hampshire, within two years.[104] These popular stoves were selected by the first New England missionaries to Honolulu, who departed in 1820 for a place where they expected that firewood would be scarce. Unfortunately, some castings were broken on the voyage out, and the stoves never functioned satisfactorily. As a result, the correspondence of the missionary women has some of the most useful descriptions of the advantages and difficulties of cooking on a James stove. As illustrated on the frontispiece to *The Experienced American Housekeeper* in 1823, these stoves had a central firebox and a fairly large baking oven; the top had two large boiling holes flanking the firebox. The advantages were proclaimed by the manufacturer: such stoves "will do all kinds of cooking, washing and heating of rooms, with a small quantity of fuel, without inconvenience of Steam—it being conducted from the Steamer, Oven and Boiler, into the pipe. It may be used with wood or coal, with grates or without. The fire passes round the Oven, Boilers, and Tea-Kettle, or under the Griddle, and is turned from one to the other by Dampers, to heat one or more at a time."[105]

James's stoves were sold with customized cooking apparatus that fitted snugly in the openings on the top of the stove. Eight sizes were available; the complete units included a cast boiler and steamer, a stew pan, two griddles, a tin tea kettle, two pudding or bread pans, two pie pans, a sheet-iron pan, a dipper, and an oven slider. The prices ranged from fifteen to fifty dollars in 1823. Five thousand sets had been sold by then, and the makers recommended the stoves for cooking in boardinghouses, in taverns, and on ships, as well as for private family use.[106]

129. A JAMES STOVE IN THE HARRISON GRAY HARRIS HOMESTEAD, WARNER, NEW HAMPSHIRE. PHOTOGRAPH, 1908. PRIVATE COLLECTION.

This stove was brought from Concord, New Hampshire, on an ox sled in February 1827 and is said to have been the first cookstove brought to Warner. It remained in use until 1908 and was described in 1915 by a woman who had cooked on it nearly all her life as "a marvel of convenience in every respect. The oven was directly over the fire, where wood twenty inches long could be used. The blaze passed under the two oval places for the kettles, and then over the oven into the funnel [pipe] so that all the heat was available and could be regulated by the dampers. . . . Down in front was a large sunken hearth unsurpassed as a place for broiling purposes. The two doors could be set wide, and as there was always a fine draught, the effect was that of an open fireplace." (Amanda Harris, "When This Old Stove Was New," Country Life *[January 1915], p. 68.) It appears that the Harris family used the large brick oven in their chimney for baking after the new stove was installed in 1827.*

The technical differences between the James stoves and those of its many competitors were fairly minor, although each manufacturer prided himself on the distinctive ornamentation of his castings. In May 1830, John Moore of Acworth, New Hampshire, received a patent for "an improved *Cooking Stove*" that was "an oval stove, having the general form of a common ten plate stove," with "nothing in it meriting particular notice, as it merely differs in the form and arrangement of its parts from a number of others," with the exception of "two flues which admit the heat under the two boilers."[107] Seeking a way to distinguish his stove from hundreds of competitors, Moore published advertisements containing endorsements from satisfied users in nine towns throughout southern New Hampshire, and he began to franchise dealers. Kimball and Page of Bradford, New Hampshire, purchased the rights to sell Moore's stoves in four counties and published in the Newport, New Hampshire, *Argus Spectator* in 1837 an advertisement that was to be sung to the tune of "Yankee Doodle":

Now ladies all and gentlemen.
We pray you give attention,
Whilst we relate a real tale
About a new invention.

One Johnny Moore of Yankee blood,
A cute and cunning fellow,
He made himself a Cooking Stove—
By gosh! It was a whaler.

Four holes upon its top it had,
And rims both big and little,
So he could boil his dinner in
Most any kind of kettle.

A darn'd great oven, too, it had,
As big as Granny's apron,
In which he always baked his bread,
While Molly fried the bacon.

And dampers, too, it had within,
To regulate the heat, sir,
And threw it round the oven where
He wished to bake his meat, sir.

It took but mighty little fire
To cook a rousing dinner;
'Twould bake his bread and boil his pot,
And warm a chilly sinner.

And all the folks "down east" declared
It was a nation's good thing,
To roast a fowl, to bake a pig,
Or boil a hasty pudding.

When Uncle Sam the story heard,
How nice 'twould cook provision,
He vowed no man such stoves should make
Without John Moore's permission.[108]

In the competitive New England stove business, marketing was everything.

Some people were distrustful of the new stoves. Susan Blunt described public reaction to one in her family's home in Thornton's Ferry, New Hampshire: "That year we had a new cooking stove, the first one in town. The neighbors said we would all be sick before Spring." The family, however, could see the advantages of new technology: "Mother was pleased with it. It was easier to cook than the fireplace. In a year or two all the neighbors had one, after they saw that we came out all right in the Spring."[109] Even frugal Ruth Bascom spent thirty dollars for a cookstove in 1819, despite her concern that such an indulgence might be unseemly for a minister's wife.

130. KITCHEN OF THE HOME OF JAMES AND JANE RUNDLET, PORTSMOUTH, NEW HAMPSHIRE, BUILT 1807–08. COURTESY OF THE SOCIETY FOR THE PRESERVATION OF NEW ENGLAND ANTIQUITIES. PHOTOGRAPH BY DOUGLAS ARMSDEN.

The kitchen is shown as last used by James and Jane Rundlet's descendants in the 1960s. A Rumford roaster is still accessible at the left of the fireplace, but the pot holes of the Rumford range at the right have been covered over to create a counter. The fire holes of the range are still accessible behind their cast-iron doors, and the hood, which was intended to capture smoke and steam and convey it to the chimney, is still in place above the inoperative range.

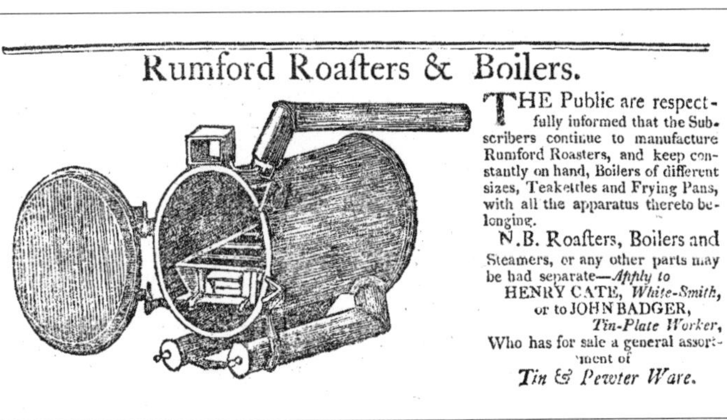

Rumford Roafters & Boilers.

THE Public are respectfully informed that the Subscribers continue to manufacture Rumford Roasters, and keep constantly on hand, Boilers of different sizes, Teakettles and Frying Pans, with all the apparatus thereto belonging.

N.B. Roafters, Boilers and Steamers, or any other parts may be had separate—*Apply to*
HENRY CATE, *White-Smith*,
or to JOHN BADGER,
Tin-Plate Worker,
Who has for sale a general assortment of
Tin & Pewter Ware.

131. "RUMFORD ROASTERS & BOILERS," ADVERTISEMENT IN THE *Portsmouth Oracle*, MAY 9, 1807. PORTSMOUTH ATHENAEUM.

On October 11, 1806, Rumford kitchens had been offered in Portsmouth "as cheap as they can be purchased in Boston" by Henry Cate, White-Smith, and John Badger, "Tin-Plate Worker," who also offered to sell roasters and boilers separately. Badger billed James Rundlet $37.49 for "Rumford works" in January 1808; in July of the same year, Henry Cate billed Rundlet $85.73 for "Rumford work &c."

None of the common early-nineteenth-century cookstoves incorporated technical improvements based on the scientific studies of fuel efficiency and radiation of heat that were conducted by Benjamin Thompson, Count Rumford, in the 1790s and applied by him to cooking ranges and roasters. Rumford's innovative suggestions were recognized as important by educated men, and they were popularized in America by being included and illustrated in the second, 1811 edition of Asher Benjamin's *American Builder's Companion.* Rumford roasters and boilers were manufactured in Boston by William Howe, who sold them for installation in private homes and taverns. Despite the fact that a complete installation usually cost over a hundred dollars, more than five hundred Rumford apparatuses were operating in New England kitchens by 1826.[110]

A Rumford range is a series of individual fireboxes enclosed in brickwork and accessible through cast-iron doors. Each fire could be regulated by adjustable dampers and was vented directly into a nearby chimney. Each firebox had a hole on top with specially fitted covered pots and kettles that extended down into the range and obtained heat from individual fires on iron grates in each firebox. Various sizes of Rumford's cooking apparatus were available, and they could be arranged in different configurations, depending on the available space. A Rumford roaster is a cast-iron cylinder with a firebox below and a series of ventilating tubes that permit close control of the speed of cooking in either damp or dry heat.[111] Unfortunately, the apparatus was so complex that few cooks were able to regulate it successfully, and it was hard to get repairs done after the original installers and manufacturers had died; consequently, many of the roasters were used only for a few years.

Changing Attitudes

As technology changed, so, too, did people's attitudes toward kitchens and toward food itself. More and more attention was given to the ideal diet and changes in cooking style in the 1830s and 40s. Some people advocated whole-grain bread, vegetarianism, temperance, and other dietary reforms. Completely enclosed kitchen ranges that cooked by radiant heat from a concealed fire were available by mid-century. All of these modern innovations seem incompatible with the popular image of the bountiful New England kitchen, but in their denial of the pleasures of traditional food and drink and the warmth of the fireside, the reformers may have contributed to the longing expressed in the mid-century re-creations of the New England kitchen as an icon of hospitality and plenty.

Some people were concerned only about the food, convinced that nothing could replace the open hearth. Caroline King remembered "the very contemptuous expression on my father's face the first time a turkey baked in a range was placed before him on the dinner table, and he always maintained that meats had a wholly different flavor and relish when they were roasted before an open fire, and his opinion was largely shared by many old-fashioned people."[112]

132. KITCHEN OF THE BELLINGHAM CAREY HOUSE, CHELSEA, MASSACHUSETTS, PHOTOGRAPH, C. 1860–90. COURTESY OF THE SOCIETY FOR THE PRESERVATION OF NEW ENGLAND ANTIQUITIES.

On the left is the kind of large kitchen range often installed in the mid-nineteenth century in the old kitchen fireplace of an urban dwelling house. In this case, the old oven has been left accessible.

But changing attitudes affected the kitchen as much as new technology. As Uncle Bill sternly admonished Aunt Lois when she wanted to move the family into the "best room" in *Oldtown Folks,* "Home means right here by mother's kitchen-fire, where she and father sit, and want to sit. You know nobody ever wants to go into that terrible best room of yours." Mrs. Stowe went on to develop this picture fully in a description of the kitchen:

> Now the kitchen was my grandmother's own room. In one . . . corner of it stood a round table with her favorite books, her great work basket, and by it a rickety rocking-chair, the bottom of which was of ingenious domestic manufacture, being in fact made by interwoven strips of former coats and pantaloons of the home circle; but a most comfortable and easy seat it made. My grandfather also had a large splint bottomed arm-chair, with rockers to it, in which he swung luxuriously in one corner of the great fireplace. By the side of its ample blaze we sat down to our family meals, and afterwards, while grandmother and Aunt Lois washed up the tea things, we all sat and chatted by the firelight. Now it was a fact that nobody liked to sit in the best room. In the kitchen each member of the family has established unto him or herself some little pet snuggery, some chair or stool, some individual nook,—forbidden to gentility, but dear to the ungenteel natural heart,—that we looked back to regretfully when we were banished to the colder regions of the best room.[113]

133. *Evening Amusements,* woodcut, c. 1820. Alexander Anderson Scrapbooks, Vol. VII, Print Collection, Miriam & Ira D. Wallach Division of Art, Prints and Photographs, The New York Public Library, Astor, Lenox and Tilden Foundations.

Previously, the "ungenteel natural heart" had lived more fully in the whole house—boiling tea, making toast, dining by many firesides. As gentility was increasing in the parlors and dining rooms, making them seem both forbidding and formal, some people preferred the old, familiar ways. The New England kitchen, which had been the center of so much work as well as fun, was idealized as a social center. As early as 1876, some of these kitchens were transformed into family living rooms, and many of them remain so to this day.

IX

The Pleasure of Our Friends and Neighbors

THE YOUNG WOMAN WHO WROTE "THE PARING (OR APPLE) BEE"—A STORY published in the Lowell *Offering* in 1845—grew up in a town that was "a famous one for frolicking, or rather the folks who lived in it were so. Old and young, church-members and all, partook largely of the spirit of agrarianism and hilarity. We used to have sewing parties, tea parties, candy parties, sugar-camp parties in the wood, parties for cracking nuts and parching corn, huskings, quilting matches and spinning frolics."

If New England households depended for their subsistence on an extended family and an interchange of goods and services among relatives and neighbors, there was also a strong web of mutual concern and lively social intercourse, which both developed out of this system and nurtured it. In New England towns there was little artifice. Relatives and neighbors entered households freely to share joys and sorrows, to offer assistance and support. The same women who had worked together as girls to spin threads, husk corn, and stitch quilts now ran their own hospitable kitchens, encouraged each other during labor, fitted each other's gowns, and had established places in the community.

Women called on each other in the kitchen, weaving room, sitting room, garden, or dooryard; men dropped in at worksites, whether they were in the field, barn, woodshed, shop, mill, or study, many seeking information, tools, or essential ingredients as well as company and offering advice and sharing news in the process. The gender lines were crossed more easily in the evening, and hospitable kitchens or sitting rooms were magnets on cold nights. Some visitors were welcomed for their sage advice, high spirits, and willing hands; others were considered tiresome busybodies. But all were integral parts of the community. It was these individuals who were the models for the central characters in stories crafted by New England authors such as Sarah Orne Jewett, Alice Brown, and Harriet Beecher Stowe. Mrs. Todd, Captain Tilley, and Grandmother Badger were real people.

The democratic kitchen of a minister and his wife grew out of their responsibility for everyone in a community, but their exalted place in a carefully defined social orbit evolved from a well-understood class structure. People like Abner Sanger ranged up, down, and around the town, borrowing, gossiping, chopping wood, running errands, helping out, fixing up, and getting by. Elizabeth Phelps moved as freely through Hadley, but her respected status as mistress of a large farm and family was understood in a different way. With power and privilege came responsibility, and Mrs. Phelps found herself called on to assist, encourage, and even care for many who were less fortunate than she. Even after Peter Bryant died and his widow found herself in increasingly straitened economic circumstances, Sarah Bryant retained her respected social position in Cummington. For these women, neighborliness required charity and service at the same time that it gave sociable pleasures.

New England diarists quite generally chronicle an active pattern of coming and going, of visiting or being visited by neighbors and relatives. This was certainly affected by seasonality. During the press of summer and fall work, people had much less time for visiting. In wintertime, especially when there was good sleighing, everyone enjoyed a lively sociability. In mud-time it was "slow going" or "impossible to stir." Women with very young children were probably at once the most restricted in their visiting and the most eager to see visitors.

Elizabeth Phelps's week beginning Sunday, September 2, 1781, may be seen as typical for someone of her rank and station. The twenty-four-year-old mother and mistress of a large household of people entertained six guests in five days, and one of them stayed overnight: "Monday Mrs. Smith of the Mills here—Tuesday Cousins Anne and Dorothy Parsons of Northampton here—in the after noon Pene and they a visit at Brother Warners. Wednesday Aunt Porter and the Col'lls wife here—my aunt stayed. Thursday Mrs. Bartlett here. Fryday my Aunt Porter went home." By Saturday Elizabeth could hardly wait to get out herself: she went "into town of errands."[1]

This kind of easy sociability must not be seen as disassociated from the conduct of daily work and business, for those who participated in these visits usually did not sit with idle hands; women often carried their sewing or knitting with them. A brisk walk or ride in the open air, followed by the pleasure of sitting down and exchanging family or neighborhood news, reading aloud, seeking advice, or exploring topics of common concern, could be combined with the satisfaction of actual accomplishment.

Large numbers of visitors came for meals or to "tarry" overnight. Laurel Ulrich tells us that in 1790, Martha Ballard entertained sixty-eight overnight guests and served ninety-eight meals to non-family members, probably many of them to men who had come to engage in business at her husband's rural sawmill.[2] As a minister's wife, Ruth Bascom also had large numbers of visitors to cope with. For several years she systematically kept track of them in an addendum to her diary in which she used a code to indicate whether people were there overnight; for breakfast, dinner, or supper; or if they came to see a member of the family. Although dinner with tea was specified separately from dinner, apparently no one came just for tea. In 1825 in the month of January alone, Mrs. Bascom served dinner to fifteen extra people and supper to seventeen, and sixteen "additional meals" were served at irregular hours. At this time the Bascom family was composed of seven people: "Mr. and Mrs. B, Louisa White, Phebe H. Denney, and Franklin Gibson" most of the time. In addition, Winthrop Gates lived with them for nine months beginning in March, Sophronia Kendall moved in with them for November and December, and both Elvira and Lysander came home on extended visits. Five more people "lodged overnight," and one of them was served breakfast. During that month, eleven people called on the minister and eight on his wife, but none of them partook of a regularly scheduled meal. The couple dined out together once and went out for supper four times, always with another family. This active pattern continued from month to month and year to year, with occasional dramatic exceptions resulting from illness or circumstance. In February 1825, nine men stopped at the Bascom parsonage after working to break out the snowy roads; Mrs. Bascom provided them with hot toddy.[3] Over the course of the years, she fed peddlers, "drunken tinkers," and "Negro basket pedlars," sometimes permitting them to sleep on a straw bed on the floor.[4] On March 23, 1826, she had a visit from "Old Lady Patch PM, still deranged & drest like the merest beggar—a Fearnough coat,* without a gown, & very little else, having given away almost every article of her clothes & refuses to wear them at any rate, believing she must suffer 'cold & hunger & nakedness' (in degrees)."[5] A minister's wife accepted whoever walked in the door.

Guests staying overnight contributed skills and labor to family work. Mothers or sisters sometime stayed for as long as six weeks when a child was born,

* Petticoat

taking over the basic household management, permitting the new mother to recover her strength and give her attention to the baby, and offering advice born of their own experience. While visiting in Cummington in September 1808, Charity Bryant cut out "a gown and spencer of black lutestring" for her sister-in-law. Charity may have had particular skill in designing and fitting gowns, or she may have had knowledge of a new style or pattern that she could best convey with her scissors. In Sarah Bryant's busy world, the help itself was welcome. The best visitors fitted easily into the family circle, lightened routine tasks through their assistance, gave special attention to children and the elderly, brought interesting news, knew different songs and games, and they told good stories.

Although Sarah Bryant's diary records many visitors, there is little evidence of their providing actual help with her family sewing. The callers must have brought their own work with them for a few hours of companionable sewing together by the fireside. Sarah Emery referred more than once to the special kind of work that Newburyport ladies took with them when they went visiting: "It was customary for the young ladies of the neighborhood to give social tea parties of an afternoon, at which we assembled at an early hour, with our go-abroad knitting work, usually fine cotton, clocked hose. Some of these clocks comprised the most elaborate patterns. After tea the knitting was laid aside. As the evening drew on the beaux began to appear, then games, or dancing, were enjoyed."[6] Young women who wished to display their superior knitting skills to potential suitors, to women who were acknowledged knitting experts, or to competitive peers were certain to select complex patterns for work that was to be done in public.[7] Plain stockings and mittens could be made at home.

Carrying knitting was by no means unique to Newburyport; diaries document the custom in Salem, Portsmouth, Hadley, and other New England towns. Ruth Bascom often carried her knitting with her; on December 28, 1825, she "called in at Mr. Gates PM with my knitting."[8] This kind of informal, drop-in visit was far more common than the boisterous tea party highlighted by Sarah Emery. Most rural women had to go home to take care of the milk, serve the evening meal, and clean up the kitchen.

Some sewing projects were also carried while visiting. It was important to select a project that would take a few hours, be relatively lightweight, and not demand much concentration. Hemming aprons, pillowcases, napkins, skirts, or small tablecloths was perfect. On September 10, 1801, Sarah Bryant made two handkerchiefs while visiting her neighbor Mrs. Austin. One could just as easily carry sleeves for a gown or the breadths of a skirt to be assembled. Sometimes, the visit itself was focused on viewing a new style, cutting and fitting a particularly difficult pattern, or sharing a clever technique. On June 15, 1810, Mrs. Bryant "made bonnets with Mrs. Snell & Briggs"; the following day she went to Mrs. Snell's to "finish" her bonnet.[9]

Whether visitors arrived or not, a period of quiet afternoon work characterized the daily schedule in many households. This was often improved by reading aloud. One author described a time when "all the family were assembled in the afternoon for their usual quiet occupations, . . . [and] all were quietly settled, the ladies with their work, and the boys with their pencils," texts for reading were suggested.[10] Susan Lesley recalled the Lyman household in Northampton, where:

> all the family were readers, the old ladies and the young; and among them were all kinds of tastes; and they did a great deal of reading aloud, while the audience were diligently sewing. Our sister Eliza would have one kind of reading going on in her room with some of the children, and the old ladies another kind in theirs. History, philosophy, poetry, novels and plays, each had its turn. I well remember hearing the "Paradise Lost" read when I was between eight and nine years old; and I received it as an authentic record of the beginning of the world, and recurred to it as such in imagination many years after. Reading was the constant resource and amusement when the more exacting business of the day was over."[11]

Frolicking

The "frolicking" described in the story about apple paring at the beginning of this chapter was more than this casual visiting, however. Frolics were usually organized in advance, involved more people, and were much more active. Jonathan Sayward described frolicking in a way that makes it also seem to have been synonymous with both festive activity and courtship. Sayward tells us that when "Edward Emerson was twenty one years old he made an entertainment for the young gentlemen and Ladies it was exceeding bad travailing notwithstanding the young Ladies were so much engaged on the Frollic that they went Knee Deep in Snow water to honor Mr Emerson and see and get sweethearts."[12] Sarah Bryant tells of attending a "nutcake frolic,"* and in York, Maine, in 1792, "27 young men & women had an entertainment after a Slaying Frollick and returned all well."[13] Other diarists speak of quilting or husking frolics, or of other types of parties that involved a period of mutual work and a display of good-natured industry followed by refreshments and dancing or

* Nutcakes are fried cakes or doughnuts.

134. *Corn Husking Frolic,* OIL ON PANEL, BY ALVIN FISHER, 1828–29. GIFT OF MAXIM KAROLIK TO THE KAROLIK COLLECTION OF AMERICAN PAINTINGS, 1815–65. COURTESY MUSEUM OF FINE ARTS, BOSTON.

A romanticized view of a popular fall event, already passing from common experience in 1829. Like other kinds of frolics, huskings were popular with young people and included courtship games. Here the artist shows an exchange between a young man who has found a red ear of corn and wants to claim a kiss, and the young woman he is approaching, who holds a withered ear of corn as a symbol of her unwillingness to be kissed.

other entertainment. The term "frolic" is usually used in ways that imply spontaneity and fun. Perhaps the most extreme example is the curious occasion described by Abner Sanger when, on a late September evening in 1779, he and two young friends engaged in what he termed a "cow-turd frolic" after raking hay."[14]

House and barn raisings required large numbers of people and were often concluded with refreshments. When Ebenezer Parkman's new barn was raised on May 15, 1752, the work was eased by "a Sufficient Number of Hands (about 70 Great and Small)." The minister had expected only "about a Score" and expressed his "hope no one went away without some refreshment. It was only Cake and Cheese and Butter etc."[15]

Although any kind of frolic was certainly popular with young people, it was the husking, quilting, and apple-paring parties that were most fondly remembered and vividly described. These were all time-consuming tasks that could be easily divided among a large group of people. Minimal skills were necessary for successful participation. Even in the mid-eighteenth century the annual husking and the occasional quilting were organized as parties for groups of ten to twenty people. In the case of husking corn—a task that needs to be done on many different farms within a fairly narrow time frame—close scheduling was necessary in order to ensure that all the necessary work was done during a brief period in the late fall. Any kind of work party must have been planned well in advance to give time to prepare ample refreshments and to have the tasks sufficiently well organized that some amount of useful work was actually accomplished. Because most husking parties were held in the evening, and some house raisings were followed by lively frolics that kept people up late at night and at which they drank too much alcohol, the next day's work was often impaired. On May 24, 1751, Ebenezer Parkman's two "impudent" eldest sons did not return from a neighbor's barn raising until late at night. There was trouble when "instead of their rising Earlier than usual that I might Send one of them this Morning to Mr. Willsons, my Sons, both of them were so sound, that when awak'd they are disturb'd."[16]

At many of these work parties mixed age groups participated, but some frolics seem to have been designed specifically as occasions for young people to come together to have a good time and to show off well-honed skills and industrious habits to potential spouses.

Not all work parties included women, though. Ebenezer Parkman regularly expected that much of his farm work, including husking, would be done as part of his ministerial support, and he was always anxious until the work was accomplished. He was almost continually short of wood, but he received only a load or two at a time. Because he expected the work to be done and the wood to be delivered, and he often had to badger people about it, Parkman seems to have felt little obligation to entertain in return.

Sometimes, however, frolics were an organized part of ministerial support. In the eighteenth century, some women held spinning parties and presented the results of a day's work to the minister and his family. In the years immediately before the American Revolution, such parties became a form of political statement supporting independence.

A story in the Lowell *Offering* in 1845 tells of less altruistic spinning parties, which must have been held in the 1820s: "Our spinning frolics usually took place in May, because then the days are long, and it was the time when we were in a post-haste hurry to get the 'sail cloth' done for market, so as to have our bonnets and white frocks made up by the first of July, or before. The paraphernalia for our spring attire was the proceeds of butter, eggs, and the socks we had knit through the winter, but we had to make tow and linen cloth to purchase our white dresses and summer bonnets." Apparently, the spinning parties began at one o'clock, after an early dinner, and concluded with tea and custard pies, and fortunetelling from the tea leaves. According to the author: "The wheels were brought together before dinner time, and every operator commenced at the same moment and 'spun like sixty,' to see which could get her stint off first." Unlike the other work frolics recalled by the author, no young men arrived for further entertainment, and the girls walked home as the sun went down, happy with their accomplishment and still thrilled by the competition.[17]

Quilting Parties

Quilting parties were much more widespread than spinning frolics, even in the eighteenth century; Abner Sanger noted evening quilting frolics in Keene as early as 1778. In Hadley, Elizabeth Phelps attended an average of six quilting parties a year before she was married in 1770. Although she participated in fewer quiltings while her children were very young, she continued to attend them and to hold them at her own house throughout her life. Sometimes there were only three or four women working together on a quilted petticoat or a bed quilt.

Sarah Bryant also made quilts and attended roughly three to five "quiltings" a year throughout most of her adult life. She participated in six quiltings in 1803, but none during the next ten years when her house was full of very young children and her elderly parents needed care. She resumed quilting after her parents died in 1813, when she made a woolen bed quilt, and the following February she "began to piece out a bed quilt." Apparently, she cut out the pieces and worked on it during a severe ice and snow storm and then put it away until summer. In August, she fixed the lining and colored it yellow, carded woolen batting, "got [it] in" the frame, and then invited some other women to help her do the actual quilting. It is not clear how many women came to help, but two of them stayed overnight and helped to finish the quilt the next day. This long process was unusual, for Mrs. Bryant usually pieced her quilts within two weeks and quilted them herself immediately after the tops were finished. One was finished in one day "by daylight."[18] By working alone in good natural light, Mrs. Bryant may have been able to produce a much more elaborate quilt than

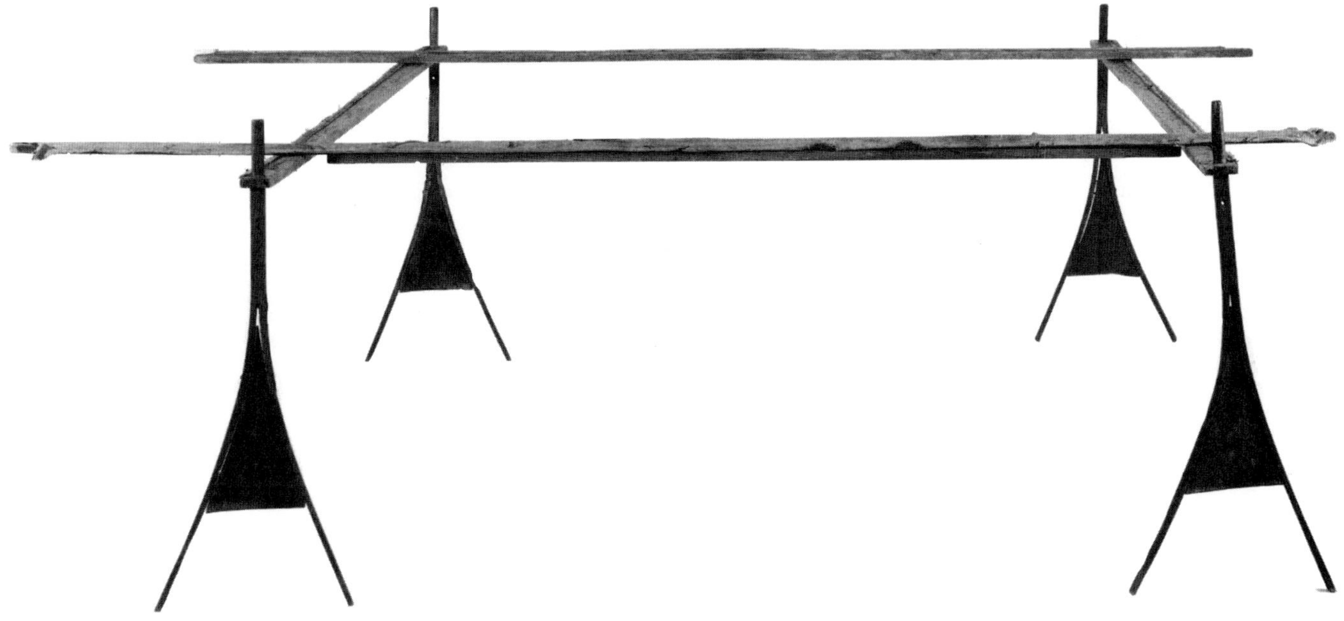

135. A QUILTING FRAME, FROM ASHLEY AND BOYDEN FAMILIES, DEERFIELD, MASSACHUSETTS, LATE EIGHTEENTH CENTURY. HISTORIC DEERFIELD, INC.

could be made by a group of inattentive, chattering women. In her diary references, Sarah Bryant never mentioned pattern names, although she sometimes differentiated between bed quilts and petticoats, and in 1830 she described making quilts of "old callicoes," some of which were "pieced in stripes," or "Pink gingham and white" and "a bedquilt for myself worsted red and black, the middle red, border pieced."[19] Mrs. Bryant's skill in drawing quilting patterns must have been recognized in Cummington, for on December 22, 1822, she "went to Mr. Briggses to draw a feather on a bed quilt," and her diary contains half a dozen drawings of patchwork and quilting patterns.[20]

Fictional accounts of quilting parties are much more dramatic. They usually describe much larger parties, with lavish refreshments, dancing, and lively games. In *Quabbin,* Francis Underwood described the refreshments at a quilting: "Mrs. Kempton's spreads were worthy of all superlatives. The tea, pale in color, but really strong, was served in delicate old china, with flesh-colored figures; and the fragrance of so many cups filled the room. There was bread and butter, hot biscuits (which were not *bis cuit* at all), waffles, peach preserves, apple and quince sauce, doughnuts, mince-pie, custard-pie, fruit-cake, sponge-cake, and mellow sage cheese. The tablecloth was like satiny snow. Everything was best and daintiest."[21] In "The Quilting Party," T. S. Arthur suggested that when a girl attended her first quilting party it was a "sign that she was looking forward to the matrimonial goal," and underscored the popularity of quilting-party games, with their titillating touches and quick kisses—activities the author called "the evening's sport."[22] As usual, it was the best that was remembered.

The partying associated with these events was the thing that was most fondly recalled by those looking back to the olden times. In "The Paring (or Apple) Bee," the author described the refreshments of "pumpkin pies, doughnuts, cheese, 'hard cider' and tea" that were served when the work was finished and things were cleaned up after the clock struck ten. Then "lively dancing commenced in the parlor," with the tunes being sung if there was no fiddler. After midnight, dancing was abandoned in favor of a variety of active games, including "The lawyer," "Drop the handkerchief," "The Juniper Tree," and "Blind Man's Buff." "Button! button who's got the button?" was the favorite, and all were happy to "whirl the [pewter] plate" with its kissing forfeits.[23]

These nostalgic reminiscences may reflect a growing concern that the cost of refreshments might outweigh the benefit of the accomplishments at work parties. Still, these established community rituals encompassed sanctioned forms of courtship behavior. By combining them with work, people fulfilled their sense of duty and assuaged their guilt at entertaining for pure pleasure.

136. QUILTING PATTERN, SARAH BRYANT DIARY, 1806. BY PERMISSION OF THE HOUGHTON LIBRARY, HARVARD UNIVERSITY.

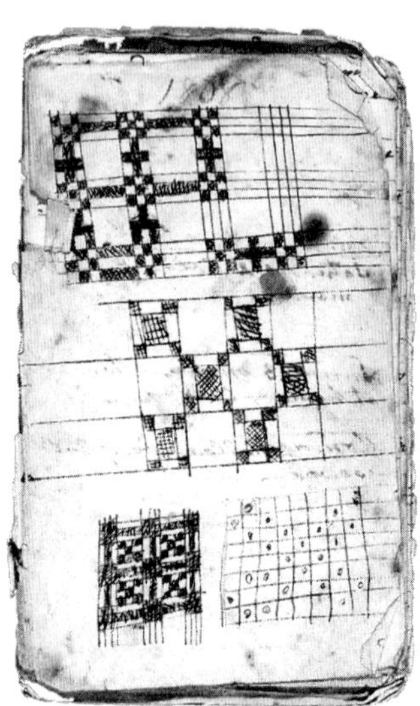

137. PATCHWORK PATTERN, SARAH BRYANT DIARY, 1806. BY PERMISSION OF THE HOUGHTON LIBRARY, HARVARD UNIVERSITY.

Ministerial and Other Professional Obligations

Until the disestablishment of the Congregational church in the early nineteenth century, each New England town was responsible for the support of the minister and his family. In return, the minister was expected to be both a spiritual and a social leader in the community—something that was extremely difficult if the family had no independent income and the level of support was inadequate. The minister's door was open to people who came to be married, to receive counsel, to discuss theology and local politics, to decide what to do in cases where charity was needed, to seek advice for marital problems or disputes between neighbors, or simply to get out of the rain. In a world where much of both normal and abnormal human behavior was regarded as evidence of original sin, the minister played an important mediating role. In all cases, his wife was expected to minister to the human needs of those who arrived at their door. In many communities, the minister's wife was also expected to offer some hospitality at noontime on Sundays to those who lived too far from the meeting house to return home to eat between the morning and afternoon services.

Trying to balance the needs of a large family and occasional distinguished visitors with the expectations of parishioners was not easy for the minister or his wife. In 1738, Ebenezer Parkman described "Mrs. Tainters high Disgust at our Dining the Sabbath before last in the Kitchen—She Surmizing that it was done with design to keep People from coming to warm themselves, which had not entered into our Thoughts, but was done because the House was Cold by the Storm, and we had no fire in the Dining Room."[24] On a rainy Sunday in July 1810, Ruth Bascom found many people hanging around after the morning meeting. She served them "toddy, bread & cheese, cider, &c" while they tarried in her kitchen.[25]

After two "mammoth loads" of wood were delivered to the Bascoms at noontime on January 3, 1824, a cold day with spitting snow, Mrs. Bascom was prepared with a meal for the "one hundred & 55 men and boys [who] took some refreshment here soldier like, it being set on a board table before the house consisting of roast beef cut in slices, boil'd potatoes, bread, cheese, biscuit & nutcakes—cider & toddy 'fore & aft'—many came as spectators . . . in short our house was thronged for several hours."[26] Four days later, with the temperature about 16 degrees, she served a similar meal outdoors to the thirty or forty men who came to unload, split, and stack the wood. Perhaps fortunately, in 1826 things were not so elaborate. On January 26, the Bascoms were presented with twenty-six cords of wood, which had to be cut, split, and stacked. Fourteen men worked at these tasks on February 1, and twenty-four "cut, sawed & piled wood" on the thirteenth. Both times Mrs. Bascom provided supper indoors for the workers, with the help of "Aunt Patty, so called" on January 31 and three other women on February 13.[27] We can be sure that fourteen or twenty-four steamy, sweaty, tired, hungry men with their wet wool clothing, muddy and snowy feet, and dirty hands did not sit decorously at one table to dine.

Professional men's wives were also occasionally responsible for much more formal entertainment of the quarterly or annual meetings of regional legal, medical, or ministerial associations. The newly married Betsy Huntington was almost overwhelmed by the amount of work necessary when she found that, indeed, she did have to entertain forty members of a ministerial association at the end of the first week she lived in Litchfield in June 1801. Perhaps hoping for some sympathy, she described it in a letter to her mother: "The worst of this association, I hope is over, after all that Mr H told me of not providing dinner for the whole, and I have had it to do—all day on saturday I was at work making pies and cake." When guests arrived to call on her, she "could not spend the time with them as I had pies and puddings to make, and all the meat for this day's dinner to cook, as it was tho't best to have a cold collation. Miss Chandler came down in the morning and has been here until now—I think I never worked harder or more constantly for two days in my life." Two days after it was over, Betsy was still cleaning up, but she found time to write a little more: "On Tuesday we had nearly forty to dine—but all things went on well and no sad accident has happen'd not so much as a glass has been broken."[28]

Betsy had been through this kind of thing before, but she hadn't paid much attention to the work involved. While visiting her future sister-in-law, Sally Parsons, in Newburyport in 1787, fifteen or twenty gentlemen of the bar were invited by Sally's uncle, Theophilus Parsons, to dine. Betsy tried to describe it in a letter to her mother: "Mrs. P. made an elegant entertainment but I can't write everything that she had—Sarah and my self drank tea and spent the evening at Miss Titcomb's—quite a large party—we return'd to this social circle just after nine—and Mrs P—gave us some of the good provision that was left at dinner."[29] The work and the details had escaped the attention of the inexperienced guest.

When the Worcester ministerial association met at the Bascoms' home in September 1830, Mrs. Bascom served a dinner of "roast beef, roast fowls, boiled ditto & pork & vegetables, tongue, apple & custard pies." She was delighted to be presented "with an elegant glass bowl of fruit & flowers & a decanter of Madeira Wine" from Mrs. Gould.[30] In preparing to provide for an event with this kind of exceptionally large number of guests, Mrs. Bascom usually arranged to have help in the kitchen and borrowed cups and saucers, plates, and glassware from close friends or neighbors.

Patriotism and Civic Duty

Across New England, within each town and village a pattern of holidays and rituals was observed. The semiannual militia training days and occasional military reviews were always occasions for masculine excess. Young people and some families flocked to observe the drilling and sham battles conducted by their uniformed neighbors. Sarah Emery recalled: "These training days were the occasion for a general frolic, especially the reviews. General training drew a motley crowd, vendors of all sorts of wares, mountebanks, and lewd women; a promiscuous assemblage, bent upon pleasure. Beyond the lines

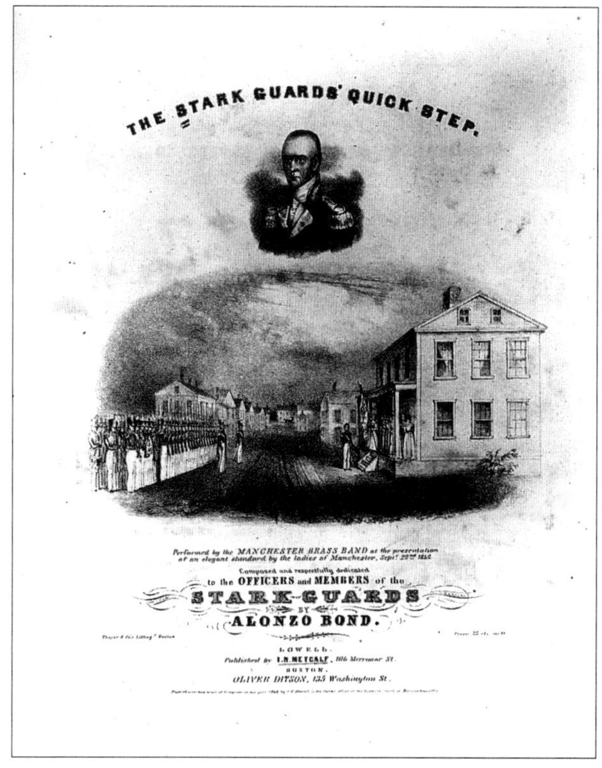

138. PICNICKING DURING A SUMMER ENCAMPMENT OF THE ROBIN-HOOD ARCHERS, SHEET-MUSIC COVER, BOSTON, 1836. COURTESY AMERICAN ANTIQUARIAN SOCIETY.

139. LADIES PRESENTING A FLAG TO THE STARK GUARDS, MANCHESTER, NEW HAMPSHIRE, SEPTEMBER 22, 1842, SHEET-MUSIC COVER, THAYER & CO., LITHOGRAPH, BOSTON, 1842. COURTESY AMERICAN ANTIQUARIAN SOCIETY.

there was always much rousing and hilarious uproar. . . . Many a poor fellow became somewhat 'onsteady' before the day had far advanced."[31]

Sarah Bryant almost never went down to the village to watch the activity of training, but she described in her diary the crowds of men who came to dinner on some of these festival days. Sometimes the victims of the terrible accidents and injuries caused by gunshot or cannon explosions were brought to her house for treatment by Dr. Bryant or he was called into the village or to a neighboring town to care for them.[32]

Fortunately, the Fourth of July was usually less violent than training day. In 1801, the Bryants "went to Worthington to keep independence—dined & supt at Esq. Woodbridges." The next year they stayed home. Because the Fourth of July in 1802 was a Sunday, patriotic observances were held on Monday. "Held a day of Independence, an Oration delivered by Dr Bryant—Esq. White & Lady here over night." In 1816, Mrs. Bryant "went to the meeting house Cullen delivered an Oration," but she also "sewed—warpt—baked" while the celebrations continued in town. Unfortunately, "Mr. Daniels [was] hurt with a cannon."[33]

Christopher Columbus Baldwin described another postponed Independence Day celebration, held in Worcester on Monday, July 5, 1830: "In the afternoon the ladies gave a public tea party in the same bower which was used on Saturday. One hundred and thirty partake and about the same number of gentlemen. Many excellent toasts were given. Musick follows each toast and the whole goes off very pleasantly. I have never seen so many pretty faces before. The ladies contributed as each one felt disposed. Some brought cake, some pies, some cherries, others furniture for the table, and all, good feeling and cheerful faces and merry hearts."[34]

Election Day was observed in some towns with a celebration for successful candidates, parades, inaugural ceremonies, church services, feasting, gun salutes, and perhaps a ball in the evening. In the country the occasion was marked with turkey shoots, bowling, cricket, and other sports. The day was considered a major occasion for hospitality in Hartford, Connecticut, and was described nicely by J. Hammond Trumbull in 1886: "All day Wednesday the country people poured into town, bringing their dinners with them or relying on the corner stands, where root and ginger beer, molasses candy, and gingerbread were sold. The houses were already full of visitors; and in the parlor—opened then if ever, or the living-room, pine boughs or branches of lilacs filled the fireplaces and a table was set with cake and wine. Hospitality was so free that the doors of some wealthy people were open to any stranger who chose to walk in and refresh himself."[35] Throughout New England, "election cake" was a special treat, and people looked forward to a taste of the extra-sweet raised cake no matter whether it was baked at home for the guests who flocked to town on that day or purchased from a street vendor.

Abner Sanger described an especially enthusiastic "election frolic" which lasted all night at Colonel Wyman's tavern in 1779; the next morning he observed "some fragments of Election frolickers gather together."[36] On a somewhat higher plane, on March 4, 1825, Dr. and Mrs. Bascom attended a party at Esquire Willard's in Ashby, Massachusetts, with ten "gentlemen and their ladies." The party lasted from mid-afternoon until nine-thirty in the evening, and Mrs. Bascom commented upon the "pleasant visit and genteel accommodations [which included] tea, bread & butter (spread), puff, variety of cake &—cordial & wine, apples & musick, viz. the Hand & large Organ . . . the flag was hoisted, cannon fired, &c. &c. in the town and the report of a great number of cannon here from . . . Wachusett mountain, where it is said Princeton & vicinity celebrate the day by burning many cords of wood—a burn of tar, rosin &c in the mountain this evening the light of which was seen this evening in many places in this town. All in *honor* of *Hon. J. Q. Adams, President of U.S.A.*"[37]

Widespread Hospitality

Aside from casual visiting, professional obligation, or particular holidays, a kind of general hospitality was widespread in New England households. Women learned to expect unannounced visitors at any time and knew that they might be called upon to take in friends who happened to be in the area at mealtime or were overtaken by darkness or a spell of bad weather. They put up sisters and brothers, aunts and uncles, cousins and cousins' cousins. Ministers' wives provided overnight hospitality for the traveling wives and daughters of other ministers even if they had never met before, so that the women did not have to stay in taverns. They opened their doors to neighbors and to strangers who were seeking information or were hungry and thirsty from walking, chasing an errant animal, looking for a lost child, or berrying. Peddlers, tinkers, vagrants, or Indian basket sellers might come to the door at mealtime or late at night. On December 5, 1782, Abner Sanger's family made room for "a little basketmaker" who "come in, lodged with us." It must have been a trying evening, for the next day Sanger commented in his diary, "Morning the idiot basketmaker goes off." Sometimes the visitor brought special talents and entertained the family. Abner Sanger's family enjoyed the time "Stephen Carpenter comes with a fife to see us."[38] Only a few strangers seemed dishonest or threatening. On May 9, 1834, Sarah Bryant was a little nervous when "a man tarried here over night called himself a sailor."[39]

While some kinds of strangers might be offered an opportunity to sleep on a straw bed spread before the kitchen fire, where the last person to go to bed at night and the first person to get up in the morning could keep track of them, people of a more elevated social station would be offered greater comfort. In crowded households, it was not unusual for overnight visitors to share beds with family members. While Mr. Bascom was in Boston on December 12, 1808, Miss Catherine Fiske called on Mrs. Bascom and "passed the evening here and slep with me."[40] Ruth Bascom also offered this kind of hospitality to other women who stayed overnight—at least once even when her husband was at home.

Not until the nineteenth century did many houses have enough room or a small enough population to set aside a special room for overnight guests, yet the

140. Parlor closet, or beaufat, built for Peter and Sarah Mills Olcott, Norwich, Vermont, c. 1789. Photograph by Jeffrey Nintzel.

"best room" was often offered to company. This tradition seems to have led to the romantic descriptions of the "spare chamber" in which "the bedstead with its heaped up feather beds and down pillows, its fine linen, fragrant with lavender, and its gorgeous or delicate bed trappings, was the chief feature. . . ."[41] Such rooms were asserted to be "jest as grand as could be, with a gret four-post mahogany bedstead and damask curtains brought over from England; but it was cold enough to freeze a white bear solid,—the way spare chambers allers is."[42] These grand rooms did exist in wealthy eighteenth-century homes, and it was only when the household population began to decline that they were set aside exclusively for guests.

No matter who came knocking at the door, or when they came, it was customary to welcome them and to offer hospitality of some sort, whether it was a mug of cider and a slab of bread and butter or a special table. Susan Blunt described a supper prepared by a kind country woman for a group of young girls who had been drenched by rain while out cranberrying: "The table looked pretty, I thought. She had taken out her best dishes that were all pink. At every plate she put a little cup plate about the size of a dollar to put our cups in when we poured out our tea into the saucer to drink. She made hot buiscuit and she gave us plenty of honey, for they kept Bees. There were three kinds of pie and cake, which we all injoyed very much."[43]

Being ready to provide instant hospitality for an undetermined number of people required the storage of special foods. In some situations the visitor could join the family meal. In others, a glass of cider, a cup of tea, or some toast and cheese would serve very well. If the food and water in the pantry were not frozen solid, it would not be hard to provide simple refreshment. Tea with cold meat or cheese and bread and butter could be served in any room that was warm. On January 12, 1785, William Pyncheon and his wife had tea with two other couples in "Mrs. Pyncheon's chamber."[44]

Fortunately, in most substantial households, parlors, sitting rooms, and dining rooms were furnished with a closet in which were stored cups and saucers, decanters of wines, glassware, and loaves of rich fruitcake, which was prized for its lasting quality as well as its flavor. The shelves of these closets were grooved so that the small serving plates called "twifflers" could be stood against the back wall and make a handsome show when the door was opened. Some of the closets had glass windows in the doors; most were equipped with a lock. Sarah Orne Jewett was convinced that such closets exuded the ripe "fragrance of hospitality."

141. THE TEMPTATIONS OF A PARLOR CLOSET, WOODCUT, IN JANE TAYLOR, *Original Poems for Infant Minds* (BOSTON, N.D.). COURTESY OF THE SOCIETY FOR THE PRESERVATION OF NEW ENGLAND ANTIQUITIES.

Parlor closets held wineglasses, decanters, tea dishes, wine, sugar, "the company pound cake," and other resources for entertaining unexpected guests. Sarah Orne Jewett characterized parlor closets by "the faint ancient odor of plum cakes and Madeira wine.

Wintertime Visiting

In wintertime, when there was some respite from heavy field and kitchen work, people felt that they had more time and were more rested. On "bright moonshine evenings" when the snow was well packed on the roads, the sound of sleigh bells announced the coming and going of neighbors for some sociable visiting. Many people took advantage of the easy traveling to visit people who lived too far away for a quick afternoon visit, sometimes even going to see people in towns five or ten miles away and returning in a single evening. Often couples ventured forth together, although men or women might also go separately. Hired girls might join the young women of the family for an evening with friends, and men of all ages resorted to taverns. After a January snowstorm in 1781, Abner Sanger was glad to get out. He felt that the weather was "very pleasant for the season," and the new snow on the icy roads made "beautiful sledding."[45] Usually, someone had to stay at home to tend the fires and the children, but some young couples packed up their babies and ventured forth as a family.

Sometimes, even necessary work could be put off for a little sociable visiting. On December 3, 1812, Ruth Bascom spent the evening with her husband and another couple riding "to Dr. Knowltons in sleigh, took tea and returned at ten." Nothing was put off long in that house, however, for when she returned, Mrs. Bascom "sewed on a cotton shirt &c. and retired at 1 o clock."[46]

Good snow also made possible lively sleighing parties, in which crowds of people traveled ten or fifteen miles to a tavern, where they enjoyed refreshments and sometimes dancing before returning home by moonlight. Such parties attracted public notice: Samuel Larkin mentioned in his diary that there had been a "great sleighing party out to Greenland" from Portsmouth in February 1840, even though he did not participate.[47]

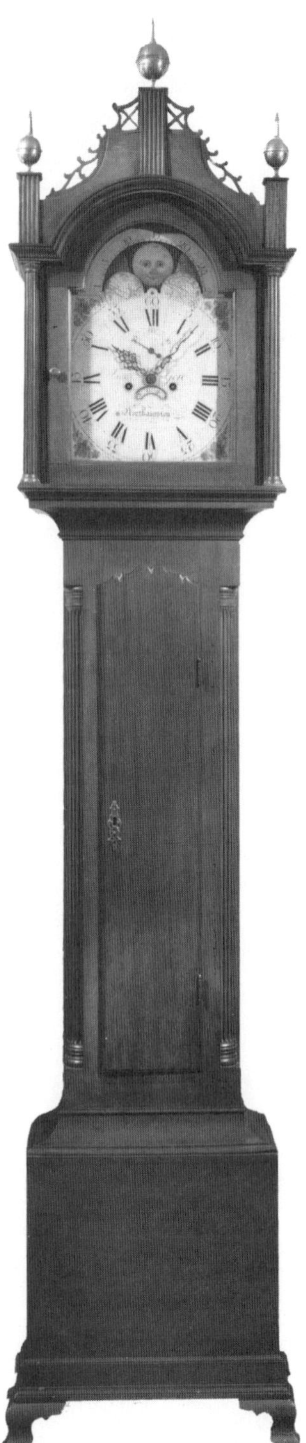

142. CLOCK FACE WITH MOON-DIAL, TALL CLOCK MADE BY GEORGE HOLBROOK, BROOKFIELD, MASSACHUSETTS, FOR MAJOR DAVID DICKINSON OF DEERFIELD, MASSACHUSETTS, C. 1800. HISTORIC DEERFIELD, INC. PHOTOGRAPHS BY AMANDA MERULLO.

A clock with a separate dial showing the phases of the moon predicted when there would be a favorable amount of light for traveling or working at night. The sharp contrast of black numerals painted on a white dial made it easier to read the time by moonlight or reflected firelight, obviating the necessity of carrying a candle to the clock to tell the time.

On February 2, 1830, Christopher Columbus Baldwin invited a young woman to accompany him on a sleighing party to Westborough with two other couples; the next evening, he took a double sleigh and rode to Leicester with a married couple and the three young women who had been with him the night before: "They sing, going and returning, which sounds very prettily. Have some hot coffee, and return at half past nine." Although the sleighing was "perfect," Baldwin did not venture out to enjoy it again until the fifth, when he joined a large party: "A sleigh ride is got up to go to Westboro. Mr. Newcomb induces me to attend. Ride with him and Mary and Catherine Robinson in a 4-horse sleigh. Leave Worcester at 3 and return at 10. Between 20 & 30 in the party. Most all married people. Mulled wine was prepared for the ladies and flip for the gentlemen, but by *mistake* the flip is carried to the ladies and they do not find their error until our flip is mostly gone, when they pronounce it very unpleasant stuff!! I find that I have been very dissipated this week and form a resolution to be more sober."[48]

The Snug Fireside

In the dead of winter, when darkness falls as early as four in the afternoon, the family drew around the fire for warmth. Winter evenings were prized as opportunities for family activities, both entertaining and instructive. The author of an article in the *New England Farmer* calculated that winter evenings, estimated to be at least three hours long and extending from September to March, added up to a period of time equal to eight twelve-hour days. The writer cautioned that this time should not be lost, but used to weld the children's affection to the domestic hearth; and he ambitiously recommended academic instruction, particularly in reading, chemistry, music, and religion. Undoubtedly many families were entertained by music and storytelling in addition to reading aloud selections from the Bible, poetry, or fiction. Unwilling to sit with idle hands, women and girls spent the time knitting or sewing, while men whittled clothespins, made candle rods, or did small repairs to tools, harnesses, or household furnishings. The Reverend Jonathan Fisher of Blue Hill, Maine, insisted that his children spend their evenings making bone buttons or some other saleable product while he read aloud. Mid-nineteenth-century parlor magazines reinforced these ideas. An author in *Godey's Lady's Book* in 1857 offered a pattern for a silk patchwork pillow, because "the time of the year is fast approaching for those happy in-door evenings with their pleasant and easy occupations which help to make home so dear, [and] we think it requisite that we should offer a suggestion for one of those tasteful works which are of ceaseless variety in their execution, and are, when completed, worthy of becoming family heirlooms."[49]

The concept of the family gathered together in the evening became one of the important focal points of the romanticization of the New England home: "Home means right here by mother's kitchen-fire, where she and father sit, and want to sit."[50] Both pictorial and verbal images of the "home so dear" stressed family unity and invariably depicted a hearthside group. By placing the group in the kitchen, ideas of agricultural bounty and frugal industry were swept into the picture. When Harriet Beecher Stowe asserted that "nobody ever wants to go into that terrible best room of yours,"[51] she acknowledged the pressures for increasing gentility and more formal social relationships that were disrupting traditional New England society. For Mrs. Stowe, Grandmother Badger's democratic kitchen was still the setting for the ideal woman—the center of a

143. FOUR GENERATIONS OF THE PECKHAM-SAWYER FAMILY, OIL ON CANVAS, BY ROBERT PECKHAM, BOLTON, MASSACHUSETTS, C. 1817. THE HAYDEN COLLECTION, COURTESY, MUSEUM OF FINE ARTS, BOSTON.

Sixteen members of the Peckham family have gathered at ten minutes before two o'clock to enjoy apples, nuts, cider, and wine. Since only ten chairs have been set out for the assembled company, the children would be expected to remain standing. On Sunday evenings in Salem, the Tucker family regularly expected callers, and at nine o'clock the hired girl brought in a tray with "apples, nuts and cake, with a decanter of wine" before the company went home.

female universe. Looking backward to an ideal home in a time that appeared simpler, Mrs. Stowe ignored its social stratification and sour smells, which had been as real as its warm hearth and vigorous mistress.

Tea and Supper Parties

Among the country gentry and the urban upper classes, entertaining had always been far more formal than the gatherings described in *Oldtown Folks.* While touring America in 1827, Mrs. Basil Hall, who noted the strict observance of the Sabbath in New England, also observed that "on Sunday evening, on the contrary, nothing is more common than a large party of friends assembling at some house, and they resume their usual occupations of work or anything else they may be employed about during the week."[52] In Boston, she was invited to have Sunday supper with the Ticknors and noted, "Many families here have a party regularly every Sunday evening, the Ticknors always have."[53] She went on to describe the evening of September 30, which she had spent "by invitation at Mrs. Theodore Sedgewick's, and met the whole clan of Sedgewicks, no less than three gentlemen of the family with their respective wives, beside their sister the authoress, and various others of the society of Stockbridge.... The refreshments... consisted of sweetmeats and cream, in the first place, then apples and grapes, thirdly, almonds and raisins, and lastly wine, and the double duty of distributing the plates and handing round the eatables devolved upon one female servant." Mrs. Hall particularly detested the American fashion for seating men and women in separate rooms and having a servant pass food around a circle of seated guests, which she had encountered previously at the home of Governor and Mrs. Clinton in Albany. At the Sedgewicks she found the circle "smaller but not less formidable than those at Albany."[54] Later, in Boston, at a small party at Mrs. Harrison Gray Otis's, Mrs. Hall found "the Albany sin of a circle prevailed a little, but not nearly to so great a degree as there, and the small numbers offered some sort of apology for this dereliction from the ease of good manners."[55]

In 1827, a Boston house servant named Robert Roberts published written directions describing the ideal procedure for formal tea parties. A tray of filled tea and coffee cups was passed by a servant, and each guest helped himself to cream and sugar from the center of the tray. Next, a tray with "cake, wafers, toast, bread and butter, &c. all neatly arranged" was passed. The trays were offered first to the most elderly lady in the room, then to the other ladies, and finally to the hostess, before being offered to the gentlemen, in the same order.[56] The empty cups were collected, rinsed out, and refilled before a second round was offered.[57]

A party given by the Quincy family in September 1824 began with tea and coffee served this way, but the circle was soon broken. After the guests had all arrived and were seated in the parlor, "coffee, tea and cake were handed round and done ample justice to." After eating, "the conversation now became general and almost deafening. Mr. and the Miss Quincys sailed around the circle, conversing with some, offering refreshments to others and attention to all. Soon the formality of the circle was broken up and the company walked hither and thither, looked at the pictures, Susan's portfolio, and a variety of boxes which were

144. THE TEA PARTY, OIL ON CANVAS, BY HENRY SARGENT, C. 1824. GIFT OF MRS. HORATIO A. LAMB IN MEMORY OF MR. AND MRS. WINTHROP SARGENT. COURTESY MUSEUM OF FINE ARTS, BOSTON.

This was an exhibition picture heralded in its day for the accuracy with which the artist had depicted a familiar scene. At the left, a servant is carrying in a large tray with cups of tea, which will be passed among the guests.

dispersed in different directions to amuse them. . . . Everyone seemed to enjoy themselves amazingly. Presently music was proposed." The evening progressed with singing around the piano and the dancing of cotillions and contradances accompanied by piano music. After the dancing some of the guests left for home, and then "a large supply of refreshments were placed on the piano, which vanished in the twinkling of an eye." After the last guest had left, the family sat down and "eat, drank and talked over the events of the evening, all agreeing it had been a delightful party, and by twelve we retired to our chambers."[58]

William Davis recalled similar occasions, called "lap teas," in the Plymouth of his youth—"glorious occasions for us boys . . . [when] an extra supply of cream was to be bought, the sugar loaf was to be divested of its blue cartridge paper covering, and chopped into squares, and sandwiches and whips and custards were to be made, of which we were sure to get preliminary tastes." In a household lacking formal servants, the boys "were permitted to carry around waiters loaded with cups of tea and plates and cream and sugar, and the various articles of food."[59]

Miss Leslie felt that it was "tedious, inconvenient, and unsatisfactory" to have the tea carried round. However, she agreed that it was better to have tea passed around by two servants if there were too many guests to be comfortable at a single table.[60] Enlisting young boys to help out in a pinch was not something she was willing to contemplate!

Caroline King also disliked the very large and formal tea parties that were "served in the parlor where the guests were sitting round in stiff stately fashion" and cups of tea and coffee and thin bread and butter and cake were passed around on large trays: "Happy then the guest who chanced to be sitting near the inevitable pier table of the day, for there were no small tables conveniently sitting round, and the chairs were very hard and high."[61] In Newburyport, this kind of entertainment was considered old-fashioned by 1821, when Mrs. Nehemiah Parsons described a party for her brother: "In the afternoon we had a tea-party, or rather an antiquarian party; it was in the real old style." The guests at this party arrived at three o'clock and spent three hours knitting stockings and talking. "At six o'clock, the tea-table was ushered in. . . . The tea was handed, each took a cup, took a sip, then the tray of cake and toast, each took a bit & took a bite, alternately, till each had disappeared; then as the tray was successively handed, commencing with the poorest, they took till they had tasted each kind of cake.[62]

Children's tea parties mimicked those of their elders, with tea being "served on trays which were handed to the children who were seated round the room. One tray was filled with cups of milk, while another had three dishes, one with thin bread and butter, one with milk biscuits, and one with cake." The tray was passed three times, and children were instructed that "first you must take the bread and butter, then the milk biscuit, and last the cake."[63]

Miss Leslie agreed that this kind of ceremony was undesirable, advising readers: "If there is ample room at table, do not have the tea carried round,—particularly if you have but one servant to hand the whole. There is no comfortable way of eating bread, butter, toast, or buttered cakes, except when seated at a table. When handed round there is always a risk of their greasing the dresses of the ladies—the greasing of fingers is inevitable—though that is of less consequence, now that the absurd practice of eating in gloves is wisely abolished among genteel people."[64]

Many people actually preferred a different kind of tea party, the type Caroline King remembered from the 1830s, when Salem was "famous in those early days for its delightful and cosy tea parties." She penned a nice description of the usual course of events:

> In the first place, we all sat down at a long table (or a round table which was cosier and merrier), upon which was spread a red cloth, or a plaided red, white and blue one, which threw into high relief the shining silver and glass, and the India blue and gold tea set of the time. There were no tray cloths then. In front of the hostess were placed two highly decorative black and gold Chinese tea trays. (We called them waiters.) On one were placed silver tea-pots for both green and black tea, and on the other larger one was the urn for hot water, and if the tea was made on the table a dainty silver or lacquer tea caddy, with the sugar bowl, cream pitcher and slop bowl belonging to the tea service and all the nankin china cups and saucers and coffee mugs spread out in shining array. The plates were placed all down the sides of the table accompanied always by pretty little "cup plates." There were no courses at these teas. Everything was put on the bountifully provided table at once. The plates were changed between meats and sweets, but the menu was spread out before you, and if you were not hungry enough to partake of the whole array, you could choose your favorite dainty. At the foot of the table where the host sat was placed the solid part of the feast—cooked oysters, and chickens or game dressed in different ways. I once saw a noble chicken pie at one of these teas. Down the middle of the table were silver cake baskets with pound, sponge and fruit cake, and these were flanked on each side by plates and small silver dishes containing different kinds of bread and hot cakes, olives, tongue, and ham. . . . Then there were cut glass dishes of many kinds of preserves, whole quinces floating in their rich clear juice being always present and damsons and pre-

145. WOMEN ENJOYING A SEATED TEA WHILE MAKING A STRONG STAND IN FAVOR OF TEMPERANCE. WOODCUT, C. 1840. ALBERT ALDEN PROOF BOOK, COURTESY AMERICAN ANTIQUARIAN SOCIETY.

> served ginger. . . . Such a table, lighted by plenty of tall silver candlesticks, and surrounded by a jocund company of merry guests, had . . . a glow and a brilliancy and an affluent charm.[65]

The cup plates deemed a necessity at the tea table supported a particularly American social ritual. Caroline King explained that "it was the custom of the day to cool your tea before drinking it by pouring it into your saucer, and these small plates were to hold the cup. And if you would be considered especially elegant, you would stick out your little finger at an angle from your hand, as you raised your saucer to your lips."[66] Catherine Beecher expected similar behavior, for she suggested that "teacup-mats, or plates, are useful also, to preserve a tablecloth from the stains of tea and coffee."[67]

It is hard to draw the line between this kind of lavish tea party and mid-afternoon dinners and the late-afternoon suppers enjoyed by the country gentry. Indeed, Susan Dickinson equated "small friendly suppers" and "tea parties" and recalled that in Amherst, Massachusetts, when the party was "too large in number to permit of seating guests about a table, a bountiful homely supper would be handed round on large trays, every one being comfortably seated, with little tables for the tea cups."[68] Jonathan Sayward described dinner parties in York, Maine, that varied in size from six to twelve, usually attended by married couples and by gentlemen accompanied by their unmarried sisters. He was

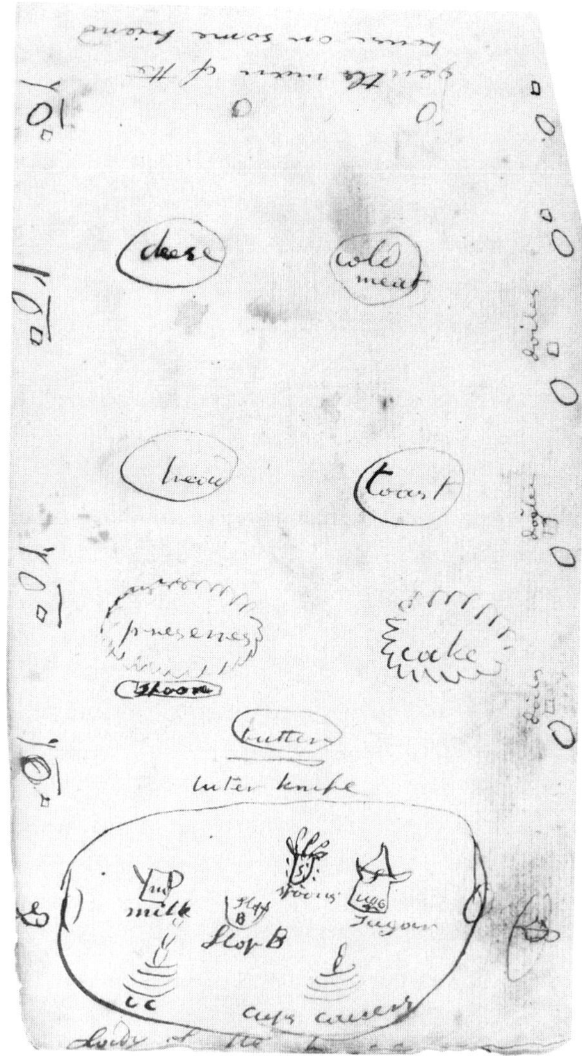

146. TABLE SETTING FOR A TEA PARTY, DRAWING BY L. FISKE, MASSACHUSETTS, C. 1850. COURTESY WINTERTHUR LIBRARY: JOSEPH DOWNS COLLECTION OF MANUSCRIPTS AND PRINTED EPHEMERA.

This table setting is based on those published in late-eighteenth- or early-nineteenth-century cookbooks, such as James Farley's Art of Cookery *(1794) and* The American Economical Housekeeper *(1823). The table was to be arranged for thirteen guests in addition to the hostess. Each individual place setting had a plate, fork, and doily. The tea service and empty cups and saucers were to be arranged on a waiter, while dishes of cheese, cold meat, toast, cake, bread, butter, and preserves were placed symmetrically on the table.*

pleased when he could account himself "hospitably entertained," when there was "a very elegant table," or when he had had an "agreeable visit."[69]

It took a woman to notice the food. On a "pleasant" spring day at the end of April 1813, Ruth Bascom went with her husband, a minister, and adopted daughter "to Esq Chambers by invitation where we dined & took tea, & met there Revds Estabrook, Foster Willington & Dr. Flint, with their ladies—Brothr D Henshaw came there & took tea also—we returned home at dusk after a very pleasant visit & Luxurious entertainment—Dined on pudding, roast veal, d[itt]o. leg pork, boiled fowls, vegetables, Asparagus, dandelions, Custard (cup), pies, preserves, wines, apples, &c. &c. &c."[70] On other occasions, Mrs. Bascom described dining with her neighbors on "steak, tea, &c.," and "at 3 on tea, sausages," and serving meals to guests of "pie," "roast beef &c," "pickled fish," "cold meat &c &c," and "stuffed veal."[71] Although much more work was involved in the preparation of the pies and other desserts, it was usually the quantity and variety of meats that received the most notice in Mrs. Bascom's diary. Even Mrs. Chambers's success in offering apples that had been successfully preserved from the previous fall in combination with the new season's first asparagus and dandelions went without comment.

Dinner parties of this sort featured two courses—one with quantities of meats, boiled vegetables, and condiments, the other of pies and a variety of desserts. Everything for each course was brought to the table at once, and people served themselves from whatever dish they could reach. Usually, the lady of the house carved the meat, which was the centerpiece of the meal. Sometimes she was the only woman present. In 1796, Dr. Bentley "supped with several of the Clergy & private gentlemen at Mr. Micah Webb, just married . . . the Lady did the honours of the house very well."[72]

Despite the apparent formality of these dinner parties, only a few homes had rooms specially furnished and exclusively used for formal dining. Sets of dining tables that could be joined into a single long table and tables that could be expanded by the addition of wooden leaves were unknown in the mid-eighteenth century and were rare even in the 1830s. The ministers and lawyers may have shared a long table at their association meetings, or they may have eaten at several independent tables, or even in more than one room. The long table could easily have been a makeshift affair of boards laid on sawhorses or barrels that were concealed under table linen.

Dining Rooms, Dining Parlors

Except in the wealthiest households, at the beginning of the nineteenth century rooms served a variety of purposes, and people were still accustomed to eating in more than one place within a house—the parlor, the sitting room, the "dining parlor," or a chamber, depending on the season and circumstance. In her reminiscences of the "first class dwellings" of Newburyport, Sarah Emery equated the dining room with the sitting room, which featured a "large mahogany sideboard."[73] As late as 1841, in her *Treatise on Domestic Economy,*

147. CHILDREN EATING IN A PARLOR OR SITTING ROOM. WOODCUT, C. 1845. ALEXANDER ANDERSON SCRAPBOOKS, VOL. IV, PRINT COLLECTION, MIRIAM & IRA D. WALLACH DIVISION OF ART, PRINTS AND PHOTOGRAPHS, THE NEW YORK PUBLIC LIBRARY, ASTOR, LENOX AND TILDEN FOUNDATIONS.

Miss Beecher commended those "who deem it wisest to enjoy the comforts of their own house, themselves, [and] select the pleasantest and largest room, and use it for both sitting and eating-room, and sometimes keeping another parlor in daily use for company."[74]

It was not customary for children to join adults at table, and they were summarily removed if an adult came to take their place. In a story in *The Mother's Book,* Mrs. Child described entering someone's "parlor unexpectedly, just as the family were seated at the supper table. A little girl, about four years old, was obliged to be removed to make room for me."[75] Young Royall Tyler "had always been accustomed from his birth to be petted by grandma and aunts, to say nothing of his doting mother, and always sat with one or the other at the table." When the united family finally set up housekeeping in Guilford, Vermont, young Royall discovered that things had changed, for "Papa set his foot down that the baby should on no account come to the table, he must go out with Molly or sit in his father's great chair by the fire, till we were done."[76]

Even at the beginning of the period under consideration, rooms called "dining rooms" were not unknown. Ebenezer Parkman referred to his "dining room" in 1753, and the 1750 Portsmouth, New Hampshire, probate inventory of wealthy George Jaffrey gives a detailed look at the contents of a dining room that was at least thirty years old. Jaffrey's dining room was furnished with three small tables (one of which was designated a tea table), six chairs, three window squabs, fireplace furniture, a pair of wooden stands, and a clock. In the adjacent parlor were two great chairs with cushions and eight smaller chairs with cushions, four window-seat cushions, an escritoire, three tables, and fireplace furniture. The parlor was certainly considered the best room, with its expensive furniture and wall decorations consisting of maps of Asia and the Mediterranean, valuable pictures of King William and Queen Mary, and thirteen mezzotints. Fourteen people could be seated in the parlor and nine in the dining room, but in each case a third of them would be seated in window seats, and all of them would be divided among small tables. Both the dining room and the parlor had built-in cupboards called "beaufats" in which were sets of burnt china, white earthen plates and dishes, a few cups and saucers, and a cracked quilted china bowl together with cruets, saltcellars, wineglasses, and a pint decanter. Jaffrey owned a considerable amount of silver, including spoons, knives, forks and canns, chafing dishes, and candlesticks, which were listed separately; but since the "case for spoons, knives and forks" was in the dining-room beaufat, perhaps those and some of the other silver were normally stored there in the lower section, which had a strong lock on its solid wooden door. In the parlor beaufat was a japanned monteith, a flowerpot, two cracked china bowls, two glass basins (one broken), a china sugar dish, two alabaster bowls with covers, four glass salvers, and a variety of other glass and china, most of it in poor condition. In Jaffrey's household, as in thousands of other prosperous New England homes of his day, meals were served on pewter plates, which were stored in the kitchen and served in the parlor, sitting room, or dining room; tea, coffee, punch, and wines were served in glass or ceramic vessels, which were conveniently stored in beaufats or cupboards in the more public first-floor rooms. There was no single long table for dining, and people expected to be seated in small groups at a number of tables wherever they ate. It would have been delightful to drink a glass of punch or a dish of tea while seated in one of the cushioned chairs near the fireplace in George Jaffrey's parlor in the wintertime, or to enjoy the same refreshment in summer while seated on a cushioned window seat beside an open window overlooking the Piscataqua River. By the time of Jaffrey's death in 1750, there was no tea table in any of the bedchambers of his house.

Although we do not know how many people lived in George Jaffrey's well-furnished home when the inventory was taken in 1750, it is clear that this house was unusual in having so many rooms without beds. Throughout the eighteenth century, a very high percentage of New England households had beds in almost every room except the kitchen; only a select few were able to afford the luxury of a parlor without a bed, much less a dining parlor as well.

Rooms specifically designated as dining rooms became more common in the last half of the eighteenth century, but even well into the nineteenth century these rooms often served as sitting rooms as well as places to eat. The dining room of the home of Ebenezer Storer in Boston in 1807 contained lolling chairs and a desk in addition to a dining table (which had two "tables to add to it") and other furnishings.[77] By the end of the eighteenth century some families owned sideboards, which offered a place to display costly articles associated with eating and drinking. Many homes had sideboards before they had dining rooms. On the "sideboard in the parlor" of William Munroe, a Boston merchant who died in 1814, were displayed a breadbasket; a china tray; four pitchers; saltcellars and spoons; plated tea, coffee, sugar, and cream pots; a plated soup ladle; plated baskets; and candlesticks.[78] Anne Clark recognized the advantages of a

148. THE DINNER PARTY, OIL ON CANVAS, BY HENRY SARGENT, C. 1821. GIFT OF MRS. HORATIO A. LAMB IN MEMORY OF MR. AND MRS. WINTHROP SARGENT. COURTESY MUSEUM OF FINE ARTS, BOSTON.

*Another popular exhibition picture, this one represents the dessert course at a meeting of the Wednesday Club, a gentlemen's club that met monthly for sumptuous midafternoon dinners in the homes of its members. A large dining table has been set up to accommodate the guests—an unusual occurrence according to Edward Everett Hale, who wrote, "Observe that this large table never appeared, unless the 'club' met with my father, except on Thanksgiving day." (*A New England Boyhood *[New York: Cassell, 1893], p. 143.)*

sideboard for such display and wrote to her sister: "Send me . . . my silver—my sideboard looks naked without it."[79]

Sideboards were as useful as beaufats or parlor closets as a convenient place to store food, wine, glassware, and serving vessels. Sarah Orne Jewett wrote an entrancing description of "a most significant odor of cake and wine" emanating from "the little closets in the sideboard" of the Brandon House in Chapter II of *Deephaven.*[80]

If a family could set up long tables for important dinner parties, the sections were usually kept with their leaves down against the long wall in the central hallway, as was the case in the house of Mr. and Mrs. Isaac Davenport on Brush Hill in Milton, Massachusetts. When Mr. Davenport died in 1828, the carpeted dining parlor contained only a dozen chairs and two pembroke tables, along with a clock, a looking glass, fireplace equipment, a china tea and coffee set, a dinner service of "India" china, and quantities of glass, some cutlery, and additional ceramics.[81] The lightweight pembroke tables could easily be moved out and the more formal dining tables brought in from the hall and set up as one long table when it was needed for a large party.

As the importance and formality of dinner parties evolved in the nineteenth century, more families established rooms that were dedicated exclusively to formal dining. Mrs. Parkes, the author of *Domestic Duties,* characterized the dining room as a place of "solid simplicity" devoted to "the *important* concerns of the table . . . and where savoury vapours give warning of the danger of delay; there no other attraction is desirable, nor scarcely any thing requisite, beyond the well arranged table, and the chairs that surround it."[82]

When Mrs. Hall dined in Boston with Mr. Webster, she found the "dinner arrangements . . . much better, according to our notions, than what we have before seen in this country," although "the company dinner hour is four o'clock, and . . . we find it rather a bore to have to dine so early, it shortens our day so much." At a dinner for twelve, "the table was not so much loaded and the servants on the whole understood their duty better."[83] Christopher Gore's butler, Robert Roberts, would have been pleased by her commendation, for serving a formal dinner party, with its succession of courses, required both hard work and organization. In his book of instructions to servants, Roberts stressed "attention and systematical neatness" as well as "convenience and taste" as the guiding factors for his very detailed instructions on changing courses, removing covers from serving dishes, assisting the carver, and efficiently supplying whatever was wanted in the course of the meal. After the first course at the Websters' dinner party, Mrs. Hall found that "there were two courses of game alone, and then followed a course of sweet things, but the Ice was put down along with the dessert which was very prettily set out on handsome china, which, by the by, they generally have."[84] Not everyone owned enough china or glassware for a large party, however. Edward F. Sise, a Portsmouth, New Hampshire, dealer in "china, glass and crockery ware," and others like him, solved this problem for some hostesses by advertising "WARE loaned to parties."[85]

Since these large dinner parties were opportunities for a family to display its wealth in handsome china and glassware and dazzling displays of silver as well as costly food and wine, Roberts also gave specific instructions for "setting out the sideboard," because "ladies and gentlemen that have splendid and costly articles, wish to have them seen and set out to the best advantage." In Boston, Mrs. Hall also admired a "beautiful set of Sevres dessert china . . . with ice pails to match" at a party at the home of Professor and Mrs. Ticknor, where she thought every part of the house was "well furnished; the stair carpeted from top

149. ENTERTAINMENT AT THE HOME OF HARRISON GRAY OTIS, BOSTON, C. 1832–38, SKETCH BY WILLIAMS MIDDLETON. COURTESY OF MIDDLETON PLACE FOUNDATION, CHARLESTON, SOUTH CAROLINA.

A fashionable evening gathering in the Otis's Beacon Street mansion.

to bottom, and altho' a few more sofas and ottomans might be a good addition the want of them is not very apparent."[86] In furnishings, the ideal, according to Robert Roberts, was "a magnificent appearance" that would "strike the eyes of every person who enters the room, with a pleasing sensation of elegance." Roberts recommended dramatic effects achieved by arranging on the sideboard all of the wineglasses in "sublime" crescents, graduated by height and centered by cruets, decanters, and the dessert grapes, with any remaining space filled in by silver spoons, which would "give the glass a brilliant display."[87]

Large displays of silver in fashionable new styles were sure to attract attention. Dr. Bentley was particularly impressed by a tea set in 1796: "At the christening of Mr. Prebble's Child, was exhibited the most elegant Service of plate at the Tea Table, which I had ever seen, & which was allowed to be the best in the Town. It was imported entire, consisting of a font of circular figure upon four legs, a coffee urn, teapot with flute & beeds, & work in relief, vases for sugar, cream, & butter with ladles, spoons, & a beautiful set of white china having only a blue sprig."[88]

The Best Room

Important rituals like christening receptions, weddings, and funerals usually took place in a family's "best room." In the eighteenth century this might, or might not, be designated a parlor. It might, or might not, contain the best bed. Either way, the best room was a place to assemble and display one's most expen-

150. MRS. REUBEN HUMPHREY, PAINTING BY RICHARD BRUNTON, C. 1796–1801. CONNECTICUT HISTORICAL SOCIETY, HARTFORD.

Mrs. Humphrey was the wife of the superintendent of Newgate Prison in East Granby, Connecticut, from 1796 to 1801, and this picture was painted by Richard Brunton while he was incarcerated there. Mrs. Humphrey's silver tea service is an obvious emblem of gentility.

sive household furnishings, entertain distinguished guests, and observe whatever degree of social ritual was appropriate for one's rank and station.

Since a well-filled feather bed with a high-post bedstead and a complete set of bed hangings usually represented the most costly article of furnishing in any household, and there was a limited amount of space, it should not be surprising that beds of this sort were featured in New England parlors throughout the eighteenth century, and in some households well into the nineteenth. Ellen Rollins described such a room in her grandparents' New Hampshire home: "The door on the other side of the entry opened into the east room. This was the 'best room' or, as my grandfather called it, the 'fore' room. Most noticeable of its furnishings was the bed, more for show than for use. It was a tall structure, built up of corn-husks and feathers, not to be leaned against or carelessly indented. Its blue and white checked canopy, edged with knotted fringe, suspended by hooks from the ceiling, was spun and dyed and woven by the women of the household."[89]

Although best rooms of this sort persisted in rural areas well into the nineteenth century, the general increase in wealth in seaport towns and throughout the New England countryside beginning in the 1790s enabled more and more people to enjoy increased amounts of personal privacy, furnish their homes more comfortably, and participate in expensive social rituals. Best beds were moved out of parlors, and these rooms were set aside exclusively for social functions.

In the homes of the wealthiest people, the most formal rooms, designated drawing rooms, were places where one could "concentrate the elegance of the whole house." Since such rooms were intended to be used as settings for lively social intercourse, it was recommended that they be furnished in a restrained and elegant way. In his 1803 *Cabinet Maker's Dictionary,* Thomas Sheraton wrote: "The walls should be free of pictures, the tables not lined with books, nor the angles of the room filled with globes; as the design of such meetings are not that each visitant should turn to his favourite study, but to contribute his part towards the amusement of the whole company. The grandeur then introduced to the drawing room, is to be considered, not as the ostentatious parade of its proprietor, but the respect he pays to the rank of his visitors."[90] By 1828, Mrs.

Parkes was disagreeing, declaring that in a drawing room, "amusement and ease are the objects desired," and thus it should be furnished in a "light and airy style" with things that can "excite lively and interesting conversation, or aid the loiterer to kill his grand enemy—time."[91] By the 1820s, the drawing rooms of wealthy Bostonians and the parlors of the country gentry seem to have been furnished with considerable uniformity. There was almost always a large looking glass over the mantel and another between the two windows on the front wall, under which was one of a pair of card tables. With ten or a dozen chairs and perhaps a sofa or a carpet and the necessary andirons and fireplace equipment,[92] these rooms came alive when they were occupied by fashionable company or lively neighbors.

Parlors and drawing rooms were places where families displayed their wealth and the polite accomplishments of their daughters. Best parlors had the most expensive furnishings and were seldom used except for elegant entertaining, piano practice, or formal occasions such as weddings and funerals. When the rooms were not in use, the furniture was formally arranged with chairs lined up around the perimeter. This is the kind of room that was ridiculed by Harriet Beecher Stowe in *Oldtown Folks:* "We had our best room, and kept it as cold, as uninviting and stately, as devoid of human light or warmth, as the most fashionable shut up parlor of modern days. . . . Now it was a fact that nobody liked to sit in the best room . . . there the sitting provisions were exactly one dozen stuffed-seated cherry chairs, with upright backs and griffen feet, each foot terminating in a bony claw, which resolutely grasped a ball. These chairs were very high and slippery, and preached decorum in the very attitudes which they necessitated, as no mortal could ever occupy them in the exercise of a constant and collected habit of mind."[93]

Such a room was like the "store-room for household treasures" in the home described by Ellen Rollins. That room was filled with "such things which had been bought with hard-earned money" and were highly prized. "Its furniture was the costliest and most modern, as well as the ugliest in the house. It was sort of a show-room. The china and glass in its cupboard were marvellously fine."[94]

In the early nineteenth century, young housekeepers were cautioned against having such showrooms—the kind that were "considered to be too fine to be habitually occupied by the family to whom they belong, and such as are kept shut up, except on particular occasions, when . . . children are seen to stare and look about them, as if they had never beheld the place before; the master of the house fidgets from one seat to another . . . it is rare that we find the album, the closeted curiosity, or even the conversation of the assembled company, having

151. EVENING AMUSEMENTS, LITHOGRAPH, C. 1845, B. F. NUTTING. PRIVATE COLLECTION.

Family and friends gathered together with the firelight augmented by two lighted candles. Although one gentleman appears to be especially interested in the activity of the young woman, the other men are gathered around one small table while one peels apples, one cracks nuts, and another reads aloud. At the other table, an older woman is knitting and a younger woman tends to her sewing while listening to her beau. The separation of men and women, the variety of activities, and the assortment of furnishings can be considered typical.

charms sufficient to dissipate that gloom."[95] The taste for such rooms had developed among the nouveau riche—people who had earned enough money to purchase the trappings of gentility but lacked the money to entertain frequently and the confidence to enjoy them thoroughly. Such a room was described by Sarah Orne Jewett in *Deephaven,* when Mrs. Patton showed her visitors "into the best room the first time we went to see her. It was the plainest little room, and very dull, and there was an exact sufficiency about its furnishings. Yet there was a certain dignity about it; it was unmistakably a best room, and not a place where one might make a litter or carry one's everyday work. You felt at once that someone valued the prim old-fashioned chairs, and the two half-moon tables, and the thin carpet, which must have needed anxious stretching to make it come to the edge of the floor." Mrs. Patton's best room was a symbol of gentility and ideal beauty, but, like its uncomfortable rocking chair, "nobody would ever wish to sit there."[96]

In some homes, formal parlors were used for prayer and reading on the Sabbath. In 1802, Zilpah Longfellow identified a particular room in her house as "the largest parlor, unfrequented by the family excepting such as retire for meditation." Unfortunately, necessity interfered with gentility; the room was taken over as a sickroom and a bed set up for Mrs. Longfellow's sister Eliza, who remained there until she died. Zilpah's sad duty increased her use of the parlor; "Hours & hours I have watched here, frequently with Stephen."[97]

Sitting Rooms

Far more comfortable, more welcoming, and more frequently used was the sitting room, the back parlor, or the family parlor. In the hierarchy of rooms, this was usually the "second-best" room. Because its furnishings usually included a rocking chair, a warm fire, and a table with Scripture and *Pilgrim's Progress* or Young's "Night Thoughts," it was used daily by the family, and it was here that they entertained their closest friends.[98] It was the proper place for the sewing table and the writing desk. Because the sitting room was used more extensively than the strictly formal parlor, Miss Beecher admired those who "select the pleasantest and largest room and use it for both sitting and eating too, and sometimes keep another parlor in daily use for company."[99] In the winter of 1825, Zilpah Longfellow wrote to her husband Stephen: "Our parlor is never quiet."[100]

In the morning, after it had been swept and dusted, and the chairs set to rights, the sitting room was an orderly place. But no matter how tidy the ideal, rooms that were used intensively became cluttered as the day went by. Margaret

152. "HON. CHARLES HUBBARD & HIS FAMILY," OIL ON CANVAS, BY CHARLES HUBBARD, CHELSEA, MASSACHUSETTS, 1841. SHELBURNE MUSEUM, SHELBURNE, VERMONT.

The forty-year-old artist has depicted himself and his wife with their family in comfortable middle-class surroundings.

Quincy gave a wonderful description of this kind of thing on a day in 1824: "On the sofa lay my shawl, hat, veil, gloves, and fan, the new edition of Racine, Jonathan Mason's open letter and Josiah's coat; on the floor appeared a pair of shoes which I had just bought for Sophia, my handkerchief and purse, which I had dropped in my flight upstairs. Before the sofa was drawn the two armchairs, from which Joseph had been speaking his oration to me, both the closet doors wide open."[101]

When one had overnight guests who had come a distance, it was usual to expect additional numbers of local callers who wished to see them or to hear news from friends and relatives in other places. Sometimes travelers brought special foods, letters, books, newspapers, or curios, all of which remained in the parlor. Sarah Joiner Lyman sent sea shells and lava specimens from her mission station in Hilo, Hawaii, to her sister Melissa in Royalton, Vermont, in 1833, telling her to keep them "to ornament the mantle piece." Eighteen years later she sent volcanic specimens, a conch shell, coral, a tapa pounder, sea shells, and other curios, expressing the hope that Melissa's "good husband" would "feel able to have a case made" for them.[102] Sarah Bryant visited Deacon Richardson's house on May 20, 1825, "to see some curiosities from the Sandwich Islands,"[103] and Abner Sanger often dropped in to see what people from afar had brought to Keene.

Victorian clutter was coming, however. A party at the Lawrences' in Boston on March 18, 1833, was described by Anna Quincy. One could see:

> Pictures of every shape, size and hue, were hung, or rather pitched upon the walls, without the slightest regard to conformity. Bookshelves filled with books and boxes and shells and stuffed birds and china pitchers and plants and flowers and sugar ornaments and bronzes and hook and eye boxes full of seals, and slates and china mandarins, two paper baskets and gold snuff boxes and bird's nests and butterflies, were all mingled, higglety pigglety. . . . I never beheld anything like it, it really seemed as Mrs. L. must have gone up into all the garrets of the museums and neighboring houses and showered down upon her hapless mansion all the old, odd things that ever were stored away. One room becoming crowded, I went into the other with Henry Davis, who seemed very dull, but could not help laughing as, at every turn, we met some oddity or other. He at last lodged me under the spreading branches of a myrtle tree, the birds, to be sure, were not singing in its branches, but a defunct bird's nest was suspended from one of them, which answered the same purpose.[104]

Dancing Parties

Any house was thrown into disarray in preparation for a large evening party with dancing and a supper. Rooms were cleared and hallways lighted with shade candlesticks to keep the candles from guttering. Arriving at a "splendid ball" in Hallowell, Maine, in 1823, one young woman found that "there were two parlors which opened into one by means of folding doors, when I went in there were about 50 young ladies and gentlemen, after we had been there 1–2 hour the folding doors were thrown open & we were desired to walk into the other parlor, where the carpet had been previously taken up, the other carpet was speedily removed & we commenced dancing to the sound of a violin and clarionet, we danced until ½ past nine, when we were marched upstairs into a room where there was a very splendid supper set out after supper coffee was handed round we then went downstairs & again commenced dancing. I got home at ½ past 11."[105] Dancing often took place at organized parties in taverns, but smaller dancing parties occurred in the parlors and kitchens of private homes as well. Not everyone approved, of course. Miss Beecher complained about dancing and balls, insisting that it was physically injurious to keep people up later than usual and necessitated one's leaving a warm room and passing through dangerous and damp night air to get home. She also cautioned that dancing in private parlors had a diminished social benefit, for "when a dancing party occupies the centre of parlors, and the music begins, most of the conversation ceases, while the young prepare themselves for future sickness, and the old look smilingly on."[106]

Dancing was often included in wedding celebrations. According to Timothy Dwight, New England weddings in the eighteenth century were "festivals of considerable significance" to which large numbers of friends and relatives were invited and at which a dinner was served before the early-evening ceremony. After the knot was tied, cake and wine were "plentifully distributed among the guests," and there was often dancing. This is the kind of joyful and hilarious wedding ceremony described in fictional accounts, perhaps beginning in 1845 with "The Country Wedding," in which the anonymous author included a description of the household preparations for a wedding: "Old clothes, worn-out baskets, broken chairs, and all things of kindred worth, had been carried out and thrown promiscuously upon one funeral pile, and there consumed. The huge fireplaces were filled to the brim with pine boughs, which were ornamented with white paper cut round, and about the size of a silver dollar, and

153. WEDDING IN A PARLOR, DETAIL FROM SHEET-MUSIC COVER, "THE LONELY AULD WIFE," LITHOGRAPH, THAYER & CO., BOSTON, 1844. COURTESY AMERICAN ANTIQUARIAN SOCIETY.

stuck on with cobbler's wax, which gave them the appearance of white rose-bushes in June. Beds were made up about six feet high, and the sand swept zigzag upon the newly scoured floors with geometrical precision. The pantry shelves now groaned beneath their load of good things cooked for the approaching festival." In the room where the ceremony would take place, "three tiers of rude benches" were placed around "three sides of it, prepared for the precious occasion." The author continued with descriptions of the clothing of the bridal pair and their guests, the feasting, dancing, games, and forfeits.[107] It was truly a frolic.

As early as 1800, the Reverend Timothy Dwight realized that these customs were changing, with smaller numbers of people invited to wedding ceremonies and a more formal kind of entertainment. When the widowed Ruth Henshaw Miles was married for a second time at her parents' house in Leicester, Massachusetts, on Wednesday, February 26, 1806, friends arrived at various times throughout the day. Mr. Bascom and Ruth's father left at noon to attend a funeral. "At night Mr. Moore [the minister] returned with Daddy—and administered the 'oath of Alegiance' to my friend E. L. Bascom & myself in presence of our family & the before mentioned friends." It must have been an old-fashioned wedding, although the diary contains no mention of any kind of refreshment or entertainment. At the first wedding Mrs. Bascom attended in Gerry, on December 28, 1808, she noticed something unusual: they "had tea carried round . . . usually roast meats & baked pudding & tea—think the former much the best way."[108] On New Year's Day in 1810, the Bascoms attended a wedding in the old style and supped on "roast turkey, beef, pies, &c" before cake and wine were served in the evening.[109] In late June of that same year, she attended another wedding, where they "sent round their tea, cake &c as is customary at weddings of late."[110] Changing standards of gentility were transforming the old country ways.

Things had not completely changed in Hadley when Elizabeth Porter Phelps attended her cousin Polly's wedding in 1808. There they had cake and wine after the three o'clock ceremony, but a cold supper was served after the newly married couple departed: "turkey, beef, roast pork, cake, and pies—a good cup of tea." Mrs Phelps pronounced it "a very nice entertainment."[111]

In 1816, Dr. Bentley observed the gender separation which had come to characterize "a fashionable display of the new Wedding Customs. The rooms were furnished elegantly & filled with Chairs. Upon entrance after sundown into the brilliantly illumined apartments four bridesmaids were ready to receive the guests, receive their outer garments & to introduce the Ladies to the Bride. Four young gentlemen had the same offices for the gentlemen. They were then seated in their respective rooms & served with the best cake & wine that could be obtained. This occasion was the marriage of the youngest d[aughter] of late G. Crowninshield, Esqr. to Mr. John Rice. The cake alone served on the occasion exceeded 130 pounds."[112]

Wedding cake became the culinary feature of these receptions instead of the variety of meats and pies served previously. By 1825, Mrs. Bascom was regularly describing wedding refreshments of "tea, toast, & cake carried round, followed by Brandy, toddy & cordial"[113] and "elegant Loaves of Cake &c."[114] When Elizabeth Margaret Carter married William Reynolds in Newburyport in 1821, her mother, sisters, and cousins made more than two hundred pounds, or fourteen loaves, of wedding cake, so that it could be passed three times with wine and lemonade to the intimate family and friends who were present at the actual wedding ceremony, and then offered to the throngs who arrived at eight o'clock for a levee, or reception, after the ceremony, and then to people to carry home. The cake was highly praised: "Its garb was purely white; Paradisical grains were scattered over its surface, & it was studded with gilded almonds. In the centre towered a beautiful collection of artificial flowers & round its body was a wreath of laurel. The groomsmen cut it up, and the Bridesmaids assisted by Old Lady Parsons handed it round; & oh it was astonishing to see how it vanished from sight; a sheet of paper was laid on each plate & a slice of cake laid upon it; soon as received, by each person, the disappearance of it was so instantaneous that we were in many instances deceived & very kindly offered a second & third piece, fearing some omission. Those who had rapidly deposited two pieces, held a third very modestly in their hands, & I do believe if any of them should give a party six months hence, Mrs. Reynolds' wedding cake will add its share of the entertainment."[115]

Wedding cakes were usually rich fruit cakes. The recipe for the cake made when Esther Chase of Deering, New Hampshire, married Dr. Michael Tubbs in 1799 calls for "seven pounds of flour, six of butter, fifty four eggs, leaving out eighteen whites to make the frosting, with fifteen pounds of currants, six of raisins, three and half of citron, a pint of brandy, two teacups of molasses, two large spoonfuls of saleratus, two large spoonfuls of mace, two of cloves, two of alspice, two of cinnamon." The manuscript receipt concludes "the above is very rich."[116] When the Carter family was preparing their fourteen loaves of cake in Newburyport in 1821, an entire day was devoted to stoning the currants "that people might not break out their teeth eating wedding cake," and Mrs. Parsons expressed her frustration with the task, concluding that "we would petetion the people of Zante to send more currants and fewer stones, for in time we feared all their island might be transported here in casks of currants."[117]

The formality with which the cake and wine were passed at early-nineteenth-century wedding ceremonies varied from place to place and according to the social sophistication of the people involved. At Northampton, Massachusetts, Mrs. Basil Hall was invited to a wedding party on October 4, 1827, where she observed "a boy bearing a tray covered with plates and two beautiful wedding cakes, of which each guest helped him or herself to a large piece, even the newly married pair seemed to have retained their appetite for plum cake, and the gentleman still had enough of his senses sufficiently about him to take proper care of his wedding suit and followed the example of the other males of the party in spreading his pocket handkerchief over his knees to protect his trousers from the grease of the cake. We next had wine handed round." At a country wedding near Holyoke, she observed the company "seated according to the American fashion as if they were pinned to the wall, and the gentlemen divided from the ladies, whether by design or accident I do not know."[118] Such a scene is far from the relaxed and easy sociability described in the stories of Sarah Orne Jewett and Harriet Beecher Stowe. As usual, these authors brought to mind the comfortable, democratic ideal while ignoring both awkwardness and incivility of rural folk or the rigor and artificial nature of upscale convention and manners. The New England of their parents' time was characterized by each.

X

The One Day Above All Others: New England Thanksgiving

MANY NEW ENGLANDERS TOOK TIME AT THE BEGINNING OF EACH YEAR to assess their situation in life and consider their many blessings. Those who kept diaries often summarized their thoughts on New Year's Day. Ruth Bascom took a moment on January 1, 1825, to note that "this year opens upon us also, surrounded by every external necessary and convenience—a warm and convenient house & outhouses—food, fuel & fire & ten thousand blessings."[1] For Mrs. Bascom, as for many of the others, home had many private satisfactions.

At Thanksgiving time, these same feelings were expressed and celebrated by many people throughout the region with feasting and festivity. The Thanksgiving holiday had achieved its traditional status long before the beginning of the nineteenth century. The editor of the Salem *Observer* explained it well in 1825, writing that "the anniversary of this good old Festival will ever be greeted with hearty welcome." Thanksgiving combined the celebration of the harvest and a review of individual and community blessings with formal and informal praise and thanks to God, the renewal of familial ties and the bonds of friendship with a jolly good time. The editor assured his readers: "This ancient holiday has become so associated with the habits and feelings of the people of New-England, that its discontinuance would now leave a painful void, which would be felt like a blight upon the heart. Time has reared no custom, which yields so wide a diffusion of temperate hilarity and sober joy. If we revert to the blithe period of our childhood, we remember it as a jubilee which was anticipated with eager expectancy, and enjoyed with unmingled delight."[2] The edi-

154. "THANKSGIVING," IN *Gleason's Pictorial Drawing Room Companion,* NOVEMBER 1852. COURTESY OF THE SOCIETY FOR THE PRESERVATION OF NEW ENGLAND ANTIQUITIES.

An emblem with a contemporary parlor scene surmounting conjecturing views of the first Thanksgiving at Plymouth and surrounded by allegorical representations of Peace, Plenty, and Liberty.

tor of the *Massachusetts Spy* felt that the proper motivation for the traditional Thanksgiving was to "show respect for the memory of our pious forefathers" to whom were owed "the many civil and religious blessings which we enjoy."[3]

Thanksgiving, of course, is a New England tradition dating back to the time of the first harvest at Plymouth in 1621. Days of public fasting and thanksgiving were proclaimed on an ad hoc basis by the Colonial governors in the seventeenth century for a variety of reasons, but the late-fall commemoration of thanksgiving gathered strength in the eighteenth century. By the 1770s, it was traditional for the individual New England governors to proclaim a Thursday in late November or early December as a day of Thanksgiving. Well before the American Revolution, the blessings enumerated by the governor and the local minister, the components of the feast, and the special details of individual family celebrations had the force of ritual.

As early as 1827, in her novel *Northwood: A Tale of New England,* Sarah Josepha Hale described the traditional feast with its array of foods featuring roasted turkey and other meats, and chicken and pumpkin pies, explaining that everyone was "proud of displaying his abundance and prosperity."[4]

Shortly after the publication of *Northwood,* Mrs. Hale campaigned vigorously to have Thanksgiving adopted as a national holiday, to be observed on the fourth Thursday in November. Mrs. Hale became the editor of *Godey's Lady's Book* in 1832, and she used the magazine as an effective propaganda vehicle in her campaign. The idea was finally adopted by Abraham Lincoln in 1863.

Thanksgiving proclamations were usually read aloud after worship on the Sunday preceding Thanksgiving day. Since the custom was well established, the day was anticipated long before the official proclamation was read, and preparations were already well under way in many families. Until Lincoln's proclamation, the holiday might be observed on different days in different states. One year, this proved an opportunity for Betsy Phelps to celebrate the holiday with both her parents and her husband, a minister who could not leave his congregation on Thanksgiving day. Her mother wrote: "As to being with you at thanksgiving we feel as if it would be very clever to unite in that grateful employment once more . . . as the days are different, ours one week before yours, that you & yours, as many as can will come & keep thanksgiving with us here—& return the next week to your own thanksgiving."[5]

Mrs. Hale felt that the choice of November for Thanksgiving celebrations was inspired. It makes "the funeral-faced month of November . . . wear a garland of joy, and instead of associating the days of fog, like our English relations, with sadness and suicide, we hail them as the era of gladness and good living."[6]

In 1834, the editor of the New Hampshire *Patriot* pointed out the signs of the approaching holiday: "The harvesting of pumpkins—the gobbling of turkeys and fatting of pigs—the buying and selling of eggs—a moderate rise in the price of molasses and spices—the increased demand for laces, ribbons and dancing pumps—the hurrying of tailors, milliners and mantua makers—frequent and important consultations of young gentlemen—whispering, flushed faces, and anxious looks among young ladies—an increase of publishments—and lastly, a string of proclamations announcing the 27th day of November as a day of Thanksgiving in New Hampshire, Massachusetts, Connecticut, and Vermont."[7]

The weather was apt to be cold, but good sleighing was not guaranteed so early in the season. Stores were closed, business was generally suspended, and the day had the aspect of a Sunday. Ministers conducted services in meeting houses, gave special consideration to their choice of texts, and labored over new sermons. Except for attending the services at the meeting house, Thanksgiving observances centered on the home and reinforced the patriarchal sense of the New England family. It was a time for family reunions and for family traditions.

Varying Observations of the Holiday

Not every Thanksgiving day was the stuff of poetry and tradition. Bad weather sometimes kept people from traveling. Not everyone could afford a rich display of food. Sarah Connell Ayer described a very simple situation in her diary in 1807: "Thursday. Was thanksgiving day. We dined without company. Caty went up to her Mothers, and staid all night. We could not go to Church on account of rain."[8]

Sarah Bryant's diary suggests variations in Thanksgiving observances over a lifetime. When newly married, she often "went to Sirs"; sometimes she and Dr. Bryant and their very young children "tarried over night" with her parents. In 1798, when Dr. Bryant was called away overnight to treat a patient, she sent her five-year-old son, Austin, "to his grand sirs" on the day before Thanksgiving, going herself with four-year-old Cullen and four-month-old Cyrus on the day itself. When the weather was poor and the roads muddy, or "bad going," Sarah Bryant did not go to meeting on Thanksgiving day but "tarried at home." Often the hired girl went home to spend Thanksgiving with her own family. If the weather was good, there might be company in the evening, usually close relatives or the Reverend James Briggs and his wife. In 1830, Sarah went to meeting, and in the evening she ventured forth "to the village to hear Miss Clark's lecture on history."[9] Whether or not the celebration was at her house, Mrs. Bryant had plenty to do. The usual laundry, churning, weaving, sewing, and other work continued during the days before the holiday. Sometimes Mrs. Bryant "baked pies" during the week before Thanksgiving, usually on Wednesday. Often she "picked fowls" on Tuesdays, which suggests that she was about to make a chicken pie.[10]

Newlyweds and unmarried young people who were away at school, working in other families, or living far away did not always return home for the holiday. Sarah Bryant's sons often came home for Thanksgiving from teaching school or studying law, but when her daughter Sarah was attending a boarding school in Northampton in 1818, she did not return home for Thanksgiving, although the distance was only twenty miles. In 1805, Charles and Elizabeth Phelps traveled to Litchfield to celebrate with Betsy and her husband, Daniel Huntington. On returning to Hadley, Mrs. Phelps wrote to her daughter: "Don't you think it is rather odd? That children generally go to their parents to keep thanksgiving—but we have been to our children."[11]

Clearly, though, the ideal was to return home if it was at all possible. In retrospect, Caroline King believed that "Thanksgiving day . . . was a much more important festival [in 1825–40] than at present, and was universally kept as a season of family reunions. No obstacle was then allowed to prevent the return to the family home of all the separated sons and daughters with their children, and great was the rejoicing when the fledged birds once more flew back to the mother nest."[12]

People did try to get home and felt both blessed and rewarded when they were able to do so. In 1806, after several years as a missionary in Ohio, the Reverend Thomas Robbins preached a Thanksgiving sermon at his own church in Windsor, Connecticut, and then traveled to his parents' home in Norfolk for the rest of the day, noting in his diary: "Have not been home at a Thanksgiving since '99. All my brothers here except James." Often, though, Robbins remained with the family with whom he boarded, and his diary reflects no great crowd. In 1812 he wrote, "our family is quite small"; in 1825, "we had no company with our own family"; and in 1832, "we have a small family; but three at dinner."[13] Perhaps these three occasions were the only ones at which the family was so small, but every family had times when the Thanksgiving table was not surrounded by a dozen or more people.

Then as now, young married couples had to decide which family they would visit on Thanksgiving day. With her son Charles and his wife Sally caring for a new baby in Boston and unable to travel safely for such a long journey,[14] Elizabeth Phelps was particularly anxious about whether her daughter Betsy would be able to return for Thanksgiving in Hadley after her marriage on New Year's Day in 1801. Mrs. Phelps must have put on the pressure early, for as soon as July, Betsy wrote to her mother reassuringly that her husband "says we must go to Hadley at Thanksgiving," but she qualified her promise by saying, "perhaps if both states keep the same day—we may set out the day after and be with you on Saturday night."[15] Since Mr. Huntington was a minister, it would be difficult, if not impossible, for him to leave his congregation on whatever day the governor of Connecticut chose to celebrate Thanksgiving. Betsy's mother did not give up, however, and wrote in mid-September: "Give my love to your beloved & ask him if I may have you, a little while before Thanksgiving to help me prepare for him & our other friends."[16] Even her father joined in. On September 28, he wrote confidently to his daughter expressing their "expectation" that she would be in Hadley at Thanksgiving time.[17] After several more letters in which her mother also urged Betsy to join the family for Thanksgiving, the younger woman made the journey to Hadley alone. Her mother was delighted and expressed her feelings in her diary: "I desire to return thanks to God for granting us the Company of our daughter Huntington through this Thanksgiving. We are unworthy but God is very kind. I feel grateful very grateful to Mr. Huntington for sparing his wife but supremely grateful to the Lord."[18] When Betsy returned to Litchfield, she carried meat, pies, and cakes with her, part of the bounty of the Phelps farm, but perhaps also a kind of peace offering to Mr. Huntington from her mother.

At Thanksgiving time in 1825, when Sarah Bryant was sharing the family homestead with her son Austin, his wife Adeline, and their young children as well as her own daughter Louisa and her younger sons Rush and John, the family scattered. Austin, Adeline, and their children went to Adeline's parents' home in Richmond, Massachusetts, from Wednesday until Monday, while Mrs. Bryant went to meeting, served a dinner of chicken and other pies, and then spent the evening at her brother's home, where they were joined by his wife's two brothers and their wives. The young people—Louisa, Rush, and John—went to a different party in the evening, at the home of their closest neighbor, Deacon Briggs.

Those who could afford to do so made a special effort to take in people who lived in small families or who had suffered some kind of adversity. In 1774, Samuel Snell and his wife and "two old country men who have no home" joined Elizabeth and Charles Phelps and their large family for supper on Thanksgiving day.[19] Some unmarried people found themselves expected guests as traditions developed. In 1829, Christopher Columbus Baldwin of Worcester dined at Governor Lincoln's, spent "the afternoon at Dr. Bancroft's frolicking, and the evening at Gov. Lincoln's." Looking back over the past six years, Baldwin found that he had developed a personal tradition of Thanksgiving celebration, which he noted in his diary: "In 1823, 1824, 1825, 1826, 1827, I eat my Thanksgiving dinners with my friend William Lincoln at his mother's. The last two years I have had it at Gov. Lincoln's, and have had my Thanksgiving supper at Gov. Lincoln's seven years in succession."[20] The following year he varied his day by borrowing a horse and sulkey, dining with a friend who had a new son, taking tea with a judge, paying an evening call on a newly married couple in a boardinghouse, and attending the Worcester lyceum to hear lectures on the proper method of reading history and "an interesting memoir of old Genl Gookin of Indian memory," but even after all that he made sure not to miss the Lincolns' party in the evening, where he had, "according to long usage, a supper."[21]

The Blessings of the Table

The reputation of New England households for their bountiful dinners at Thanksgiving time was well established by the end of the eighteenth century. A popular account, reprinted in many newspapers, estimated

> the good things consumed in New-England on Thanksgiving day,—The number of families [being] about 250,000.
>
> | | |
> |---|---:|
> | A Turkey or goose for every two families | 125,000 |
> | Two pair of Chickens to a family | 1,000,000 |
> | And a pair for chicken-pie to each family | 500,000 |
> | Roasted Pigs, say | 10,000 |
> | Pumpkin-pies, at least ten to a family | 2,500,000 |
> | Apple d^{o} and tart—an equal number | 2,500,000 |
>
> To these should be added roast beef, joints of pork or mutton, and many small dishes occasionally used but not reducible to a fair estimate.[22]

In order to fulfill the expectations of their families and to meet their own high standards, there was a great deal of work to be done. Caroline King remembered that "preparations for the reception of the homecomers were

155. FANEUIL HALL MARKET BEFORE THANKSGIVING, IN *Gleason's Pictorial Drawing Room Companion*, DECEMBER 6, 1851. COURTESY OF THE SOCIETY FOR THE PRESERVATION OF NEW ENGLAND ANTIQUITIES.

made for weeks before hand. Stores of food sufficient for an army were bought, for everything was laid on large lines then. The pie closet was filled with apple, mince, squash and cranberry pies, and plum and Marlborough puddings, and the store closet was filled with good things."[23] Expecting her children for Thanksgiving in 1810, Elizabeth Phelps began cooking early, and "soon, all my cooking had reference to my dear children's visit, how often did I say to myself 'this and this we will eat now, but that and that I hope to feed upon, with my children' two chicken pies I made (and do guess they are good ones)."[24]

Storekeepers throughout the region made certain that their stock of winter goods was on hand in plenty of time for Thanksgiving shopping, and many ordered extra supplies of special foods. In late November 1804, Samuel Holland advertised "*articles necessary for Thanksgiving*" in the Greenfield *Gazette:* "St Croix & Jamaica Rum, French and Cider Brandy, Gin, Molasses, Loaf & Brown Sugars, by the 100 wt. or less, Hyson-Souchong & Bohea Teas, Pepper, Ginger, Pimento, Cinnamon, Nutmegs, Box Raisins, Coffee, Chocolate, and many other articles."[25]

Featuring turkey or chicken pie at Thanksgiving is certainly related to the fact that often the major butchering of the winter was done the following week, and fresh beef or pork was simply unavailable in many households. Preparing pies and cleaning the house for Thanksgiving took time, and few people were willing to undertake the tremendous amount of work involved in cutting up a whole cow or pig, making sausages, and dealing with heads, feet, organ meats, and tallow until the holiday was over. In describing the Thanksgiving dinner in *Northwood,* Mrs. Hale did not explain how the Romolee family had been able to prepare a sirloin of beef, a leg of pork, and a joint of mutton to go with their turkey, goose, and pair of ducklings. Offering such variety was important in developing her image of the family's agricultural success, but it would have created chaos in the kitchen.

Although it was easy enough for country people to kill a chicken or a turkey, city dwellers relied on markets for the necessary meat and poultry. Caroline King remembered that in Salem, Massachusetts, "for the week before Thanksgiving the farmers used to come in from the country, with carts full of poultry, or loads of wood drawn by mild melancholy eyed oxen, and stand round the market place, and up each side of Essex Street from Central to Washington Street, waiting for customers, who were not wanting."[26] Dr. Bentley confirmed this with many observations about the availability and price of goods in the Salem market, and the situation was the same in other seaport towns and cities. In Portsmouth, New Hampshire, Samuel Larkin observed on December 4, 1839, that it was "very pleasant, & the Market overloaded with Poultry—for the lovers of good eating on Thanksgiving day—provisions of all kinds has fallen in price by nearly one half."[27] The following year, the Portsmouth market was again well stocked with poultry for Thanksgiving, and Larkin noted "an unusual quantity" and "generally very good—prices from 6 to 9 cents" [per pound].[28] Zilpah Longfellow vividly described the situation in Portland, Maine: "Tomorrow is our Thanksgiving and the turkeys & ducks are flying up and down the street in everybody's hands."[29]

Market demand sometimes drove up prices, and abuses were not unknown. On the day before Thanksgiving in 1802, William Bentley observed: "Markets higher this day than yesterday. Turkies at 9/*d,* or 12½ cents, ducks at 4/6, 75 cents a pair. The rise has happened several years."[30] In 1805, turkeys were only ten cents a pound in the Salem market, and Bentley observed: "The Salem Thanksgiving market creates a great demand for poultry. Few other articles feel the benefit of this market. Every person of every condition reckons upon fowls, geese, ducks or Turkies."[31]

So universal was the reliance on poultry for the Thanksgiving table that a popular story about it was published in 1828: "It is said that turkeys were sold in the market in Boston, on the morning of Thanksgiving day, for twenty-five cents a pound. . . . One man who bought a fine turkey a day or two previous,

156. *Making Thanksgiving pies in the Allen House kitchen,* DEERFIELD, MASSACHUSETTS. PHOTOGRAPH BY FRANCES S. AND MARY E. ALLEN. POCUMTUCK VALLEY MEMORIAL ASSOCIATION, DEERFIELD, MASSACHUSETTS.

This carefully posed photograph features women in historical costume engaged in the quintessential kitchen activity of preparation for Thanksgiving, pie making.

carried it into the market and resold it, concluding to make his Thanksgiving dinner on beef. This man could not have been a full-blooded Yankee. What, go without turkey on Thanksgiving day, when you had made sure of one at a reasonable price? The thing is incredible."[32]

And the Pies!

If turkey and chicken pies were the features of the first course at Thanksgiving dinner, it was pies alone that starred in the second act. An enormous quantity and variety of pies were expected, and in some ways they were a measure of a successful Thanksgiving dinner. Harriet Beecher Stowe felt that "the making of pies, at this period assumed vast proportions that verged on the sublime. Pies were made by the forties and fifties and hundreds, and made of everything on the earth and under the earth. . . . Pumpkin pies, cranberry pies, huckleberry pies, cherry pies, green currant pies, peach, pear, and plum pies, custard pies, apple pies, Marlborough-pudding pies,* pies with top crusts, pies without, pies adorned with all sorts of fanciful fluting and architectural strips laid across and around, and otherwise varied, attested to the boundless fertility of the feminine mind, when once let loose in a given direction."[33]

Both mincemeat and plum puddings required raisins, and these, too, were considered essential to a successful feast. "Raisins are a *sine qua non* in celebrat-

* Marlborough pies usually combine apples with lemon custard. They were considered a regional specialty, and many families cherished their own unique recipe.

ing a New England Thanksgiving," affirmed the *Massachusetts Spy* in November 1830. "These annual festivals approach, and since the 1st instant, there have been received, in five vessels from Malaga, 7614 casks, 800 half casks, 439 quarter casks, 7772 boxes, 1766 half boxes and 745 quarter boxes raisins; and more are expected."[34]

In preparation for the baking, the currants and raisins needed to be carefully examined and seeds and stones removed. Loaves of sugar needed to be pounded to a fine granular texture and spices pulverized. In *Oldtown Folks,* Mrs. Stowe defined these as children's tasks: "For as much as a week beforehand, 'we children' were employed in chopping mince for pies to a most wearisome fineness, and in pounding cinnamon, allspice, and cloves in a great 'lignum-vitae' mortar; and the sound of this pounding and chopping re-echoed throughout all the rafters of the old house."[35]

Mrs. Stowe's vivid picture of kitchen activity at Thanksgiving time continued: "In the old corner of the great kitchen, during all these days, the jolly old oven roared and crackled in great volcanic billows of flame, snapping and gurgling as if the old fellow entered with joyful sympathy into the frolic of the hour; and then, his great heart being once warmed up, he brooded over successive generations of pies and cakes, which went in raw and came out cooked, till butteries and dressers and shelves and pantries were literally crowded with jostling abundance."[36]

157. THE BASEMENT KITCHEN, NO. 2 CHESTNUT STREET, SALEM, C. 1850–56, DRAWING, BY L. J. BRIDGMAN AT THE DIRECTION OF JOHN ROBINSON, SALEM, 1915, USING ACTUAL MEASUREMENTS. COURTESY OF THE SOCIETY FOR THE PRESERVATION OF NEW ENGLAND ANTIQUITIES.

Elinor Stearns recalled that in a similar kitchen on the day before Thanksgiving, "the Rumford oven was in full blast, the matches were taken out of the boiler top, the fire lighted beneath; even the wash-boiler was called into service and the whole battery was engaged.... The pride of the kitchen was the battery of boilers and ovens with fire-boxes beneath them on either side of the fireplace. First came the copper wash-boiler, with its individual fire-box, ready for Monday observances; next to it was the ham boiler, a two story affair of thick tin, constructed above and topped by a smaller, detachable steamer for plum puddings and the like, but being seldom used, it served to hold the stock of sulphurous matches; this, too, had its own fire-box below. Beyond the large, open fire-place, again with an individual fire-box, was the Rumford oven, always in great demand just before Thanksgiving and Christmas." (Old Time New England *13 [January 1923]: 31.)*

The Day Itself

An unusual quantity of cooking required extra supplies of split and dry firewood and oven wood. More would be needed to keep the parlor at a comfortable temperature throughout the festival day. Abner Sanger found the necessity worth mentioning in his diary, when he "cut wood at the door for Thanksgiving."[37]

"Everything that could possibly be prepared the night before, was put in order, that there might be as little manual labor in store for the day of the feast as possible, and only a few hands might be detained from attending church,"[38] wrote an anonymous author in 1842. In 1809, Mrs. Phelps took a moment a little after four o'clock on the afternoon before Thanksgiving to review her situation: "All the things are done, that can be done now—the chicken pies are out of the oven, and I never saw any done better, Polly has gone home well loaded, and well pleased. . . . I must attend to supper as I am maid."[39]

On Thanksgiving morning, there was still more to be done. Animals needed

158. PREPARING FOR THANKSGIVING, IN *Ballou's Pictorial*, DRAWING, BY W. L. CHAMPNEY, NOVEMBER 24, 1858. COURTESY OF THE SOCIETY FOR THE PRESERVATION OF NEW ENGLAND ANTIQUITIES.

This was described as "a genuine New England scene": "A large, old-fashioned room, at once perhaps, kitchen and sitting room, and here the preparations for the genial anniversary are being made... on the right side of the picture... we see a huge fireplace, which a sturdy yeoman is filling with stout cord wood sticks... hard by is a table, whereon that most delicious of New England delicacies—and, alas! the most indigestible, mince-pie is being prepared by a neat-handed Phillis. Nor, we may be sure, is the generous pumpkin-pie forgotten.... There has been sad havoc in the poultry-yard, we fear, for there is a strong representation of the juvenile force of the family engaged in plucking certain bipeds of their feathers.... Conspicuous in the centre of the picture is the presiding goddess of the feast, or rather, the culinary priestess of its mysteries, vested with high authority.... This picture will remind many of our city readers of the days of auld lang syne and revive the dear home scenes of happy youth to which no after-scenes will ever compare."

to be fed and cows milked. Fires were lighted, and hungry people tried to eat a light breakfast. Jacob Abbott affirmed that "the morning repast is frugal, and yet the appetite is excited by some little foretaste of what is to come."[40] Rooms not normally used were heated; if the day was very cold, fires had to be started in the early morning. Harriet Beecher Stowe sketched a vivid picture in *Oldtown Folks:* "The best room on this occasion was thrown wide open, and its habitual coldness was warmed by the burning down of a great stack of hickory logs, which had been heaped up unsparingly since morning."[41]

For many people, morning attendance at meeting was an important part of Thanksgiving day. Ministers prepared special sermons, often reviewing current events of national and local importance and speaking out on the duties of Christians in relation to political action—topics they seldom addressed at the regular weekly religious meeting. In the nineteenth century, special music was often prepared by the choir or singing school. The ministers seem to have viewed a full meeting and a generous collection of money as a sign of their Thanksgiving success. In some churches the Thanksgiving collection was designated for a particularly needy group; during the 1830s, Thomas Robbins's church at Mattapoisett collected money, and sometimes wood, for "poor widows."[42]

Although Edward Everett Hale asserted that "every human being went to 'meeting' on the morning of Thanksgiving Day, the boy of four years included,"[43] that was not always the case. On Thanksgiving in 1835, the Reverend Thomas Robbins noted: "Meeting rather thin. Not cold. The people here have been much accustomed to consider this and the Fast as secular days."[44]

Robbins was disgusted to report that in some towns, "not a few are found, who desecrate the day by entire devotion to amusements. The Bowling Alley is thronged by dissolute loungers. The idle and dissipated congregate for field sports and shooting-matches and pass the day in deeds of cruelty and sin."[45] Especially in newly settled areas, some men devoted Thanksgiving morning to hunting or to turkey shoots, such as the one held in 1783 in Warren, New Hampshire, where hens and turkeys were tied to stakes and men paid four and a half pence to shoot at a hen from a distance of eight rods or nine pence to shoot at a turkey from ten rods. Usually the birds were freshly killed before being mounted on the stakes, and if a man hit a bird, it was his to take home. It is hard to imagine a woman waiting until halfway through the morning to know if someone would succeed in shooting a turkey and bring it home for her to cook for an occasion as important as Thanksgiving day itself. These trophies were probably hung in a cold, secure barn until they could be singed, plucked, and dealt with later in the week.

The Dinner

Whether people went to meeting or indulged in active sports, there was still work to do in the kitchen and parlor on Thanksgiving morning. Some women stayed home from meeting to finish the preparations. Sarah Emery recalled that her "Aunt Hannah set the table with the best napery and ware."[46]

To accommodate large numbers of people, sometimes two tables would be set up for dinner, while in other families the children would be expected to stand and reach between their elders for their share of food. In the household described by Mrs. Hale in *Northwood,* every child was able to sit at the table for Thanksgiving dinner—an unusual occurrence, which added dignity to their perception of the festival. In the Hale household in Boston, "there would be a side table for the children at which the oldest cousin in a manner presided, with his very funny stories, with his very exciting lore."[47] Sometimes a favorite aunt presided at the children's table, entertaining the young people with stories and word games while trying to keep them in their places through the long meal.

The dinner itself was the centerpiece of the day—the culmination of tremendous effort on the part of the women of the family. The meal, with its abundance of food, might last as long as two hours, and all were expected to eat more than their fill. In many families, certain foods made their appearance on the table only at Thanksgiving time, and so it seemed that Thanksgiving dinner was "always the same."[48] Edward Everett Hale explained the importance of the meal itself as a symbol: "Had we children been asked what we expected on Thanksgiving Day we should have clapped our hands and said that we expected a good dinner. As we had a good dinner every day of our lives their answer shows simply that children respect symbols and types. And indeed there were certain peculiarities in the Thanksgiving dinner which were not on common days."[49]

159. THANKSGIVING DINNER, WOODCUT, C. 1840. ALEXANDER ANDERSON SCRAPBOOKS, VOL. IV, PRINT COLLECTION, MIRIAM & IRA D. WALLACH DIVISION OF ART, PRINTS AND PHOTOGRAPHS. THE NEW YORK PUBLIC LIBRARY, ASTOR, LENOX AND TILDEN FOUNDATIONS.

In this family, the patriarch has assumed his place at the head of the table and has begun to carve some meat even before the turkey is delivered. With such a large crowd, the children stand behind and between the seated adults, reaching over their shoulders to secure their share of the feast.

In Boston, as Mr. and Mrs. Hale described it, "you began with your chicken pie and your roast turkey. You

160. A NEW ENGLAND THANKSGIVING DINNER, IN *Gleason's Pictorial Drawing Room Companion,* DECEMBER 6, 1851. COURTESY OF THE SOCIETY FOR THE PRESERVATION OF NEW ENGLAND ANTIQUITIES.

ate as much as you could, and then you ate what you could of mince pie, squash pie, Marlborough pie, cranberry tart, and plum pudding. Then you went to work on the fruits as you could. . . . Dates, prunes, raisins, figs and nuts held a much more prominent place in a handsome dessert than they do now."[50]

In Portsmouth, New Hampshire, Sarah Rice Goodwin recalled that someone had "spread out the pies (except the mince which were served hot) on the piano with the raisins, grapes, nuts, oranges, etc." For the dinner, "a long table was spread in the largest room with a table cloth of finest damask which hung in rich folds, and at every plate was a beautifully ironed napkin, a small roll and a tall glass of currant jelly. The silver and glass seemed to take on a higher polish and a large glass pyramid crowned the center of the table covered with almond custards and small glasses of strawberries and cream. This pyramid had belonged to Governor Benning Wentworth and was broken many years ago. . . . The dinner began with a ham, handsomely decorated, at one end of the table and a large roast turkey at the other. Chickens and ducks followed, with celery dressed and undressed. Then plum pudding with delicious sauce. This was succeeded by pies and these by fruits of every sort that could be procured. After this coffee and tea."[51]

According to William Bentley, "A Thanksgiving is not complete without a turkey. It is rare to find any other dishes but such as turkies & fowls afford before the pastry on such days & puddings are much less used than formerly." The turkeys were generally smaller than those of today, but a kingly bird was usually selected for the Thanksgiving feast. William Bentley's Thanksgiving turkeys in 1803 were pronounced "excellent . . . the best raised in our country which I have ever seen, from 14 to 20 pounds."[52] On November 31, 1837, the Dwinnell family of Danvers, Massachusetts, sat down with four guests to "a Table loaded with a Turkey whose weight was 18 lbs,"[53] and in 1841, Nathaniel and Sophia Hawthorne shared a five-pound turkey that she had cooked, "sentence for sentence," from the recipe in Miss Leslie's cookbook.[54]

To accompany the turkey and the chicken pie, a wide variety of vegetables was "all piled together in jovial abundance upon the smoking board."[55] Hostesses brought out different kinds of pickles, and preserves, the nicest and finest butter and cheese, a variety of breads, and perhaps honey. These foods were all placed on the table at once, with no flowers or table ornaments. The food itself was ornament enough, and the chicken pie was usually considered the centerpiece. In the feast described by Mrs. Hale, "plates of pickles, preserves and butter, and all the necessary seasonings filled the interstices on the table, leaving hardly sufficient room for the plates of the company, a wine glass and two tumblers for each, with a slice of white bread lying on one of the inverted tumblers."[56]

After this came the array of pies, cakes, tarts, custards, and other desserts, which had been the focus of attention in the kitchen for days. The selection of pies varied from house to house, but apple, mince, and Marlborough pies were perhaps the most popular. Edward Everett Hale asserted that "in any old and well-regulated family in New England, you will find there is a traditional method for making the Marlborough pie, which is a sort of lemon pie, and each good housekeeper thinks that her grandmother left a better receipt for Marlborough pie than anybody else did. We had Marlborough pies at other times, but we were sure to have them on Thanksgiving Day; and it ought to be said that there was no other day on which we had four kinds of pies on the table and plum pudding besides."[57]

Until the temperance movement began to have an impact in about 1840, hard cider, beer, and stronger liquors were a natural part of the Thanksgiving celebration, as they were of any other dinner. In *Northwood,* Mrs. Hale wrote: "On the sideboard was ranged a goodly number of decanters and bottles; the former filled with currant wine, and the latter with excellent cider and ginger beer."[58]

Thanksgiving Charity

At Thanksgiving time it was customary for donations of food and wood to be made to the clergy. In Litchfield, Connecticut, on the day before Thanksgiving in 1818, the Reverend Lyman Beecher received six pounds of butter, six pounds of lard, two pounds of tea, five dozen eggs, eight pounds of sugar, a large pig, a large turkey, four cheeses, and three turkeys.[59] The Bascoms received a six-pound cheese, a shank of lamb, and a forequarter of mutton during the week before Thanksgiving in 1825, but no one provided them with a turkey. When Betsy Phelps returned to Litchfield from her Thanksgiving visit to Hadley in 1801, she brought food from her parents. Still, she was pleased when soon after her arrival, "Mrs. Tallmadge's black boy brought us a fine turkey, so that with all our pies, puddings and cakes, we shall be able to keep thanksgiving again." On the following Monday, she received additional gifts of beef and a spare-rib from families who were butchering—so much meat that she was "obliged to salt some of it" so it wouldn't spoil.[60]

It was only fitting that while they were enjoying such lavish entertainment, families should provide for those who were less fortunate. Many prepared special baskets to be given to the poor or to those who might not otherwise be able to enjoy a Thanksgiving feast. In Portsmouth, John Lord remembered "a row of as many as 20 or 30 women receiving gratuities in the kitchen the day before the great New England festival."[61] Such benevolence was impressive to the young. Jacob Abbott recalled the "gratified pride" he had felt as his "mother stowed in the basket the little package of tea, with the pies and other little comforts which I was to carry to the lonely widow, to the hungry family in the neighborhood."[62] Lydia Sigourney described a particular benevolence toward native Americans. In *Sketches of Connecticut Forty Years Since,* she produced a word-picture of "the practice of the household of Madam L——— to make a large quantity of pastry expressly for the natives of Mohegan. This secured an almost universal attendance of the females, who holding a neat basket of their own manufacture, would thankfully receive in it the luxury for their expectant families."[63] In Salem in 1818, Dr. Bentley observed: "The private bounty to the poor was great on the occasion [of Thanksgiving]. All who did apply were supplied abundantly.... The poor who applied were decent in their cloathing & manners & nothing reproachful was to be seen in the streets during the day."[64]

At the King household in Salem, "for two days before Thanksgiving Day our back door was besieged by pensioners, who all came with the same whining

161. THANKSGIVING CHARITY, DRAWING, BY L. J. BRIDGMAN AT THE DIRECTION OF JOHN ROBINSON, SALEM, 1915. COURTESY OF THE SOCIETY FOR THE PRESERVATION OF NEW ENGLAND ANTIQUITIES.

A window bar "placed across the backs of two Windsor Chairs served to hold the scales set up the day before Thanksgiving to weigh out butter and sugar for poor families of the town." This drawing and the one in figure 157 were done to illustrate a Thanksgiving story for children that was never published.

request, 'Please give me something for Thanksgiving.' My mother always had ready a store of rice, flour, Indian meal and apples, which were dispensed to the crowd, while the more favored family retainers were given in addition tea, sugar, raisins, and oftentimes a pair of chickens or a turkey. Each one brought a stout pillow case into which the measure of rice would be poured, and then a strong twine tied tightly round the outside to separate it from the flour, which came next, and so on to the extreme capacity of the pillow case."[65]

The daughter of the household also remembered: "It used to be a great joke for the young people of those days to dress up in shabby clothes, and on the night before Thanksgiving to go round as beggars, imposing on their friends, and I remember the glee with which my friend Lucy used to describe her working upon her mother's sympathy to such a degree, by her eloquent and lifelike personification of a poor widow with two small children to support, that her pillowcase was overbrimming with good things, and such friendly and searching offers of help were made, that the situation became embarrassing."[66]

Thanksgiving Frolicking

After the great feast was over, it was time to enjoy the company that had assembled from near and far. In some households there was only sober reflection, but for most people it was time for frolicking. Some women remained in the kitchen to organize the leftovers and begin the dishwashing, while others moved to the parlor; some men slipped out to do their evening barn chores, and someone did the milking. As darkness fell, the fires were built up and an unusual number of candles were lighted. There were toasts and songs and games. During part of the afternoon, children looked at picture books and other parlor treasures, which, according to Hale, "we could not always see. The Hogarths were out, the illustrated books of travel, the handsome annuals which were rather too fine for our hands at other periods."[67] Few remained quiet for long, and soon lively games erupted. Led by aunts and uncles, distant cousins, or older brothers and sisters, the children ransacked the house from cellar to attic, seeking hidden treasures, playing tricks on each other, telling scary stories, or playing games. Hunt the slipper, blindman's buff, and run round the chimney were all popular. Sarah Goodwin recalled lively games of blindman's buff and hide-and-seek in which girls hid in an unlighted chimney, badly soiling their best dresses.[68] In Leicester, Massachusetts, in 1791, young Ruth Henshaw "spent the eve in plays."[69]

If the weather cooperated, people might venture forth for a Thanksgiving sleigh ride; some attended informal dancing parties at private homes or organized Thanksgiving balls. Like other aspects of the holiday, these activities were apt to be multigenerational, with the eldest leading the first sets of a reel or benignly watching the activities of the young. As usual, Abner Sanger took note of what was going on in Keene: "Thanksgiving Day . . . There is a frolic at Major Willard's. Esther Scovill at it."[70] In larger towns and cities there was a considerable amount of visiting in the evening, and some families held an open house, with a supper and music of the type described above by Christopher Columbus Baldwin. It was not unusual for a couple to decide to be married on Thanksgiving day, when all the family were assembled, and this meant that wedding anniversaries were also observed at Thanksgiving time, even though the dates might not always coincide.

Although it is images of family unity that prevail in literary descriptions and in reminiscences about Thanksgiving, people often chose to associate with friends of their own generation in the evening. Just before ten o'clock on Thanksgiving day in 1796, young Charles Phelps found time to write to his beloved Sally, and he explained what had happened to the members of the family since they had arisen from the dinner table: "My father & Mother crossed the river over into Hatfield to pass the evening with Parson Lyman and his wife . . . my Grandmother is safely stowed away in a farther corner of the house, wrapt up in merry slumbers to be sure . . . my sisters . . . are tripping it away at two miles distance to the sprightly sounds of a rustic *twi tweedler* . . . Lydia & Polly have prevailed upon Seth to put the team horses into the old sleigh and are at this moment . . . enjoying all the transport of a *Thanksgiving Sleighride* . . . John, the Scotch gardener, by the kitchen fireside . . . is managing the 'Gentle Shepherd' as well as could be expected." The family had scattered, but Charles was well aware of family tradition as he penned his letter by "an old family clock" on "an old-fashioned desk which once belonged to my maternal grandfather."[71] Two years later, the family circle was broken when Charles's grandmother died and his mother wrote: "One is missing of our family who will never return, every year since my birth I have kept Thanksgiving with my mother to this—but no more—a long farewell. O Lord Bless us that are alive."[72]

A Most Meaningful Day

No matter how they might occupy themselves during the evening, Thanksgiving reminded everyone of the importance of the family. The patriarch and matriarch had a central role in the festivities. One author wrote: "The queen of this palace on Thanksgiving Day was Grandma Pratt. Every one paid his respects first to her." After dinner was over and the young people tired of

162. THE FAMILY OF JAMES NEWTON, PHOTOGRAPHED BY ELY AND POPKINS ON THANKSGIVING DAY 1860, GREENFIELD, MASSACHUSETTS. POCUMTUCK VALLEY MEMORIAL ASSOCIATION, DEERFIELD, MASSACHUSETTS.

Photography made it possible to capture the images of the great family that gathered from far and wide to celebrate Thanksgiving day.

their noisy games, "they gathered about in a far-reaching circle, and clamored for grandma's stories of their fathers and grandfathers, and of her own youth."[73]

Thanksgiving conversation often revolved around family history, and the fine points of genealogy were debated. People enjoyed hearing stories of the olden times, tender reminiscences, and news of absent family members. Traditions and stories were handed on to the next generation. Some people were the targets of merciless teasing and the kind of cruel jokes that are perpetuated in families. Young parents had made the journey home in order to teach their children these things and to demonstrate family unity. For these reasons, Jacob Abbott "blessed him who invented the 'Thanksgiving.' "[74]

By the time the day was over, people were pleased to express their satisfaction with more than a good dinner. According to Dr. Bentley, Thanksgiving in Salem in 1817 was "as well observed for us as any I have known. No unseasonable or unsuitable noises in the streets. The field sports were innocent, the walks quiet, & the temper of the people happy."[75] Others were grateful if no tensions arose within the family: "Thanksgiving day—& a most delightful day it has been—very much like a pleasant May day & every body seems in good spirits."[76]

Elizabeth Phelps often expressed her concern that the true meaning of Thanksgiving not be lost in all the hustle and bustle. After completing her kitchen preparations for the holiday in 1808, she took a moment to reflect in a letter to her daughter: "I fear I am not half prepared for the business of tomorrow—cooking eno' is done but is the heart prepared properly with gratitude to the giver of all good."[77] Finding time for reflection amidst the hectic responsibilities of the day was not easy.

On Thanksgiving morning, November 21, 1793, seventy-five-year-old Samuel Lane of Stratham, New Hampshire, offered up a special prayer:

> as I was Musing on my Bed being awake as Usual before Daylight; recollecting the Many Mercies and good things I enjoy for which I ought to be thankful this Day; some of which I have Noted after rising as follows viz:
>
> > The Life & health of myself and family, and also of so many of my Children, grand Children and great grandchildren; also of my other Relations and friends & Neighbors, for Health peace and plenty amongst us.
> >
> > for my Bible and Many other good and Useful Books, Civil & Religious Priviledges, for the ordinances of the gospel; and for my Minister.
> >
> > for my Land, House and Barn and other Buildings, & that they are preserv'd from fire & other accidents.

> for my wearing Clothes to keep me warm, my Bed & Beding to rest upon.
>
> for my Cattle, Sheep & Swine & other Creatures, for my support.
>
> for my Corn, Wheat, Rye Grass and Hay; Wool, flax, Syder, Apples. Pumpkins, Potatoes, Cabages, tirnips, Carrots, Beets, peaches and other fruits.
>
> For my Clock and Watch to measure my passing time by Day and by Night,
>
> Wood, Water, Butter, Cheese, Milk, Pork, Beefe, & fish, &c
>
> for Tea, Sugar, Rum, Wine, Gin, Molasses, peper, Spice & Money for to bye other Necessaries and to pay my Debts & Taxes &c.
>
> for my Lether, Lamp oyl & Candles, Husbandry Utensils, & other tools of every sort &c &c &c.
>
> Bless the Lord O my Soul and all that is within me Bless his holy Name. Bless the Lord O my Soul and forget not all his benefits, who Satisfieth thy mouth with good things &c.[78]

Elizabeth Phelps would have agreed. "Betsy," she asked in 1809, "should not every day be a Thanksgiving day?"[79]

Acknowledgments

GROWING UP IN THE WESTERN RESERVE, THE DAUGHTER OF ONE NEW Englander and the granddaughter of another, I was steeped early in old-fashioned traditions and a nostalgic view of the New England way of life. At least once a week a postcard from my grandmother arrived, bearing the image of an historic house or village scene. Visiting picturesque villages and historic house museums was an established part of every summer vacation. When my dream of attending college in New England was fulfilled at Pembroke College in Brown University, professors David Lovejoy and Elmer Cornwell fostered my interest in social history, and Lea Williams provided the opportunity to work for a full year as a research assistant in the Edward Carrington House with its treasure trove of decorative arts, family and business manuscripts, and China Trade material. Fortunately, my professors also encouraged me to pursue graduate study, and I was accepted into the Winterthur Program, where Charles Montgomery challenged me to sharpen my research skills and to think about the public presentation of historic houses in new ways.

Early in my curatorial career, I came to know Abbott Lowell Cummings and was introduced to the rich collections of the Society for the Preservation of New England Antiquities, where my husband has been curator for more than twenty-five years and I now serve as director. My interest in material-culture studies and of well-documented family collections and photographic archives has found both stimulus and endless opportunity at SPNEA. Through SPNEA I have also had the immense good fortune to get to know both Bertram K. and

Nina Fletcher Little, who have introduced me to many ideas and sources of information as well as been unfailingly helpful in my search for photographs and documentation.

The basic questions addressed by this book I had framed during my sixteen years at Old Sturbridge Village as a member of the Curatorial Department. I uncovered much of the primary source material for the early-nineteenth-century portions during my tenure at the village. I would be remiss if I did not acknowledge my great appreciation for the professional encouragement and collegial atmosphere I found at Old Sturbridge Village while working with Barnes Riznik, Richard Rabinowitz, and my former colleagues in the Curatorial Department, John Curtis, Frank White, Henry Harlow, and Donna Baron; in the Research Department, John Worrell, Jack Larkin, Caroline Sloat, Myron Stachiw, Ted Penn, and Catherine Fennelly; as well as the experience and insights of many who have worked in the Interpretation Department, especially Warren Leon, Mark Sammons, Margaret Piatt, and the late Aphia Crockett. Theresa Percy and Jennie Miller in the Village Research Library have continued to be helpful with research requests and bibliographical inquiries.

Over the years I have been an avid reader of New England diaries, letters, and literature. I am fortunate to have been able to prepare or consult on the household furnishings and interpretive plans for a number of important historic sites, sometimes drawing on the research of others. These projects have contributed to my understanding of the New England home in the period before the Civil War. Perhaps the most revealing have been the work associated with the refurnishing of the Asa Knight store and the reinterpretation of center village houses at Old Sturbridge Village, but I have also participated in many other projects and have learned from people associated with them, especially: the Mission Houses in Honolulu, with Peggie Schleiff and Debbie Pope; Lloyd Manor, a property of the Society for the Preservation of Long Island Antiquities, with Hope Alswang and John Kirk; the houses of the Webb-Deane-Stevens Museum in Wethersfield, Connecticut, with Kevin Sweeney and Helen Lewis; the Salisbury Mansion in Worcester, Massachusetts, with William Wallace, Ann Riggs, Susan Myers, and Marylou Davis; the Concord Museum with Dennis Fiori, Ned Cooke, and David Wood; and the Prudence Crandall House in Canterbury, Connecticut.

As a member of the Advisory Committee and, since 1981, the Board of Trustees of Historic Deerfield, Inc., I have had opportunities to work closely with curators Peter Spang and Philip Zea. In the Memorial Libraries David

Proper was always helpful with manuscripts and photographs, and in the office of Academic Programs, J. Ritchie Garrison was generous in sharing research. At the Pocumtuck Valley Memorial Association, also in Deerfield, Suzanne Flynt and Margery Howe have been particularly helpful in leading me to important objects and useful information.

Over the years I have also had opportunity to work with colleagues on exhibition planning, reviewing research, evaluating object selections, and helping to shape exhibition scripts. At the Albany Institute of History and Art and Historic Cherry Hill, Connie Frisbee (now Frisbee-Houde) reviewed the Van Rensselaer family collections with me as we planned "Not Just Another Pretty Dress." In Hartford, I had the opportunity to work with the archives assembled by Bill Hosley and Betsy Fox for the exhibition and catalogue *The Great River* at the Wadsworth Athenaeum in 1985.

Throughout the many years that this has been a work in progress, many individuals have been helpful in providing access to manuscripts and museum collections, arranging to have photographs made, answering questions, and straightening out convoluted genealogical patterns. I am deeply grateful to those I have named here and to many others who patiently endured a quick visit or a telephone call, responded to my letters of inquiry, or undertook a bit of research in a place where I was unable to do it myself. In so doing, each of these people has advanced my understanding of New England's material culture and, thus, has made an important contribution to the final form of this book. I would particularly like to thank Lorna Condon and David Bohl at the SPNEA archives; Georgia Barnhill, Thomas Knowles, Nancy Burkett, and Barbara Simmons at the American Antiquarian Society; Donald Fennimore, Charles Hummel, and Bea Taylor at Winterthur; Sarah Lytle at Middleton Place; Susan Lisk and Susan Wojewoda at the Porter-Phelps-Huntington Foundation; Donald Kelley at the Boston Athenaeum; Celia Oliver, Polly Mitchell, and Laura Luckey at the Shelburne Museum; Donna-Belle Garvin, Bill Copely, and Steve Cox at the New Hampshire Historical Society; Richard Kugler and Judy Lunt at the Whaling Museum of the New Bedford Historical Society; Jane Porter, Kevin Shupe, and Ronan Donohoe at the Portsmouth Athenaeum; Anne Golovin and Rodris Roth at the National Museum of American History; Elsie Racz at the Bryant Homestead; and Thomas Parker at the Bostonian Society.

I am also grateful to Paige Adams Savery, my former intern at Old Sturbridge Village and now in the Print and Photograph Department at the Connecticut Historical Society, who continues to share research findings with me, among them her translations of segments of the very interesting diary of Julia Evelina Smith.

Many other individuals have contributed ideas and information that have been helpful in the development of this book—so many, in fact, that I want to apologize to any who feel they should have been acknowledged here. This is clearly a lifework, and the following friends, neighbors, students, and colleagues have all had a part in it: Beth Bower, Wendy Cooper, Carl Crossman, Jay Cantor, Claire Dempsey, Jonathan Fairbanks, Dean and M'Lou Fales, the late Anne Farnam, Wendell and Elizabeth Donaghy Garrett, James Garvin, Ed McCarron, the late Mary Martin, Christopher Monkhouse, Florence Montgomery, Barbara Nachtigall, the late Donn and Doris Purvis, Janet Low Rigby, Peter Thornton, Laurel Thatcher Ulrich, Morton Vose, Charles B. Wood, III, and Elizabeth Ingerman Wood.

I am especially grateful to Richard Candee, who has always shared ideas and been helpful with sources and sharpening ideas, and who was also kind enough to read the finished manuscript and offer helpful suggestions, some of which have been incorporated into the final manuscript.

Throughout the years that this book has been on my desk, Jane Garrett has been a patient and encouraging editor. Her faith in the finished product is largely responsible for its final appearance.

Finally, I am deeply grateful to the trustees and staff of Strawbery Banke, and especially to President Herbert A. Grant, Jr., for conspiring to ensure that time was set aside for completion of the text. Without their understanding and support, this book would not be finished yet.

Most of all, I am grateful to my family—to Tom and Tim for their patience in growing up with all of this, to Tom for lending me his powerful computer when I really needed it, to Sarah for her wonderful insights and for sharing her exciting new research, and, of course, to Richard, who opened my eyes to so many things, who helped me through the times when I thought I would never bring this to completion, and who knows more than I shall ever know about New England history and material-culture and never fails to share it with me and with others.

Notes

ABBREVIATIONS

AAS: American Antiquarian Society, Worcester, Mass. • Bentley: *The Diary of William Bentley, D.D.,* 4 vols. (Gloucester, Mass., 1962). • CHS: Connecticut Historical Society, Hartford. • EPP: Elizabeth Porter Phelps. • EPP diary: Manuscript diary of Elizabeth Porter Phelps, in the Porter-Phelps-Huntington Family Papers at the Amherst College Library, Amherst, Mass. Extensive selections from it were edited by Thomas Eliot Andrews and published as "The Diary of Elizabeth (Porter) Phelps, 1763–1805," *New England Historical and Genealogical Register* 18–22 (1964–68). • EWP: Elizabeth Whiting Phelps (who married Daniel Huntington on Jan. 1, 1800, and became EWPH). • EWPH: Elizabeth Whiting Phelps Huntington. • MHS: Massachusetts Historical Society, Boston. • NHHS: New Hampshire Historical Society, Concord. • OSV: Old Sturbridge Village, Sturbridge, Mass. • PA: Portsmouth Athenaeum, Portsmouth, N.H. • Parkman: Francis G. Wallett, ed., *The Diary of Ebenezer Parkman, 1703–1782: First Part, Three Volumes in One, 1719–1755* (Worcester, Mass., 1974). • Parkman (Forbes): Harriette M. Forbes, ed., *The Diary of Rev. Ebenezer Parkman of Westborough, Mass. . . .* (Westborough, 1899). • PFP: Porter-Phelps-Huntington Family Papers, Amherst College Archives, Amherst, Mass. • PVMA: Pocumtuck Valley Memorial Association, Deerfield, Mass. • Pyncheon: Fitch Edward Oliver, ed., *The Diary of William Pyncheon of Salem* (Boston and New York, 1890). • RevTR: Increase N. Tarbox, ed., *Diary of Thomas Robbins, D.D., 1796–1854* (Boston, 1882). • RHB: Journals of Ruth Henshaw Bascom, American Antiquarian Society, Worcester, Mass. • RIHS: Rhode Island Historical Society. • Sanger: Lois Stabler, ed., *Very Poor and of a Low Make: The Journal of Abner Sanger* (Portsmouth, N.H., 1986). • Smith: Diary of Julia Evelina Smith, Glastonbury, Conn., 1828, Connecticut Historical Society. I am grateful to Paige Adams Savery for sharing with me her translation from the original French. • SPNEA: Society for the Preservation of New England Antiquities, Boston. • SSB: Diary of Sarah Snell Bryant: 1794, Trustees of Reservations, Bryant Homestead, Cummington, Mass.; 1795–1836. By permission of the Houghton Library, Harvard University, Cambridge, Mass. (bms, AM 1438). • Tyler: Frederick Tupper and Helen Tyler Brown, eds., *Grandmother Tyler's Book: The Recollections of Mary Palmer Tyler (Mrs. Royall Tyler), 1775–1866* (New York, 1925).

PREFACE

1. See especially Elizabeth Donaghy Garrett, *At Home: The American Family, 1750–1870* (New York, 1990); Gerald W. R. Ward and William N. Hosley, Jr., *The Great River* (Hartford, 1985); Laura Sprague, *Agreeable Situations* (Kennebunk, Maine, 1987); "House and Home," *Dublin Seminar for New England Folklife Annual Proceedings* (Boston, 1988); and Edgar deN. Mayhew and Minor Myers, Jr., *A Documentary History of American Furnishings to 1915* (New York, 1980).
2. Bettye Hobbs Pruitt, "Self-Sufficiency and the Agricultural Economy of Eighteenth-Century Massachusetts," *William and Mary Quarterly* 3d ser., 41 (July 1984): 333–64, and Carol Shammas, "How Self Sufficient Was Early America?," *Journal of Interdisciplinary History* 13 (Autumn 1982): 2, 247–72.
3. Laurel Thatcher Ulrich, *A Midwife's Tale* (New York, 1990) and "Housewife and

Gadder: Themes of Self-Sufficiency and Community in Eighteenth-Century New England," in *"To Toil the Livelong Day": America's Women at Work, 1780–1980*, ed. Carol Groneman and Mary Beth Norton (Ithaca and London, 1987), pp. 21–34.

4. Christopher Monkhouse, "The Spinning Wheel as Artifact, Symbol, and Source of Design," in *Victorian Furniture,* ed. Kenneth L. Ames (Philadelphia, 1982), pp. 154–72.

5. Sarah Bryant kept her diary until shortly before her death in 1847. The volume for 1794 is owned by the Trustees of Reservations at the Bryant Homestead in Cummington, Massachusetts; the remainder of the diary is in the Houghton Library at Harvard University. The entries for each year are written in a separate volume, most of them apparently folded and stitched by Sarah herself.

6. EPP Diary. The Phelps Family Correspondence is owned by the Porter-Phelps-Huntington Foundation, Inc., and is on deposit in the Special Collections Department of the Amherst College Library, Amherst, Mass. I am grateful to Edward McCarron for bringing it to my attention.

7. Ruth Henshaw Bascom's journals are at the American Antiquarian Society in Worcester, Massachusetts. I am grateful to Miss Catherine Fennelly, former director of publications at Old Sturbridge Village, for calling my attention to these journals and for permitting me to read portions of her typescript. I am also grateful to William Joyce and Nancy Burkett of the American Antiquarian Society for their assistance as I worked with many of the original volumes.

8. For further biographical information on Ruth Henshaw Bascom, see Mary Eilen Fouratt, "Ruth Henshaw Bascom: Itinerant Portraitist," *Worcester Art Museum Journal* 5 (1981–82): 57–65.

9. Bentley, vol. 1, p. 16, entry for April 23, 1793.

CHAPTER I

1. J. H. Temple, *History of the Town of Whately, Mass. . . . 1660–1871* (Boston, 1872), p. 66.

2. Caroline Howard King, *When I Lived in Salem, 1822–1866* (Brattleboro, Vt., 1937), p. 16.

3. Mrs. Elizabeth Orne (Paine) Sturgis, "Recollections of the 'Old Tucker House,' 28 Chestnut Street, Salem," *Essex Institute Historical Collections* 74 (April 1938): 2, 141. Both of these women were born in Salem in the 1820s and wrote their recollections about 1900.

4. "Really, I can see now that the old house was the remote but firm center of it all." Barrett Wendell, writing of the importance of the family homestead in "Recollections of My Father, Jacob Wendell II," typescript, PA.

5. The proprietors of New Hampshire lands required that new settlers construct houses of at least 16 feet square, each with a chimney, within a year of settlement in order to be granted title to their lands. Apparently, some houses were even less substantial than this. The homes of poor people living between York and Wells, Maine, in 1787 were described as "cottages which could not be exceeded in miserable appearance by any of the most miserable in Europe. . . . Glass was not to be seen. Few of the huts were framed and few had floors. The Crotches supported a few slabs, under which the inhabitants lived." (Bentley, vol. 1, p. 64; entry for June 4, 1787.)

6. Michael Steinitz, "Rethinking Geographical Approaches to the Common House: The Evidence from Eighteenth Century Massachusetts," in *Perspectives in Vernacular Architecture,* vol. 3, ed. Thomas Carter and Bernard L. Herman (Columbia, Mo., 1989), pp. 16–26. See also Edward M. Cook, Jr., *Ossipee, New Hampshire, 1785–1985: A History* (Ossipee, N.H., 1989), pp. 104–5.

7. S. G. Goodrich [Peter Parley], *Recollections of a Lifetime, or Men and Things I Have Seen* (New York, 1856), p. 96.

8. Bentley, vol. 1, p. 286; entry for Aug. 15, 1791.

9. Mrs. Basil Hall, quoted in Una Pope-Hennessy, *The Aristocratic Journey* (New York, 1931), p. 78.

10. Eliza S. M. Quincy, *A Memoir of the Life of Eliza S. M. Quincy* (Boston, 1861), p. 61.

11. Susanna Rowson, *An Abridgement of Universal Geography . . .* (Boston, [1805]), p. 181.

12. Sarah Anna Emery, *Reminiscences of a Nonagenarian* (Newburyport, Mass., 1879), preface.

13. Emery, p. 177. On May 19, 1780, darkness descended at noon on much of New England as smoke from western forest fires filtered sunlight. There was great consternation among the people; some believed doomsday was at hand. David Ludlum, *The Country Journal New England Weather Book* (Boston, Mass., 1976), p. 122.

14. The material culture of the Robbins family can be studied in the collections of the Society for the Preservation of New England Antiquities, Boston, Mass.; the Textile Department of the Museum of Fine Arts, Boston; the Essex Institute, Salem, Mass.; and the Lexington Historical Society, Lexington, Mass.

15. A drawing had been made shortly before the house was destroyed by fire on Dec. 29, 1810. (Samuel Adams Drake, *Old Landmarks of Boston* [Boston, 1900], p. 252.)

16. Boston *Post,* Dec. 15 and 21, 1858. Considerable attention had been called to the birthplace during the sesquicentennial commemoration of Benjamin Franklin's birth in 1854. Although the old house on Milk Street was no longer standing, Nathaniel Shurtleff's description of it in *A Topographical and Historical Description of Boston* (Boston, 1871), pp. 615–25, was based on a drawing made before demolition and confirmed that the house had only a parlor and a kitchen on the first floor and a single chamber on the second.

17. Address of George Sheldon, *Pocumtuck Valley Memorial Association Annual Report,* Deerfield, Mass., 1878.

18. Amelia F. Miller, foreword to *A History of Deerfield Massachusetts,* by George Sheldon (facsimile of the 1895–96 edition) (Deerfield, Mass., 1972), n.p.

CHAPTER II

1. Sarah Anna Emery, *Reminiscences of a Nonagenarian* (Newburyport, Mass., 1879), pp. 270–2.

2. Ibid., p. 55.

3. Sarah Emery described the usual motivation for remarriage when in "the second year of her widowhood, aunt Hannah Stickey married Mr. Samuel Noyes, . . . a widower with four children." She said: "This good man needed a wife, his children needed a mother, she could supply this need. Cheerfully and lovingly her life's work was assumed." (Ibid., p. 79.)
4. Ibid., p. 6.
5. Ibid., p. 108.
6. Ibid., p. 289.
7. Katherine Henshaw journal, Feb. 14 and May 16, 1804, AAS.
8. RHB, March 10 and 18, 1807.
9. RHB, Jan. 1, 1812.
10. RHB, Jan. 24, March 13, June 6, and June 8, 1813.
11. Elizabeth W. Phelps to Charles Phelps, Hadley, Feb. 16, 1798, PEP (box 12, folder 15).
12. "The Diary of Elizabeth (Porter) Phelps," *New England Historical and Genealogical Register* (January 1967): 65; entry for April 8, 1798. Three additional wagonloads of "Mrs. Hitchcock's furniture" had been sent to Brimfield on March 11.
13. Sarah D. Phelps to EPP, Boston, June 21, 1801, and Charles Phelps to EPP, Hadley, Sept. 10 and 22, 1801; Charles Phelps to EWPH, Hadley, Sept. 28, 1801; PFP (box 10, folder 6; box 12, folder 15).
14. The Bryant children were Austin, born in April 1793; William Cullen, known to his mother as Cullen, born Nov. 3, 1794; Cyrus, born July 12, 1798; Sarah, born July 24, 1802; Peter Rush, known to his mother as Rush and later called Arthur, born Nov. 28, 1803; Charity Louise, named for Peter Bryant's sister Charity and known as Louisa, born Dec. 20, 1805; and John, born July 7, 1807.
15. The term "social childbirth" is introduced in Richard W. and Dorothy C. Wertz, *Lying-In: A History of Childbirth in America* (New York, 1977), p. 2. For a discussion of midwifery and the rituals of childbirth in late-eighteenth-century New England, see Laurel Thatcher Ulrich, *A Midwife's Tale* (New York, 1990).
16. "Diary of Mary Vial Holyoke," in *The Holyoke Diaries,* ed. George Francis Dow (Salem, Mass., 1911, p. 77).
17. "Pleasant Memories," memoirs of Sarah Parker Rice Goodwin, 1889, Goodwin Family Papers, Thayer Cumings Research Library, Strawbery Banke Museum, Portsmith, N.H., pp. 25–6.
18. RHB, May 13, 1812.
19. Susan I. Lesley, *Recollections of My Mother* (Boston, 1899), pp. 192–3.
20. Ibid., p. 164. Letter to Abby, May 15, 1823.
21. Harrison Gray Otis to Sally Foster Otis, Feb. 21, 1798. Harrison Gray Otis Papers, MHS.
22. The value of the basket and its contents was 3-12-0. Rockingham County, N.H., Probate Records, Exeter, N.H.
23. EPP to EWPH, Boston, Sept. 24, 1801, PFP (box 6, folder 1).
24. "Diary of Mary (Vial) Holyoke," p. 77.
25. Ibid., p. 66. Of all the births attended by Martha Moore Ballard in late-eighteenth-century Hallowell, Maine, and vicinity, the name of only one child, "Hyrum" Belcher, born Feb. 23, 1790, was recorded in her diary. (Ulrich, *A Midwife's Tale,* p. 394.)
26. *The Young Mother, or Management of Children in Regard to Health* (Boston, 1839), p. 257.
27. Inventory of Ebenezer Rockwood, Esq., Boston, 1815, Suffolk County Probate Office, Boston, Mass.
28. "The Passing of the Spare Chamber," *Atlantic Monthly* (January 1899): 140–1.
29. Sally Phelps to EPP, Boston, Dec. 29, 1801, PFP (box 10, folder 6).
30. RevTR, vol. 2, pp. 32, 34.
31. Emery, *Reminiscences,* pp. 80–1.
32. Priscilla Robertson, *Lewis Farm: A New England Saga* (Norwood, Mass, 1950), p. 6.
33. Alice Jones, *In Dover on the Charles* (Boston, 1904), p. 43.
34. Quoted in [Abbott Lowell Cummings], "Notes on Furnishing a Small New England Farmhouse," *Old Time New England* (Winter 1958), p. 76.
35. RevTR, vol. 1, p. 803.
36. Sanger, Sept. 13, 19, and 25 and Nov. 14, 1780. On Dec. 29 the diary entry is, "Go home to the Cresty farm and fetch up a jag of trumpery (viz., beds and goods) and unload them at Ezra Metcalf's."
37. SSB, Feb. 18 and 19, 1807.
38. William Cullen Bryant II and Thomas G. Voss, eds., *The Letters of William Cullen Bryant,* vol. 1 (New York, 1975), p. 10. See also SSB, March 6, 1806: "Joseph Richards came here to study physick."
39. EPP diary, Oct. 20 and 27, 1782.
40. EPP to EWPH, Hadley, Dec. 15, 1809, PFP (box 6, folder 4).
41. Sanger, Oct. 5, 1794.
42. RHB, Dec. 29 and 30, 1802, and Jan. 1, 1803.
43. Bentley, vol. 2, p. 169. He was speaking of "Madam Lambert, aet. 90 next May."
44. Bentley, vol. 1, p. 168; entry for Dec. 22, 1795.
45. Emery, *Reminiscences,* p. 84.
46. Susan H. Dickinson, "Two Generations of Amherst Society," in *Essays on Amherst's History* (Amherst, Mass., 1978), pp. 180–1.
47. RHB, June 14, 1814.
48. Goodwin, "Pleasant Memories."
49. Harriet Beecher Stowe, *Oldtown Folks* (Boston, 1869), p. 28.
50. EPP diary, July 17, 1773, PFP.
51. Lesley, *Recollections,* p. 39.
52. EPP to EWPH, Hadley, Dec. 15, 1809, PFP (box 6, folder 4).
53. Charles Lane Hanson, ed., *A Journal for the Years 1739–1803* by Samuel Lane of Stratham, New Hampshire (Concord, N.H., 1937), p. 31.
54. Ulrich, *A Midwife's Tale,* p. 81.
55. Emery, *Reminiscences,* p. 245.
56. Jack Larkin, *The Reshaping of Everyday Life, 1790–1840* (New York, 1988), p. 13.
57. Journal of Jonathan Sayward, AAS.
58. Sturgis, *Recollections,* pp. 113–14.
59. EPP to EWPH, Hadley, May 4, 1815, PFP (box 6, folder 5).
60. EWPH to EPP, Litchfield, March 18, July 22, Sept. 30, and Oct. 8, 1801, PFP (box 13, folder 1).
61. Account book of Consider Dickinson, Deerfield, Mass., 1806–23, PVMA.

62. Account book of Mary Barrell, York, Maine, 1835–51, SPNEA.
63. Blanche Brown Bryant and Gertrude Elaine Baker, eds., *The Diaries of Sally and Pamela Brown, 1832–1838* . . . (Springfield, Vt., 1970), p. 12; entry for May 31, 1833.
64. SSB, June 27 and Sept. 1, 1807.
65. SSB.
66. Sturgis, *Recollections,* p. 114. A tire is an enveloping apron which opens up the back.
67. Emery, *Reminiscences,* p. 335.
68. *New England Farmer,* July 26, 1837, p. 33.
69. RevTR, vol. 1, p. 752.
70. RevTR, vol. 1, p. 997.
71. EPP diary, Jan. 25, 1767.
72. EPP diary, Sept. 22–Oct. 2, 1768.
73. Ann Taves, ed., *Religion and Domestic Violence in Early New England: The Memoir of Abigail Abbott Bailey* (Bloomington and Indianapolis: Indiana Univ. Press, 1988), p. 58. Mr. Bailey also abused his daughter, and eventually Abigail was successful in suing him for divorce.
74. Bentley, vol. 2, p. 212; entry for Jan. 22, 1797. Bentley has expressed shock despite the high rates of premarital pregnancy in New England in the 1790s.
75. SSB, Dec. 6, 1800.
76. Emery, *Reminiscences,* p. 39.
77. Parkman, p. 207.
78. Lesley, *Recollections,* p. 40.
79. EPP to EWPH, March 31, 1812, PFP (box 6, folder 5).
80. Goodwin, "Pleasant Memories," p. 25.
81. S. J. Hale, *The Good Housekeeper* (Boston, 1839), p. 126.
82. Lydia Maria Child, *The American Frugal Housewife* (Boston, 1832), p. 92.
83. Catharine Beecher, *A Treatise on Domestic Economy* (Boston, 1841), p. 201.
84. Quoted in G. W. Allen, *Waldo Emerson* (New York, 1982), p. 366.
85. Hanson, *Journal . . . by Samuel Lane,* p. 35.

CHAPTER III

1. RHB, March 27–May 30, 1805.
2. Joseph Fish to John and Mary Noyes, Aug. 17, 1759, Silliman Family Papers, Yale University Library, New Haven, Conn.
3. Jannette Lasansky, *A Good Start: The Aussteier or Dowry* (Lewisburg, Penn.: Oral Traditions Project, 1990), pp. 12–13. Lasansky discusses this in a Pennsylvania context, but her comments about the origins of the idea of a "hope chest" apply to New England as well.
4. Charles Lane Hanson, ed., *A Journal for the Years 1739–1803 by Samuel Lane of Stratham, New Hampshire* (Concord, N.H., 1937), pp. 28–9.
5. Lane Family Papers, NHHS.
6. Nathan Howe account book, Shrewsbury, Mass., privately owned.
7. *North American Review* 151 (1890): 746–69.
8. Tyler, p. 180.
9. Ibid., p. 217.
10. Ibid., pp. 210–11.
11. EPP to Sarah Parsons, Hadley, Sept. 18, 1799, PFP (box 12, folder 19).
12. Sarah Parsons Phelps journal, PFP (box 11, folder 7).
13. Lane Family Papers.
14. Marylynn Salmon, *Women and the Law of Property* (Chapel Hill, N.C., and London, 1986), pp. 140–43.
15. For abundant examples of definition of dower rights, consult the published probate records of the New England states or original court documents. For further explanation, see Gloria L. Main, "Widows in Rural Massachusetts on the Eve of Revolution," in *Women in the Age of the American Revolution,* 67–90, and Barbara McLean Ward, "Women's Property and Family Continuity in Eighteenth-Century Connecticut," in *Early American Probate Inventories: The Dublin Seminar for New England Folklife Annual Proceedings, July 11 and 12, 1987* (Boston, 1989).
16. Will of Jonathan Sayward, filed 1797, York County Probate Court, Alfred, Maine, docket 16674, vol. 17, p. 345ff, copy in the files of SPNEA.
17. Will of Ebenezer Snell, Cummington, Mass., 1813, Hampshire County Probate Office.
18. SSB, Sept. 11, 1813.
19. Robert Haas, ed., "The Forgotten Courtship of David and Marcy Spear, 1785–1797," *Old Time New England* 52, no. 3 (Jan.–March 1962): 61–74.
20. "Patch" is a New England regionalism that refers to the kinds of brightly printed glazed cottons also known as furniture prints or furniture chintzes. The word was particularly favored in Boston, Salem, Newburyport, Portsmouth, and other towns north of Boston.
21. Lydia Maria Child, *Hints to Persons of Moderate Fortune* (Boston, 1832).

CHAPTER IV

1. Harriet Beecher Stowe, *Oldtown Folks* (Boston, 1869), p. 274.
2. *The Book of the Seasons* (Boston, 1842).
3. G[ustavius?] Tuckerman in Boston to Elizabeth Tuckerman Salisbury in Worcester, Dec. 19, 1818, Salisbury Family Papers, AAS.
4. *Book of the Seasons,* p. 31.
5. Samuel Larkin diary, Portsmouth, N.H., March 17, 1840, Larkin House, Monterey, Calif.
6. Joseph K. Ott, "John Innes Clark and His Family: Beautiful People in Providence," *Rhode Island History* (Fall 1973): 128.
7. Sarah Anna Emery, *Reminiscences of a Nonagenarian* (Newburyport, Mass., 1879), p. 312.
8. Elizabeth Orne (Paine) Sturgis, "Recollections of the 'Old Tucker House,' 28 Chestnut Street, Salem," *Essex Institute Historical Collections* 74 (April 1938): 126.
9. Bentley, vol. 4, p. 627; entry for Nov. 1, 1819.
10. Tyler, p. 320.
11. RevTR, vol. 2, p. 396; entry for Dec. 17, 1835. Robbins's ink was also frozen on Dec. 28, 1826 (vol. 2) p. 37.
12. Pyncheon, p. 259; entry for Dec. 12, 1786.
13. Jonathan Sayward diary, AAS; entry for July 16, 1787.
14. Pyncheon, p. 282; entry for Aug. 30, 1787.

15. RevTR, vol. 1, p. 645; entry for Oct. 14, 1815.
16. RevTR, vol. 1, p. 639; entry for Sept. 5, 1815.
17. Christopher Columbus Baldwin, *Diary* (Worcester, Mass., 1971), p. 15.
18. SSB, note at the conclusion of 1833.
19. RevTR, vol. 2, p. 299; entry for March 6, 1833.
20. RevTR, vol. 1, p. 435; entry for April 25, 1818, and similar comments, Vol. 2, pp. 50, 52, and 53 concerning the spring of 1827. Waistcoat and stockings, Jonathan Sayward diary, entry for June 4, 1783.
21. SSB, May 23 and 28, 1818.
22. Susan I. Lesley, *Recollections of My Mother* (Boston, 1899), p. 90.
23. Ibid., p. 343; entry for Feb. 10, 1840.
24. Providence Mutual Fire Insurance Company policy book, RIHS, p. 514.
25. Clarissa Packard, *Recollections of a Housekeeper* (New York, 1834), pp. 98–9.
26. Smith, Feb. 26, 1828.
27. RevTR, vol. 1, p. 807.
28. *Book of the Seasons,* pp. 41, 59.
29. "During those early years on cold winter days, mother hung bedding back . . . making an inner circle near the fire for the little ones to play in." (Reminiscences of Nancy Knight Fogg, b. 1835, in Robert H. Nylander, "The David Hubbard House, Hancock, New Hampshire," *Old Time New England* 49 [Winter 1959]: 79–83).
30. Stowe, *Oldtown Folks,* p. 275.
31. Parkman, Feb. 17, 1780.
32. Charles Lane Hanson, ed., *A Journal for the Years 1739–1803 by Samuel Lane of Stratham, New Hampshire* (Concord, N.H., 1937), p. 91.
33. Tyler, p. 199.
34. RHB, April 10, 1826.
35. Stowe, *Oldtown Folks,* p. 275.
36. Mrs. [Lydia Maria] Child, *The American Frugal Housewife* (Boston, 1832), p. 16.
37. Parkman, Feb. 19, 1737.
38. Lesley, *Recollections,* p. 53.
39. Smith, Oct. 2, 1828.
40. Sanger, p. 540.
41. RevTR, vol. 2, p. 762; entry for Dec. 21, 1844.
42. Ibid., p. 769; entry for Feb. 7, 1845.
43. Samuel Griswold Goodrich [Peter Parley], *Recollections of a Lifetime* (New York, 1856), 133.
44. Probate Inventory of John Sparhawk, recorded in Rockingham County, N.H., vol. 29, p. 178, includes globes, a telescope, a spyglass, hydrostatic balance scales, a hydrometer, prisms, and a magnifying mirror, in addition to a thermometer.
45. Portsmouth *Oracle,* Dec. 21, 1805.
46. Rev. Timothy Dwight, *Travels in New England and New York,* vol. 1 (Cambridge, Mass., 1960), p. 55.
47. Horace Clark diary, OSV; entry for Feb. 19, 1836.
48. RevTR, vol. 1, p. 476; entry for May 6, 1811.
49. RevTR, vol. 1, p. 689; entry for March 18, 1843; vol. 2, p. 736; entry for May 17, 1844.
50. RevTR, vol. 2, p. 930; entry for Feb. 3, 1849.
51. RevTR, vol. 1, p. 695; entry for Feb. 14, 1817.
52. RevTR, vol. 1, p. 729.
53. George Atkinson Ward, ed., *Journal and Letters of Samuel Curwen . . .* (New York, 1842), p. 45; London, Jan. 29, 1776.
54. *New England Farmer,* Dec. 20, 1823.
55. Dwight, *Travels,* vol. 1, p. 75.
56. *New England Farmer,* Dec. 20, 1823.
57. SSB, March 4, 1826.
58. RevTR, vol. 2, p. 566; entry for April 10, 1840.
59. Ibid., p. 370; entry for Jan. 9, 1835.
60. Clarence Cook, ed., *A Girl's Life Eighty Years Ago* (New York, 1883), p. 88. Letter of Eliza Southgate, Portland, Maine, Jan. 24, 1802.
61. New Hampshire *Gazette,* Jan. 25, 1760.
62. Pyncheon, pp. 2–3; entry for Jan. 26, 1776, and p. 328, entry for Feb. 28, 1789.
63. Timothy Dwight, *Travels in New England and New York* (Cambridge, 1960), p. 140.
64. Bentley, vol. 3, p. 332; entry for Dec. 10, 1807.
65. Dwight, *Travels,* vol. 1, p. 140.
66. Joseph and Laura Lyman. *The Philosophy of Housekeeping* (Hartford, 1867), pp. 534–5.
67. Sanger, p. 184.
68. Ibid., March 17, 1778; Feb. 17, 1781; Nov. 16, 1782; and other entries.
69. Sullivan Dorr Family expense book, vol. 1, John Hay Library, Brown University, Providence, R.I.
70. Parkman, p. 267; entries for Jan. 27 and 29, 1753.
71. Parkman, Nov. 30, 1779.
72. *New England Farmer,* Jan. 24, 1824.
73. RHB, Jan. 3 and 7, 1824.
74. RevTR, vol. 2, p. 300; entries for March 15 and 19, 1833.
75. Ibid., p. 566, entry for April 10, 1840: "Finished my large pile of wood to lie over the summer"; p. 514, entry for Nov. 17, 1838; p. 955, entry for Nov. 1, 1849.
76. Mary Ellen Chase, *Jonathan Fisher: Maine Parson, 1768–1847* (New York, 1948), p. 130.
77. Tyler, pp. 153–6.
78. John Greenleaf Whittier's image of the "clean-winged hearth" in "Snowbound" referred to the task of brushing up ashes with a dried turkey wing to which the feathers were still attached. Such wings were often kept on the kitchen mantel, where they were always handy.
79. Edith E. W. Gregg, ed., *The Letters of Ellen Tucker Emerson* (Kent, Ohio, 1982), vol. 1, p. 176.
80. See, for example, the chimney corner in the kitchen of the Harrison Gray Harris Homestead, Warner, N.H., in figure 129.
81. RevTR, vol. 1, p. 723; entry for Dec. 6, 1817.
82. Thomas C. Hubka, *Big House, Little House, Back House, Barn: The Connected Farm Buildings of New England* (Hanover, N.H., 1984), pp. 6, 67.
83. Emery, *Reminiscences,* p. 334.
84. Pyncheon, p. 150; entry for April 21, 1783.
85. Tyler, p. 319.
86. Parkman, p. 286.
87. New Hampshire *Gazette,* April 4, 1763.
88. Parkman; entries for Jan. 26 and 27, 1780.

89. Connecticut *Courant,* March 6, 1805.
90. Leander W. Cogswell, *History of the Town of Henniker* (Henniker, N.H., 1880), pp. 263–5.
91. RHB, March 28 and 31, 1826.
92. Connecticut *Courant,* Jan. 23, 1816.
93. Pyncheon, p. 23.
94. RHB, March 11, 1826.
95. *New England Farmer,* Dec. 23, 1825, p. 171.
96. RevTR, vol. 1, p. 960; entry for March 29, 1824.
97. See, for example, New Hampshire *Gazette,* April 15, 1768, and Oct. 6, 1799.
98. RevTR, vol. 2, p. 553; entry for Dec. 20, 1839.
99. William T. Davis, *Plymouth Memories of an Octagenarian* (Plymouth, Mass., 1906), p. 483.
100. Stowe, *Oldtown Folks,* p. 274.
101. Ibid., pp. 262–4.
102. Sanger, Dec. 19, 1793.
103. Hanson, *Journal . . . by Samuel Lane,* p. 30; entry for Dec. 6, 1742.
104. Jonathan Sayward diary, AAS; typescript at SPNEA.
105. Tyler, pp. 316–18.
106. "The Diary of Isaiah Thomas, 1805–1828," in *Transactions of the American Antiquarian Society* 9 (Worcester, Mass., 1909); entry for Dec. 6, 1816.
107. Martha Moore Ballard, "Diary," *The History of Augusta,* ed. C. E. Nash (Augusta, 1904), entry for Jan. 22, 1806.
108. Greenfield *Gazette,* Jan. 16, 1802. I am grateful to Ritchie Garrison, formerly of Historic Deerfield, Inc., for sharing this reference with me.
109. RHB, Nov. 24, 1809, and other related entries.
110. Helen B. Lewis, "Textiles Owned in Wethersfield 1750–1800 as Evidenced by Contemporary Estate Inventories," Unpublished research paper filed at the Webb-Deane-Stevens Museum, May 1981. Similar studies for Deerfield, Massachusetts, and Providence, Rhode Island, offer comparable statistics.
111. Bentley, vol. 4, p. 373; entry for Feb. 12, 1816.
112. A. F. M. Willich, *The Domestic Encyclopaedia,* 1st American ed., vol. 2 (Philadelphia, 1804), p. 299.
113. "Edward J. Carpenter's Journal," *Proceedings of the American Antiquarian Society* 98, no. 2 (1988): 344–6.
114. Carol F. Karlsen and Laurie Crumpacker, eds., *The Journal of Esther Edwards Burr, 1754–1757* (New Haven, 1984), p. 79.
115. Henry Reed Stiles, *Bundling: Its Origin, Progress and Decline in America* (1871; reprint, Cambridge, Mass., n.d.). See also Ellen K. Rothman, *Hearts and Hands* (New York, 1984), pp. 44–9, and Laurel Thatcher Ulrich and Lois K. Stabler, " 'Girling of it' in Eighteenth-Century New Hampshire," in *Families and Children: The Dublin Seminar for New England Folklife Annual Proceedings 1985* (Boston), pp. 24–36.
116. Stiles, *Bundling,* p. 67.
117. Ibid., p. 92.
118. Abbott Lowell Cummings cites fifteen warming pans located in kitchens, two in unspecified first-floor locations, and only one in a chamber in Suffolk County homes inventoried between 1750 and 1775. (*Rural Household Inventories* [Boston, 1960].)
119. Nineteen out of thirty-two households cited by Cummings owned warming pans between 1750 and 1775; one family owned two!
120. *Diary of Isaiah Thomas,* p. 259.
121. Stowe, *Oldtown Folks,* p. 341.
122. Mrs. Cornelius, *The Young Housekeeper's Friend* (Boston, 1848), p. 183.
123. Pyncheon, p. 320; entry for Oct. 30, 1788.
124. Stewart Mitchell, ed., *New Letters of Abigail Adams, 1788–1801* (Boston, 1947), p. 74; Adams to Mary Cranch, Philadelphia, Oct. 30, 1791.
125. Francis W. Underwood, *Quabbin* (Boston, 1893; rpt. 1986), p. 22.
126. Parkman, p. 228.
127. Noah Blake diary, PVMA; entry for Dec. 2, 1805.
128. RHB, Nov. 1, 1810.
129. Sanger. See entries for Oct. 3–4, 1774; Nov. 26, 1777; Nov. 9, 17, and 18, 1779; Nov. 12, 1781; and Nov. 13, 18, and 21, 1782, among others.
130. Miss [Eliza] Leslie, *The House Book,* 6th ed. (Philadelphia, 1841), p. 322.
131. Ibid., p. 323.
132. Providence *Journal,* Feb. 17, 1831.
133. Memorandum of Elizabeth Babcock Leonard by her mother, "The Life, from birth of a child of cultured parents of means," PVMA.
134. New Hampshire *Gazette,* Dec. 7, 1793.
135. Joyce Butler, "The Longfellows: Another Portland Family," unpublished paper, pp. 12–13. Courtesy of the author.
136. Tyler, pp. 319–20.
137. Francis Mason, ed., *Childish Things: The Reminiscences of Susan Baker Blunt* (Grantham, N.H., 1988), p. 33.

CHAPTER V

1. SSB, March 22 and April 16 and 19, 1825.
2. A Lady, *The Housekeeper's Book* (Philadelphia, 1838), p. 21.
3. Anne Clark Kane to Mrs. John Innes Clark, Providence, June 17, 1812. Quoted in Joseph K. Ott, "John Innes Clark and His Family: Beautiful People in Providence," *Rhode Island History* 32 (Nov. 1973): 4, 127–8.
4. Rev. Timothy Dwight, *Travels in New England and New York,* vol. 4 (Cambridge, Mass., 1969), p. 335.
5. Bentley, vol. 2, p. 55; entry for Aug. 19–Sept. 5, 1793.
6. Caroline Davidson, *Woman's Work Is Never Done* (London, 1982), p. 117.
7. Catherine Beecher, *A Treatise on Domestic Economy* (Boston, 1841), p. 109.
8. Susan I. Lesley, *Recollections of My Mother* (Boston, 1899), p. 415.
9. Smith, Jan. 5, 1828.
10. RHB, Jan. 20, 1812.
11. Sanger, p. 118.
12. RevTR, vol. 1, p. 550; entry for May 1, 1813.
13. RevTR, vol. 2, p. 435.
14. Bentley, vol. 2, p. 413; entry for Feb. 11, 1802. Dr. Bentley has copied extracts from

remarks in Capt. John White of Salem's Almanacs, 1774–1790.

15. H. C. Brown, *Grandmother Brown's Hundred Years, 1827–1927* (Boston, 1929), p. 92.

16. Sylvester Judd, *History of Hadley* (Springfield, Mass., 1905), pp. 294–5.

17. Sanger, Dec. 15, 1775; April 16 and Nov. 13 and 24, 1779; Oct. 26 and Nov. 14 and 29, 1782, and other entries.

18. George Channing, *Early Recollections of Newport, R.I., from the Year 1793 to 1811* (Newport, 1868), pp. 267–8.

19. Greenfield *Gazette,* July 14, 1796.

20. Connecticut *Courant,* Feb. 5, 1812.

21. EPP to EWPH, Hadley, March 2, 1801, PFP (box 6, folder 1).

22. Based on comparisons of rural storekeepers' inventories done by Caroline Fuller Sloat at Old Sturbridge Village, 1970–74.

23. Harriet Beecher Stowe, *Poganuc People* (Boston, 1878), pp. 162–3.

24. A Lady, *A New System of Domestic Cookery* (Boston, 1807), p. viii.

25. Francis Mason, ed. *Childish Things: The Reminiscence of Susan Baker Blunt* (Grantham, N.H., 1988), p. 35.

26. Ibid.

27. Ibid.

28. *New England Farmer* 1829, p. 283.

29. Lydia Maria Child, *The American Frugal Housewife* (Boston, 1832), p. 114. See also Beecher, *Treatise,* pp. 306–7.

30. *New England Farmer,* April 15, 1825, p. 301.

31. Eliza A. Storr, "A Leaf," *History and Proceedings of the Pocumtuck Valley Memorial Association* 1 (1873):158–9.

32. Elizabeth Tuckerman Salisbury to Stephen Salisbury, II, June 2, 1818; Salisbury Family Papers, box 18, folder 4, AAS. I am grateful to Bill Wallace and Anne Riggs for sharing this reference with me.

33. RevTR, vol. 2, pp. 637, 672, 820.

34. "Diary of Elizabeth Fuller," in Francis Everett Blake, *History of the Town of Princeton, Massachusetts* (Princeton, Mass., 1915), pp. 304, 307.

35. RHB, Feb. 22, 1812.

36. Connecticut *Courant,* Aug. 9, 1790; New Hampshire *Gazette,* Nov. 3, 1791.

37. Robert Roberts, *The House Servant's Directory: A Facsimile of the 1827 Edition* (Waltham, Mass., 1977), p. 27.

38. Ibid., p. 21.

39. RevTR, vol. 2, p. 924.

40. Sturgis, p. 126.

41. Pyncheon, p. 145; entry for Feb. 5, 1783.

42. RHB, Nov. 24, 1829.

43. Bentley, vol. 2, pp. 4, 46–47. As early as the 1770s, the Stratton Tavern in Northfield, Massachusetts, had a similar system of wooden water pipes, which led water from a spring on a nearby hillside into the barn, a cistern in a still house, and the tavern itself. Evidence of the system was excavated by a team of archaeologists from Old Sturbridge Village in 1979. See: John E. Worrell, "Scars Upon the Earth: Physical Evidence of Dramatic Social Change at the Stratton Tavern" in *Proceedings of the Conference on Northeastern Archaeology,* ed. James A. Moore (Amherst, Mass., 1980); and J. Ritchie Garrlson, *Landscape and Material Life in Franklin County, Massachusetts* (Knoxville, Tenn., 1991), pp. 171–5.

44. Bentley, vol. 2, pp. 206, 212, 218, 222–3ff; Charles Brewster, *Rambles about Portsmouth,* first series, 2nd ed. (Portsmouth, N.H., 1873), pp. 242–3.

45. Bentley thought that "the effect from the excrement below" attracted lightning in summer storms. (Bentley, vol. 1, p. 309; entry for Sept. 24, 1791.)

46. Beecher, *Treatise,* p. 272.

47. Ibid., p. 294.

48. Abbott Lowell Cummings, for example, cites five chamber pots in room-by-room inventories taken in Suffolk County, Massachusetts, 1675–1775. (*Rural Household Inventories* [Boston, 1964].)

49. EPP to Elizabeth W. Phelps, Hadley, Nov. 4, 1797, PFP (box 6, folder 1). Mrs. Phelps continued, "'Tis now about .8. but we shall all be rested by the morning I hope. & find the morrow a Sabbath of rest."

50. EPP to EWPH, Hadley, June 13, 1801, PFP (box 6, folder 1).

51. Judd, *History,* p. 374.

52. Sanger, April 3, 1778; Dec. 7 and 8, 1779; April 27, 1780.

53. Harriet Beecher Stowe, *Oldtown Folks* (Boston, 1869), p. 61.

54. Mason, *Childish Things,* p. 26.

55. M. R. G., "A Country Wedding," Lowell *Offering,* March 1845, pp. 49–52; Sarah Anna Emery, *Reminiscences of a Newburyport Nonagenarian* (Newburyport, Mass., 1879), p. 10.

56. Stowe, *Oldtown Folks,* p. 23.

57. Emery, *Reminiscences,* p. 23.

58. Ellen H. Rollins [E. H. Arr], *New England Bygones* (1883, rpt. Stockbridge, Mass., 1977), p. 66.

59. Milton Meltzer, *Tongue of Flame* (New York, 1965), pp. 155–6. During the same year, Mrs. Child cooked 360 dinners and 362 breakfasts, wrote 235 letters and 6 newspaper articles, read aloud, mended, and sewed garments for freedmen and hospital patients as well as her own family, and spent two weeks making and quilting a "starred crib quilt."

60. Miss [Eliza] Leslie, *The House Book* (Philadelphia, 1843), p. 336.

61. Ibid.

62. Sanger, May 21, 1781.

63. Spring cleaning was often the target of heavy-handed humorists who cast themselves in the role of husbands seeking to avoid the hard work and turmoil.

64. Smith, May 2, 5, 6, 24, and 28 and Aug. 13, 14, and 15, 1828.

65. Account book of an anonymous Roxbury, Massachusetts, upholsterer, 1840s, formerly in the collection of the Roxbury Historical Society but destroyed by fire since my research was completed.

66. *Salem Directory* (Salem, 1846).

67. J. Hammond Trumbull, *The Memorial History of Hartford County, Connecticut, 1633–1884* (Boston, 1886), p. 589.

68. Blanche B. Bryant and Gertrude E. Baker, eds., *The Diaries of Sally and Pamela Brown, 1832–1838. Hyde Leslie, 1887* (Springfield, Vt., 1970). Diary of Pamela Brown, May 29, 1837.

69. Beecher, *Treatise,* p. 341. She recommended beating carpets with "pliant whips."

70. Abigail Adams to Mary Cranch, New York, May 6, 1791, in *New Letters of Abigail Adams, 1788–1801*, ed. Stewart Mitchell (Boston, 1947), p. 73.
71. Edward Everett Hale, *A New England Boyhood* (New York, 1893).
72. Beecher, *Treatise*, p. 359.
73. RevTR, vol. 1, p. 929.
74. Smith, July 26, 1828.
75. Beecher, *Treatise*, p. 361.
76. *How to Do Things Well and Cheap. For Domestic Use. By One Who Knows* (Boston, 1845), pp. 9–10, and Mrs. E. A. Howland, *The New England Economical Housekeeper* (Worcester, Mass., 1845), p. 94.
77. Leslie, *House Book*, pp. 316–18.
78. A Lady, *Housekeeper's Book*, p. 21; Beecher, *Treatise*, p. 376.
79. Beecher, *Treatise*, p. 307.
80. Child, *Frugal Housewife*, p. 13; Leslie, *House Book*, p. 9.
81. Roberts, *House Servant's Directory*, p. xiii.
82. Beecher, *Treatise*, p. 312.
83. Howland, *Economical Housekeeper*, p. 100; Roberts, *House Servant's Directory*, pp. 93–4.
84. *Columbian Centinel*, June 11, 1825.
85. Stowe, *Oldtown Folks*, p. 63.
86. Child, *Frugal Housewife*, pp. 16–17.
87. Beecher, *Treatise*, p. 376.
88. Child, *Frugal Housewife*, p. 21.
89. *New England Farmer*, Aug. 10, 1831, p. 27.
90. Sanger, June 17, 1794.
91. Christopher Clark, ed., "Journal of Edward Jenner Carpenter," *American Antiquarian Society Proceedings* 98, no. 2 (1988): 388.
92. *New England Farmer*, Aug. 3, 1831, p. 21.
93. *New England Farmer*, 1826, p. 331.
94. Beecher, *Treatise*, p. 349.
95. Calvert Vaux, *Villas and Cottages* (New York, 1864), p. 68.
96. Miss [Eliza] Leslie, *The Behaviour Book* (Philadelphia, 1856), p. 26.
97. A Lady, *Housekeeper's Book*, pp. 24–5.
98. RHB, Sept. 29 and 30 and Oct. 1 and 8, 1829.
99. Bryant and Baker, *Diaries*, p. 28. Diary of Pamela Brown, Dec. 16, 1835.
100. Sanger, Nov. 16, 1775; April 6, 1776; Dec. 5, 1777; Jan. 1, 1781; April 24, 1782.
101. Laura Fish Judd, *Honolulu* . . . (Honolulu, 1928), p. 12.
102. RHB, Feb. 2, 1829.
103. *New England Farmer*, Oct. 18, 1837, p. 117.
104. A Lady, *Housekeeper's Book*, pp. 184–5.
105. Elihu to Hannah Hoyt, Jan. 30, 1804; June 4, 1808; Nov. 26, 1816; June 9, 1817; Jan. 23, 1818; Jan. 23, 1820; Feb. 16, 1828; and others. Hoyt Family Papers, PVMA. The Jan. 23, 1818, note includes this request: "Shall want you to send back my shirts & stockings by Mr. Barbard the next time he comes down, or by someother conveyance so I can get them soon—(send also the bag)— . . . P.S. My bag of dirty cloaths will consist of Shirts, Hkfs, Stockings, one Waistcot, Newspapers, other papers & one book."
106. *New England Farmer*, Feb. 10, 1841.
107. Some particularly careful estate appraisers also made use of linen marks to identify specific items and assign relative values. In the 1783 inventory of the estate of Sarah Wells, the widow of Dr. Thomas Wells of Deerfield, Massachusetts, for example, the appraisers listed "1 pr. linen do. [sheets] No. 1," which they valued at fourteen shillings, as well as seven other pairs of sheets, with values ranging from three shillings to eleven shillings and ninepence. Mrs. Wells's linen and cotton pillow biers, diaper table cloths, cotton diaper towels, and linen towels were all similarly enumerated and appraised, with the embroidered marks used to identify each specific item.
108. RHB, Oct. 1, 1829.
109. "Mrs. Richardson washed yesterday & ironed this day till 10 evening. I cleansed gowns, muslins &c, brought little to pass." (RHB, Oct. 1, 1829.)
110. Sanger, Nov. 8, 1794.
111. According to William Pyne's *British Costumes* (London, 1805), in Scotland, the term "bucking" referred to stepping into the laundry tubs and treading the clothes with bare feet. There is no evidence that this is what Rhoda was doing, however. The *Oxford English Dictionary* includes "washtub" as a definition for the word "buck."
112. Beecher, *Treatise*, p. 311.
113. Child, *Treatise*, p. 17.
114. Child, *Treatise*, p. 23.
115. Sanger, March 25, March 27, April 1, and Nov. 20, 1782.
116. Beecher, *Treatise*, pp. 313–14.
117. Emery, *Reminiscences*, p. 7.
118. David Brown diary, Hubbardston, Mass., May 9, 1791, AAS.
119. *Columbian Centinel*, Jan. 6, 1827.
120. Child, *Treatise*, p. 17.
121. One "cloath horse," valued at 2/2, was sold to Mr. Warner at the "Vendue of sundry Goods belonging to Col. John Tufton Mason, Esq. at his Mansion House in Portsmouth," June 12, 1766. (Warner House Papers no. 56, PA.)
122. "Directions for using Arnold's Patent Washing Machine. Made and Sold by Anson Merriman. Southington" (Conn.), 1831. Broadside at CHS. I am grateful to Caroline Sloat for sharing this reference with me.
123. SSB, March 10, 1798.
124. Sarah J. Hale, *The Good Housekeeper* (Boston, 1839), p. 119.
125. Child, *Treatise*, p. 17.
126. EPP to EWPH, March 20, 1801, PFP (box 6, folder 1).
127. This practice apparently offered great temptation to a thief in Newburyport in 1812, who "striped a large clothes horse of the week's ironing." (Emery, *Reminiscences*, p. 284.)
128. RHB, Aug. 3 and 4, 1829.

CHAPTER VI

1. EPP to EWPH, Aug. 6, 1802, PFP (box 6, folder 2).
2. Sanger, p. 5.
3. Ibid.
4. *The Mirror of the Graces* (London, 1815), p. 35.
5. Anne Usher to Harriet Clark, June 1790, RIHS.

6. Richard L. Bushman and Claudia L. Bushman, "The Early History of Cleanliness in America," *Journal of American History* 74, no. 4: 1213–38.
7. William A. Alcott, *The Young Man's Guide,* 14th ed. (Boston, 1839), p. 88.
8. Beecher, *Treatise,* pp. 103–4.
9. Ibid., p. 103.
10. Ibid., p. 360.
11. Although scented "wash balls" were imported from England in the eighteenth century and domestic toilet soaps were advertised in New England newspapers and stocked in country stores by at least 1810, they were seldom used for general bathing. These small cakes of highly perfumed soap were considered cosmetics and were valued more for the way in which they would beautify the skin than for their cleansing qualities. Most people were content with a splash of cold water and a hard rub with a towel.
12. Beecher, *Treatise,* p. 361.
13. Sarah Anna Emery, *Reminiscences of a Nonagenarian* (Newburyport, Mass., 1879), p. 32.
14. [Hiram Munger], *The Life and Religious Experience of Hiram Munger* (Chicopee Falls, Mass., 1856), p. 36.
15. Tyler, p. 194.
16. *Twice Married: A Story of Connecticut Life* (New York and London, 1855), p. 186.
17. William T. Davis, *Plymouth Memories of an Octagenarian* (Plymouth, Mass., 1906), p. 281.
18. "The Will of George Rea Curwen (1823–1900)," *Essex Institute Historical Collections* 36 (1900): 253.
19. Portsmouth *Oracle,* Aug. 16, 1806.
20. Bentley, pp. 250, 255; entries for April 21 and 28, 1791.
21. The auction was held at the fourth house in Quincy Place, Boston (*Columbian Centinel,* April 26, 1823).
22. Beecher, *Treatise,* p. 102.
23. Ibid.
24. RHB, June 30, 1810.
25. RHB, April 15 and 18, 1829.
26. RHB, May 28 and 30, 1829.
27. RHB, Oct. 9, 1830.
28. Mrs. Ellen Strong Bartlett, "Bits from Great Grandmother's Journal," *Connecticut Magazine* 1 (1893): 3, 270.
29. EWP to Charles Phelps, Hadley, July 1, 1796; April 1797; May 19 and 30, 1797; PFP (box 12; folder 15).
30. Emery, *Reminiscences,* p. 106.
31. For good examples, see Alice Morse Earle, ed., *Diary of Anna Green Winslow: A Boston School Girl of 1771* (Boston and New York, 1894), and Clarence Cook, ed., *A Girl's Life Eighty Years Ago: Letters of Eliza Southgate Bowne* (New York, 1883).
32. EWP to EPP, Aug. 30, 1797, PFP (box 13, folder 1).
33. EWP to Charles Phelps, Hadley, Dec. 18, 1797, PFP (box 12, folder 15). Elizabeth continued, "My guittar too is the subject of conversation—many times but I make light of it—for I have not attempted to play before any company yet—I fancy I make some progress—but it requires much time and attention—you must suppose that I am much attached to it from my natural fondness for musick."
34. Anne Elizabeth or Harriet Clark to Mrs. John Inness Clark, New York, early 1800s. Joseph K. Ott, "John Inness Clark and His Family: Beautiful People in Providence," *Rhode Island History* 32 (Nov. 1973): 4, 130.
35. Helen Morgan, ed., *A Season in New York, 1801: Letters of Harriet and Maria Trumbull* (Pittsburgh, 1969), p. 87.
36. EWP to Charles Phelps, Hadley, May 30, 1797, PFP (box 12, folder 15).
37. On Dec. 30, 1774, Abner Sanger talked of "buying old shirts of Jacob Day."
38. Emery, *Reminiscences,* p. 16.
39. Filania Dickinson's cloak is in the collections of PVMA. Jane C. Nylander, "Textiles, Clothing, and Needlework," in *The Great River,* ed. Gerald W. R. Ward and William N. Hosley, Jr. (Hartford, 1985), fig. 257, pp. 387–8.
40. Sarah Orne Jewett's story of "The Dulham Ladies" explores false notions of gentility and the transmission of taste; while the situation is absurd, it has the ring of truth.
41. Rev. Timothy Dwight, *Travels in New England and New York,* vol. 1 (Cambridge, Mass., 1960), p. 60.
42. William Cullen Bryant to Peter Bryant, Bridgewater, Mass., April 27, 1815. William Cullen Bryant II and Thomas G. Voss, eds., *The Letters of William Cullen Bryant* (New York, 1975), vol. 1, p. 55.
43. Ibid., p. 145; William Cullen Bryant to Sarah Snell Bryant, Great Barrington, Mass., Sept. 15, 1823.
44. Susan I. Lesley, *Recollections of My Mother* (New York, 1899), pp. 251–2.
45. Will of Dr. Peter Bryant, 1820, Hampshire County Probate Office, Springfield, Mass.
46. S. G. Griffin, *A History of the Town of Keene* (Keene, N.H., 1904; rpt. 1980), p. 333.
47. Simple loose dresses fitted by gathering the fabric on a drawstring around the neck. Coolers were made with both long and short sleeves; there was no waistband.
48. RHB, March 20 and 23, 1813.
49. RHB, June 20 and 21, and Aug. 5 and 6, 1805.
50. RHB, Sept. 23, 1807: "Mrs. Joshua Lamb here & Brought Mrs. Brigham's mourning bonnet to make. I sat up nearly all night & made it." Feb. 4, 1808: "Hear of Mrs. Powers death . . . began to make bonnet for her daughters—set up till after one!"
51. RHB, June 17, 1813.
52. RHB, March 7, 1814.
53. Cook, *A Girl's Life,* p. 22. Eliza Southgate to Octavia, Boston, Feb. 7, 1800.
54. RHB, Feb. 9, 1806.
55. RHB, March 12, 1814.
56. EPP to EWPH, Hadley, Aug. 6, 1802, PFP (box 6, folder 1).
57. EWPH to EPP, Litchfield, March 18, 1801, PFP (box 13, folder 1).
58. Actually, the development of less expensive fabrics and the mechanical sewing machine only increased it. People expected more clothing, and it was much more closely fitted and elaborately trimmed.

CHAPTER VII

1. SSB, Aug. 21, 1824.
2. These ideas are well defined in Carol Shammas, "How Self Sufficient was Early

America?," *Journal of Interdisciplinary History* 13 (Autumn 1982): 2, 247–72. Since 1982, many others have completed regional studies further refining this important point.
3. Asa Talcott account book, CHS, 1773–76.
4. Charles Lane Hanson, ed., *A Journal for the Years 1739–1803 by Samuel Lane of Stratham, New Hampshire* (Concord, N.H., 1937), p. 5.
5. Parkman (Forbes), pp. 97–98.
6. SSB, Jan. 11–14, 1832.
7. "Work inside the house was termed house-work, earning, and sitting work." (Alice Jones, *In Dover on the Charles* [Boston, 1906], p. 47.)
8. Francis W. Underwood, *Quabbin* (Boston, 1893), pp. 20–1.
9. Eliza Buckminster Lee, *Sketches of a New England Village in the Last Century* (Boston, 1838), p. 19.
10. W. R. Cochrane, *History of the Town of Antrim, New Hampshire, from Its Earliest Settlement, to June 27, 1877* (Manchester, N.H., 1880), p. 275.
11. For example: "The spinning wheel was in every house, and the loom in every neighborhood, and almost every article of clothing was the product of female industry." See Theron Wilmot Crissey, comp., *History of Norfolk* (Conn.) (Everett, Mass., 1900), p. 223.
12. Horace Bushnell, "The Age of Homespun," in *Work and Play* (New York, 1864), quoted in Christopher Clark, "Household Economy, Market Exchange and the Rise of Capitalism in the Connecticut Valley, 1800–1860," *Journal of Social History* 13, no. 2 (Winter 1979): 169.
13. Shammas, "How Self Sufficient," p. 257.
14. Reprinted in the Hampshire *Gazette,* Jan. 28, 1789.
15. William Hillhouse to John Chester, Montville, Conn., Sept. 6, 1791, in ed., *Industrial and Commercial Correspondence of Alexander Hamilton,* ed. Arthur Harrison Cole (Chicago, 1928), p. 18.
16. Research report by Charlotte Stiverson, Historic Deerfield, Inc., Deerfield, Mass., 1981.
17. Shammas points out that the letter was first published in the *American Museum* in Philadelphia in 1787.
18. Tyler, pp. 282–3.
19. Susan I. Lesley, *Recollections of My Mother* (Boston, 1899), p. 115.
20. Grace Rogers Cooper, *The Copp Family Textiles* (Washington, D.C., 1971).
21. Elihu to Hannah Hoyt, Boston, Jan. 25, 1805, Hoyt Family Papers, PVMA.
22. "The Paring (or Apple) Bee," Lowell *Offering,* Nov. 1845.
23. RHB, Aug. 29 and Dec. 7, 1791.
24. Sarah Anna Emery, *Reminiscences of a Nonagenarian* (Newburyport, Mass., 1879), p. 9.
25. Connecticut *Courant,* March 6, 1805. Account of a fire that completely consumed the house of Deacon Ephraim How and his family and was caused by drying undressed flax too near the hearth.
26. Underwood, *Quabbin,* pp. 20–1.
27. Testimony of Joanna Dresser, Rowley, Mass., in Massachusetts Historical Society, Miscellaneous Papers 12.
28. Francis Everett Blake, *History of the Town of Princeton, Massachusetts* (Princeton, Mass., 1951), pp. 311–22.
29. RHB, Feb. 21, 1791.
30. Josiah Howes Temple and George Sheldon, *A History of the Town of Northfield, Massachusetts . . . ,* vol. 1 (Albany, N.Y., 1875), p. 161.
31. Hampshire *Gazette,* Oct. 4, 1815.
32. Lee, *Sketches,* p. 6.
33. RHB, Dec. 7, 1791.
34. RHB, March 18, 1797.
35. SSB, Feb. 2–April 17, 1797.
36. Blake, *History,* pp. 311–22.
37. Emery, *Reminiscences,* pp. 8–9.
38. Ibid., p. 6.
39. Inventory, Estate of Peter Bryant, Cummington, Mass., 1820, Hampshire County Probate Court, Springfield, Mass.
40. SSB, July 14–19, 1820.
41. SSB, Nov. 7, 1823.
42. SSB, Feb. 14, 1820.
43. SSB, May 11, 1820.
44. *New England Farmer,* Nov. 5, 1830, p. 213.

CHAPTER VIII

1. Field Family Papers, PVMA.
2. Will of Samuel Denney, Georgetown, Maine, probated Sept. 16, 1772. William D. Patterson, ed. *The Probate Records of Lincoln County, Maine, 1760 to 1800* (Portland, Maine, 1895), pp. 56–7.
3. Patterson, p. 300.
4. S. G. Goodrich [Peter Parley], *Recollections of a Lifetime* (New York, 1856), p. 67.
5. Harriet Beecher Stowe, *Oldtown Folks* (Boston, 1869), p. 61.
6. Catharine Beecher, *A Treatise on Domestic Economy* (Boston, 1841), p. 369.
7. Sanger, May 5, 1781.
8. Francis W. Underwood, *Quabbin* (Boston, 1893), p. 80.
9. Stowe, *Oldtown Folks,* p. 295.
10. Susan I. Lesley, *Recollections of My Mother* (Boston, 1899), p. 417.
11. Sanger, Aug. 22, 1776.
12. Ibid., Aug. 14, 1821.
13. Hampshire *Gazette,* Sept. 3, 1788.
14. Sarah Anne Emery, *Reminiscences of a Nonagenarian* (Newburyport, Mass., 1879), p. 7.
15. RHB, July 22, 1830.
16. EWPH to EPP, Litchfield, March 18 and Dec. 13, 1801, PFP (box 13, folder 1).
17. Caroline Howard King, *When I Lived in Salem, 1822–1866* (Brattleboro, Vt., 1937), p. 98.
18. Lesley, *Recollections,* p. 417.
19. Francis Mason, ed., *Childish Things: The Reminiscence of Susan Baker Blunt* (Grantham, N.H., 1988), p. 26.
20. David Brown diary, Hubbardston, Mass., May 16, 1791, AAS.
21. Emery, *Reminiscences,* p. 8.
22. EPP to EWP, Hadley, Nov. 1, 1797. PFP (box 6, folder 2).
23. *New England Farmer,* July 28, 1841.
24. Underwood, *Quabbin,* p. 324.
25. Reminiscence of Lyndon Freeman (1811–60), Sturbridge, Mass., OSV.

26. Elihu Hoyt in Boston to Hannah Hoyt in Deerfield, June 6, 1819. Hoyt Family Papers, PVMA.
27. Bentley, vol. 3, p. 331; entry for Nov. 8, 1807.
28. Alice Brown sketched a vivid picture of such a nooning in her short story "The Mortuary Chest."
29. William Jones account book, Rye Historical Society, Rye, N.H.
30. Mary Ellen Chase, *Jonathan Fisher: Maine Parson, 1768–1847* (New York, 1948), p. 131.
31. Underwood, *Quabbin*, p. 9.
32. New Hampshire *Gazette*, Nov. 18, 1756; April 1, 1757; June 10, 1757.
33. For a summary of foodstuffs available in eighteenth-century Deerfield, Massachusetts, see Daphne L. Derven, "Wholesome, Toothsome, and Diverse: Eighteenth-Century Foodways in Deerfield, Massachusetts," in *Foodways in the Northeast: The Dublin Seminar for New England Folklife Annual Proceedings 1982* (Boston, 1984), pp. 47–63. For Boston, see advertisements summarized in George Francis Dow, *The Arts and Crafts in New England, 1704–1775, Gleanings from Boston Newspapers* (Topsfield, Mass., 1927), pp. 252–4, 292–6.
34. "Moses Hodgkins commenced driv'g my Cow, & took the Heifer down with him. I agree[d] to give him 9[00] for the Season." (Jacob Wendell diary, Portsmouth, N.H., May 25, 1829, PA.)
35. Papers relating to the Daniel Street market, PA.
36. Samuel Larkin diary, Portsmouth, N.H., Feb. 1, 1839, Larkin House, Monterey, Calif.
37. King, *Salem*, pp. 109–10.
38. Emery, *Reminiscences*, pp. 23–4.
39. Sanger, Dec. 8, 1780, and Jan. 30, 1781.
40. Ibid., Nov. 3 and 5, 1793; April 23, 1794; Sept. 2 and March 6, 1793; March 17, 1792; May 5 and Aug. 22, 1794.
41. SSB, Oct. 8 and 16, 1833.
42. "Forenoon Rhoda bakes. She went up to Carpenter's for emptyings." (Sanger, Jan. 8, 1776.)
43. Mrs. Cornelius, *The Young Housekeeper's Friend; or, A Guide to Domestic Economy and Comfort* (Boston, 1848), p. 19.
44. Sarah Emery recalled "brightly painted red painted oven lids" in her home in Newbury. (Emery, *Reminiscences*, p. 6.)
45. Cornelius, *Housekeeper's Friend*, p. 19.
46. Laurel Ulrich, *A Midwife's Tale* (New York, 1990), p. 85.
47. SSB, Oct. 30, 1826; Dec. 8, 1827; and subsequent references.
48. EPP to EWP, Nov. 4, 1797, PFP (box 6, folder 1).
49. Mrs. S. J. Hale, *The Good Housekeeper* (Boston, 1839), p. 120.
50. SSB, Sept. 11 and 13, 1819.
51. Portsmouth *Oracle*, Nov. 24, 1810. I am grateful to Kathleen Shea and Deborah Burrows for sharing this reference with me.
52. *Columbian Centinel*, Feb. 27, 1808.
53. Salem *Gazette*, Oct. 19, 1849, quoted in Dorothy Burnett Porter, "The Remonds of Salem, Massachusetts: A Nineteenth-Century Family Revisited," in *Proceedings of the American Antiquarian Society* 95, no. 2 (Oct. 1985): 272.
54. EPP to EWPH, Hadley, Nov. 13, 1810. PFP (box 6, folder 4).
55. Will of Peter Bryant, Cummington, Mass., 1820, Hampshire County Probate Office, Springfield, Mass.
56. Emery, *Reminiscences*, p. 7.
57. EPP to EWPH, June 13, 1801, PFP (box 6, folder 1).
58. SSB, June 1, 1814, and June 15, 1826.
59. According to Stephen Walkley, whose family in Southington, Connecticut, kept five cows and shared milk with another family who kept four, "The milk from nine cows would make a cheese about eight inches in diameter and four inches high." ("Furnishing a Small New England Farmhouse," *Old Time New England* [Winter 1958], p. 83.)
60. RHB, July 28 and 30 and Aug. 3 and 14, 1810.
61. Emery, *Reminiscences*, p. 8.
62. Thomas Walter Ward, Jr., to Sarah Henshaw Ward Putnam, June 14, 1847, Ward Papers, AAS. Quoted in Andrew H. Baker and Holly Izard Peterson, "Farmers' Adaptations to Markets in Early Nineteenth-Century Massachusetts," in *The Farm: The Dublin Seminar for New England Folklife Annual Proceedings 1986* (Boston, 1988).
63. Underwood, *Quabbin*, p. 21.
64. SSB, Oct. 1, 1822, and Sept. 29, 1825.
65. Underwood, *Quabbin*, p. 22.
66. Jonathan Sayward journal, March 14, 1797, AAS. Typescript at the Old York Historical Society, York, Maine, and SPNEA.
67. EPP to EWPH, Hadley, Nov. 15, 1805. PFP (box 6, folder 2).
68. SSB, Nov. 24, 1803.
69. RHB, Jan. 8, 1812.
70. EWPH to EPP, Litchfield, Dec. 30, 1802, PFP (box 13, folder 11).
71. Bentley, vol. 2, p. 214; entry for Feb. 13, 1797.
72. Bentley, vol. 4, p. 548; entry for Sept. 24, 1818.
73. Sanger, Oct. 31, 1794.
74. Lemuel Shattuck, *The Domestic Book-Keeper* (Boston, 1843), p. 18.
75. Emery, *Reminiscences*, p. 32.
76. Bentley, vol. 3, p. 140; entry for Feb. 13, 1805.
77. William T. Davis, *Memories of a Plymouth Octagenarian* (Plymouth, Mass., 1906), p. 19.
78. King, *Salem*, p. 98.
79. Elihu Hoyt in Boston to Hannah Hoyt in Deerfield, Mass., March 5, 1826, Hoyt Family Papers, PVMA.
80. Sanger, May 28, 1775.
81. Sanger, Oct. 19, 1774; Nov. 27 and 19, 1780; and Oct. 28, 1782.
82. Sanger, Oct. 21 and Nov. 8, 1775; Nov. 28 and 29, 1777; and Oct. 31 and Nov. 6, 1778.
83. EPP to EWPH, Hadley, Nov. 18, 1804. PFP (box 6, folder 2).
84. Underwood, *Quabbin*, p. 21. See also Frank Smith, *A History of Dover* (Dover, N.H., 1897), p. 76.
85. Goodrich, *Recollections*, p. 80.
86. SSB, Dec. 31, 1808.
87. Charles Lane Hanson, ed., *A Journal for the Years 1739–1803 by Samuel Lane of Stratham, New Hampshire* (Concord, N.H., 1937), p. 76.

88. SSB, April 5, 1820.
89. SSB, April 3, 1830.
90. "The Diary of an Apprentice Cabinetmaker: Edward Jenner Carpenter's Journal, 1844–5," ed. Christopher Clark, *Proceedings of the American Antiquarian Society* 98, no. 2 (1988): 325.
91. RevTR, vol. 2, p. 278; entry for Sept. 5, 1832.
92. RHB, Aug. 7, 1830; EPP diary, Sept. 1, 1780.
93. EWP to EPP, Aug. 30, 1797, PFP (box 13, folder 1).
94. RHB, Aug. 7, 1830.
95. Chase, *Jonathan Fisher,* p. 143.
96. RevTR, vol. 2, pp. 312, 346.
97. EWPH to EPP, Litchfield, Oct. 24, 1801, PFP (box 13, folder 1).
98. Daniel Huntington to Charles Phelps, Litchfield, Oct. 26, 1801, PFP (box 10, folder 1).
99. Underwood, *Quabbin,* p. 22.
100. SSB, note at the end of Dec. 1825.
101. *New England Farmer,* Nov. 5, 1830, p. 123.
102. I have seen only one copy of this broadside; it belongs to the owner of a late-eighteenth-century house in Vermont who found it folded up in the pantry, where it had apparently been for many years.
103. William J. Keep, "Early American Cooking Stoves," *Old Time New England* 22, no. 2 (October 1931): 76; Frank J. White, "Stoves in Nineteenth Century New England," *Magazine Antiques* 116 (Sept. 1979): 9, 592–9.
104. New Hampshire *Sentinel,* Nov. 23, 1817.
105. New Hampshire *Patriot and State Gazette,* Oct. 12, 1819.
106. Information from "Hide Your Fire in an Iron Cage," lecture by Frank J. White, OSV.
107. *Franklin Institute Journal* 10 (1830): 75.
108. *Argus Spectator,* Jan. 28, 1837.
109. Mason, *Childish Things,* p. 33.
110. Inventory of the Estate of Joseph Howe, tinplate worker, 1818, Suffolk County Probate Records, docket 25685, Boston, Mass.; account book of Henry Cate, ironworker, Portsmouth, N.H., PA.
111. Benjamin Rumford, *Collected Works of Count Rumford, edited by Sanborn C. Brown,* vol. 2, *Practical Applications of Heat* (Cambridge, 1969).
112. King, *Salem,* p. 24.
113. Stowe, *Oldtown Folks,* p. 64.

CHAPTER IX

1. EPP diary, Sept. 2, 1781.
2. Laurel Ulrich, *A Midwife's Tale* (New York, 1990), pp. 94–5.
3. RHB, Feb. 5, 1825.
4. RHB, April 3 and 6, 1826. Mrs. Bascom's diary contains many similar references over the years.
5. RHB, March 23, 1826.
6. Sarah Anna Emery, *Reminiscences of a Nonagenarian* (Newburyport, Mass., 1879), p. 77.
7. Some New England women today attend town meeting with their knitting, and multicolored Scandinavian or complicated textural patterns are favored for the same reason.
8. RHB, Dec. 28, 1825. Bear in mind that although she reported calling "at Mr. Gates," she was probably calling on Mrs. Gates.
9. SSB, June 15, 1810. Mrs. Snell and Mrs. Briggs were Sarah Bryant's nearest neighbors; Mrs. Snell was her sister-in-law, Ebenezer's wife.
10. *The Book of the Seasons* (Boston, 1842), p. 47.
11. Susan I. Lesley. *Recollections of My Mother* (Boston, 1899), p. 41.
12. Jonathan Sayward journal, Jan. 23, 1786, AAS.
13. Ibid., Jan. 3, 1792.
14. Sanger, Sept. 21, 1779.
15. Parkman, May 15, 1752.
16. Ibid., May 24–25, 1751.
17. M. R. G., "The Paring (or Apple) Bee," Lowell *Offering,* Nov. 1845, pp. 268–9.
18. SSB, March 2, 1830.
19. SSB, Feb. 9 and 24 and March 1, 2, 9, and 19, 1830.
20. SSB, Dec. 13, 1822.
21. Francis W. Underwood, *Quabbin* (Boston, 1893), p. 204.
22. T. S. Arthur, "The Quilting Party," *Godey's Magazine and Lady's Book,* Sept. 1849, pp. 185–6.
23. M. R. G., "The Paring (or Apple) Bee."
24. Parkman, Oct. 5, 1738.
25. RHB, July 8, 1810.
26. RHB, Jan. 3, 1824.
27. RHB, Jan. 26 and 31, and Feb. 1 and 13, 1826.
28. EWPH to EPP, Litchfield, June 12–20, 1801, PFP (box 13, folder 1).
29. EWP to EPP, Newburyport, Oct. 4, 1787, PFP (box 13, folder 1).
30. RHB, Sept. 21, 1830.
31. Emery, *Reminiscences,* p. 57.
32. SSB, Sept. 30, 1819; Sept. 28, 1821; and other references.
33. SSB, July 4, 1801; July 5, 1802; and July 4, 1816.
34. Christopher Columbus Baldwin, *Diary, 1829–1835* (Worcester, Mass., 1971), p. 69.
35. J. Hammond Trumbull, *The Memorial History of Hartford County, Connecticut, 1633–1884* (Boston, 1886), pp. 589–90.
36. Sanger, May 27 and 28, 1779.
37. RHB, March 4, 1825.
38. Sanger, Jan. 8, 1776.
39. SSB, May 9, 1834.
40. RHB, Dec. 12, 1808.
41. Caroline Howard King, *When I Lived in Salem, 1822–1866* (Brattleboro, Vt., 1937), pp. 185–6.
42. Harriet Beecher Stowe, "The Ghost in the Cap'n Brown House," Sam Lawson's *Oldtown Fireside Stories* (Boston, Mass., 1872).
43. Francis Mason, ed., *Childish Things: The Reminiscence of Susan Baker Blunt* (Grantham, N.H., 1988), p. 41.
44. Pyncheon, p. 204.
45. Sanger, Jan. 15, 1781.
46. RHB, Dec. 3, 1812.
47. Samuel Larkin diary, Portsmouth, N.H., Feb. 7, 1840, Larkin House, Monterey, Calif.
48. Baldwin, *Diary,* pp. 51–2.
49. *Godey's Lady's Book and Magazine,* Jan. 1857, p. 72.
50. Harriet Beecher Stowe, *Oldtown Folks* (Boston, 1869), p. 64.

51. Ibid.
52. Mrs. Basil Hall to "My Dearest Jane," Stockbridge, Mass., Oct. 2, 1827, in Una Pope-Hennessey, *The Aristocratic Journey* (New York, 1931), p. 78.
53. Ibid., p. 105.
54. Ibid., p. 78.
55. Ibid., pp. 90–1. For further discussion of social rituals and entertainment, see Barbara Carson, *Ambitious Appetites: Dining, Behaviour and Patterns of Consumption in Federal Washington* (Washington, D.C., 1990).
56. Robert Roberts, *The House Servant's Directory* (Boston, 1827). Roberts does not suggest that the ladies and gentlemen would be seated in separate rooms, pp. 62–3.
57. Ibid., p. 62.
58. M. A. DeWolfe Howe, *The Articulate Sisters: Passages from Journals and Letters of the Daughters of President Josiah Quincy of Harvard University* (Boston, 1946), pp. 77–82.
59. William T. Davis, *Plymouth Memories of an Octagenarian* (Plymouth, Mass., 1806), p. 330.
60. Miss Leslie, *The Behaviour Book: A Manual for Ladies* (Philadelphia, 1856), p. 34.
61. King, *Salem*, p. 107.
62. [Anna Quincy Thaxter Parsons], "A Newburyport Wedding One Hundred Years Ago," *Essex Institute Historical Collections*, Oct. 1951, p. 316.
63. King, *Salem*, p. 103.
64. Leslie, *Behaviour Book*, p. 34.
65. King, *Salem*, pp. 105–6.
66. Ibid., p. 105.
67. Catherine Beecher, *A Treatise on Domestic Economy* (Boston, 1841), p. 351.
68. Susan H. Dickinson, "Two Generations of Amherst Society," in *Essays on Amherst's History* (Amherst, Mass., 1978), p. 174.
69. See, for example, Jonathan Sayward diary, Jan. 17, 1789; Sept. 17, 1790; and Jan. 5, 1792.
70. RHB, April 29, 1813.
71. RHB, Jan. 6 and 7, 1814; several references in 1812; Jan. 17, 1810; Sept. 28, 1811; and March 10 and May 23, 1812.
72. Bentley, vol. 2, p. 207; entry for Dec. 6, 1796.
73. Emery, *Reminiscences*, p. 244.
74. Beecher, *Treatise*, p. 338.
75. Lydia Maria Child, *The Mother's Book* (Boston, 1831), p. 48.
76. Tyler, p. 233.
77. Inventory of Ebenezer Storer, Boston, 1807, Suffolk County Probate Court.
78. Inventory of William Munroe, Boston, 1814, Suffolk County Probate Court. I am grateful to Wendy Cooper for sharing this reference with me.
79. Anne Clark Kane to Harriet Clark, *Rhode Island History*, Fall 1973, p. 20.
80. Sarah Orne Jewett, *Deephaven* (1877, rpt. New Haven, Conn., 1966), p. 46.
81. Inventory of Isaac Davenport, Esq., Milton, Mass., 1828, Dedham County Probate Court.
82. Mrs. William Parkes, *Domestic Duties; or, Instructions to Young Married Ladies . . .*, 3d American ed. from the 3d London ed. (New York, 1829), p. 173.
83. Pope-Hennessy, *Aristocratic Journey*, pp. 87, 90.
84. Ibid., p. 87.
85. New Hampshire *Gazette*, March 10, 1839. The New England Glass Company in Boston also advertised "Ware loaned for parties, &c." in the *Columbian Centinel*, Jan. 5, 1825.
86. Pope-Hennessy, *Aristocratic Journey*, p. 89.
87. Roberts, *House Servant's Directory*, pp. 44–60.
88. Bentley, vol. 2, p. 188; entry for June 19, 1796.
89. Ellen H. Rollins [E. H. Arr], *New England Bygones* (New York, 1883), pp. 70–1. Examples of this type of blue-and-white-checked linen used for bed hangings survive at SPNEA, OSV, the Litchfield Historical Society, and other New England historical collections.
90. Thomas Sheraton, *The Cabinet Maker's Dictionary*, vol. 1 (London, 1803), p. 218.
91. Parkes, *Domestic Duties*, p. 173.
92. Inventory of the Estate of John Joy, Boston, Mass., 1814, Suffolk County Probate Court.
93. Stowe, *Oldtown Folks*, pp. 63–4.
94. Rollins, *Bygones*, p. 75.
95. A Lady, *The Housekeeper's Book* (Philadelphia, 1838), pp. 15–16.
96. Sarah Orne Jewett, *Deephaven* (Boston, 1877), p. 62.
97. Joyce Butler, "The Wadsworths: A Portland Family" (unpublished paper, 1986), p. 33.
98. Lydia H. Sigourney, *Sketches of Connecticut, Forty Years Since* (Hartford, 1824), p. 21.
99. Beecher, *Treatise*, p. 328.
100. Butler, "Wadsworths," p. 18.
101. Howe, 65.
102. Sarah Joiner Lyman to Melissa Joiner, Hilo, Aug. 21, 1833, and Sarah Joiner Lyman to Melissa Joiner Hall, Hilo, Oct. 21, 1850. Margaret Greer Martin, comp., *Sarah Joiner Lyman of Hawaii: Her Own Story* (Hilo, Hawaii, 1970), pp. 18, 129.
103. SSB, May 20, 1825.
104. Howe, *Articulate Sisters*, p. 196.
105. Emma Huntington Nason, *Old Hallowell on the Kennebec* (Augusta, Maine, 1909), p. 274, quoted in Laura Fecych Sprague, ed., *Agreeable Situations* (Kennebunk, Maine, 1987), p. 109.
106. Beecher, *Treatise*, p. 254.
107. "The Country Wedding," Lowell *Offering*, March 1845, p. 50.
108. RHB, Dec. 28, 1808.
109. RHB, Jan. 1, 1810.
110. RHB, June 27, 1810.
111. EPP to EWPH, Hadley, Dec. 15, 1808, PFP.
112. Bentley, vol. 4, p. 423; entry for Nov. 22, 1816.
113. RHB, Feb. 22, 1825.
114. RHB, Nov. 27, 1825.
115. "Newburyport Wedding," pp. 4, 317, 325–27.
116. NHHS.
117. "Newburyport Wedding," p. 317.
118. Pope-Hennessy, *Aristocratic Journey*, p. 81.

CHAPTER X

1. RHB, Jan. 1, 1825.
2. Quoted in the *Columbian Centinel*, Nov. 23, 1825.

3. *Massachusetts Spy,* Nov. 27, 1816.
4. Mrs. S. J. Hale, *Northwood: A Tale of New England* (Boston, 1827).
5. EPP to EWPH, Hadley, Nov. 4, 181?, PFP (box 6, folder 5).
6. Sarah J. Hale, *Traits of American Life* (Philadelphia, 1835), p. 209.
7. New Hampshire *Patriot,* Nov. 10, 1834.
8. *Diary of Sarah Connell Ayer* (Portland, Maine, 1910), p. 28.
9. Although it is interesting that a public lecture was given on Thanksgiving day, Miss Clark may have seemed a near relative to Sarah, for she was the sister of the stepmother of Sarah's beloved granddaughter, Ellen Shaw.
10. SSB, entries for Thanksgiving, 1795–1835.
11. EPP to EWPH, Hadley, Dec. 6, 1805, PFP (box 6, folder 2).
12. Caroline Howard King, *When I Lived in Salem, 1822–1866* (Brattleboro, Vt., 1937), p. 108.
13. RevTR, Nov. 6, 1806; Nov. 12, 1812; Nov. 25, 1825; and Nov. 29, 1832.
14. Sally Phelps to EPP, Boston, Dec. 29, 1801, PFP (box 10, folder 6).
15. EWPH to EPP, Litchfield, July 22, 1801, PFP (box 13, folder 1).
16. EPP to EWPH, Hadley, Sept. 18, 1801, PFP (box 6, folder 1).
17. Charles Phelps to EWPH, Hadley, Sept. 28, 1801, PFP (box 10, folder 6).
18. EPP diary, Nov. 22, 1801.
19. EPP diary, Dec. 11, 1774.
20. Christopher Columbus Baldwin, *Diary, 1829–1835* (Worcester, Mass., 1971), pp. 42–3.
21. Ibid., pp. 82–3.
22. Hampshire *Gazette,* Dec. 23, 1801; reprinted from the New York *Commercial Advertiser.*
23. King, *Salem,* pp. 108–9.
24. EPP to EWPH, Hadley, Dec. 19, 1810. PFP (box 6, folder 4). Alas, the children were unable to come home for the holiday, and when this letter was written, the pies were still unopened.
25. Greenfield *Gazette,* Nov. 19, 1804.
26. King, *Salem,* p. 111.
27. Samuel Larkin diary, Dec. 4, 1839. Larkin House, Monterey, Calif.
28. Ibid., Dec. 11, 1840.
29. Zilpah to Mary Longfellow, Dec. 3, 1845, in Joyce Butler, "The Longfellows: Another Portland Family" (unpublished paper, 1986).
30. Bentley, vol. 2, p. 458; entry for Nov. 24, 1802.
31. Bentley, vol. 3, p. 202; Nov. 27–28, 1805.
32. *Freedom's Sentinel,* Dec. 12, 1828.
33. Stowe, *Oldtown Folks* (Boston, 1869), p. 340.
34. *Massachusetts Spy,* Nov. 17, 1830.
35. Stowe, *Oldtown Folks,* p. 338.
36. Ibid., p. 341.
37. Sanger, Dec. 12, 1781.
38. *The Book of the Seasons* (Boston, 1842).
39. EPP to EWPH, Hadley, Nov. 29, 1809, PFP (box 6, folder 4).
40. Jacob Abbott, *New England and Her Institutions: By One of Her Sons* (Boston, 1835), p. 139.
41. Stowe, *Oldtown Folks,* p. 346.
42. RevTR, Nov. 28, 1833; Dec. 3, 1835; Dec. 1, 1836; Nov. 30, 1837; Nov. 29, 1838; Nov. 28, 1839; and Nov. 26, 1840.
43. Edward Everett Hale, *A New England Boyhood* (New York, 1893), p. 140.
44. RevTR, vol. 2, p. 435.
45. Abbott, *New England,* p. 139.
46. Sarah Anna Emery, *Reminiscences of a Nonagenarian* (Newburyport, Mass., 1879), p. 10.
47. E. E. Hale, *New England Boyhood,* p. 143.
48. King, *Salem,* p. 112.
49. E. E. Hale, *New England Boyhood,* p. 140.
50. Ibid., pp. 144–5.
51. Sarah Parker Rice Goodwin, "Pleasant Memories," Memoirs of Sarah Parker Rice Goodwin, 1889, Goodwin Family Papers, Strawbery Banke Museum, Portsmouth, N.H.
52. Bentley, vol. 3, p. 264; entry for Nov. 26, 1806; vol. 3, p. 63; entry for Dec. 1, 1803.
53. "Extracts from the Diary of Joseph Porter Dwinnell, 1837–1838," *Historical Collections of Danvers, Massachusetts* 26 (1938), entry for Nov. 31, 1837.
54. James R. Mellow, *Nathaniel Hawthorne in His Times* (Boston, 1980), p. 216.
55. Stowe, *Oldtown Folks,* p. 347.
56. S. J. Hale, *Northwood,* p. 110.
57. E. E. Hale, *New England Boyhood,* pp. 140–1.
58. S. J. Hale, *Northwood,* p. 116.
59. Charles Beecher, ed., *Autobiography, Correspondence, etc., of Lyman Beecher, D.D.,* vol. 1 (New York, 1865), p. 378, letter to his son Edward.
60. EWPH to EPP, Litchfield, Dec. 13, 1801, PFP.
61. Ferenc M. Szasz, ed., "John Lord's Portsmouth," *Historical New Hampshire* 44 (Fall 1989): 3, 145.
62. Abbott, *New England,* p. 138.
63. Lydia H. Sigourney, *Sketches of Connecticut, Forty Years Since* (Hartford, 1824), pp. 155–6.
64. Bentley, vol. 4, pp. 562–3, entry for Dec. 3, 1818.
65. King, *Salem,* pp. 110–11.
66. Ibid., p. 111.
67. E. E. Hale, *New England Boyhood,* p. 142.
68. Goodwin, "Pleasant Memories."
69. Ruth Henshaw, diary, Nov. 17, 1791.
70. Sanger, Nov. 28, 1782.
71. Charles Phelps to Sarah Parsons, Hadley, Dec. 15, 1796, PFP (box 10, folder 6). His mother's only comment in her diary about all this is, "In the Eve. Mr. Phelps & I visit Mr. Lyman . . . almost the whole family into town."
72. EPP diary, Nov. 25, 1798; p. 68.
73. Anna Fuller, "Old Lady Pratt," in *Pratt Portraits* (New York, 1897), pp. 240–1.
74. Abbott, *New England,* p. 138.
75. Bentley, vol. 4, p. 489; entry for Nov. 4, 1817.
76. Samuel Larkin diary, Dec. 5, 1839.
77. EPP to EWPH, Hadley, Nov. 26, 1808, PFP (box 6, folder 3).
78. Charles Lane Hanson, ed., *A Journal for the Years 1739–1803 by Samuel Lane of Stratham, New Hampshire* (Concord, N.H., 1937), pp. 21–2.
79. EPP to EWPH, Hadley, Nov. 29, 1809, PFP.

Bibliography

BOOKS

Abbott, Jacob. *New England and Her Institutions: By One of Her Sons.* Boston: R. B. Seeley and W. Burnside, 1835.

Abbott, John. *The Mother at Home; or, Principles of Maternal Familiarity Illustrated.* Boston: Crocker & Brewster, 1833.

Abell, Mrs. L. G. *The Skillful Housewife's Book; or, Complete Guide to Domestic Cookery, Taste, Comfort and Economy.* New York: D. Newell, 1846.

Adams, Hannah. *A Memoir of Miss Hannah Adams, Written by Herself, with Additional Notices, by a Friend.* Boston: Gray and Bowen, 1832.

Alcott, William A. *The Young House-Keeper; or, Thoughts on Food and Cookery.* Boston: George W. Light, 1838.

———. *The Young Man's Guide.* 1833. Rev. 14th ed. Boston: Perkins and Marvin, 1839.

———. *The Young Mother; or, Management of Children in Regard to Health.* Rev. 2d ed. Boston: Light and Stearns, 1836.

———. *The Young Wife.* Boston: G. W. Light, 1837.

Allen, Gay Wilson. *Waldo Emerson.* New York: Penguin Books, 1982.

All Sorts of Good Sufficient Cloth: Linen Making in New England, 1640–1860. North Andover, Mass.: Merrimack Valley Textile Museum, 1980.

American Ladies' Memorial: The Indispensable Home Book for the Wife, Mother, Daughter; in Fact Useful to Every Lady throughout the United States. Boston: 60½ Cornhill, 1850.

An American Lady. *The Ladies' Hand-Book of Millinery and Dressmaking, with Plain Instructions for Making the Most Useful Articles of Dress and Attire.* New York: J. S. Redfield, 1844.

Arr, E. H. [Ellen Hobbs Robbins]. *New England Bygones.* Philadelphia: Lippincott, 1883. Reprint. Stockbridge, Mass.: Berkshire Traveller Press, 1977.

Baldwin, Christopher Columbus. *Diary, 1829–1835.* Worcester, Mass.: American Antiquarian Society, 1971.

Ballard, Martha Moore. "Diary, 1795–1812." In *The History of Augusta,* edited by Charles Elventon Nash, 229–464. Augusta, Maine: Charles Nash and Sons, 1904.

Barnes, Emily R. *Narratives, Traditions and Personal Reminiscences.* Boston: G. H. Ellis, 1888.

Beecher, Catharine. *Miss Beecher's Domestic Receipt Book.* New York: Harper, 1846.

———. *A Treatise on Domestic Economy.* Boston: Marsh, Capen, Lyon and Webb, 1841.

Beecher, Catherine, and Stowe, Harriet Beecher. *The American Woman's Home.* New York: J. B. Ford and Company, 1869.

Beecher, Charles, ed. *Autobiography, Correspondence, etc. of Lyman Beecher, D.D.* New York: Harper and Brothers, 1865.

Beecher, Henry Ward. *Norwood; or Village Life in New England.* New York: Scribner, 1869.

Belden, Louise Conway. *The Festive Tradition: Table Decoration and Desserts in America, 1650–1900.* New York: Winterthur Museum, 1983.

Benes, Peter, ed. *Early American Probate Inventories: The Dublin Seminar for New England Folklife Annual Proceedings 1987.* Boston: Boston University, 1989.

———. *Foodways in the Northeast: The Dublin Seminar for New England Folklife Annual Proceedings 1982.* Boston: Boston University, 1984.

———. *House and Home: The Dublin Seminar for New England Folklife Annual Proceedings 1988.* Boston: Boston University, 1990.

———. *Old Town and the Waterside: Two Hundred Years of Tradition and Change in Newbury, Newburyport and West Newbury, 1635–1835*. Newburyport, Mass.: Historical Society of Old Newbury, 1986.

———. *Two Towns: Concord and Wethersfield: A Comparative Exhibition of Regional Culture, 1635–1850*. Vol. 1. Concord, Mass.: Concord Antiquarian Society, 1982.

Benjamin, Asher. *American Builder's Companion*. 1806. Rev. 6th ed. Charlestown, Mass., 1811. Reprint. New York: Dover Publications, 1971.

The Diary of William Bentley, D. D. 4 vols. 1911. Reprint. Gloucester, Mass.: Peter Smith, 1962.

Bishop, J. Leander. *A History of American Manufactures from 1608* to *1860*. 3 vols. Philadelphia: Edward Young, 1866.

The Book of the Seasons. Boston: B. B. Mussey, 1842.

Brewster, Charles. *Rambles about Portsmouth. First Series. Sketches of Persons, Localities, and Incidents of Two Centuries. Principally from Tradition and Unpublished Documents*. 2d. ed. Portsmouth, N.H.: Lewis W. Brewster, 1873.

Brightman, Anna. *Window Treatments for Historic Houses, 1700–1850*. Preservation Leaflet Series, no. 14. Washington, D.C.: National Trust for Historic Preservation, 1968.

Brown, Alice. *The County Road*. 1906. Reprint. Ridgewood, N.J.: Gregg Press, 1968.

———. *Tiverton Tales*. 1899. Reprint. Ridgewood, N.J.: Gregg Press, 1967.

Brown, Harriet Connor. *Grandmother Brown's Hundred Years, 1827–1927*. Boston: Little, Brown, 1929.

Brown, Sanborn C. *Benjamin Thompson, Count Rumford*. Cambridge: M.I.T. Press, 1979.

Brown, William C., ed. *The Mother's Assistant, and Young Lady's Friend*. Boston: William C. Brown. 8 vols. 1842–1846.

Bryant, Blanche B., and Gertrude E. Baker, eds. *The Diaries of Sally and Pamela Brown, 1832–1838. Hyde Leslie 1887*. Springfield, Vt.: William L. Bryant Foundation, 1970.

Bryant, William Cullen II, and Thomas G. Voss. *The Letters of William Cullen Bryant*. Vol. 1, 1809–1836. New York: Fordham University Press, 1975.

Buckingham, Joseph T. *Personal Memoirs and Recollections of Editorial Life*. Boston: Ticknor, Reed and Fields, 1852.

Buell, Joy Day, and Richard Buell, Jr. *The Way of Duty: A Woman and Her Family in Revolutionary America*. New York: Norton, 1984.

Bushman, Richard L. *The Refinement of America. Persons, Houses, Cities*. New York: Knopf, 1992.

Carpenter, Esther Bernon. *South-County Neighbors*. Boston: Roberts Brothers, 1887.

Carson, Barbara. *Ambitious Appetities: Dining, Behavior and Patterns of Consumption in Federal Washington*. Washington, D.C.: American Institute of Architects Press, 1990.

Channing, George C. *Early Recollections of Newport, R.I., from the Year 1793 to 1811*. Newport: A. J. Ward, C. E. Hammett, Jr., 1868.

Chase, Mary Ellen. *Jonathan Fisher: Maine Parson, 1768–1847*. New York: Macmillan, 1948.

Child, Lydia Maria. *The American Frugal Housewife*. Boston: Carter, Hendee and Company, 1832. Reprints. Worthington, Ohio: Worthington Historical Group, 1965; Cambridge, Mass.: Applewood Books, n.d.

———. *The Girl's Own Book*. New York: Clark, Austin and Company, 1833.

———. *The Mother's Book*. Boston, 1831. Reprint. Cambridge, Mass.: Applewood Books, n.d.

Clark, Charles E. *The Eastern Frontier: The Settlement of Northern New England*. New York: Knopf, 1970.

Cole, Arthur Harrison, ed. *Industrial and Commercial Correspondence of Alexander Hamilton, Anticipating His Report on Manufactures*. Chicago: A. W. Shaw Company, 1928.

Cook, Clarence, ed. *A Girl's Life Eighty Years Ago: Letters of Eliza Southgate Bowne*. New York: Scribner's, 1883.

Cook, Edward M., Jr. *Ossipee, New Hampshire, 1785–1985*: A History. Portsmouth, N.H.: Peter Randall for the Town, 1989.

Cooke, Edward S. *Upholstery in America and Europe from the Seventeenth Century to World War I*. New York and London: Norton, 1987.

Cooper, Grace Rogers. *The Copp Family Textiles*. Washington, D.C.: Smithsonian Institution Press, 1971.

Copley, Esther. *Cottage Comforts*. 13th ed. London: Simpkin and Marshall, 1836.

Cornelius, Mrs. *The Young Housekeeper's Friend; or, A Guide to Domestic Economy and Comfort*. Boston: John M. Whittemore, 1848.

Cott, Nancy. *The Bonds of Womanhood: "Woman's Sphere" in New England, 1780–1835*. New Haven: Yale University Press, 1977.

Cowan, Ruth Schwartz. *More Work for Mother: The Ironies of Household Technology from the Open Hearth to the Microwave*. New York: Basic Books, 1983.

Cummings, Abbott Lowell, comp. *Bed Hangings: A Treatise on Fabrics and Styles in the Curtaining of Beds, 1650–1850*. Boston: Society for the Preservation of New England Antiquities, 1961.

———. *Rural Household Inventories*. Boston: Society for the Preservation of New England Antiquities, 1964.

Davidson, Caroline. *A Woman's Work Is Never Done: A History of Housework in the British Isles, 1650–1950*. London: Chatto and Windus, 1982.

Davis, William T. *Plymouth Memories of an Octagenarian*. Plymouth, Mass.: Memorial Press, 1906.

Diary of Sarah Connell Ayer. Portland, Maine: Lefavor-Tower Company, 1910.

Dow, George Francis. *The Arts and Crafts in New England, 1704–1775*. Topsfield, Mass.: Wayside Press, 1927. Reprint. New York: DaCapo Press, 1967.

———. *The Holyoke Diaries, 1709–1856.* Salem, Mass.: Essex Institute, 1911.

Downing, Alexander Jackson. *The Architecture of Country Houses.* 1850. Reprint. New York: Dover Publications, 1969.

Drake, Samuel Adams. *Old Landmarks of Boston.* Boston: Little, Brown, and Co., 1900.

Dr. Bentley's Salem: Diary of a Town. Salem: Essex Institute, 1977.

Dublin, Thomas, ed. *Farm to Factory: Women's Letters, 1830–1860.* New York: Columbia University Press, 1981.

Dudden, Faye E. *Serving Women: Household Service in Nineteenth Century America.* Middletown, Conn.: Wesleyan University Press, 1981.

Dwight, Timothy, Rev. *Travels in New England and New York,* 4 vols. Cambridge, Mass.: Belknap Press, 1960.

Earle, Alice Morse. *Customs and Fashions of Old New England.* New York: Charles Scribners' Sons, 1893.

———. *Diary of Anna Green Winslow, a Boston School Girl of 1771.* Boston and New York: Houghton, Mifflin and Company, 1894.

———. *Home Life in Colonial Days.* New York: Grosset and Dunlap, 1898.

Eastman, Sophie C. *In Old South Hadley.* Chicago: Blakely Printing Company, 1912.

Eisler, Benita, ed. *The Lowell Offering: Writings by New England Mill Women, 1840–1845.* New York: Harper Colophon Books, 1977.

Emery, Sarah Anna. *My Generation.* Newburyport, Mass.: Moses H. Sargent, 1893.

———. *Reminiscences of a Nonagenarian.* Newburyport, Mass.: William H. Huse and Company, 1879. Reprint. Bowie, Md.: Heritage Books, 1978.

The Experienced American Housekeeper, or Domestic Cookery Formed on the Principles of Economy for the Use of Private Families. New York: Johnstone & Van Norden, 1823.

Farrar, Mrs. John. *The Young Lady's Friend.* Rev. ed. New York: Samuel and William Wood, 1849.

Fisher, David Hackett. *Growing Old in America.* New York: Oxford University Press, 1977.

Flaherty, David H. *Privacy in Colonial New England.* Charlottesville: University Press of Virginia, 1972.

Forbes, Harriette M., ed. *The Diary of Rev. Ebenezer Parkman of Westborough, Mass. for the Months of February, March, April, October and November 1737, November and December of 1778, and the Years of 1779 and 1780.* Westborough, Mass.: Westborough Historical Society, 1899.

———. *The Hundredth Town: Glimpses of Life in Westborough, 1717–1817.* Boston: Press of Rockwell and Churchill, 1889.

Fowler, John, and John Cornforth. *English Decoration in the Eighteenth Century.* Princeton, N.J.: Pyne Press, 1974.

Fuller, Anna. *Pratt Portraits.* New York: G. P. Putnam's Sons, 1897.

Fuller, Elizabeth. "Diary." In Francis Everett Blake, *History of the Town of Princeton, Massachusetts.* Vol. 1, 302–23. Princeton, Mass.: 1951.

Garrett, Elisabeth Donaghy. *At Home: The American Family, 1750–1870.* New York: Abrams, 1990.

Garrison, J. Ritchie. *Landscape and Material Life in Franklin County, Massachusetts, 1770–1860.* Knoxville: The University of Tennessee Press, 1991.

[Gilman, Samuel]. *Memoirs of a New England Village Choir, with Occasional Reflections. By a Member.* Boston: S. G. Goodrich, 1829.

Goodrich, Charles A. *The Family Encyclopedia; or Compendium of Useful Knowledge.* Hartford, Conn.: Wm. Jas. Hamersley, 1850.

Goodrich, S[amuel] G. [Peter Parley]. *Peter Parley's Method of Teaching Arithmetic.* Boston: Cater and Hendee, 1834.

———. *Recollections of a Lifetime; or, Men and Things I Have Seen.* New York: Arundel Print, 1856.

———. *A System of Universal Geography, Popular and Scientific.* Boston: Carter, Hendee & Co., 1832.

Gregg, Edith E. W., ed. *The Letters of Ellen Tucker Emerson.* 2 vols. Kent, Ohio: Kent State University Press, 1982.

Grier, Katherine C. *Culture and Comfort: People, Parlors, and Upholstery, 1850–1930.* Rochester, N.Y.: Strong Museum, 1988.

Griffin, S. G. *A History of the Town of Keene.* Keene, N.H.: Sentinel Publishing Company, 1904. Reprint. Bowie, Md.: Heritage Books, 1980.

Groneman, Carol, and Mary Beth Norton, eds. *"To Toil the Livelong Day": America's Women at Work, 1780–1980.* Ithaca, N.Y.: Cornell University Press, 1987.

Gross, Robert. *The Minutemen and Their World.* New York: Hill and Wang, 1976.

Grover, Kathryn, ed. *Dining in America, 1850–1900.* Amherst: University of Massachusetts Press, 1987.

Hale, Edward Everett. *A New England Boyhood.* New York: Cassell Publishing Company, 1893.

Hale, Mrs. S. J. *The Good Housekeeper; or, The Way to Live Well and to Be Well While We Live.* Boston: Weeks, Jordan and Company, 1839.

———. *Northwood: A Tale of New England.* 2 vols. Boston: Bowles and Dearborn, 1827.

Hanson, Charles Lane, ed. *A Journal for the Years 1739–1803 by Samuel Lane of Stratham, New Hampshire.* Concord, N.H.: New Hampshire Historical Society, 1937.

Harris, Amanda B. *Old School Days.* Chicago: Interstate Publishing Company, 1886.

Hartley, Miss Florence. *The Ladies' Handbook of Fancy and Ornamental Work.* Philadelphia: J. W. Bradley, 1859.

Heninger, Mary Lynn Stevens. *A Century of Childhood, 1820–1920.* Rochester, N.Y.: Strong Museum, 1984.

Holt, Mrs. Elizabeth F. *From Attic to Cellar; or, Housekeeping Made Easy.* Salem, Mass.: Salem Press, 1892.

Howe, Julia Ward. *Reminiscences, 1819–1899.* Boston: Houghton, Mifflin, 1900.

How to Do Things Well and Cheap, for Domestic Use. By One Who Knows. Boston: Tappan, 1845.

Howe, M. A. DeWolfe, ed. *The Articulate Sisters: Passages from Journals and Letters of the Daughters of President Josiah Quincy of Harvard University.* Cambridge: Harvard University Press, 1946.

Howland, Mrs. E. A. *The New England Economical Housekeeper and Family Receipt Book.* Worcester, Mass.: S. A. Howland, 1845.

Hubka, Thomas C. *Big House, Little House, Back House, Barn: The Connected Farm Buildings of New England.* Hanover, N.H.: University Press of New England, 1984.

Jewett, Sarah Orne. *Country By-Ways.* Boston: Houghton, Mifflin and Company, 1881.

———. *The Country of the Pointed Firs.* Boston and New York: Houghton, Mifflin and Company, 1896.

———. *Deephaven.* Boston: James R. Osgood and Company, 1877.

Jones, Alice Hanson. *American Colonial Wealth: Documents and Methods.* 3 vols. New York: Arno Press, 1977.

Jones, Alice J. *In Dover on the Charles.* Newport, R.I.: The Milne Printery, 1906.

Judd, Laura Fish. *Honolulu. . . .* Honolulu: Honolulu *Star Bulletin,* 1928.

Judd, Sylvester. *History of Hadley.* Springfield, Mass.: H. R. Huntting and Company, 1905.

Karlsen, Carol F., and Laurie Crumpacker. *The Journal of Esther Edwards Burr, 1754–1757.* New Haven: Yale University Press, 1984.

King, Caroline Howard. *When I Lived in Salem, 1822–1866.* Brattleboro, Vt.: Stephen Day Press, 1937.

Kissam, Richard S., M.D. *The Nurse's Manual and Young Mother's Guide.* Hartford, Conn.: Cooke and Company, 1834.

The Ladies' Hand-Book of Baby Linen . . . with Additions by an American Lady. New York: J. S. Redfield, 1844.

A Lady. [McDougall, Frances Harriet (Whipple) Green] *The Housekeeper's Book.* Philadelphia: William Marshall, 1838.

A Lady. *A New System of Domestic Cookery, Formed upon Principles of Economy, and Adapted to the Use of Private Families.* Boston: William Andrews, 1807.

A Lady. [Mrs. Rantoul]. *On the Treatment of Infants.* Boston: L. C. Bowles, 1832.

A Lady. *The Workwoman's Guide.* London: Simpkin, Marshall and Company, 1838. Reprint. Guilford, Conn.: Old Sturbridge Village and Opus Publications, 1986.

A Lady. *The Young Lady's Friend.* Boston: American Stationer's Company, 1837.

The Ladies' Indispensable Assistant. New York: Published at 128 Nassau St., 1852.

The Ladies' Work-Table Book, Containing Clear and Practical Instructions in Plain and Fancy Needlework, Embroidery, Knitting, Netting and Crochet with Numerous Engravings, Illustrative of the Various Stitches in Those Useful and Fashionable Employments. Philadelphia: G. B. Zeiber and Company, 1847.

Larcom, Lucy. *A New England Girlhood.* 1889. Reprint. Boston: Northeastern University Press, 1986.

Larkin, Jack. *Children Everywhere.* Sturbridge, Mass.: Old Sturbridge Village, 1987.

———. *The Reshaping of Everyday Life, 1790–1840.* New York: Harper and Row, 1988.

Lasansky, Jeannette. *A Good Start: The Aussteier or Dowry.* Lewisburg, Penn.: Oral Traditions Project, 1990.

Leavitt, Judith Walzer. *Brought to Bed: Childbearing in America, 1750–1950.* New York: Oxford University Press, 1986.

Lee, Eliza Buckminster. *Sketches of a New England Village in the Last Century.* Boston: James Munroe and Company, 1838.

Lesley, Susan I. *Recollections of My Mother, Anne Jean Lyman of Northampton.* Boston: Houghton, Mifflin and Company, 1899.

Leslie, Miss [Eliza]. *The Behaviour Book: A Manual for Ladies.* 7th ed. Philadelphia: W. P. Hazard, 1853.

———. *The House Book: A Manual of Domestic Economy.* 6th ed. Philadelphia: Carey and Hart, 1843.

Little, Nina Fletcher. *Country Arts in Early American Homes.* New York: Dutton, 1975.

———. *Little by Little.* New York: Dutton, 1984.

Little, William. *The History of Warren: A Mountain Hamlet, Located among the White Hills of New Hampshire.* Manchester, N.H.: W. E. Moore, 1870.

Livermore, Mary. *The Story of My Life.* Hartford, Conn.: 1899.

Loudon, John Claudius. *An Encyclopaedia of Cottage, Farm and Villa Architecture and Gardening.* London: Rees, Orme, Brown, Green and Longman, 1833.

Lovell, Malcolm, ed. *Two Quaker Sisters: From the Original Diaries of Elizabeth Buffum Chase and Lucy Buffum Lovell.* New York: Lineright, 1937.

Ludlum, David. *The Country Journal New England Weather Book.* Boston: Houghton, Mifflin Company, 1976.

Lung, Peter. *A Brief Account of the Life of Peter Lung.* Hartford, Conn.: William S. March, 1816.

Lyman, Joseph, and Laura Lyman. *The Philosophy of Housekeeping.* Hartford, Conn.: Goodwin and Betts, 1867.

Macdonald, Anne L. *No Idle Hands: The Social History of American Knitting.* New York: Ballantine Books, 1988.

Martin, Glenna. *"Just a Housewife": The Rise and Fall of Domesticity in America.* New York: Oxford University Press, 1987.

Martin, Margaret Greer, comp. *Sarah Joiner Lyman of Hawaii: Her Own Story.* Hilo, Hawaii: Lyman House Memorial, 1970.

Martineau, Harriet. *Retrospect of Western Travel.* 3 vols. London: Saunders and Otley, 1838.

Mason, Francis, ed. *Childish Things: The Reminiscence of Susan Baker Blunt.* Grantham, N.H.: Tompson and Rutter, 1988.

Mayer, Lance, and Guy Myers. *The Devotion Family: The Lives and Personal Possessions of Three Generations in Eighteenth Century Connecticut.* New London, Conn.: Lyman Allen Museum, 1991.

Mayhew, Edgar deN., and Minor Myers, Jr. *A Documentary History of American Interiors from the Colonial Era to 1915.* New York: Scribner, 1980.

McMurray, Sally. *Families and Farmhouses in Nineteenth Century America: Vernacular Design and Social Change.* New York: Oxford University Press, 1988.

Mellow, James R. *Nathaniel Hawthorne and His Times.* Boston: Houghton, Mifflin, 1980.

Meltzer, Milton. *Tongue of Flame.* New York: Dell, 1965.

Melville, Herman. "I and My Chimney"; "The Apple Tree Table." (1853–1856) in *Selected Writings of Herman Melville.* New York: The Modern Library, 1952.

Merrifield, Mrs. *Dress as a Fine Art.* Boston: J. P. Jewett and Co., 1854.

The Mirror of the Graces. New York: I. Riley, 1815.

Mitchell, Stewart, ed. *New Letters of Abigail Adams, 1788–1801.* Boston: Houghton, Mifflin Company, 1947.

Montgomery, Florence. *Printed Textiles: English and American Cottons and Linens, 1700–1850.* New York: Viking Press, 1970.

———. *Textiles in America, 1650–1870.* New York: Norton, 1984.

Morgan, Helen, ed. *A Season in New York, 1801: Letters of Harriet and Maria Trumbull.* Pittsburgh: University of Pittsburgh Press, 1969.

[Moulton], Ellen Louise Chandler. *This, That and the Other.* Boston: Phillips, Sampson, and Company, 1854.

[Munger, Hiram]. *The Life and Religious Experience of Hiram Munger, including many singular circumstances connected with camp-meetings and revivals.* Chicopee Falls, Mass.: the author; Boston, Office of the "Crisis," 1856.

Mussey, Barrows, ed. *Yankee Life by Those Who Lived It.* New York: Alfred A. Knopf, 1947.

New England Directory, 1849. Boston: L. C. and H. L. Pratt, 1849.

Norton, Mary Beth. *Liberty's Daughters: The Revolutionary Experience of American Women, 1750–1850.* Boston: Little, Brown, 1980.

Nye, Alvan Crocker. *A Collection of Scale-Drawings, Details and Sketches of What Is Commonly Known As Colonial Furniture.* New York: William Helburn, 1895.

Oliver, Fitch Edward, ed. *The Diary of William Pyncheon of Salem.* Boston and New York: Houghton, Mifflin, 1890.

Packard, Clarissa. [Caroline Howard Gilman] *Recollections of a Housekeeper.* New York: Harper and Brothers, 1834.

Parkes, Mrs. William. *Domestic Duties; or, Instructions to Young Married Ladies. . . .* 3d American ed. from the 3d London ed. New York: J. and J. Harper, 1829.

Patterson, William D., ed. *The Probate Records of Lincoln County, Maine, 1760–1800.* Portland, Maine: Maine Genealogical Society, 1895.

Pierce, Josephine. *Fire on the Hearth: The Evolution and Romance of the Heating-Stove.* Springfield, Mass.: Pond-Ekberg Company, 1951.

Pope-Hennessey, Una, ed. *The Aristocratic Journey: Being the Outspoken Letters of Mrs. Basil Hall Written during a Fourteen Months' Sojourn in America, 1827–1828.* New York: G. P. Putnam's Sons, 1931.

Primo, Terri L. *Winter Friends: Women Growing Old in the New Republic.* Urbana and Chicago: University of Illinois Press, 1990.

Quincy, Eliza S. M. *A Memoir of the Life of Eliza S. M. Quincy.* Boston: John Wilson and Son, 1861.

Ring, Betty. *Let Virtue Be a Guide to Thee.* Providence, R.I.: Rhode Island Historical Society, 1983.

Roberts, Robert. *The House Servant's Directory. A Facsimile of the 1827 Edition.* Waltham, Mass.: Gore Place Society, 1977.

Robertson, Priscilla. *Lewis Farm: A New England Saga.* Norwood, Mass.: privately printed, 1950.

Root, Grace Cogswell, ed. *Father and Daughter: A Collection of Cogswell Family Letters and Diaries, 1772–1830.* West Hartford, Conn.: American School for the Deaf, 1924.

Rowson, Susanna. *An Abridgement of Universal Geography.* Boston: John West, [1805].

Salmon, Marylyn. *Women and the Law of Property in Early America.* Chapel Hill: University of North Carolina Press, 1986.

Schauffler, Robert Haven. *Thanksgiving.* New York: Moffat, Yard and Company, 1907.

The Seamstress. . . . New York: J. S. Redfield, 1847.

Sedgewick, Catherine. *Life and Letters,* ed. by Mary E. Dewey. New York: Harper and Brothers, 1872.

Shattuck, Lemuel. *The Domestic Book-Keeper and Practical Economist. . . .* Boston: Published by the Author, 1843.

Sheldon, Asa. *Life of Asa G. Sheldon: Wilmington Farmer.* Woburn, Mass.: E. T. Moody, 1862. Reprinted as *Yankee Drover.* Hanover, N.H.: University Press of New England, 1988.

Sheldon, George. *A History of Deerfield, Massachusetts.* 2 vols. 1895–96. Reprint. Somersworth, N.H.: New Hampshire Publishing Company; Deerfield, Mass.: Pocumtuck Valley Memorial Association, 1972.

Sheraton, Thomas. *The Cabinet Maker's Dictionary.* London, 1803. Reprint. New York: Praeger, 1970.

[Sigourney, Mrs. Lydia] *Sketches of Connecticut Forty Years Since.* Hartford: Oliver D. Cooke and Sons, 1824.

———. *Letters to Young Ladies.* New York: Harper and Brothers, 1838.

An Orphan. [Amelia Simmons]. *American Cookery.* Hartford: Hudson and Goodwin, 1796. Reprint. New York: Oxford University Press, 1958; Mineola, N.Y.: Dover Publications, 1984.

Sklar, Kathryn Kish. *Catherine Beecher: A Study in American Domestic Economy.* New Haven and London: Yale University Press, 1973.

Sloat, Caroline, ed. *The Old Sturbridge Village Cookbook.* Chester, Conn.: Globe Pequot Press, 1984.

Smith, Barbara Clark. *After the Revolution: The Smithsonian History of Everyday Life in the Eighteenth Century.* New York: Pantheon Books, 1985.

Smith, Frank. *A History of Dover, Massachusetts. . . .* Dover: Published by the Town, 1897.

Sprague, Laura Fecych, ed. *Agreeable Situations: Society, Commerce and Art in Southern Maine, 1780–1830.* Kennebunk, Maine: Brick Store Museum, 1987.

Stabler, Lois, ed. *Very Poor and of a Low Make: The Journal of Abner Sanger.* Portsmouth, N.H.: Peter E. Randall for the Historical Society of Cheshire County, 1986.

Stewart, Randall, ed. *The Notebooks of Nathaniel Hawthorne.* New Haven, Conn.: Yale University Press, 1933.

Stiles, Henry. The *History and Genealogies of Ancient Windsor, Connecticut.* 2 vols. Hartford: Case, Lockwood & Brainard Co., 1891–92.

Stiles, Henry R. *Bundling: Its Origin, Progress and Decline in America.* 1871. Reprint. Cambridge, Mass.: Applewood Books, n.d.

Stowe, Harriet Beecher. *House and Home Papers.* Boston: Ticknor and Fields, 1865.

———. *Poganuc People.* New York: Fords, Howard and Hulbert, 1878.

———. *Sam Lawson's Oldtown Fireside Stories.* Boston: J. R. Osgood, 1872.

———. *Oldtown Folks.* Boston: Fields, Osgood, 1869.

———. *The Pearl of Orr's Island.* Boston: Houghton, Mifflin, 1884.

Strasser, Susan. *Never Done: A History of American Housework.* New York: Pantheon Books, 1982.

Swan, Susan Burrows. *Plain and Fancy: American Women and Their Needlework, 1750–1850.* New York: Holt, Rinehart and Winston, 1977.

Tarbox, Increase N., ed. *Diary of Thomas Robbins, D.D., 1796–1854.* 2 vols. Boston: T. Todd, 1882.

Taves, Ann, ed. *Religion and Domestic Violence in Early New England: The Memoir of Abigail Abbott Bailey.* Bloomington and Indianapolis: Indiana University Press, 1989.

Taylor, Jane. *Wouldst Know Thyself: Of the Outlines of Human Physiology, Designed for the Youth of Both Sexes.* New York: George F. Cooledge and Brother, 1858.

Teller, Thomas, ed. *The Pleasant Journey, and Scenes in Town and Country.* New Haven: S. Babcock, 1845.

Temple, J. J. *History of the Town of Whately, Mass. . . . 1660–1871.* Boston: Printed for the Town by T. R. Marvin & Son, 1872.

Temple, Josiah Howes, and George Sheldon. *A History of the Town of Northfield, Massachusetts. . . .* 2 vols. Albany, N.Y.: J. Munsel, 1875.

Thompson, Benjamin [Count Rumford]. *Collected Works of Count Rumford.* Edited by Sanborn C. Brown. 2 vols. Cambridge, Mass.: Belknap Press, 1969.

Trollope, Frances. *Domestic Manners of the Americans.* London and New York, 1832.

Trumbull, J. Hammond. *The Memorial History of Hartford County, Connecticut, 1633–1884.* 2 vols. Boston: Edward L. Osgood, 1886.

Trumbull, James R. *History of Northampton.* 2 vols. Northampton, Mass.: Gazette Printing Company, 1898.

Tryon, Rolla Milton. *Household Manufactures in the United States, 1640–1860.* Chicago, 1917. Reprint. New York: Augustus M. Kelley, 1966.

Tucker, William Howard. *History of Hartford, Vermont, July 4, 1761–April 4, 1889.* Burlington, Vt.: 1889.

[Philleo, Calvin Wheeler]. *Twice Married: A Story of Connecticut Life.* New York and London: Dix and Edwards, 1855.

Tyler, Mary Palmer. *Grandmother Tyler's Book: The Recollections of Mary Palmer Tyler (Mrs. Royall Tyler), 1775–1866.* Edited by Frederick Tupper and Helen Tyler Brown. New York: G. P. Putnam's Sons, 1925.

Ulrich, Laurel Thatcher. *Good Wives: Image and Reality in the Lives of Women in Northern New England, 1650–1750.* New York: Knopf, 1982.

———. *A Midwife's Tale: The Life of Martha Ballard, Based on Her Diary, 1785–1812.* New York: Knopf, 1989.

Underwood, Francis W. *Quabbin: The Story of a Small Town, with Outlooks on Puritan Life.* Boston: Lee and Shepard, 1893. Reprint. Boston: Northeastern University Press, 1986.

Vanderpoel, Emily Noyes. *Chronicles of a Pioneer School.* Cambridge, Mass.: University Press, 1903.

Vaux, Calvert. *Villas and Cottages.* 1864. Reprint. New York: Dover, 1970.

Wagenknecht, Edward. *Mrs. Longfellow: Selected Letters and Journals of Fanny Appleton Longfellow (1817–1861).* New York: Longmans, Green and Company, 1956.

Walett, Francis G., ed. *The Diary of Ebenezer Parkman, 1703–1872. First Part, 1719–1755.* Worcester, Mass.: American Antiquarian Society, 1974.

Wansey, Henry. *The Journal of an Excursion to the United States of North America in the Summer of 1794.* Salisbury, Eng., 1796. Reprint. New York, 1969.

Ward, Barbara McLean, ed. *A Glimpse into the Shadows: Forgotten People of the Eighteenth Century.* Winterthur, Del.: Winterthur Museum, 1987.

Ward, George Atkinson. *Journal and Letters of the Late Samuel Curwen, Judge of Admiralty, etc., An American Refugee in England, from 1775* to *1784. . . .* New York: C. S. Francis and Company, 1842.

Ward, Gerald W. R., and William N. Hosley, Jr. *The Great River: Art and Society of the Connecticut Valley, 1635–1820.* Hartford: Wadsworth Athenaeum, 1985.

Webster, Thomas, and Mrs. William Parkes. *An Encyclopaedia of Domestic Economy.* New York: Harper and Brothers, 1848.

Wertz, Richard W., and Dorothy C. Wertz. *Lying-In: A History of Childbirth in America.* New York: Free Press, 1977.

Wheeler, Gervase. *Rural Homes; or, Sketches of Houses Suited to American Country Life.* New York: Charles Scribner, 1851.

Whitehill, Walter M., ed. *Journals of Hezekiah Prince, Jr., 1822–1828.* New York: Crown, 1965.

Williams, Susan. *Savory Suppers and Fashionable Feasts: Dining in Victorian America.* New York: Pantheon Books, 1985.

Willich, A. F. M. *The Domestic Encyclopaedia; or, A Dictionary of Facts, and Useful Knowledge.* 2 vols. London, 1802. 1st American ed. Philadelphia, 1804.

Wright, Meredith. *Put on thy Beautiful Garments: Rural New England Clothing, 1783–1800.* East Montpelier, Vt.: Clothes Press, 1990.

The Young Mother, or Management of Children. Boston: Light and Stearns, 1836.

Zeiber, G. B. *The Ladies' Work Table Book.* Philadelphia: G. B. Zeiber, 1847.

ARTICLES

Adrosko, Rita J. "Eighteenth-century American Weavers: Their Looms and Their Products." In *Irene Emery Roundtable on Museum Textiles, 1975 Proceedings.* Washington, D.C.: Textile Museum, 1976: 105–25.

Andrews, Thomas Eliot, ed. "Diary of Elizabeth Porter Phelps, 1763–1805." *New England Historical and Genealogical Register* 18–22 (1964–68).

Arthur, T. S. "The Quilting Party." *Godey's Magazine and Lady's Book,* Sept. 1849, 185–86.

Benes, Peter. "Sleeping Arrangements in Early Massachusetts: The Newbury Household of Henry Lunt, Hatter." *Early American Probate Inventories: Annual Proceedings of the Dublin Seminar for New England Folklife* 12 (1989): 140–52.

Blundell, Barbara Adams. "Setting Up House in 1821: An Account Book of Elizabeth Margaret Carter of Newburyport." *Essex Institute Historical Collections* 113 (January 1977): 1, 16–28.

Bonfield, Lynn A. "The Production of Cloth, Clothing and Quilts in Nineteenth Century New England Homes." *Uncoverings* 2 (1981): 77–96.

Boyett, Tanya. "Thomas Handasyd Perkins: An Essay on Material Culture." *Old Time New England* 70 (1980): 45–62.

Brewer, Priscilla. " 'We Have Got a Very Good Cooking Stove': Advertising, Design and Consumer Response to the Cookstove, 1815–1880." *Winterthur Portfolio* 25 (Spring 1990): 1, 35–54.

Brightman, Anna. "Window Curtains in Colonial Boston and Salem." *Antiques,* Aug. 1964, 184–7.

———. "Woolen Window Curtains: Luxury in Colonial Boston and Salem." *Antiques,* Dec. 1964, 722–7.

Brown, Jerald E. "From Shoemaker to Esquire: The Trade of Samuel Lane, 1752–1768." *Retrospection* 3 (1990): 2, 45–63.

Bushman, Richard L., and Claudia L. Bushman. "The Early History of Cleanliness in America." *Journal of American History* 74: 4, 1213–38.

Calvert, Karin. "Children in American Family Portraiture, 1670 to 1810." *William and Mary Quarterly* 98 (1988): 2, 303–94.

Clark, Christopher. "The Diary of an Apprentice Cabinetmaker: Edward Jenner Carpenter's 'Journal,' 1844–45." *Proceedings of the American Antiquarian Society* 98 (1988): 2, 303–94.

———. "The Household Economy, Market Exchange and the Rise of Capitalism in the Connecticut Valley, 1800–1860." *Journal of Social History* 13 (Winter 1979): 2, 169–99.

Cooke, Edward S., Jr. "Domestic Space in the Federal Period Inventories of Salem Merchants." *Essex Institute Historical Collections* 116 (October 1980): 4, 248–264.

Crompton, Robert Donald, ed. "A Philadelphian Looks at New England, 1820: Excerpts from 'Journal of a Journey by Sea from Philadelphia to Boston' by William Wood Thackara, 1791–1839." *Old Time New England* 50 (January–March, 1960): 3, 57–71.

[Cummings, Abbott Lowell]. "Notes on Furnishing a Small New England Farmhouse." *Old Time New England* 48 (Winter 1958): 3, 65–84, iv.

Delorme, Eleanor P. "James Swan's French Furniture." *Antiques,* March 1975, 452–61.

Derven, Daphne L. "Wholesome, Toothsome, and Diverse: Eighteenth Century Foodways in Deerfield, Massachusetts." *Foodways in the Northeast: Annual Proceedings of the Dublin Seminar for New England Folklife* 7 (1982): 47–63.

Destler, Chester McArthur. "The Hartford Woolen Manufactory: The Story of a Failure." *Connecticut History* 14 (June 1974): 8–32.

Dickinson, Susan H. "Two Generations of Amherst Society, c. 1900." In *Essays on Amherst's History.* Amherst, Mass.: Vista Trust, 1978: 168–88.

Dodge, Katherine. "A Federalist Dowry." *Old Time New England* 44 (Winter 1954): 3, 79–83.

Dublin, Thomas. "The Hodgdon Family Letters: A View of Women in the Early Textile Mills." *Historical New Hampshire* 33 (Winter 1978): 4, 283–95.

Dunn, Richard S. "Servants and Slaves: The Recruitment and Employment of Labor." In *Colonial British America: Essays in the New History of the Early Modern Era.* Edited by Jack P. Greene and J. R. Pole. Baltimore: Johns Hopkins University Press, 1984.

"Expences of the Wedding Outfit of Sarah Williams Barrett (1798–1864), Daughter of John and Martha (Dickinson) Barrett of Northfield, Mass., afterwards Mrs. Thomas Shephard, May 8, 1821." *Old Time New England,* no. 78 (January 1935): 111–12.

"Extracts from the Diary of Joseph Porter Dwinnell, 1837–38." *Historical Collections of Danvers, Mass.* (1938).

Farnam, Anne. "A Society of Societies: Associations and Voluntarism in Early Nineteenth Century Salem." *Essex Institute Historical Collections* 113 (July 1977): 3, 181–90.

Fouratt, Mary Eileen. "Ruth Henshaw Bascom: Itinerant Portraitist." *Worcester Art Museum Journal* 5 (1981–82): 57–65.

Garrett, Wendell D. "The Furnishings of Newport Houses, 1780–1800." *Rhode Island History* 18 (1959): 1–19.

G., M. R. "The Paring (Apple) Bee." *Lowell Offering* 5 (November 1845): 268–9.

Gura, Philip F. "The View From Quabbin Hill." *New England Quarterly,* March 1987, 92–106.

Haas, Robert Bartlett, ed. "The Forgotten Courtship of David and Marcy Spear, 1785–1787." *Old Time New England* 52 (Jan.–March 1962): 3, 61–74.

Hale, Sarah J., ed. *American Ladies' Magazine.* Philadelphia, 1836.

Hall, Elton W. "New Bedford Furniture." *Magazine Antiques* 113 (May 1978): 5.

Hammond, Charles A. "Producing, Selecting, and Serving Food at the Country Seat." *Foodways in the Northeast: Annual Proceedings of the Dublin Seminar for New England Folklife* 7 (1982): 80–93.

Harris, Amanda. "When This Old Stove Was New." *Country Life.* January 1915. Clipping at the Pillsbury Free Library, Warner, N.H.

Huse, Caleb and Henry. "The Coffin House in the Early Nineteenth Century." *Old Time New England* 27 (October 1936): 2, 69–72.

Jobe, Brock. "Urban Craftsmen and Design." In *New England Furniture: The Colonial Era.* Edited by Brock Jobe and Myrna Kaye, 3–46. Boston: Houghton, Mifflin, 1984.

Larkin, Jack. "The View from New England: Notes on Everyday Life in Rural America to 1850." *American Quarterly* 34 (Fall 1982): 3, 242–61.

Little, Nina Fletcher. "The Blyths of Salem: Benjamin, Limner in Crayons and Oil, and Samuel, Painter and Cabinetmaker." *Essex Institute Historical Collections* 108 (1972): 49–57.

Lockwood, Rose. "Birth, Illness, and Death in Eighteenth Century New England." *Journal of Social History* 12 (1978): 111–28.

MacFarlane, Lisa Watt. "The New England Kitchen Goes Uptown: Domestic Displacements in Harriet Beecher Stowe's New York." *New England Quarterly* 64 (June 1991): 2, 272–91.

Main, Gloria L. "Probate Records as a Source for Early American History." *William and Mary Quarterly* 31 (January 1975): 1, 88–99.

———. "Widows in Rural Massachusetts on the Eve of the Revolution." In *Women and the American Revolution.*

Martin, Margaret E. "Merchants and Trade of the Connecticut River Valley, 1750–1820." *Smith College Studies in History* 24, nos. 1–4 (Oct. 1938–July 1939).

McMahon, Sarah. "A Comfortable Subsistence: The Changing Composition of Diet in Rural New England." *William and Mary Quarterly* 42, 3d series (Jan. 1984): 1, 26–65.

Miller, George L. "Marketing Ceramics in North America: An Introduction." *Winterthur Portfolio* 19 (Spring 1984): 1, 1–6.

Monkhouse, Christopher. "The Spinning Wheel as Artifact, Symbol, and Source of Design," *Victorian Furniture,* Kenneth L. Ames, ed. Philadelphia: Victorian Society in America, 1982: 154–72.

"A Newburyport Wedding One Hundred and Thirty Years Ago." *Essex Institute Historical Collections* 87 (October 1951): 4, 309–32.

Norton, Mary Beth. " 'My Resting Reaping Times': Sarah Osborn's Defense of Her 'Unfeminine' Activities, 1767." *Signs* 2 (Winter 1976): 515–19.

Nylander, Robert Harrington. "The David Hubbard House, Hancock, New Hampshire." *Old Time New England* 49 (Winter 1959): 3, 79–83.

Ott, Joseph K. "John Innes Clark and His Family: Beautiful People in Providence." *Rhode Island History* 32 (Nov. 1973): 4, 123–132.

"The Passing of the Spare Chamber." *Atlantic Monthly* (January 1899): 140–41.

Pendery, Stephen R. "The Archaeology of Urban Foodways in Portsmouth, New Hampshire." *Foodways in the Northeast: Annual Proceedings of the Dublin Seminar for New England Folklife* 7 (1982): 9–27.

Philachantis [pseud.]. "Directions for the Breeding and General Treatment of Canary-Birds," *Ackermann's Repository,* May 1804, 77–80.

Porter, Dorothy. "The Remonds of Salem, Massachusetts: A Nineteenth-Century Family Revisited." *Proceedings of the American Antiquarian Society* 95 (Oct. 1985): 2, 259–95.

Pruitt, Bettye Hobbs. "Self-Sufficiency and the Agricultural Economy of Eighteenth-Century Massachusetts. *William and Mary Quarterly* 41, 3d series (July 1984): 333–64.

Rhodes, Elizabeth A. "The Furnishing of Portsmouth Houses, 1770–1775." *Historical New Hampshire* 28 (Spring 1973): 1, 1–20.

Roth, Rodris. "The New England, or 'Old Time,' Kitchen Exhibit at Nineteenth Century Fairs." In *The Colonial Revival in America,* 159–83. New York: Norton for the Winterthur Museum, 1985.

———. "Tea Drinking in Eighteenth Century America: Its Etiquette and Equipage." *United States Museum Bulletin 225.* Contributions from the Museum of History and Technology. Washington, D.C.: Smithsonian Institution, 1961: paper 19, 1–30.

Rumford, Beatrix T. "How Pictures Were Used in New England Houses, 1825–1850." *Antiques* 106 (Nov. 1974), 827–35.

Shammas, Carol. "How Self Sufficient Was Early America?" *Journal of Interdisciplinary History* 13 (Autumn 1982): 2, 247–72.

Spillman, Jane Shadel. "Cup Plates in Early America." *Magazine Antiques* 104 (August 1973): 2, 216–19.

Stachiw, Myron, and Nora Pat Small. "Tradition and Transformation: Rural Society and Architectural Change in Nineteenth-Century Central Massachusetts." *Perspectives in Vernacular Architecture* 3 (1989): 135–48.

Stearns, Elinor. "A Kitchen of 1825 in a Thriving New England Town." *Old Time New England* 13 (Jan. 1923): 3, 125–30.

Steinitz, Michael. "Rethinking Geographical Approaches to the Common House: The Evidence from Eighteenth-Century Massachusetts." *Perspectives in Vernacular Architecture* 3 (1989): 16–26.

Sturgis, Elizabeth Orne. "Recollections of the 'Old Tucker House,' 28 Chestnut Street, Salem." *Essex Institute Historical Collections* 74 (April 1938): 2, 108–41.

Sweeney, Kevin M. "Furniture and the Domestic Environments of Wethersfield, Connecticut, 1639–1800." *Connecticut Antiquarian* 36 (Dec. 1984): 2, 10–39.

Szasz, Ferenc M. "John Lord's Portsmouth." *Historical New Hampshire* 44 (Fall 1989): 3, 142–3.

Teller, Barbara Gorely. "Ceramics in Providence, 1750–1800." *Antiques* 94 (October 1968): 570–7.

Ulrich, Laurel Thatcher. "Housewife and Gadder: Themes of Self-Sufficiency and Community in Eighteenth-Century New England." In *"To Toil the Livelong Day": America's Women at Work, 1780–1980.* Edited by Carol Groneman and Mary Beth Norton. Ithaca: Cornell University Press, 19.

Vickers, Daniel. "Competency and Competition: Economic Culture in Early America." *William and Mary Quarterly* 47, 3d series (Jan. 1990): 1, 3–29.

Ward, Barbara McLean. "Women's Property and Family Continuity in Eighteenth-Century Connecticut." *Early American Probate Inventories: Annual Proceedings of the Dublin Seminar for New England Folklife* 12 (1989): 74–85.

Welles, Winifred. "The Downstairs Bedroom." *Atlantic Monthly,* July 1937, 65–8.

Wenger, Mark. "Gender and the Eighteenth Century Meal." In *A Taste of the Past: Early Foodways of the Albemarle Region, 1585–1830.* Edited by Barbara E. Taylor, 21–33. Elizabeth City, N.C.: Museum of the Albemarle, 1991.

Wetherell, Charles. "The Letterbook of George Boyd, Portsmouth, New Hampshire, Merchant-Shipbuilder, 1773–1775. Part I." *Historical New Hampshire* 46 (Spring 1991): 1, 3–53.

"The Will of George Rea Curwen (1823–1900)." *Essex Institute Historical Collections* 36 (1900): 253.

White, Frank G. "Stoves in Nineteenth Century New England." *Magazine Antiques* 116 (September 1979): 9, 592–9.

Zea, Philip. "Rural Craftsmen and Design." In *New England Furniture: The Colonial Era.* Edited by Brock Jobe and Myrna Kaye. 47–72. Boston: Houghton, Mifflin, 1984.

NEWSPAPERS

Columbian Centinel, Boston, 1805–35.

Connecticut *Courant,* Hartford, 1768–1820.

Farmer's Monthly Visitor, Concord, N.H., 1840–41.

Freedom's Sentinel, Athol, Mass., 1828.

Greenfield *Gazette,* Greenfield, Mass., 1792–1820.

Hampshire *Gazette,* Northampton, Mass., 1788–1828.

Massachusetts Spy, Worcester, Mass., 1800–50.

New England Farmer, Boston, 1820–42.

New Hampshire *Gazette,* Portsmouth, N.H., 1757–1839.

New Hampshire *Patriot and State Gazette,* Concord, N.H., 1819.

New Hampshire *Sentinel,* Keene, N.H., 1817.

Portsmouth *Oracle,* Portsmouth, N.H., 1798–1806.

Providence *Daily Journal,* Providence, R.I., 1831.

Providence *Gazette,* Providence, R.I., 1806–30.

MANUSCRIPTS

American Antiquarian Society, Worcester, Mass.
- Alden Proof Book
- Salisbury Family Papers
- Ward Family Papers

Amherst College Library, Amherst, Mass.
- Phelps Family Papers

Baker Library, Harvard Business School, Cambridge, Mass.
- Jacob Wendell Papers

New Hampshire Historical Society, Concord, N.H.
- Lane Family Papers
- Langdon Papers
- Letterbook (transcript) of Governor John Wentworth, 1768–1820

Old Sturbridge Village, Sturbridge, Mass.
- Reminiscence of Lyndon Freeman, 1811–60
- Diary of Horace Clark, 1836–37

Pocumtuck Valley Memorial Association, Deerfield, Mass.
- Hoyt Family Papers
- Dickinson Family Papers
- "The Life, from birth, of a child of cultured parents of means." Memorandum of Elizabeth B. Leonard, 1841–1850.

Portsmouth Athenaeum Manuscript Collections, Portsmouth, N.H.
- Warner House Papers
- Wendell Family Papers MS. 25
  - Jacob Wendell: Diary
  - Jacob Wendell: Daniel St. Market Records

Rhode Island Historical Society, Providence, R.I.
- Correspondence and Family Papers of John Inness Clark
- Sullivan Dorr Papers
- Carrington Papers
- Providence Mutual Fire Insurance Company Policy Books

Strawbery Banke, Inc., Portsmouth, N.H.
- Chase Family Papers

Yale University Library, New Haven, Conn.
- Silliman Papers

ACCOUNT BOOKS

Anonymous Roxbury, Mass., upholsterer, 1841–45. Formerly owned by the Roxbury Historical Society, since destroyed by fire.

Mary Barrell, York, Maine, 1831–51. Society for the Preservation of New England Antiquities.

Henry Cate, blacksmith and ironmonger, Portsmouth, N.H. [1807–17]. Portsmouth Athenaeum.

George Davidson, painter, Boston, 1796–97. Old Sturbridge Village.
John Doggett, looking glass, carpet, and print dealer, Boston, 1822–24. Letter-book, Winterthur Museum Library.
Sullivan Dorr, Providence, R.I. 1819–49. Family Account Book, Brown University Library
Diadama Harwood, farmer's wife and dressmaker, Bennington, Vt., 1825. Winterthur Museum Library.
Nathan Howe, farmer, Shrewsbury, Mass., 1849. Privately Owned.
William Jones, tavern keeper, Rye, N.H., 1761–1800. Rye Historical Society.
Ruby Packard, housekeeper, Cummington, Mass., 1818–28. Pocumtuck Valley Memorial Association, Henry N. Flynt Library, Deerfield, Mass.
Samuel Perkins painter, Boston, 1811–24, Baker Library, Harvard Business School, Cambridge, Mass.
Samuel Pierce, Jr., metalworker and stove dealer, Greenfield, Mass., 1834–35. Historic Deerfield, Henry N. Flynt Library, Deerfield, Mass.
Asa Talcott, tailor, Glastonbury, Conn., w. 1773–85. Connecticut Historical Society.

DIARIES

Ruth Henshaw Bascom, Leicester, Gerry, and Ashby, Mass., and elsewhere, 1794–1847. American Antiquarian Society.
David Brown, 1791. Westmoreland, N.H., and Hubbardston, Mass. American Antiquarian Society.
Sarah Snell Bryant (1766–1847), Cummington, Mass., 1794, Bryant Homestead, Trustees of Reservations; 1796–1835, Houghton Library, Harvard University.
Katherine Henshaw, Leicester, Mass., 1804–05. American Antiquarian Society.
Samuel Larkin, Portsmouth, N.H., 1839–49. Larkin House, Monterey State Historic Park, California State Park System.
Julia Evelina Smith. Translation from French by Paige Adams Savery. Connecticut Historical Society.
Jonathan Sayward, York, Maine, 1760–99. American Antiquarian Society. Transcript at Society for the Preservation of New England Antiquities.
Jacob Wendell, Portsmouth, N.H., 1829. Portsmouth Athenaeum.
Mary Hoyt Wilson, Hoyt Family Papers, Pocumtuck Valley Memorial Association.

PROBATE RECORDS

Hampshire County, Mass.
Typescripts of all Deerfield inventories, 1750–1800, Henry N. Flynt Library, Historic Deerfield, Inc.
Jonathan Ashley, Deerfield, 1787
Peter Bryant, Cummington, 1820
John Catlin, Deerfield, 1766
John Hinsdale, Deerfield, 1788
Samuel Munn, Jr., Greenfield, account taken 1784
Ebenezer Snell, Cummington, 1813
Rockingham County, N.H.
Katherine Dean, will, proved 1766
George Jaffrey, 1750
Samuel Moffatt, 1768
John Moffatt, 1786
John Peirce, 1815
Suffolk County, Mass.
James Bowdoin, 1811
David Hinckley, 1825
John Joy, 1814
John Osborne, inventory, 1819
Daniel Sargent
David Spear (21949), inventory, 1803 v. 101, p. 459
David S. Spear (22508, non compos mentis), inventory, 1806 v. 104, p. 1; guardian's account, v. 104, pp. 13–15
Isaac Stevens (32220), v. 116, p. 214.
Worcester County, Mass.
Transcript of all room-by-room inventories taken before 1850, compiled by William Wallace.
York County, Maine
Jonathan Sayward, will, d. 1797

UNPUBLISHED PAPERS

Joyce Butler. "The Longfellows: Another Portland Family." 1986.
———. "The Wadsworths: A Portland Family." 1986.
Mary Eileen Egan. "Ruth Henshaw Bascom: New England Portraitist." Honors thesis, College of the Holy Cross, 1980.
Sarah L. Giffen. "And Mr. Wildes Sailed for the West Indies." 1987.
Debra Hashim. "Bed Hangings for the John Brown House: An Inventory Study." Paper prepared for the Rhode Island Historical Society, January 1980.
Helen Roelker Lessler. "The World of Abigail Brackett Lyman." Master's thesis, Tufts University, 1986.
Helen B. Lewis. "Textiles Owned in Wethersfield, 1750–1800, As Evidenced by Contemporary Estate Inventories." Webb-Deane-Stevens Museum, May 1981.

Index

Numerals in *italics* indicate illustrations.

abolition, 11
account books, 166–7
Adams, Abigail, 97, 122
Adams, John Quincy, 235
Adams, Richard, 184–5
adopted children, 24–6, 36
advice books, 113, 120, 197, 212–13
agriculture, 41–2, 63, 77–8, 80–1, 116, 164, 181, 207–8; food exchanges, 193–5; laborers, 41–3, *43*; work exchanges, 164, 165, 166
alcohol, 35, 36, *36*, 114, *128*, 193, 194, 227, 238, 244, 260, 276
Alcott, William A., xi, 145
Alexander, Francis, painting by, *43*
Allen, Frances and Mary, 13; photograph by, *270*
American Revolution, 82, 169, 170, 178, 227, 263
Amherst, Massachusetts, *39*, 244
antiquarians, 4–6, 11–19
Antrim, New Hampshire, 168
ants, 126
apples, 183, 197, 207, 210–11, 225, 226
applesauce, 210–11
apprentices, 43, 44
architecture, 6–7, 16, *70–1*, 72, 98; *see also* house(s)
Arnold, Ann, *44*
art, domestic images in, xi, xiii, xiv, 11–19, 45, 47, 167; *see also specific artists*
Arthur, T. S., 229–30
attics and garrets, 14, *14*, 23, 97, 128, 174, 203
Augusta, Maine, 198, 204
autumn, 77, 120, 128–9, 178, 222
Ayer, Sarah Connell, 77, 264

baby clothes, xi, 14, 31, 158, 162, 171
Bailey, Abigail, 49
Baker, Alice, *19, 168*
baking, 140, 161, 196–7, *197*, 198–9, *199*, 270–1
Baldwin, Christopher Columbus, 77, 234, 238, 267, 279
Ballard, Martha, 93, 198, 204, 223
Ballou's Pictorial, 101, 272
barn(s), 6, 23, 81, 116; raising, 226, 227
Barre, Massachusetts, 72
Barrell, Mary and Elizabeth, 7
Bascom, Ezekiel Lysander, xii, 24–5, 86
Bascom, Ruth Henshaw, xi, xii–xiv, *xiv*, 24–5, 40, 54–5, 73, 167, 234; diary of, xii–xiv, 25, 28, 37, 45, 80, 91, 94, 98, 106, 111–14, 129, 132, 134, 142, 150, 159–60, 174, 176–7, 189, 201, 203, 209–10, 216, 223–4, 231, 235, 237, 245, 258, 261
bathing, 85, 143, 144–8, *144–8*
beaufat, 236, *236*, 237, *237*, 247, 248, 249
bed(s), 30–2, 55, 56, 61, 62, 68, 69, 72, 148, 247, 248; best, 236, 251–2; childbirth, 27–30, *30*; cradles, 6, 16, 31–2, *32*, 37, *38*; curtains and hangings, 94–5, *94–5*, 123–4, 252; on fire, 93–5, *95*; lying in, *124*; making, 113, 116, 117, 123–4; shared, 47, 93, 95–6, 235; trundle-, 31, 93; warming, 95–6
bedbugs, 126
bedding, xi, 15, 56–7, 60, 61–2, 64, 68–9, 88, 122–4, 133, *133*, 143; cleaning, 104, 122–4, 133, 148; warming, 95–6
bedroom(s), 17, *29–30*; bathing in, 145–6; best room, 236, 251–2; for childbirth, 27–31; for food storage, 96–7; warming of, 78, 88, 92–6
Beecher, Catharine, xi, 114, 122–3, 144, 145–6, 161, 213, 244, 255, 257; *A Treatise on Domestic Economy*, 29, 52, 105–6, 135, 137, 138
beef, 190, 192, 193, 194, 203, 204, 268
bellpulls, *51*
Benes, Peter, 24
Benjamin, Asher, *American Builder's Companion*, 217
Bentley, William, xiv, 9, 32, 49, 76, 84, 94, 104, 106, 114, 192, 204, 205, 251, 259, 269, 276, 277, 281

best room, 236, 251–4
Bible, 6, 37, 255
birth(s), xii, 10, 12, 26–31, 223–4; baskets, 30
black servants, *44*, 45, 46, 48, *189*
Blake, Noah, 97–8
blinds, exterior, 128, *129*
Blunt, Susan, 110, 119, 190, 216, 236
boarders, 25, 32–3, 34–5, 132
bonnets, 13, 149, 150, 152, 153, 154, 156, 225, 227, 228; mourning, xiv, 159, 160
Boston, x, 10, 11, 16, *17*, 31, *33*, 44, 49, 54, 60, 66, 68, *70–1*, 82, 111, 122, 125, 132, 138, 147, 152–6, 160, 189, 192, 194, 199, 204, 218, 240–1, 248, 251, 253, *268*, 274
Boston Weekly Magazine, The, *112*
Boyd, George, 188
Brattleboro, Vermont, 170, 173
bread(s), 187–8, 189, 191, 192, 212, 218, 229, 243; baking, 196–7, *197*, 198–9
breakfast, 187–8, *188*, 192, 223
breastfeeding, 26, 29, 30, *30*, 31, 158
brick ovens, 197–9, 205, *215*
Bristol, Rhode Island, 144
British ceramics, 72
British textile industry, 149, 162, 168–9, 171–2
brooms, 118–20
Brown, Alice, xi, 222
Brown, Moses, *35*, 78
Brunton, Richard, paintings by, *123*, *252*
Bryant, Austin, 36, 159, 180, 181, 208, 264, 266
Bryant, Cyrus, 36, 158, 159, 264
Bryant, Peter, 24, 33, 35, 36, 39, 152, 158–9, 178, 180, 200, 222, 264
Bryant, Rush, 36, 152, 158–9, 266
Bryant, Sarah Snell, xi–xii, *xii*, xiv, 24, 26–7, 33, 47, 54, 73, 116–18, 222; diary of, xi–xii, 27–31, 35, 49–51, 65, 77–8, 83, 97, 103, 111, 118, 126, 128, 130, 133–5, 139, 140, 42, 149, 151–2, 155–61, 163, 166, 177–82, 197–212, 224, 225, 228–9, *230*, 233, 256, 264–6
Bryant, William Cullen, xii, 35–6, 152, 155, 158, 159, 210, 264
Bumstead & Son Warehouse, Boston, *70*
bundling, 95–6
Burnham house, Melrose, Massachusetts, *125*
butchering, 117–18, 164–5, 187, 197, 203–4, 268
butter, 104, 163, 193, 199–202, *200–2*
Cabot, James Elliott, watercolor by, *8*
cake(s), 196–9, 212, 229, 234, 241–3; wedding, 199, 257, 259–60
candle(s), 72, 105, 106–8, *108*, 109, *109*, 110–12, 238; dipped, 13, 50, 109–11, 140; making, 109–11, 117; molded, 110, 111
candlesticks, 67, 108, *108–9*, 111–13, 248
candlewood, 107
carding wool, 174, 179
Carey house, Chelsea, Massachusetts, *219*
carpets, 70, 100, 103, 119, 121–2, 174, 179, 181
Carter, Elizabeth Margaret, 68–72, 259
cast-iron stoves, 99–100, *100*, 101–2, 198
cellar(s), 97, *115*, 128; banking, 97–8
census, 22
chair(s), x, xi, 6, *6*, *9*, 55, 62, 64, 67–9, 72, 248; best room, 253, 254; coverings, 124, 129; Plymouth, *16*; sitting room, 255, 256; Windsor, *35*
chamber pots, 70, 105, 113, 114, 116
chambersticks, 108, *108*, *109*
Champney, J. Wells, painting by, *22*
Chandler, Winthrop, painting by, *94*
charity, 10–11, 113, 222; Thanksgiving, 277–8, *278*
cheese, 167, 192–4, 199–202, *202*, 203
chest of drawers, 57
chicken, 204, 268–70, 274–6
Child, Lydia Maria, xi, 119, 126, 136, 139; *The American Frugal Housewife*, 52, 140, 213
children, x, xi, 22–3, 26–32, 51, 54, *76*, 90, 107, 111, 132, *134*, *136*, 190, 224, 237, 253, 274, 279; adopted, 24–6, 36; birth of, xii, 10, 12, 26–31, 223–4; care of, 28–32, *29–33*; clothing for, 149, 157–62, 169, 171; death of, 30–1, 90, 94; in fires, 90–1, *92*, 93–5, 100–1, 108; tea parties of, 242–3; and transfers of property, 58–65; washing, 144, *144*, 145
chimney(s), 78–9, 85, 88, 97–102, 127, 218; fires, 91–2
Christmas, 8
churns, x, 6, 200, *200–2*
Civil War, ix, 5, 127
Clark, John Innes, 75, 152–3
cleanliness, standards of, 103–6, 118, 121, 132
clocks, 6, 16, 62, 63, 65, *137*, *238*
clothes, 10, 13, 35, 42, 44, 56, 58, 63, 78, 133, 143–62, *270*; aprons and frocks, 143, 179–80; baby, xi, 14, 31, 158, 162, 171; basic, 156–9; bonnets, xiv, 13, 149–56, 159, 160; British influence on, 10, 149, 162; children's, 149, 157–62, 169, 171; cleaning, 104–5, 130–42, *130–42*, 143, 161; cloaks, 154–6, 157, 158; cotton, 142, 156, 172, 174, 179, 182; fashion, 152–6, 160, 162; gowns, 143, 149, 150–60, 180; linen, 133, *133*, 140, 143, 147, 156, 169; mending, 161–2; men's, 143, 149, 151–62; mourning, xiv, 10, 39–40, 159–60, *160*; servants', 44, *44*, 47–8, 51, 52; sewing, 148–53, 157, *157*, 159–62, *162*, 224–5; and textile production, 148–50, 167–74, 179–82; types of, 133–4; underwear, 156–8; wardrobe composition, 148–50; wedding, 14, 159, 162; woolen, 133, 140, 149, 167–82
clotheslines, 138–9
coal, 82, 88, 90, 96, 213
coats of arms, 14
coffee, 187, 190, 194, 241–5
Coffin house, Newbury, Massachusetts, *24*, *191*, *201*
coffins, 39–41, *39–41*
Coleman, Emma, 13; photographs by, *19*, *168*, *185*
college, 22, 35–6
Concord, Massachusetts, 17, 52, 88, 98, 132
Connecticut, x, 17, 23, 32, 40, 48, 55–7, 79, 82, 91, 99, 122, 169, 252, 264
Cook, Clarence, *The House Beautiful*, *16*
cookbooks and receipts, 186, 196, 211–13
cooking, *see* food and cooking
cookstoves, 213–15, *214–15*, 216–17, *217*, 218
Copp family textiles, 172
corn, 196, 207, 208, 212; husking frolics, 44, 225–6, *226*, 227
Corné, Michel Felice, drawing by, *136*
cotton fabrics and clothing, 142, 156, 168, 172, 174, 179, 182
courtship, 95–6, 224–5, *226*, 227–30
cradles, 6, 16, 31–2, *32*, 37, *38*
credit systems, 116, 163–7, 172, *173*, 174, 193–5, 202, 221
Cummington, Massachusetts, xi, 24, 77, 83, 103, 155, 193, 206, 222, 229
cups and saucers, xi, 62, *71*, 75, *192*, 232, 236, 243–4, *245*
Currier and Ives, 4; prints, *75*
Cushing house, Hingham, Massachusetts, *4*
Cutts, Sarah, *37*, 38

dairying, xii, 62, 104, 105, 116, 117, 120, 167, 199–202, *200–2*
dancing, 225, 230, 242; parties, 257–60
Davis, William, 92, 146, 242
day laborers, 41–2, *43*, 84, 131, 166
death(s), xiv, 10, 12, 39–41, *39–41*, 53, 63; in fires, 90–1, 93, 94; of husbands, 54–5, 63; of infants, 30–1; mourning clothes, xiv, 10, 39–40, 159–60
Deerfield, Massachusetts, 13, 15, 17, *18*, 19, *19*, 46, 89, 97, 133, *168*, 171, 183, 206, 270
Denney, Samuel, 184–5
diaries, xi–xiv, 8, 81, 116–17, 166–7, 176; *see also specific authors*
Dickinson, Consider, 46, 47, 183
Dickinson, Susan, 39, 244
diet and nutrition, 84, 187–93, 218
dining rooms, 248–50
dinner, 188–91, *189–90*, 192–3, 223; parties, 240–51, *241–51*
dishes and china, 61, 62, *71*, 72, 190, *190*, 232, *245*, 246–51
dishwashing, 79, 85, 113, *115*, 117
doctors, 28, 35, 165
domestic textile production, 57, 149–50, 163, 167–71, 172–82
dower right, 62–5
dowry, 59, 62; *see also* marriage portion
drawing rooms, 252–3
dresser, *191*
dressing, *144*
dressing table, 72
dummyboards, *45*
dusting, 118–20
Dwight, Timothy, xiii, 81, 104, 155, 257–8; *Travels in New England and New York*, 84
dyes, 177–8, 180

Eakins, Thomas, *The Courtship*, 12
East Windsor, Connecticut, 79, 122
economy, x, xi, 10, 47, 73, 105, 143, 169; credit systems and work exchanges, x, 163–7, 193–5
Edouart, Auguste, silhouettes by, *33*
education, 10, 25, 32, 35–6, 44
elderly, the, 33–5, *34–5*, 36, 65, 154, 224
Election Day, 234
embroidery, *40*, 151, *160*
Emerson, Lidian, 52
Emerson, Ralph Waldo, 52, 98
Emery, David, 20–1
Emery, Sarah Anna Smith, xi, xiv, 11–12, 20–4, 33, 37–9, 44–8, 75, 119, 146, 154, 177, 188, 191, 196, 201, 205, 224, 232, 274; *Reminiscences of a Nonagenarian*, 11–12, *12*, *21*, 202
England, 10, 54, 58, 62, 82; textiles in, 149, 162, 168–9, 171–2; trade with New England, 10, *71*, 72, 169
Enneking, John, painting by, *115*
exhibitions of household objects, 15–19
extended family structure, 20–6, 30–6, 43, 221
exterminators, *126*

factories, 73, 173–4, 182
family, 20–53, 76, 103, 149, 163–4; births and child care, 26–32, *29–33*; caring for the sick, 36–9, *37–9*; extended, and shared living quarters, 20–6, 30–6, 43, 63–5, 221; fireside, *76*, 77–98, *101*, 102; and funerals, 39–41, *39–41*; portraits, *23*; and servants, 41–52, *42–51*; at Thanksgiving, 264–82; transfers of property in, 58–65; widows and elders, 33–4, *34–5*, 36; work exchanges, 163–7, 172–4
Faneuil Hall Market, Boston, *268*
Farley, James, 245
fashion, 43; clothing, 152–4, *154*, 155–6, 160, 162; household, 66–8
featherbeds, 122–3
Felton, O., engraving by, *76*
Field, Samuel, 183–4
fire(s), 10, 76–102, 107, 113, 127, 128, 140, 185–6, 197; bedroom, 78, 88, 92–6; hazards, 88–92, *90–2*, 93–5, *95*, 100–1, 108, 139, 174, 175; kitchen, 78–80, 85, 88, 89, 92; management, 84, 85, *85*, 87–8; stove, 99–102
fireboards, 127, 128, *128*, *129*
fireplace(s) and hearth(s), 6, 7, *13*, 15, 16, *16–17*, 24, 55, 63, 68, 74, 76, *76*, 77–98, *101*, 102, 103, 105, 107, 118, 127, 128, *129*, *168*, *175*, *185*, *191*, *212*, 213, 218, 253, *254*, *271*, *272*; for baking, 197, *197*, 198–9; cooking, 185, *185*, 186–7, 197–9, 213; and socializing, 239–40; technological improvements in, 99–102
firewood, 64, 80–3, *83*, 84–5, *85*, 86–8, 99, 131, 213, 214, 272
fish, 184, 187, 193, 194, 203, *204*, 205–6
Fisher, Alvin, painting by, *226*
Fisher, Jonathan, 87, 193, 210, 239
Fisher's Improved House-Keeper's Almanac and Family Receipt Book, *204*
flags, 17
flax, 13, 90, 167–80, 182
floor(s): cleaning, 113, 117, 118–22; coverings, 70, *89*, 100, 103, 119, 121–2, 174, 181
flour, 196, 197, 198, 212
food and cooking, xii, 21, 28, 50, 51, 62, 72, 77, 79–80, 85, 104, 105, 113, 116, 117, 120, 125, 140, 183–220; baking, 196–7, *197*, 198–9, *199*; and changing attitudes, 218–20; cookbooks and receipts, 211–13; cookstoves, 213–15, *214–15*, 216–17, *217*, 218; dairying, 199–202, *200–2*; diet and nutrition, 184, 187–93, 218; exchanges, 164, 184, 193–5, 201, 202; fireplace cooking, 185, *185*, 186–7, 197–9, 213; fish, 205–6; fruits, 209–11; funeral, 40–1; grocery store, 193–4, *194*, 195; maple sugaring, 208–9, *209*; meat, 202–4, *204*, 205; and socializing, 223, 226, 229–32, 234, 236–7, 240–60; in springtime, 209; storage and preservation, 96–7, 103–4, 125, 128, 184, 188, 195–6, 203–4, 207–8, 213; Thanksgiving, 261, 264–6, 267–70, *270*; vegetables, 206–8; wedding, 257–60
Forbes, Mrs. Robert Bennett, *33*
forks, 62, 72, 190, *190*, *245*, 248
Forty Acres farm, Hadley, Massachusetts, *xiii*, 25, 41–2, 60, 197
Franklin, Benjamin, 16; birthplace of, 16, *17*, 175
Franklin stoves, 99–100
freezing food, 96, 97, 103
frolics, 176, 225–6, *226*, 227–8, 232; Thanksgiving, 278–80
fruit(s), 97, 103, 128, 183, 194, 207–8, 209–11; trees, 77, 79
fuel, 82–8
Fuller, Elizabeth, 111, 176, 177
funerals, xiv, 10, 39–41, *39–41*, 53, 159, 253
furniture, 55–73; best room, 251–4; cleaning, 121, 124; dining room, 248–50; sitting room, 255–6; taste and fashion, 66–8; *see also specific furniture*

gardens, 79, 207
geese, picking, 117–18
gender roles, xi, 11, 113, 221
genealogy, 14, 281
Gill, Moses, 42
glassware, 72, 232, 236, 247–51
Glastonbury, Connecticut, 80, 164
Gleasons' Pictorial Drawing Room Companion, 262, 268, 275
Glyson, William, *94*
Godey's Lady's Book, 59, *76,* 113, 239, 263
Goodrich, Samuel, 8–9, 185, 207–8; *Recollections of a Lifetime,* 81
Goodwin, Sarah, 28, 40–1, 51, 275, 279
groceries, 193–4, *194,* 195
Gullager, Christian, painting by, *34*

Hadley, Massachusetts, xii, xiii, 25–6, 42, 60, 86, 107, 118, 152, 173, 189, 197, 204, 224, 228, 258, 266
Hale, Edward Everett, 122, 249, 273, 274, 276
Hale, Sarah Josepha: *The Good Housekeeper,* 52; *Northwood: A Tale of New England,* 263, 269, 274, 276
Hamilton, Alexander, 169
Harris homestead, Warner, New Hampshire, *215*
Hartford, Connecticut, 17, 111, 121, 192, 234
harvest, 44, 128, 261, 263
Heade, Martin Johnson, painting by, *35*
hearth rugs, 88, *89,* 100
heating systems, 76–102
herbs and spices, 194, 208
Hinckley, Benjamin, 138
historical exhibitions, 15–19
"The Hobby Horse" (painting), *113*
holidays, 8, 44, 53, 232–4, 261–82; *see also* Thanksgiving
Holten house privy, Danvers, Massachusetts, *116*
homespun textiles, 57, 167–71, 172–82
hope chests, 57–8
hospitality, 10–11, 75, 76, 80, 218, 222, 230–2, 234–7, 277–8
house(s), 6–8, 23, 58; banking of, 97–8, 103; cleaning, 103–5, 116–24; heating, 76–102; ownership of, 58, 63–5; raisings, 226, 227; shared, 20–6, 32–3, 63–5; taste and fashion, 66–8; types and construction, 6–7, 98; *see also specific houses and rooms*
housekeeping, 43–5, 54–73; hope chests, 57–8; marriage portions, 58–62, 66; servants, 41–52, *42–51;* taste and fashion, 66–8; transfers of property, 58–66
houseplants, 100, *129*
housework, 103–42; bedding, 122–4; fire and water, 113–16; laundry, 130–42; and light, 106–13; routines of, 116–18; scrubbing and scouring, 118–22; spring cleaning, 103–5, 120–4; standards of cleanliness, 103–6, 118 121, 132; summertime, 125–30
Howland, Esther, *The New England Economical Housekeeper, 212,* 214, *214*
Hoyt, Elihu, 132–3, 172, 192, 206
Hubbard, Charles, painting by, *255*
Humphrey, Reuben, *123,* 252
Humphrey, Mrs. Reuben, 252
Huntington, Betsy Phelps, 45–6, 161–2, 189, 204, 231–3, 265, 266
husking parties, 44, 225–6, *226,* 227
husk mattress, 123

Illinois, xi, 36, 73, 181, 182
illness, 9, 10, 22, 30, 36–9, *37–9*
imported textiles, 57, 148–9, 164, 169, 171–2
income-producing labor, xiii–xiv, 116, 163–7, 172, *173,* 174, 181, 193–5, 202
Independence Day celebrations, 233–4
Indians, 4, 15, 45, 277
industrialization, 5, 69–73, 99, 142, 149, 163, 173–4, 178, 182, 218–20
insects, 122, 125–6, *126,* 127
ironing, 130, *130,* 134, 140, *140,* 141, *141,* 142, 161
ironware, 62, 186–7

Jaffrey, George, 247–8
James, William T., 214
James stoves, 214–15, *214–15*
Jewett, Sarah Orne, x, xi, 3–4, 38, 52, 222, 237, 260; *Deephaven,* 249, 254
Judd, Sylvester, *History of Hadley,* 107

Keene, New Hampshire, 81, 114, 192, 204, 214, 228, 279
kerosene, 111, 112–13
King, Caroline, xi, 189, 195, 218, 242, 243, 265, 267, 269; *When I Lived in Salem,* 5, 243–4
kitchen(s), *13,* 15, 16, *16,* 17, 23, 51, 52, 75, 103, 131, *185, 191, 201, 212, 215, 217, 219,* 239–40, *271, 272;* bathing in, 146–7; changing attitudes in, 218–20; cleaning, 119, 120; cooking, 183–220; equipment, 62, 64, 65, 72, *73,* 190, *191;* fires, 78–80, 85, 88, 89, 92; scullery, *115;* spinning in, 175; visiting in, 221, 222
knitting, 116, 149, 150, *150,* 162, 173, 180, 222, 224
knives, 62, 72, 190, *190,* 248

Lady Pepperrell house, Kittery Point, Maine, *38*
lamb, 203
lamp(s), 72, 108, *109,* 112–13, *112–13;* oil, 112–13, *113;* staircase, *109*
lamp rugs, 113, *113*
land ownership, 58–65
Lane, Samuel, 43, 53, 58–9, 61–2, 79, 93, 134, 166, 186, 190, 208, 281
Larkin, Samuel, 195, 237, 269
laundry, xii, 28, 42, 50, 68, 70, 72, 85, 104, 105, *115,* 116, 117, 120, 130–42, *130–42,* 143, 161, 166, 167; hanging and drying, *136,* 137, *137,* 138–9, *142;* methods and equipment, 133–7; soap, 135–7; washing machines, *138,* 139, *139,* 140
lawyers, 35, 36, 81, 165
Lee, Eliza Buckminster, 168
Leicester, Massachusetts, 28, 37, 176, 258, 279
Lesley, Susan, 41, 78, 106, 225
Leslie, Eliza, 113, 123, 128, 145, 213, 242, 243, 276; *The American Girl's Book,* 113; *The House Book,* 98, 113, 120, 132
light, 106–13, 150, 177, 228; candle, 106–11, 112; lamp, 108, *109,* 112–13, *112–13*
Lincoln, Abraham, 263
linen(s), 168–82; bed and table, 56–7, 60, 64, 69–70, 88–9, 104, 133, *133,* 140, 142, 143, 169, 172, 179, 181; body, 133, *133,* 140, 143, 147, 156, 169

Litchfield, Connecticut, 17, 45, 161, 204, 231, 277
literature, xi–xii, 1, 10; domestic images in, 3–6, 11–12, 19, 45, 74, 76, 167; *see also specific authors and books*
Longfellow, Henry Wadsworth, "The Courtship of Miles Standish," 3, 15
Longfellow, Zilpah, 101, 254, 255, 269
looking glasses, 69, 125–6, 146, 253
looms, 176–82
lye, 135–7
"lying-in," 27–9
Lyman, Anne Jean, 28–9, 80, 155–6, 187

Maine, x, 7, 13, 17, 87, 88, 93, 184
maple sugaring, 77, 165, 187, 208–9, *209*
marking, 150
marriage(s), xiii, 12, 20, 21, 45, 54, 66, 95, 229–30, 265–6; and extended families, 20–6, 30, 32–6; and hope chests, 57–8; and housekeeping, 54–73; social order in, 8; and transfers of property, 58–66
marriage portion, 58–62, 66
Massachusetts, x–xiv, 4–5, 11–25, 32, 42, 59, 60–1, 66, 68, 77, 79, 83, 86, 91, 99, 104, 107, 132, 147, 152, 166, 169, 170, 181, 182, 204, 264
Massachusetts Spy, 169, 182, 263, 271
meat(s), 184, 186, 187, 188, 189, *189,* 190, 192–4, 198, 202–4, *204,* 205, 218, 268–9; salted, 203, 205
medical care, 10, 36–9, *37–9,* 116; and childbirth, 27–30
Memorial Hall, Deerfield, Massachusetts, 17, *19*
mending, 161–2
mental illness, 36–7, *37*
middle class, x, 51–2, 73, 105, 113, 120, 255
midwifery, 27, 28, 30, 166
Miles, Asa, 24, 54, 159–60
milk, 187–8, 191, 192, 200–2, 243
ministers, 9, 15, 32, 35, 40, 150, 155, 165, 192–3, 263, 264, 265, 273; social obligations of, 222–3, 227, 230–2, 235; wood supply of, 81, 86–7
missionaries, xi, 132, 214, 256
Moore, John, 215–216
moral values, 8–10, 105, 114, 117, 155, 169–70
mosquitoes, 126–7
moths, 104, 122, 124
Moulthrop, Reuben, painting by, *150*
mourning clothes, xiv, 10, 39–40, 159–60, *160*
Mullins, Priscilla, *15*
museums, 3, 15–19
music, 233–4, 239, 242, 253, 257–60; sheet-, *6, 90, 130, 134, 142, 233, 258*

names, 8
Newburyport, Massachusetts, 11, 12, *21, 24,* 44, 60, 68, 152, 192, 205, 224, 232, 242, 259, 260
New England Farmer, 82, 110, 126, 132, 182, 239
New Hampshire, x, xii, 7–9, 17, 28, 41, 43, 49, 58, 61, 79, 81, 89, 90, 99, 104, 114, 119, 168, 194, 215–17, 252, 264
New Haven, Connecticut, 84, 107
newspapers, xi, 44, 48, 89, 90, 91, 99, 122, 148, 169, 170, 171, 172–3, 182, 215, 261, 268
New Year's Day, 261
New York, 10, 73, 153
Northampton, Massachusetts, 28–9, 51, 78, 107, 152, 170, 187, 189, 225, 260
Noyes, Mary Fish, 55–7

Ohio, 73, 182, 265
oil lamps, 112–13, *113*
"olden time," 11–19
old maids, 21, 22
orphans, 22, 24–6, 36
Otis, Harrison Gray, 29, 241; home of, *251*
Otis, Sally Foster, 29
oven(s), 197–9, 211, *219,* 271; brick, 197–9, 205, *215;* tin kitchens, 205, *212*

Packard, Ruby, 47, 78
paintings, xi, xiv, 125; domestic images in, 4–6, 12–14, 45; dummyboards, *45;* family portraits, *23; see also specific artists*
Parkes, Mrs., *Domestic Duties,* 250, 253
Parkman, Ebenezer, 50, 79, 80, 86, 89, 97, 166, 226, 227, 231
parlor(s), 15, *15,* 16, 17, 39, *64,* 65, 66, 67, 76, 78, 99–100, *112,* 122, *127, 129,* 236, 242; back, 255–6; socializing in, 247–8, 251–60
parlor closet, 236, *236,* 237, *237,* 247–9
paternal wills, 58–9, 63–5, 158–9
patriotism and civic duty, 232–3, *233,* 234–5
Peckham, Robert, painting by, *240*
Peckham-Sawyer family, *240*
peddlers, *73,* 118, 223, 235
Pennsylvania, 88, 99
Peter Parley's First Book of Arithmetic, 194, 199
Peterson's Magazine, 59
pewter, 190, *190, 191,* 248
Phelps, Charles, xiii, 25–6, 60, 151, 207, 266, 267, 279–80
Phelps, Elizabeth Porter, xi, xii, xiv, 25–6, 33, 54, 116–17, 265–8, 279; diary of, xii, 25–6, 30–7, 41–2, 45, 48–9, 51, 60, 108, 117, 133, 141–4, 151–2, 161, 189, 191, 198–200, 207, 210, 222, 228, 258, 263, 266, 272, 281–2
Phelps, Sally Parsons, xiii, 60, 279
Philadelphia, 10, 16, 29
photography, 4, 12, 13, 280
pies, 183, 189, 197–9, 203, 207, 212, 229; Thanksgiving, 267–70, *270,* 271, 275, 276
Pilgrims, 15, *16*
Pilgrim's Progress, 10, 255
Pillsbury place, Newburyport, Massachusetts, 20–1, *21*
pitchers, *173,* 248
Plymouth, Massachusetts, 15, *16,* 17, 146, 206; Thanksgiving at, *262,* 263
politics, ix, 35, 227, 233–5
pork, 192, 193, 203, 204, 268
Portland, Maine, 101, 269
Portsmouth, New Hampshire, 28, 30, 75, 81, 83, 89–90, 99, 111, 114, 147, 192, 195, 199, 204, 217, 224, 237, 269, 275, 277
pots and kettles, 15, 62, *62,* 90, 178; bathing, 145–7; chamber, 70, 105, 113, 114, 116; cooking, *185,* 186–7, 198, 213, 214, 218; laundry, 134, *134, 137*
poultry, 194, 204, 205, 267–70, 273–5
pregnancy, 26–31, 116, 117, 131, 158
privacy, ix, 64–5, 68, *94,* 252

privies, 114–16, *116*, 146
property ownership and transfer, 58–66
Providence, Rhode Island, 75, 85, 144
puddings, 189, 191, 198–9, 212, 268–70, 275
Punderson, Prudence, *40*
Pyncheon, William, 76–7, 83–4, 89, 91, 97, 113, 236

quilting, 13, 44, 56, 57, 58, 61, 172, 221, 225–7; frame, 228, *229;* parties, 228–30; patterns, *230*

Randolph, Mary, *The Virginia Housewife,* 212–13
reading, 107, *107,* 112, 225
religion, xii, 8–10, 35, 44, 86–7, 239; ministerial obligations, 230–2; observances and ceremonies, 9–10, 15, 40, 105, 192–3, 230, 240, 254, 273
Rhode Island, 75, 85, 128, 144, 188
rising, hours of, 105–6
Robbins, Ammi Ruhamah, *150*
Robbins, Thomas, 32, 33, 48, 76, 77, 79, 81, 82, 83, 86–8, 92, 106, 111, 112, 122, 150, 209, 210, 265, 273
Robbins family textiles, 172
Robbins homestead, East Lexington, Massachusetts, *14*
Roberts, Robert, xi, 111, 112, 241, 250–1
Rogers, John, sculpture by, *15*
routines, work, 116–18
Rumford, Count, 99, 217–18
Rumford roasters and boilers, 217, *217,* 218, 271
Rundlett kitchen, Portsmouth, New Hampshire, *217*
Russell, Joseph, watercolors by, *129, 188–9*

Salem, Massachusetts, 5–6, 17, 31–2, 37, 44, 76, 83, 94, 114, *115,* 121, 147, 189, 192, 204–6, 224, 240, 243, 261, 269, 271, 277
Salisbury, Elizabeth, *34,* 75, 111
salt, 194, 203, 205, 206
samplers, 14, 151
sand, scouring, 118, 119
Sanger, Abner, 34–7, 81, 84, 85, 93, 98, 106–7, 116, 118, 120, 126, 131, 134–6, 144, 153, 187–8, 192, 196, 203–6, 208, 222, 228, 234–7, 256, 279
Sargent, Henry: *The Dinner Party, 249; The Tea Party, 241*
Sayward, Elizabeth, 63–5
Sayward, Jonathan, 44, 47, 63–5, 77, 85, 93, 225, 244–5
Sayward House, York, Maine, *7, 64*
scrubbing and scouring, 118–22
scullery, *115*
seasons, x, 7, 11, 29, 74–102, 103, 165, 184; and annual cycle of textile production, 174–82; and visiting, 222; *see also specific seasons*
self-sufficiency, x, 8, 149, 164, 167, 169–71, 182
servants, 20–1, 22, 32, 41–52, *42–51,* 78, 111, 112, 113, 131, *189,* 241
sewing, xii, xiii–xiv, 27, *29,* 44, 47, 50–1, 57, 73, 80, 116, 117, *140,* 150–1, *151,* 152–3, 166–7, 222, 224–5, 239; clothes, 148–53, 157, *157,* 159–62, *162;* mending, 161–2; quilting parties, 228–30; tailoring, 164–6
sewing machine, 142
Shapleigh, Frank, 4, 12; paintings by, *13*
shared living spaces, 20–6, 30–6, 43, 63–5
sheet-music covers, *6, 90, 130, 134, 142, 233, 258*
Sheldon, George, 17, 19, 176; *The Little Brown House on the Albany Road, 168*
Sheraton, Thomas, *Cabinet Maker's Dictionary,* 252
shower bath, 147, *148*
sideboards, 248–51
silhouettes, *33*
Simmons, Amelia, *American Cookery,* 212
sitting rooms, 99–100, 103, 221, 236, 248, 255–6
slaves, xii, 22, 43, 44, *44,* 45
sledding, 75, 83–4, 222, 237–8, 264, 279
slepping, hours of, 105–6, *108*
Smith, Julia, 79, 80, 106, 120–2, 134
Smith house, West Newbury, Massachusetts, 11–12, *12,* 21, 23
smoke domes, 99–100, *100, 109*
soap, 104, 118, 135–7; making, 117, 135–7, 187
"social childbirth" rituals, 27–8
social classes, x, 8, 10–11, 43, 45, 51–2, 73, 105, 113, 117, 120, 195, 253–5
social life, 221–60; best room, 236, 251–4; courtship, 95–6, 224–5, *226,* 227–30; dancing parties and weddings, 257–60; frolics, 176, 225–6, *226,* 227–32, 278–80; hospitality in, 222, 230–2, 235–7; husking parties, 44, 225–6, *226,* 227; ministerial and professional obligations, 230–2; in parlors and sitting rooms, 251–6; patriotism and civic duty, 232–3, *233,* 234–5; quilting parties, 228–30; tea and supper parties, 223, 224, 234, 240–51, *241–51;* visiting, 27–30, 60, 95, 152–3, 184–5, 221–5, 235–8, 256; wintertime, 237–40
Southbridge, Massachusetts, *43*
Southington, Connecticut, 23, 34, 55–7, 172
Spear, David, 66–8
Spear, Marcy Higgins, 66–8
spinning, 50–1, 57, 80, 96–7, 116, 118, 166–8, *168,* 169–75, *175,* 176–82; parties, 227, 228
spinning sheels, x, 6, 15, *15,* 16, 17, 80, 118, 167–8, *168,* 169–71, 175, *175,* 176, 178, 182, *185*
Spooner, Grover, table by, *72*
spoons, 60, 62, 190, 248
spring, 77–8, 103, 120, 178, 179; cleaning, 103–5, 120–4; foods, 209
standing stool, *92, 136*
stepfamilies, 22, 36
Stone, Ellen, 14–15, 172
stores and markets, *70–1,* 109, 152, 172–3, 182, 193–4, *194,* 195, 199, *199,* 204, 268, *268,* 269
storytelling, 107, 239
stoves, 15, 76, 99–100, *100,* 101–2, 213–14; cook, 213–15, *215,* 216–17, *217,* 218; technological improvements in, 99–102
Stowe, Harriet Beecher, xi, 79, 85, 222, 239–40, 260, 270, 271; *Oldtown Folks,* 3, 32, 41, 52, 74, 92–3, 96–7, 118, 119, 125–6, 185–6, 187, 219–20, 240, 253, 271, 273; *Poganuc People,* 109
Stratham, New Hampshire, 43, 61, 166
straw matting, 122
Sturbridge, Massachusetts, 172, 192
Sturgis, Elizabeth, 44–45, 112
Sturgis, Eliza Orne, 5–6, 76
Sturgis, Mrs. Russell, *33*

summer, x, 29, 77, 121–30, *125–9,* 174, 222
supper, 191, 192, *192,* 223; parties, 240–51, *241–51*

table(s), xi, *9,* 55, 62, 68–9, 72, *72,* 113, 253; dining, *189–92,* 248–9, *249,* 250; for ironing, 140, *141;* setting, 116, 117; for tea parties, *245*
table linens, 56–7, 60, 64, 69–70, 88–9, 104, 133, *133*
tailoring, 164–6
tallow, 108, 109, *109,* 110–11, 135–6
Taylor, Jane: *Original Poems for Infant Minds, 237; Woulds't Know Thyself, 124, 145*
tea, ix, 21, 37, 39, 112, 170, 187, 190, 191, *192,* 194, 228, 236, *252;* parties, 223–4, 234, 240–1, *241,* 242–5, *244–5*
teachers, xiii, 10
temperance, 11, *36, 128,* 218, 244, 276
textiles and weaving, xii, xiii, 13, 15, 27, 47–51, 56–7, 80, *89,* 94–7, 116, 123–4, 133, 142, 163–82; annual cycle of work, 174–82; British influence on, 149, 162, 168–9, 171–2; clothing, 143–62, 167–74, 179–82; domestic production, 57, 149–50, 163, 167–71, 172–82; dyeing, 177–8, 180; homespun, 57, 167–71, 172–82; imported, 57, 148–9, 164, 169, 171–2; and industrialization, 69–70, 142, 148–9, 163, 173–4, 178, 182; linen, 56–8, 60–2, 69–70, 133, *133,* 168–79
Thanksgiving, 8, 13, 44, 53, 97, 195, 198, 261–82; charity, 277–8, *278;* dinner, 274–6, *274–5;* food, 267–70, *270,* 271–81; frolics, 278–80; observances, 264–7; at Plymouth, *262,* 263
thermometers, 75, 76, 81–2, 93
tin kitchens, 205, *212*
transportations, 62, 164; winter, 75, 83–4, 222, 237–8, 264, 279
trunks, 55–7; hope chests, 57–8; marriage portion, 58–62
tubs, bathing, 145–7, *147*
turkey, 204, 205, 218; Thanksgiving, 264, 267–70, 273–6
tyers, 179–80
Tyler, Mary Palmer, 59–60, 76, 80, 87, 89, 93, 101–2, 146, 170–1

Underwood, Francis, *Quabbin,* 3, 167, 175, 187, 191, 193, 201, 202, 207, 211, 229
upholstered furniture, 121, 124
upper classes, x, 43, 51, 55, 73, 85, 109, 195, 212, 236, 240, 253–4
urbanization, ix, 5, 112, 115, 122, 152–3, 192, 194, 199
Usher, Anne, 144–5

Vaux, Calvert, 128
vegetables, 103–4, 128, 184–9, *189,* 190, 193, 194, 206–9
Vermont, 59, 60, 104, 170, 264
visiting, 60, 95, 152–3, 184–5, 221–5, 235–8, 256; after childbirth, 27–30; Thanksgiving, 264–82; wintertime, 237–40

wages, 73; credit systems, 116, 163–7, 172, *173,* 174, 193–5, 202, 221; for servants, 45, 46–7
wallpaper, 67–8, *70,* 127
warming pans, 15, 62, 96
Warner, New Hampshire, 17, 215
War of 1812, 169
washing, *see* laundry
washing machines, *138,* 139, *139,* 140
Washington, George, 12, 160
washstands, *144,* 145–7
washtubs, 134, *134,* 136, 137, *137*
water and wells, 79, 104, 105, 113–16, 130, *131,* 165; for bathing, 144–8; for laundry, 130–2, 134, 140; piped systems, 114, *115,* 132
water buckets, 113, *114,* 134, *134*
weather, x, xi, 7, 9, 13, 74–102, 264; autumn, 77, 120, 128–9; records, 81–2; spring, 77–8, 103–5, 120–4, 209; summer, x, 29, 77, 121, 122, 123, 124, 125–30, 174; winter, x, 7, 29, 74–102, 130–1, 195, 203–4
weaving, *see* textiles and weaving
wedding(s), 32–3, 53, 57–8, 68, 253, 257–8, *258,* 259–60; cake, 199, 257, 259–60; clothes, 14, 159, 162; and marriage portion, 58–62, 66
Wendell, John, 89–90
West, the, xii, 6, 73
Westborough, Massachusetts, 79, 86
West Newbury, Massachusetts, 11, *12,* 23
Wheeler, Gervase, *Rural Homes, 141*
Wheelock farm, Southbridge, Massachusetts, *43*
Whitefield, Edwin, watercolors by, *131*
Whittier, John Greenleaf, 3
widowhood, xii, xiii, 5, 22, 24, 33–4, *41,* 54, 184; and property ownership, 58, 63–5
Wilbur family textiles, 172
wild game, 204–5
Willey house, Crawford Notch, New Hampshire, 7, *8,* 9, *9*
Williams, Eliza, 89
Williams College, 36, 155
wills, xi, 63, 184; paternal, 58–9, 63–5, 158–9; and right of dower, 63–5
Wilson's patent stove, *100*
window(s), 104, 118, 121; coverings, *123,* 124, 125, *125,* 128, *129*
winter(s), x, 7, 29, 74–102, 103, 113, 130–1, 178, 179, 195, 203–4, 222, 231; clothing, 156, 157; heating, 76–102; socializing, 237–40
Wolcott, Eveline, 32–3
wood, *see* firewood
Wood, Thomas Waterman, "On Guard," *32*
woolen fabrics and clothing, 133, 140, 149, 167–82
Worcester, Massachusetts, 34, 91, *91,* 169, 192, 204, 232
work exchanges, 163–7, 172, *173,* 174, 221

Yale University, 81
York, Maine, *7,* 13, 17, 47, 64, 225, 244

A Note About the Author

Jane C. Nylander received her A.B. from Pembroke College, Brown University, and her M.A. from the Winterthur Program in Early American Culture, University of Delaware. From 1962 to 1969 she was curator at the New Hampshire Historical Society; from 1969 to 1985, curator of textiles and ceramics at Old Sturbridge Village and from 1985 to 1986, senior curator. From 1986 to 1992 she was the director of the Strawbery Banke Museum. She is currently the director of the Society for the Preservation of New England Antiquities, which has its headquarters in Boston, Massachusetts. She has written more than sixty articles and reviews, has organized several major exhibitions, serves on a number of museum boards and advisory councils, and is an adjunct assistant professor of history at the University of New Hampshire. For her joint authorship of *The Great River,* published in 1985 by the Wadsworth Atheneum, she won the Charles F. Montgomery Award of the Decorative Arts Society of the Society of Architectural Historians. She is also the author of *Fabrics for Historic Buildings,* now in its fourth edition.

A Note on the Type

This book was set in Granjon, a type named in compliment to Robert Granjon but neither a copy of a classic face nor an entirely original creation. George W. Jones based his designs on the type used by Claude Garamond (c. 1480–1561) in his beautiful French books. Granjon more closely resembles Garamond's own type than does any of the various modern types that bear his name.

Robert Granjon began his career as type cutter in 1523. The boldest and most original designer of his time, he was one of the first to practice the trade of type founder apart from that of printer. Between 1557 and 1562 Granjon printed about twenty books in types designed by himself, following, after the fashion, the cursive handwriting of the time. These types, usually known as *caractères de civilité,* he himself called *lettres françaises,* as especially appropriate to his own country.

Composed by North Market Street Graphics,
Lancaster, Pennsylvania
Printed and bound by Arcata Martinsburg,
Martinsburg, West Virginia
Designed by Anthea Lingeman